Microsoft® PowerPoint 2010

COMPLETE

by Pasewark and Pasewark*, Bunin, Morrison

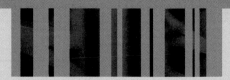

Microsoft® PowerPoint 2010

COMPLETE

by Pasewark and Pasewark*, Bunin, Morrison

William R. Pasewark, Sr., Ph.D.
Professor Emeritus, Business Education, Texas Tech University

Scott G. Pasewark, B.S.
Occupational Education, Computer Technologist

William R. Pasewark, Jr., Ph.D., CPA
Professor, Accounting, Texas Tech University

Carolyn Denny Pasewark, M.Ed.
National Computer Consultant, Reading and Math
Certified Elementary Teacher, K-12 Certified Counselor

Jan Pasewark Stogner, MBA
Financial Planner

Beth Pasewark Wadsworth, B.A.
Graphic Designer

Connie Morrison, M.A.
Consultant, Encore Training, Inc.

Rachel Biheller Bunin
Contributing Author

*Pasewark and Pasewark is a trademark of the Pasewark LTD.

COURSE TECHNOLOGY
CENGAGE Learning™

Australia • Brazil • Japan • Korea • Mexico • Singapore • Spain • United Kingdom • United States

COURSE TECHNOLOGY
CENGAGE Learning™

Microsoft PowerPoint 2010 Complete
Pasewark and Pasewark, Bunin, Morrison

Author: Connie Morrison

Contributing Author: Rachel Biheller Bunin

Executive Editor: Donna Gridley

Product Manager: Allison O'Meara McDonald

Development Editors: Karen Porter, Fran Marino, Katherine T. Pinard

Associate Product Manager: Amanda Lyons

Editorial Assistant: Kim Klasner

Senior Content Project Manager: Catherine DiMassa

Associate Marketing Manager: Julie Schuster

Director of Manufacturing: Denise Powers

Text Designer: Shawn Girsberger

Photo Researcher: Abigail Reip

Manuscript Quality Assurance Lead: Jeff Schwartz

Manuscript Quality Assurance Reviewers: Green Pen QA, Susan Pedicini, Marianne Snow

Copy Editor: Michael Beckett

Proofreader: Green Pen Quality Assurance

Indexer: Sharon Hilgenberg

Art Director: Faith Brosnan

Cover Designer: Hannah Wellman

Cover Image: © Neil Brennan / Canopy Illustration / Veer

Compositor: GEX Publishing Services

For product information and technology assistance, contact us at
Cengage Learning Customer & Sales Support, 1-800-354-9706
For permission to use material from this text or product, submit all requests online at **www.cengage.com/permissions**.
Further permissions questions can be e-mailed to
permissionrequest@cengage.com.

Library of Congress Control Number: 2010943255

Hardcover
ISBN-13: 978-1-111-52953-6
ISBN-10: 1-111-52953-1

Course Technology
20 Channel Center Street
Boston, Massachusetts 02210
USA

Cengage Learning is a leading provider of customized learning solutions with office locations around the globe, including Singapore, the United Kingdom, Australia, Mexico, Brazil, and Japan. Locate your local office at:
international.cengage.com/region

Cengage Learning products are represented in Canada by Nelson Education, Ltd.

To learn more about Course Technology, visit **www.cengage.com/coursetechnology**

To learn more about Cengage Learning, visit **www.cengage.com**

Any fictional data related to persons or companies or URLs used throughout this book is intended for instructional purposes only. At the time this book was printed, any such data was fictional and not belonging to any real persons or companies.

Printed in the United States of America
1 2 3 4 5 6 7 15 14 13 12 11

ABOUT THIS BOOK

Microsoft PowerPoint 2010 Complete is designed for beginning users of Microsoft PowerPoint 2010. Students will learn to use the application through a variety of activities, simulations, and case projects. *Microsoft Access 2010 Complete* demonstrates the tools and features for this program in an easy-to-follow hands-on approach.

This self-paced step-by-step book with corresponding screen shots makes learning easy and enjoyable. End-of-lesson exercises reinforce the content covered in each lesson and provide students the opportunity to apply the skills that they have learned. It is important to work through each lesson within a unit in the order presented, as each lesson builds on what was learned in previous lessons.

Illustrations provide visual reinforcement of features and concepts, and sidebars provide notes, tips, and concepts related to the lesson topics. Step-by-Step exercises provide guidance for using the features. End-of-lesson projects concentrate on the main concepts covered in the lesson and provide valuable opportunities to apply or extend the skills learned in the lesson, and instructors can assign as many or as few of the projects at the end of the lesson as they like.

The lessons in the **Introductory PowerPoint** unit introduce students to presentation graphics software and teach them how to create professional-looking PowerPoint presentations. Working with the program, they learn how to enter text and graphics to create slides they can use when delivering a presentation. Students learn how to edit and enhance slides. They insert and link information from other programs such as Word and Excel, insert sound and video to enhance the slides, and create SmartArt and WordArt on the slides. Students learn how to animate objects on the slides and add transitions to the slide show to create exciting presentations. They learn how to run slide shows and deliver custom shows as well as share presentations through email and broadcasting on the Internet.

The lessons in the **Advanced PowerPoint** unit build on the skills and features introduced in the Introductory PowerPoint unit. The lessons emphasize the importance of clarity in a presentation and how to use PowerPoint features to create a presentation that will effectively deliver a message. The exercises provide extensive practice working with tables and charts, using visual and sound objects, and customizing slide designs and slide layouts. The unit also provides comprehensive coverage and practice importing and exporting information to other applications and sharing and delivering presentations in a business or professional environment.

To complete all lessons and End-of-Lesson material, this book will require approximately 16 hours.

Start-Up Checklist

Hardware

- Computer and processor 500-megahertz (MHz) processor or higher
- Memory: 256 megabytes (MB) of RAM or higher
- Hard disk: 3.5 gigabyte (GB) available disk space
- Display 1024 × 768 or higher-resolution monitor

Software:

- Operating system: Windows XP with Service Pack 3, Windows Vista with SP1, or Windows 7

INSIDE THIS BOOK

Creating a Photo Album

The Photo Album feature creates a new presentation for a group of pictures. After you identify the pictures to be included in the photo album, the pictures are arranged on individual slides. You can choose the number of pictures to show on each slide. Photo album templates with preformatted slide borders and picture placeholders are also available at Office.com, or you can create your own template using special effects including themes, transitions, colorful backgrounds, and specific layouts. You can easily rearrange the order of the slides, add captions to the pictures on the slides, format all pictures in black and white, and add frames around the pictures. To provide information about the photos, you can insert text boxes between slides.

You can enhance the appearance of the photos by adjusting the brightness and contrast. You can also recolor the photos and apply artistic effects. If necessary, you can rotate a photo to change from landscape orientation to portrait orientation.

TIP

PowerPoint provides several sample photo album templates that provide a variety of slide layouts for positioning photos. To access the sample templates, click the File tab, and then click New. Under Available Templates and Themes, click the Sample templates icon.

Step-by-Step 7.7

1. If necessary, open a new blank presentation. Click the **Insert** tab. In the Images group, click the **New Photo Album** button. The Photo Album dialog box opens, as shown in **Figure 7–16**.

FIGURE 7–16
Photo Album dialog box

2. Under Insert picture from, click **File/Disk**. The Insert New Pictures dialog box opens. If necessary, navigate to the drive and folder where your Data Files are stored. Select the following filenames: (*Hint*: Click the first filename, press and hold **Ctrl**, and then click the remaining filenames.)

   A perfect catch!.jpg

   Focus.jpg

   Let's play!.jpg

   Nap time.jpg

   Run fast.jpg

3. When the five files are selected, click **Insert**.

Step-by-Step Exercises offer "hands-on practice" of the material just learned. Each exercise uses a data file or requires you to create a file from scratch.

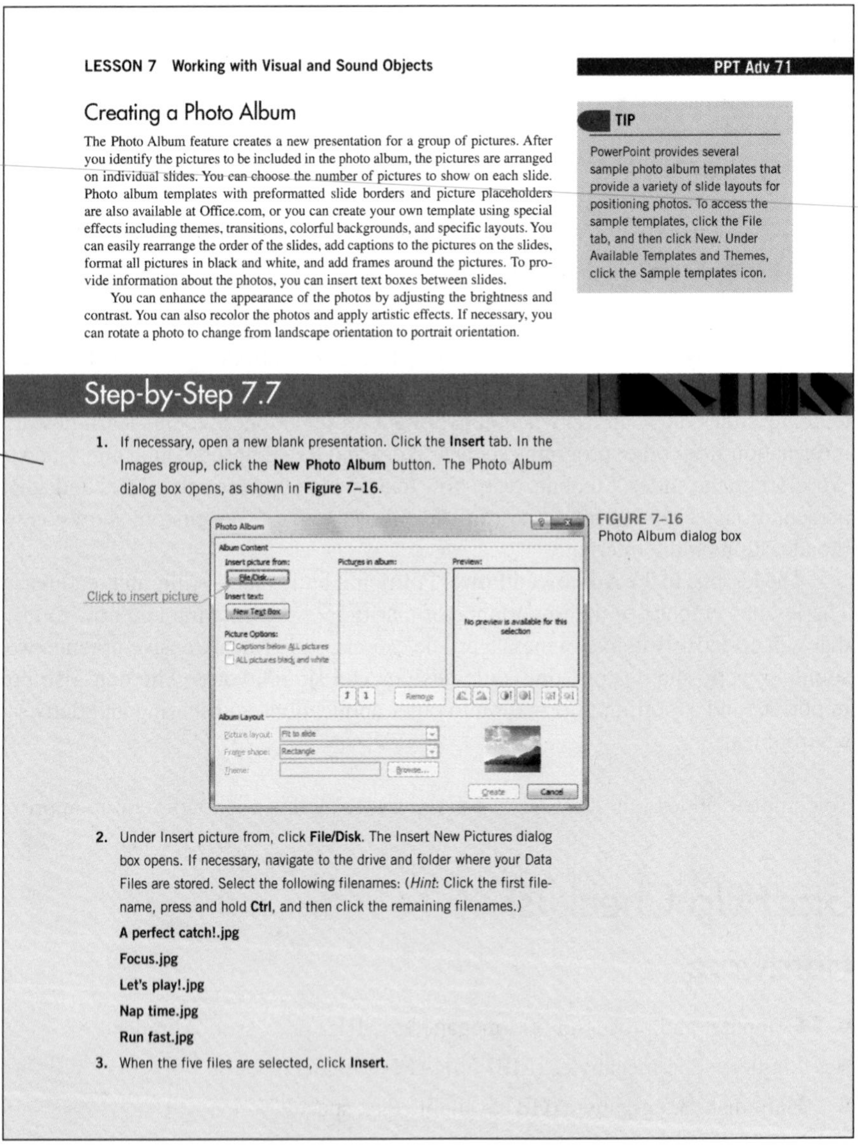

Lesson opener elements include the **Objectives, Suggested Completion Time**, and **Vocabulary Terms**.

End of Lesson elements include the **Summary, Vocabulary Review**, **Review Questions, Lesson Projects**, and **Critical Thinking Activities**.

Instructor Resources Disk

ISBN-13: 978-0-538-47523-5
ISBN-10: 0-538-47523-4

The Instructor Resources CD or DVD contains the following teaching resources:

The Data and Solution files for this course.

ExamView® tests for each lesson.

Instructor's Manual that includes lecture notes for each lesson and references to the end-of-lesson activities and Unit Review projects.

Answer Keys that include solutions to the end-of- lesson and unit review questions.

Critical thinking solution files that provide possible solutions for critical thinking activities.

Copies of the figures that appear in the student text.

Suggested Syllabus with block, two quarter, and 18-week schedule.

Annotated Solutions and Grading Rubrics.

PowerPoint presentations for each lesson.

Spanish glossary and Spanish test bank.

Appendices that include models for formatted documents, an e-mail writing guide, and a letter writing guide.

Proofreader's Marks.

ExamView®

This textbook is accompanied by ExamView, a powerful testing software package that allows instructors to create and administer printed, computer (LAN-based), and Internet exams. ExamView includes hundreds of questions that correspond to the topics covered in this text, enabling students to generate detailed study guides that include page references for further review. The computer-based and Internet testing components allow students to take exams at their computers, and save the instructor time by grading each exam automatically.

Microsoft Office Specialist

The Microsoft Office Specialist Program enables candidates to show that they have something exceptional to offer—proven expertise in certain Microsoft programs. The Microsoft Office Specialist certification exams validate specific skill sets within each of the Microsoft Office system programs. Exams are available for Windows Vista, Word, Excel, PowerPoint, Access, Outlook, and SharePoint. The Microsoft Office Specialist Certification exams focus on the candidate's ability to apply multiple skill sets to complete more complex tasks. This book has been approved as courseware for the Microsoft Office Specialist PowerPoint Certification exam.

Online Companion

This book uses an Online Companion Web site that contains valuable resources to help enhance your learning.

- Student data files to complete text projects and activities
- Key terms and definitions for each lesson
- PowerPoint presentations for each lesson
- Additional Internet boxes with links to important Web sites
- Link to CourseCasts

CourseCasts

CourseCasts—Learning on the Go. Always Available…Always Relevant.

Want to keep up with the latest technology trends relevant to you? Visit our site to find a library of podcasts, CourseCasts, featuring a "CourseCast of the Week," and download them to your mp3 player at http://coursecasts.course.com.

Our fast-paced world is driven by technology. You know because you're an active participant—always on the go, always keeping up with technological trends, and always learning new ways to embrace technology to power your life.

Ken Baldauf, a faculty member of the Florida State University Computer Science Department, is responsible for teaching technology classes to thousands of FSU students each year. He knows what you want to know; he knows what you want to learn. He's also an expert in the latest technology and will sort through and aggregate the most pertinent news and information so you can spend your time enjoying technology, rather than trying to figure it out.

Visit us at http://coursecasts.course.com to learn on the go!

SAM 2010 SAM

SAM 2010 Assessment, Projects, and Training version 1.0 offers a real-world approach to applying Microsoft Office 2010 skills. The Assessment portion of this powerful and easy to use software simulates Office 2010 applications, allowing users to demonstrate their computer knowledge in a hands-on environment. The Projects portion allows students to work live-in-the-application on project-based assignments. The Training portion helps students learn in the way that works best for them by reading, watching, or receiving guided help.

- SAM 2010 captures the key features of the actual Office 2010 software, allowing students to work in high-fidelity, multi-pathway simulation exercises for a real-world experience.

- SAM 2010 includes realistic and explorable simulations of Office 2010, Windows 7 coverage, and a new user interface.

- Easy, Web-based deployment means SAM is more accessible than ever to both you and your students.

- Direct correlation to the skills covered on a chapter-by-chapter basis in your Course Technology textbooks allows you to create a detailed lesson plan.

- SAM Projects offers live-in-the-application project-based assignments. Student work is automatically graded, providing instant feedback. A unique cheating detection feature identifies students who may have shared files.

- Because SAM Training is tied to textbook exams and study guides, instructors can spend more time teaching and let SAM Training help those who need additional time to grasp concepts

Note: This textbook may or may not be available in SAM Projects at this time. Please check with your sales representative for the most recent information on when this title will be live in SAM Projects.

About the Pasewark Author Team

Pasewark LTD is a family-owned business with more than 90 years of combined experience authoring award-winning textbooks. They have written over 100 books about computers, accounting, and office technology. During that time, they developed their mission statement: To help our students live better lives.

Pasewark LTD authors are members of several professional associations that help authors write better books. The authors have been recognized with numerous awards for classroom teaching and believe that effective classroom teaching is a major ingredient for writing effective textbooks.

Connie Morrison, M.A., Consultant, Encore Training, Inc.

Connie Morrison has more than 35 years of combined experience in education and educational publishing. She began her career teaching business education at the high school and college levels, and then became an education consultant in the publishing industry. Connie currently works as a consultant for Encore Training, Inc., providing staff training and professional development.

This book represents a true team effort, and it was a pleasure working with everyone. My appreciation goes to all the members of the team who made this book possible. I owe special thanks to the following individuals: Donna Gridley, Allison O'Meara, and Cathie DiMassa for their direction and support in the development of this book; Karen Porter, for her meticulous editing and valuable input; and my family, Gene, Al, Amy, and Chris, for their continued support.— **Connie Morrison, M.A. Consultant, Encore Training, Inc.**

From the Contributing Author

With deep appreciation, I would like to thank my professional and talented co-authors; Kitty, Jess, and Robin for their support, friendship, expertise, and laughs as well as the team at Course Technology-Cengage Learning for working tirelessly to produce this excellent book. Thanks to Donna Gridley for making this all happen. Thanks to the editorial and production team, Allison O'Meara McDonald, Amanda Lyons, Kim Klasner, and Cathie DiMassa for their management and production skills. A special thanks to my family—David, Jennifer, Emily, and Michael—for their endless support, love, and good humor through it all.— **Rachel Biheller Bunin**

Microsoft Office 2010 Advanced
Casebound
ISBN-13: 978-0-538-48129-8
Hard Spiral
ISBN-13: 978-0-538-48142-7
Soft Perfect
ISBN-13: 978-0-538-48143-4

Microsoft Excel 2010 Complete
Hardcover
ISBN-13: 978-1-111-52952-9

Microsoft Word 2010 Complete
Hardcover
ISBN-13: 978-1-111-52951-2

Microsoft Access 2010 Complete
Hardcover
ISBN-13: 978-1-111-52990-1

CONTENTS

INTRODUCTORY UNIT

INTRODUCTORY MICROSOFT POWERPOINT 2010 UNIT

ADVANCED MICROSOFT POWERPOINT 2010 UNIT

What is the Microsoft® Office Specialist Program?

The Microsoft Office Specialist Program enables candidates to show that they have something exceptional to offer—proven expertise in certain Microsoft programs. Recognized by businesses and schools around the world, over 4 million certifications have been obtained in over 100 different countries. The Microsoft Office Specialist Program is the only Microsoft-approved certification program of its kind.

What is the Microsoft Office Specialist Certification?

The Microsoft Office Specialist certification validates through the use of exams that you have obtained specific skill sets within the applicable Microsoft Office programs and other Microsoft programs included in the Microsoft Office Specialist Program. The candidate can choose which exam(s) they want to take according to which skills they want to validate.

The available Microsoft Office Specialist Program exams include*:

- Using Windows Vista®
- Using Microsoft® Office Word 2007
- Using Microsoft® Office Word 2007 – Expert
- Using Microsoft® Office Excel® 2007
- Using Microsoft® Office Excel® 2007 – Expert
- Using Microsoft® Office PowerPoint® 2007
- Using Microsoft® Office Access® 2007
- Using Microsoft® Office Outlook® 2007
- Using Microsoft SharePoint® 2007

The Microsoft Office Specialist Program 2010 exams will include*:

- Microsoft Word 2010
- Microsoft Word 2010 Expert
- Microsoft Excel® 2010
- Microsoft Excel® 2010 Expert
- Microsoft PowerPoint® 2010
- Microsoft Access® 2010
- Microsoft Outlook® 2010
- Microsoft SharePoint® 2010

What does the Microsoft Office Specialist Approved Courseware logo represent?

The logo indicates that this courseware has been approved by Microsoft to cover the course objectives that will be included in the relevant exam. It also means that after utilizing this courseware, you may be better prepared to pass the exams required to become a certified Microsoft Office Specialist.

For more information:

To learn more about Microsoft Office Specialist exams, visit www.microsoft.com/learning/msbc

To learn about other Microsoft approved courseware from Course Technology, visit www.cengage.com/coursetechnology

* The availability of Microsoft Office Specialist certification exams varies by Microsoft program, program version and language. Visit www.microsoft.com/learning for exam availability.

POWERPOINT 2010 COMPLETE DATA FILES GRID

APPLICATION	LESSON	DATA FILE	SOLUTION FILE
INTRODUCTION	1	Class Descriptions.docx	Blackfoot Resort.pptx
		Clients.accdb	Final Spectrum Follow-up.docx
		Historic Preservation.pptx	First Qtr Sales.xlsx
		January Sales.xlsx	Historic Housing.pptx
		JC's Data.mdb	JC's Updated Data.accdb
		Sales Report.xlsx	Revised Sales Report.xlsx
		Spectrum Follow-up.docx	Updated Class Descriptions.docx
		Employees\Tam	Updated Clients.accdb
POWERPOINT	1	Tornadoes.pptx	Tornado Report Solution.pptx
		Network.pptx	Network Summary Solution.pptx
			Critical Thinking 1-1 Sample Solution.pptx
			Critical Thinking 1-2 Sample Solution.pptx
			EMT Rosewood Solution.pptx
POWERPOINT	2	EMT.potx	EMT Class Spring Session Solution.pptx
		EMT Class.pptx	EMT Class Spring Session– Copy Solution.pptx
		FirstAid.jpg	Critical Thinking 2-1 Sample Solution.pptx
		Rose.jpg	Critical Thinking 2-2 Sample Solution.pptx
		911.wav	Critical Thinking 2-2 Sample Solution.pptx
POWERPOINT	3	DogsAndCats.pptx	Animal Shelter - Solution.pptx
			DogsAndCats Palace.pptx
		History of Cotton.pptx	History of Cotton Report Solution.pptx
		Cotton Gin.jpg	Internet Company Research Sample Solution.pptx

POWERPOINT *(continued)*

APPLICATION	LESSON	DATA FILE	SOLUTION FILE
POWERPOINT	3	Highway.jpg	My New Company Sample Solution.pptx
		Potato Chip Plant.jpg	
		Sky.jpg	
		Truck.jpg	
		cribbedding.mpg	
POWERPOINT	4	Planet Facts.docx	Astronomy Club Solution.pptx
		Planet Number of Moons.docx	Many Moons Solution.pptx
		The Moons of Jupiter.docx	Our Solar System Solution.pptx
		Planets.xlsx	Solar System Handouts Solution.docx
		Sun Facts.pptx	Critical Thinking 4-1 Sample Solution.pptx
			Critical Thinking 4-1 Sample Solution.pptx
			Package Solar System – Solution (not provided-this is a CD file)
POWERPOINT	UNIT REVIEW	Coffee Prices.xlsx	Java Cafe Info.pptx
		Java Cafe.pptx	Project 3 Template Presentation.pptx
			Project 4 Template Presentation.pptx
			States Project 1.pptx
			States Project 2.pptx
POWERPOINT	5	1950 Paint.docx	AEP.dic
		Coasting.pptx	Before 1950.docx
		Employee Manual.pptx	Coaster Terms.docx
		Lead Poisoning.pptx	ET.dic
		Lightning.pptx	Final Lead Poisoning.pptx
		RRP.docx	Revised Coasting 1.pptx
		Terms.docx	Revised Coasting 2.pptx
			Revised Coasting 3.pptx
			Revised Coasting 4.pptx

POWERPOINT *(continued)*

APPLICATION	LESSON	DATA FILE	SOLUTION FILE
POWERPOINT	5		Revised Coasting 5.pptx
			Revised Coasting 6.pptx
			Revised Coasting 7.pptx
			Revised Coasting 8.pptx
			Revised Employee Manual.pptx
			Revised Lightning.pptx
			RRP Rule.docx
POWERPOINT	6	Byron Chart.pptx	Q1 Expenses.xlsx
		Coaster History.pptx	Rate of Loss.xlsx
		Deer Creek Inn.pptx	Revised Byron Chart.pptx
		Expenses.xlsx	Revised Coaster History 1.pptx
		Financial Review.pptx	Revised Coaster History 2.pptx
		Loss Rate.xlsx	Revised Coaster History 3.pptx
		Next Year.xlsx	Revised Coaster History 4.pptx
		Organization.pptx	Revised Organization.pptx
		Wetlands.pptx	Revised Wetlands.pptx
			The Year Ahead.xlsx
			Updated Deer Creek Inn 1.pptx
			Updated Deer Creek Inn 2.pptx
			Updated Deer Creek Inn 3.pptx
			Updated Deer Creek Inn 4.pptx
			Updated Deer Creek Inn 5.pptx
			Updated Financial Review.pptx
POWERPOINT	7	A perfect catch!.jpg	Final Motocross.pptx
		Blue.jpg	Hawaiian Sunsets.pptx
		Bright horizon.jpg	Pet Photo Album.pptx
		Charlie.jpg	Pet Photo Album.wmv
		Cuddles.jpg	Revised Dynamic Park.pptx
		Dynamic Park.pptx	Revised Dynamic Park.wmv
		Focus.jpg	Revised Happy Tails 1.pptx

POWERPOINT *(continued)*

APPLICATION	LESSON	DATA FILE	SOLUTION FILE
POWERPOINT	7	Frisbee fun.wmv	Revised Happy Tails 2.pptx
		Happy Tails.pptx	Revised Happy Tails 3.pptx
		Kylie.jpg	Revised Happy Tails 4.pptx
		Let's play!.jpg	Revised Happy Tails 5.pptx
		Motocross.pptx	Revised Happy Tails 6.pptx
		Motocross.wmv	Revised Happy Tails 7.pptx
		MX Finish.jpg	Revised Happy Tails 8.pptx
		MX Jump.jpg	Revised Happy Tails 9.pptx
		MX Start.jpg	Revised Service.pptx
		Nap time.jpg	
		Pink horizon.jpg	
		Run fast.jpg	
		Service.pptx	
		Sunset fog.jpg	
		Sunset high waves.jpg	
		Sunset silhouette.jpg	
		Sunset trees.jpg	
		Sunset waves.jpg	
		Taffy.jpg	
		Yellow sunset.jpg	
POWERPOINT	8	Building Renovation.pptx	Building Renovation Design.potx
		Grand Canyon.jpg	Custom Template yn.potx
		National Parks.pptx	Final Building Renovation.pptx
		Time Management.pptx	Final Time Management.pptx
			National Parks Draft 1.pptx
			National Parks Draft 2.pptx
			National Parks Draft 3.pptx
			National Parks Draft 4.pptx
			National Parks Draft 5.pptx

DATA FILES

POWERPOINT *(continued)*

APPLICATION	LESSON	DATA FILE	SOLUTION FILE
POWERPOINT	8		National Parks Draft 6.pptx
			National Parks Draft 7.pptx
			National Parks Draft 8.pptx
			National Parks Draft 9.pptx
			National Parks Draft 10.pptx
			National Parks Draft 11.pptx
			National Parks Handout.docx
			Organized Five Rules.pptx
POWERPOINT	9	Blood Drive.pptx	Community Service Outline.rtf
		Community Service.pptx	County Parks Outline.rtf
		County Parks.pptx	Final Preserving Wetlands.pptx
		Donations.xlsx	Revised Community Service 1.pptx
		Food Bank.pptx	Revised Community Service 2.pptx
		Items.docx	Revised Community Service 3.pptx
		Long-Term Care.docx	Revised Community Service 4.pptx
		Park Visitors.xlsx	Revised Community Service 5.pptx
		Participation.xlsx	Revised Community Service 6.pptx
		Popular County Parks.accdb	Revised Community Service 7.pptx
		Preserving Wetlands.pptx	Revised Community Service 8.pptx
		Visitor Centers.docx	Revised County Parks 1.pptx
		Volunteer Participation.accdb	Revised County Parks 2.pptx
		Wetlands Outline.docx	Revised Long-Term Care.docx
			Revised Park Visitors.xlsx
			Revised Volunteer Participation.accdb
			Title Slide.jpg
			Updated Donations.xlsx
			Updated Items.docx
			Updated Participation.xlsx
			Wetland Losses.jpg

DATA FILES

POWERPOINT *(continued)*

APPLICATION	LESSON	DATA FILE	SOLUTION FILE
POWERPOINT	**10**	Festival Reviewer A.pptx	Festival CD (folder with Presentation Package folder, AUTORUN.INF, and Revised Festival 7.pptx)
		Festival.pptx	Final Karate (folder with Presentation Package folder, AUTORUN.INF, and Revised Karate 2.pptx)
		Karate 1.pptx	Revised Festival 1.pptx
		Karate 2.pptx	Revised Festival 2.pptx
		Karate Reviewer A.pptx	Revised Festival 3.pptx
		Scarecrow 1.pptx	Revised Festival 4.odp
		Scarecrow 2.pptx	Revised Festival 4.ppsx
			Revised Festival 4.pptx
			Revised Festival 4.xps
			Revised Festival 5.pptx
			Revised Festival 6.pptx
			Revised Festival 7.pptx
			Revised Festival 8.pptx
			Revised Festival 9.pptx
			Revised Festival Picture.pptx
			Revised Karate 1.pptx
			Revised Karate 2.pptx
			Revised Karate 3.pptx
			Revised Scarecrow 1.pdf
			Revised Scarecrow 1.pptx
			Revised Scarecrow 2.pptx
POWERPOINT	UNIT REVIEW	1 meter.avi	Current Client Survey.xlsx
		3 meter.avi	Diving Videos.pptx
		10 meter.avi	Guide.jpg
		Buffalo.jpg	Revised Cabins.pptx
		Cabins.pptx	Revised Codes.pptx
		Client Survey.xlsx	Revised Fire Instructions.pptx
		Codes.pptx	Revised Insurance 1.pptx

POWERPOINT *(continued)*

APPLICATION	LESSON	DATA FILE	SOLUTION FILE
POWERPOINT	UNIT REVIEW	Diving.pptx	Revised Insurance 2.pptx
		Elephant.jpg	Revised Insurance 3.pptx
		Fire Instructions.pptx	Revised Insurance 4.pptx
		Insurance Overview.docx	Revised Insurance 5.pptx
		Leopard.jpg	Revised Insurance 6.pptx
		Lion.jpg	Revised Insurance 6.wmv
		New Insurance.pptx	Revised Insurance 6.xps
		Rhinoceros.jpg	S-P Template.potx
			The Big 5a.pptx
			The Big 5b.pptx
			The Big 5c.pptx
			The Big 5d.wmv
			WWCR.dic

ADVANCED

INTRODUCTION

LESSON 1   **2 HRS.**

Microsoft Office 2010 and the Internet

LESSON 1

Microsoft Office 2010 and the Internet

■ **OBJECTIVES**

Upon completion of this lesson, you should be able to:

- Apply basic Microsoft Word, Excel, Access, PowerPoint, and Outlook features.

- Search for information on the World Wide Web.

- Evaluate Web sites.

- Bookmark favorite Web sites.

- Manage the history of the Web sites visited.

■ **VOCABULARY**

bookmark

browser

hits

keywords

search engine

wildcard

Microsoft Office 2010 is a complete set of computer applications that equips you with the tools you need to produce a variety of documents and files, and to help streamline your everyday computing activities. This course focuses on the more complex and advanced capabilities of the Word, Excel, Access, PowerPoint, and Outlook applications.

This lesson provides a review of basic application features and will help you refresh your application skills. In this lesson, you will also learn more about how to access resources on the World Wide Web.

Applying Word Features

As you know, Microsoft Word is a powerful, full-featured word processor with comprehensive writing tools. You've already learned many of the basic features that enable you to complete common word-processing documents. The Word lessons in this course will introduce you to features that will enable you to further enhance the appearance of your documents and save time preparing and editing documents. Developing a document often involves multiple team members, and Word offers several tools to help you share documents and effectively collaborate on projects.

However, before you begin to explore these and other advanced features in Word, complete the following Step-by-Step, which provides a review of many basic Word skills.

Step-by-Step 1.1

1. Launch Word and then open the **Class Descriptions.docx** file from the drive and folder where your Data Files are stored. Save the document as **Updated Class Descriptions**, followed by your initials.

2. Edit the document as shown in **Figure 1–1**.

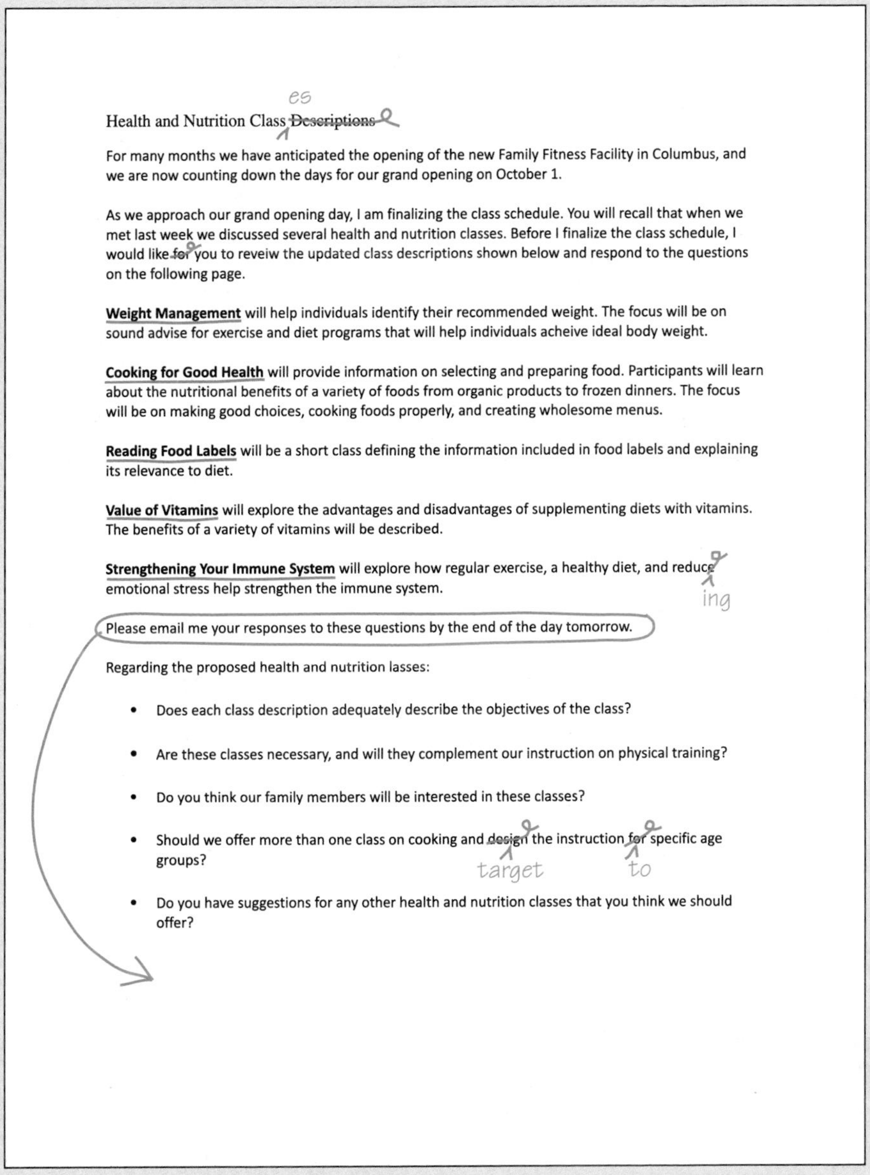

Health and Nutrition Class ~~Descriptions~~ *es*

For many months we have anticipated the opening of the new Family Fitness Facility in Columbus, and we are now counting down the days for our grand opening on October 1.

As we approach our grand opening day, I am finalizing the class schedule. You will recall that when we met last week we discussed several health and nutrition classes. Before I finalize the class schedule, I would like for you to reveiw the updated class descriptions shown below and respond to the questions on the following page.

Weight Management will help individuals identify their recommended weight. The focus will be on sound advise for exercise and diet programs that will help individuals acheive ideal body weight.

Cooking for Good Health will provide information on selecting and preparing food. Participants will learn about the nutritional benefits of a variety of foods from organic products to frozen dinners. The focus will be on making good choices, cooking foods properly, and creating wholesome menus.

Reading Food Labels will be a short class defining the information included in food labels and explaining its relevance to diet.

Value of Vitamins will explore the advantages and disadvantages of supplementing diets with vitamins. The benefits of a variety of vitamins will be described.

Strengthening Your Immune System will explore how regular exercise, a healthy diet, and reduce *ing* emotional stress help strengthen the immune system.

Please email me your responses to these questions by the end of the day tomorrow.

Regarding the proposed health and nutrition lasses:

- Does each class description adequately describe the objectives of the class?

- Are these classes necessary, and will they complement our instruction on physical training?

- Do you think our family members will be interested in these classes?

- Should we offer more than one class on cooking and *target* design the instruction *to* for specific age groups?

- Do you have suggestions for any other health and nutrition classes that you think we should offer?

FIGURE 1–1
Edits for document in
Step-by-Step 1.1

3. Center and bold the title, and then change the font to Arial 18 point. Change the title text to all uppercase.

4. Select the paragraphs that describe the five classes and format all the paragraphs with a left indent of 0.5" and a right indent of 5.5" (0.5" from the right margin).

5. Select the list of bulleted questions at the end of the document and apply the number format (1., 2., 3.) to create an enumerated list.

6. Position the insertion point anywhere in the first numbered paragraph and add space after the paragraph. Then use the Format Painter feature to copy the new paragraph format to the other paragraphs in the numbered list.

7. Search for the word *email* and replace it with **e-mail**.

8. Change the document margins to **Office 2003 Default** setting (1" top and bottom and 1.25" left and right).

9. Position the insertion point in front of the paragraph that begins *Regarding the proposed...* and insert a page break.

10. Create a header for only the second page of the document. Use the Blank (Three Columns) format for the header, and then type the title **Health and Nutrition Classes** in the center of the header.

11. Check the document for spelling and grammar and make any necessary corrections. The spelling checker doesn't catch mistypes if they are the same as correctly spelled words.

12. Save the changes. Close the document, and then exit Word.

Applying Excel Features

Excel is the spreadsheet application in the Office suite. As you've discovered, spreadsheets are used for entering, calculating, and analyzing data. You should now be familiar with the basic features for creating, editing, and formatting worksheet information. Excel's advanced features enable you to perform complex calculations and in-depth analysis that you'd normally leave up to an economist or mathematician! With Excel's data analysis tools, you can generate reports, charts, and tables that are every bit as professional looking and accurate as those created by the experts. In this course, you'll also learn how to share workbooks with colleagues.

Before you venture into the advanced features of Excel, complete the following Step-by-Step, which provides a review of the Excel basic skills.

Step-by-Step 1.2

1. Launch Excel and then open the **Sales Report.xlsx** file from the drive and folder where your Data Files are stored. Save the workbook as **Revised Sales Report**, followed by your initials.

2. Go to cell M5 and type the column heading **TOTAL**.

3. Go to cell M6 and enter a formula to calculate the sum of the numbers in cells B6:L6. Fill the formula down through cell M12.

4. Go to cell A14 and type the row heading **TOTAL**.

5. Go to cell B14 and enter a formula to calculate the sum of the numbers in cells B6:B13. Fill the formula across through cell M14.

6. Insert a new column to the left of the *TOTAL* column. In the new column, type the heading **Dec**, and then enter the following data in the new column:

   61258

   50211

   61858

   50212

   61855

   50215

   61852

7. Copy the formula in cell L14 and paste it in cell M14.

8. Merge and center the title *Division Sales Report* over cells A1:N1. Format the title text bold and italic, and change the font size to 14 point.

9. Delete rows 2 and 3.

10. Format the column and row headings bold, and then center the column headings.

11. Apply a currency format to all the numeric data, with no decimal points. If necessary, automatically adjust the column widths.

12. Create a 3-D pie chart on a new sheet, using only the data in the cell ranges A4:A10 and N4:N10. Add the title **Total Sales by Division** to the chart and apply a chart style of your choice.

13. Format the worksheet to fit on one page in landscape orientation.

14. Save the changes. Close the file, and then exit Excel.

Applying Access Features

Access is the database application in the Office suite that is used for storing and organizing information. Databases are made up of objects, including tables, queries, forms, and reports. You now should be familiar with the basic techniques for creating these objects. In the advanced lessons, you will learn about features that give you even more control over how database records are viewed, edited, and professionally analyzed. You'll learn how to streamline data entry and editing and to present the data in an attractive, reader-friendly manner.

Before you begin exploring advanced features in Access, walk through the following Step-by-Step to review the application's basic features.

Step-by-Step 1.3

1. Launch Access and open the **JC's Data.accdb** file from the drive and folder where your Data Files are stored. Save the database as **JC's Updated Data**, followed by your initials.

2. Open the EMPLOYEE table in Design View. Between the *Employee ID* and *Last Name* fields, insert a new field titled **Department**. Define the field data type as **Text**.

3. Save the changes to the table and then switch to Datasheet View.

4. Sort the table alphabetically by last name and then update the records to include the department name in which each employee works:

Dominquez:	**Marketing**
Gonzalez:	**Administrative**
Keplinger:	**Sales**
Mann:	**Accounting**
Pullis:	**Accounting**
Thomsen:	**Sales**
Ti:	**Marketing**
Wong:	**Sales**

5. Sort the table by Employee ID, and then add a new record to the table and enter the following information:

Employee ID:	**9**
Department:	**Sales**
Last Name:	**Barkin**
First Name:	**Dave**
Salary:	**$145,000**
Home Phone:	**608-555-5121**
Date Hired:	**3/24/13**

6. Adjust the column widths to show all the data, and then show the table in Print Preview.

7. Change the page layout to **Landscape** and close Print Preview. Save the changes and close the table.

8. Open the PRODUCTS table and filter the data to show only those products with a price greater than $10. The filter should produce eleven records. Remove the filter and close the table. When prompted, save the changes.

9. Use the Form Wizard to create a form based on the EMPLOYEE table.

   a. Include all the fields in the form.

   b. Select the **Columnar** layout.

   c. Name the form **EMPLOYEE FORM**.

10. Use the Report Wizard to create a report based on the EMPLOYEE table.

   a. Include all the fields except *Salary* and *Date Hired*.

   b. Group the records by **Department**.

   c. Sort the records in ascending order by **Last Name**.

   d. Apply the **Stepped** layout and **Portrait** orientation.

   e. Name the report **EMPLOYEE TELEPHONE REPORT**.

11. Close the report and the form, and then exit Access.

Applying PowerPoint Features

PowerPoint is a presentation graphics program that enables you to create presentation materials for a variety of audiences, including slide shows using a projector and online presentations that everyone on a network can view. In the PowerPoint unit, you will explore some of its more advanced features. To make your presentations more interesting and effective, PowerPoint provides tools to add multimedia effects to your slides. The many customizing features PowerPoint offers enable you to create your own color schemes, backgrounds, and design templates. When preparing for your final presentation, PowerPoint has many options for distributing your slide show, including sharing via e-mail or presenting it remotely over a Web page or network.

Before you explore these advanced PowerPoint features, complete the following Step-by-Step to review your PowerPoint skills.

Step-by-Step 1.4

1. Launch PowerPoint, and then open the **Historic Preservation.pptx** file from the drive and folder where your Data Files are stored. Save the presentation as **Historic Housing**, followed by your initials.

2. On the title slide, replace *Your Name* with your own first and last names.

3. Add a new slide after the title slide, using the **Two Content** layout for the new slide.

4. In the title placeholder, type **Stabilization**. In the text placeholder on the left, type the following two lines of text. The text should automatically be formatted with bullets.

   Reestablish structural stability.

   Maintain essential form.

5. Move slide #5 (with the title *Resources)* so it is the last slide in the presentation.

6. Add graphics to slides 2–9. If possible, search Office.com for the graphics. *Hint*: Try search terms such as *house*, *fix*, *historic*, *tools,* and *blueprints*.

7. Apply a built-in design, and, if desired, change the color theme and/or fonts.

8. Apply a transition to all slides in the presentation. Adjust the timing of the transitions as needed.

9. Apply custom animations to the text and graphics on slides 2–10 to control when and how the objects appear.

10. Run the slide show and observe your transitions and animations, and make any necessary changes.

11. Save your changes. Close the presentation, and then exit PowerPoint.

Applying Outlook Features

Outlook is a desktop information management application. As you already know, using Outlook helps you keep track of e-mail messages, appointments, meetings, contact information, and tasks you need to complete. In this course, you will explore some of Outlook's more advanced features. You will learn about features that make it even easier to manage contact information, manage e-mails, and communicate with others. You will also learn about many features and tools that make it easier for you to schedule events and track progress on tasks.

Before you explore Outlook's advanced features, complete the following Step-by-Step to review the basic skills and features for Outlook.

Step-by-Step 1.5

1. Launch Outlook. Open a new journal entry and enter the information below. Then start the timer and leave the journal entry open.

   Subject: **Step-by-Step 1.5**

   Entry type: **Task**

2. Open the Contacts folder. Create a new contact group and name the group **Fitness Trainers**.

3. Add the following contacts to the new group and save the group.

Name:	**Sharon McKee**
E-mail:	**smckee@familyfit.xyz**
Name:	**Ronald DeVilliers**
E-mail:	**rdevillers@familyfit.xyz**
Name:	**Alisa Mandez**
E-mail:	**amandez@familyfit.xyz**

4. Create a new e-mail message. Send the message to the Fitness Trainers group, and type **Health and Nutrition Classes** in the Subject box. Then type the following in the message area:

   Please review the attached document and give me your feedback by the end of the day tomorrow.

5. Attach your solution file **Updated Class Descriptions.docx** to the e-mail message, and save the e-mail message as a draft. Do not attempt to send the e-mail.

6. Create the following two notes:

   Upload the health and nutrition class descriptions to the Web site.

   Confirm yoga class schedule with Bonnie.

7. Open the Calendar and show the calendar for a week from the current date. Create an appointment with your dentist for 10 a.m. and set a reminder. The appointment should last 45 minutes.

8. Open the Tasks folder and create the following new task. Give the task high priority and specify that it be completed within a week.

   Gather information for dental bills to submit for insurance.

9. Delete the dentist appointment.

10. Delete the contact group and contacts you created, and then delete the e-mail draft.

11. Delete the insurance task.

12. Delete the two notes.

13. Return to the journal entry and pause the timer. Make note of how much time you spent on this activity, and then delete the journal entry.

14. Exit Outlook.

Accessing Internet Resources

Microsoft Office 2010 is designed to give you quick and easy access to the World Wide Web, regardless of which Office application you are currently using. A *browser* is a program that connects you to remote computers and gives you the capability to access, view, and download data from the Web. Microsoft's browser program is Microsoft Internet Explorer.

▶ **VOCABULARY**
browser

Searching for Information and Evaluating Web Sites

Each day, millions of people use the World Wide Web to find information. To get the information they're looking for, they must navigate through an enormous amount of data. As a result, even with high-speed connections and powerful search engines, searching for specific information can be very time consuming.

ADVANCED   Introduction Unit

search engine

keywords

hits

wildcard

A *search engine*, such as Microsoft's Bing, is a tool designed to find information on the Web. When you enter *keywords*, words that describe the information you are seeking, the search engine generates a list of Web sites that potentially match the search criteria. These search results (the best matching Web sites) are often referred to as *hits*. Searches often produce a long list of hits; if you wish to narrow the search results, you need to be more specific in the keywords that you provide. **Table 1–1** describes several options for refining a search so you can find information quickly and effectively.

TABLE 1–1   Options for refining searches

SEARCH OPTIONS	DESCRIPTION
Capitalization	If you want the results to include occurrences of both upper and lowercase letters, enter the keywords using all lowercase letters. However, if you want to narrow your results to words that begin with capital letters (such as Central Intelligence Agency) or all capital letters (such as CIA), enter the keywords with the same capitalization.
Plurals	Most search engines consider singular keywords as both singular and plural. For example, results for the keyword *agent* will include hits with the word *agents*. If you want the results to include only hits with a plural word, be sure the keyword is plural.
Phrases	Search for a group of words by including quotation marks before and after the sequence of words. With the quotation marks, only hits with all of the words in the exact same sequence will appear in the results. Without the quotation marks, the results will include hits that contain all or most of the words anywhere within a Web site.
Operators	Narrow or broaden the search using operators including *+*, *&*, *and*, *-*, *not*, and *or*. For example, if you are searching for information about international exchange students, use the following keywords in the search engine to exclude hits for currency exchange rates: **+international +exchange +students -currency** or **international and exchange and students not currency**
Related pages	Many search engines provide options to include hits for Web pages with similar information. Look for links such as *Similar pages*, *Also try*, or *Related searches*.
Truncation	Some search engines support the use of a symbol, sometimes referred to as a **wildcard**, that allows for variations in the spelling of words. When an asterisk (*) symbol is used in a word, the search results include hits with alternate spellings for the word at the point that the asterisk appears. For example, *extra** generates hits for Web pages with *extra*, *extras*, *extract*, and *extraordinary*.
Domains	You can limit search results to a specific domain, such as an educational institution or a government Web site. For example, to find information about environmental research at an educational institution, in the search engine, enter the following keywords: **+domain:edu +environmental +research** or **domain:edu and environmental and research**

When the search results appear, read the information carefully before clicking any of the links. You can determine the validity of some of the hits by looking at the URLs. For example, if you're looking for information about deadlines for filing forms for personal income taxes, you want to click a link that includes IRS in the URL. Also, domain name extensions help to identify the type of entity. **Table 1–2** shows common domain extensions and the type of entity related to them.

TABLE 1–2 Common domain extensions

DOMAIN EXTENSIONS	DESCRIPTIONS
.com	Commercial business
.edu	Educational institution
.gov	Governmental institution
.org	Nonprofit organization
.mil	Military site
.net	Network site
.us	Abbreviation that indicates a country; for example: .us (United States), .ja (Japan), .uk (United Kingdom), .ca (Canada), and .hk (Hong Kong)

EXTRA FOR EXPERTS

Most search engines include links that provide information about advanced search features. Be sure to access these links to learn how to make your searches more effective.

▶ **TIP**

Clicking a link on a Web site can distract you and take you off task. Before you click a link, try to determine if the link will take you where you want to go. If you click a link and see that the target is not what you expected, click the Back button to return to the previous Web page and stay on task.

Just about anyone can publish information on the Web—often for free, and usually unmonitored. So how do you know if you can trust the information that you find? When you depend on the Web for sources of information, it is your responsibility to determine the integrity and validity of the information and its source. **Table 1–3** provides questions that will guide you through an evaluation process.

TABLE 1–3   A guide for evaluating information on the Web

QUESTIONS TO ASK	WHAT TO CONSIDER
Is the information relevant to my query?	The information should help you to accomplish your goals and objectives. Make sure you analyze the information and determine if it meets your needs.
Is the information current?	Check for a date on the Web page that indicates when the information was last updated.
Is the Web site published by a company or an entity, or is it a personal Web site?	The URL often includes a company name. If you are familiar with the company or entity, consider whether you trust information from this source. If you are not familiar with the company, or the individual, look for links such as *About Us*, *Background*, or *Biography*.
What is the purpose of the Web site?	Use the domain name to identify the type of Web site. For example: a domain name ending with .com is a business, and the intent of the Web site is to sell or promote a product or service.
Who is the author?	Look for information that explains who the author is and how the author is connected to the subject. Verify that the author is qualified to address the subject. Individuals sometimes falsify their credentials, so research the author's background and confirm that the author is credible. For example, if information at the Web site indicates that the author is a professor at a university, go to the university Web site and check the faculty roster.
Is the author biased in his/her opinion?	When looking for facts, be sure the author provides objective viewpoints and cites information with credible sources.
Is the Web site presented professionally?	Information should be well organized and presented accurately, free from spelling and grammar errors.
Are the links legitimate and credible?	Confirm that links are up to date. Links to a credible Web site, such as a business or an organization, do not mean that the business or organization approves of or supports the content on the linked Web page.

Step-by-Step 1.6

1. If necessary, log onto the Internet and open your browser.

2. In the address bar, type **www.bing.com** and then press **Enter** to open the Bing search engine.

3. In the Bing search box, type **lake tahoe ski** and then click the **Search** button, or press **Enter**.

4. Note that the number of hits is indicated at the top of the search results. Scroll down and review the first set of results. Each link provides a brief preview of the Web page content, and the keywords are highlighted in the preview. Occurrences of the word *skiing* may also appear highlighted in the previews.

5. Edit the text in the search box to read **+lake +tahoe +ski -water**. Click the **Search** button, or press **Enter**. Scroll down through the first set of results. Note that the number of hits is greatly reduced, and the word *water* is not found in any of the previews.

6. Edit the text in the search box to read **"lake tahoe water ski"** and then click the **Search** button, or press **Enter**. Note that the number of hits is considerably less because adding more keywords often narrows the search.

7. Delete the text in the search box and then type **domain:org and tahoe and ski**. Click the **Search** button, or press **Enter**. Scroll down through the first set of results. Notice every URL has a .org extension.

8. Type **www.nasa.gov** in the address bar and then press **Enter**. The NASA home page opens.

9. Navigate the Web site and find the following information:
   a. the date when the site was last updated
   b. NASA locations
   c. blogs
   d. the names of the authors of the site's articles and blogs
   e. any available information about the authors' backgrounds
   f. information for contacting NASA

10. Return to the home page for the NASA Web site.

11. Leave the NASA Web site open for the next Step-by-Step.

Revisiting Web Sites

As you rely more and more on the Web as a primary source of information on any topic, you'll find that there are sites you visit frequently or that you know you'll want to access again. You can create a bookmark for quick and easy access to a Web page. A *bookmark* is a link that navigates you to the Web page, and it is saved in a Favorites folder. You can create additional folders inside the Favorites folder to keep the list of sites organized.

▶ VOCABULARY
bookmark

ADVANCED   Introduction Unit

Your browser keeps track of the sites you have visited, so you can also quickly revisit a site by selecting the Web site from the History list. The History list can be organized by date, site, most visited, and the order the sites were visited on the current day. You can easily delete the History list, as well as temporary Internet files, cookies, form data, and passwords.

Step-by-Step 1.7

The following steps describe bookmarking Web pages using Internet Explorer features. If you are not using Internet Explorer as your browser, you can still explore the features for creating the bookmarks, but these steps will not exactly describe your browser features.

1. If necessary, log onto the Internet, open your Internet Explorer browser, and open **www.nasa.gov**. Or navigate to the NASA home page, if necessary.

2. Click the **Favorites** button on the Command bar in the upper-left corner of the screen, as shown in **Figure 1–2**.

FIGURE 1–2
Favorites button on
the Internet Explorer browser

3. If necessary, click the **Favorites** tab to show a list of your favorite sites. Your favorites list will be different than the one shown in **Figure 1–3**.

FIGURE 1–3
Folders on the Favorites tab

4. Click the **Add to Favorites** button to open the Add a Favorite dialog box shown in **Figure 1–4**.

FIGURE 1–4
Add a Favorite dialog box

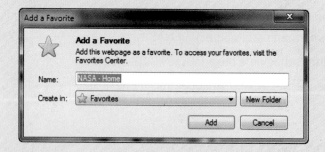

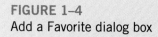

TIP

You can also quickly add Web sites to the Favorites folder using the shortcut keys Ctrl+D.

5. In the Name text box, *NASA - Home* appears. Leave the name as is and click **New Folder** on the dialog box. The Create a Folder dialog box similar to the one shown in **Figure 1–5** opens. In the Folder Name text box, type **Research** and then click **Create**. The Add a Favorite dialog box is still open. Click **Add**.

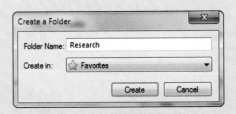

FIGURE 1–5
Create a Folder dialog box

6. Click the **Favorites** button to show your list of favorites. Click the new folder **Research** and you will see the *NASA - Home* site. You can move favorites into folders by dragging the site name to the desired folder.

7. Click the **History** tab on the Favorites pane. Click the **View By...** button at the top of the History list, and then click **View By Order Visited Today**. Notice that the NASA Web page is included in the list of documents and Web sites accessed today. Click the **View By...** button at the top of the History list again, then click **View By Most Visited**. The list is rearranged.

8. Right-click one of the Web sites in this list, click **Delete** in the shortcut menu, and then click **Yes** to confirm the deletion.

9. Click the **Favorites** button, and on the History tab, click any one of the site names on the History list. The Web page opens.

10. Click the **list arrow** at the right side of the address bar in the browser, as shown in **Figure 1–6**. A history of accessed Web sites is displayed, as well as a list of favorite sites. Click anywhere outside the History list to close it.

FIGURE 1–6
History and Favorites lists on the address bar

Click to display history of accessed Web sites and favorite sites

11. Click the **Safety** button on the browser toolbar, as shown in **Figure 1–7**.

Safety button

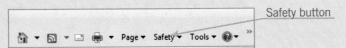

FIGURE 1–7
Safety button on browser toolbar

12. Click **Delete Browsing History** to open the dialog box in **Figure 1–8**. If necessary, change the settings so they match those shown in the figure, and then click **Delete**.

FIGURE 1–8
Delete Browsing History
dialog box

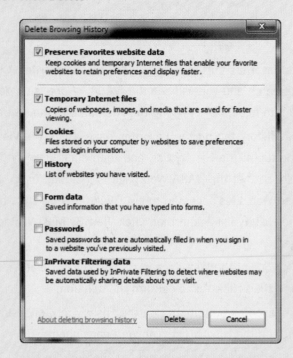

13. Click the **Favorites** button. Click the **Favorites** tab, and in the Favorites list, right-click the **Research** folder, and then click **Delete** in the short-cut menu. Click **Yes** to confirm the deletion.

14. Close Internet Explorer.

SUMMARY

In this lesson, you learned:

- Microsoft Word is a powerful, full-featured word processor. Its advanced features enable users to further enhance the appearance of documents and save time preparing and editing documents. Developing a document often involves multiple team members, and Word offers several tools to help you share documents and effectively collaborate on projects.

- Excel is the spreadsheet application in the Microsoft Office suite. Spreadsheets are used primarily for calculating and analyzing data, and Excel's advanced features enable you to perform complex calculations and in-depth analysis. Excel includes many features that enable you to generate accurate and professional-looking reports, charts, and tables.

- Access is the database application in the Office suite. Databases are used for storing and organizing information. The advanced features in Access give you more control over how database records are viewed, edited, and professionally analyzed. Effectively designed forms and reports help to streamline data entry and editing.

- Microsoft PowerPoint is a presentation graphics program that enables you to create materials for presentations of many kinds. Its advanced features include several tools for customizing slide designs and using multimedia effects to enhance your content. Remote publishing features in PowerPoint enable you to share presentations over the Internet or a network.

■ Microsoft Outlook is a desktop information management program that provides several tools for scheduling appointments and meetings, managing and delegating tasks, and communicating with others. Advanced features help you customize the tools to fit your needs.

■ An enormous amount of information is available on the World Wide Web. Effective search strategies not only save you time, but they also lead you to more relevant sources.

■ When you depend on the Web for sources of information, it is your responsibility to determine the integrity and validity of the information and its source.

■ You can bookmark Web sites that you visit frequently and save the links to the Favorites folder. You can create additional folders to organize your Favorites list.

■ You can also quickly revisit a site by selecting the Web site from the History list, which can be organized by date, site, most visited, and the order the sites were visited on the current day.

 ## VOCABULARY REVIEW

Define the following terms:

bookmark   hits   search engine
browser   keywords   wildcard

 ## REVIEW QUESTIONS

MATCHING

Match the most appropriate application in Column 2 to the application described in Column 1.

Column 1

_____ 1. A graphics application with multimedia capabilities that can be used to create materials to present and share information with others

_____ 2. An application designed for entering, calculating, and analyzing data

_____ 3. An application used for storing and organizing information

_____ 4. A desktop information management application

_____ 5. An application that provides comprehensive writing tools for sharing information with others

Column 2

A. Microsoft Outlook

B. Microsoft PowerPoint

C. Internet Explorer

D. Microsoft Word

E. Microsoft Excel

F. Microsoft Access

MULTIPLE CHOICE

Select the best response for the following statements.

1. A _____ is a program that gives you the capability to access, view, and download data from the Web.

   A. search engine   C. browser

   B. Web page   D. tracking device

2. _____ are used to broaden or narrow an online search.

   A. Keywords   C. Operators

   B. Phrases   D. all of the above

3. Non-profit organizations commonly use the _____ extension in the domain name.

   A. .net   C. country abbreviation

   B. .org   D. .com

4. _____ are the results generated by a search engine.

   A. Hits   C. Wildcards

   B. Domains   D. Quick links

5. You can organize your Internet Explorer History list based on _____.

   A. the date sites were accessed   C. the order in which sites were visited today

   B. the names of the sites   D. all of the above

WRITTEN QUESTIONS

1. Explain how the search results are affected when you include quotation marks before and after a group of words when entering keywords in a search engine.

2. Explain how the domain name can help you identify the purpose of a Web site.

3. Give an example of when you would include operators with the keywords in a search engine.

4. How can you validate that a Web site author has credibility?

5. Name some examples of related pages options provided by some search engines.

■ PROJECTS

If you have a SAM 2010 user profile, your instructor may have assigned an autogradable version of the indicated project. If so, log into the SAM 2010 Web site at *www.cengage.com/sam2010* to download the instruction and start files.

PROJECT 1–1

1. Launch Word, then open the **Spectrum Follow-up.docx** data file from the drive and folder where your Data Files are stored. Save the document as **Final Spectrum Follow-up**, followed by your initials.

2. Make the edits indicated in **Figure 1–9**.

3. Change the left and right margins to 1.25 inches.

4. Justify the alignment of the paragraphs in the body of the letter.

5. Indent the bulleted list .5 inches from the left margin.

6. Adjust the paragraph spacing as needed to fit the entire document on one page.

7. Proofread and check for spelling and grammar errors, and make any necessary corrections.

8. Save the changes and leave the document open for the next project.

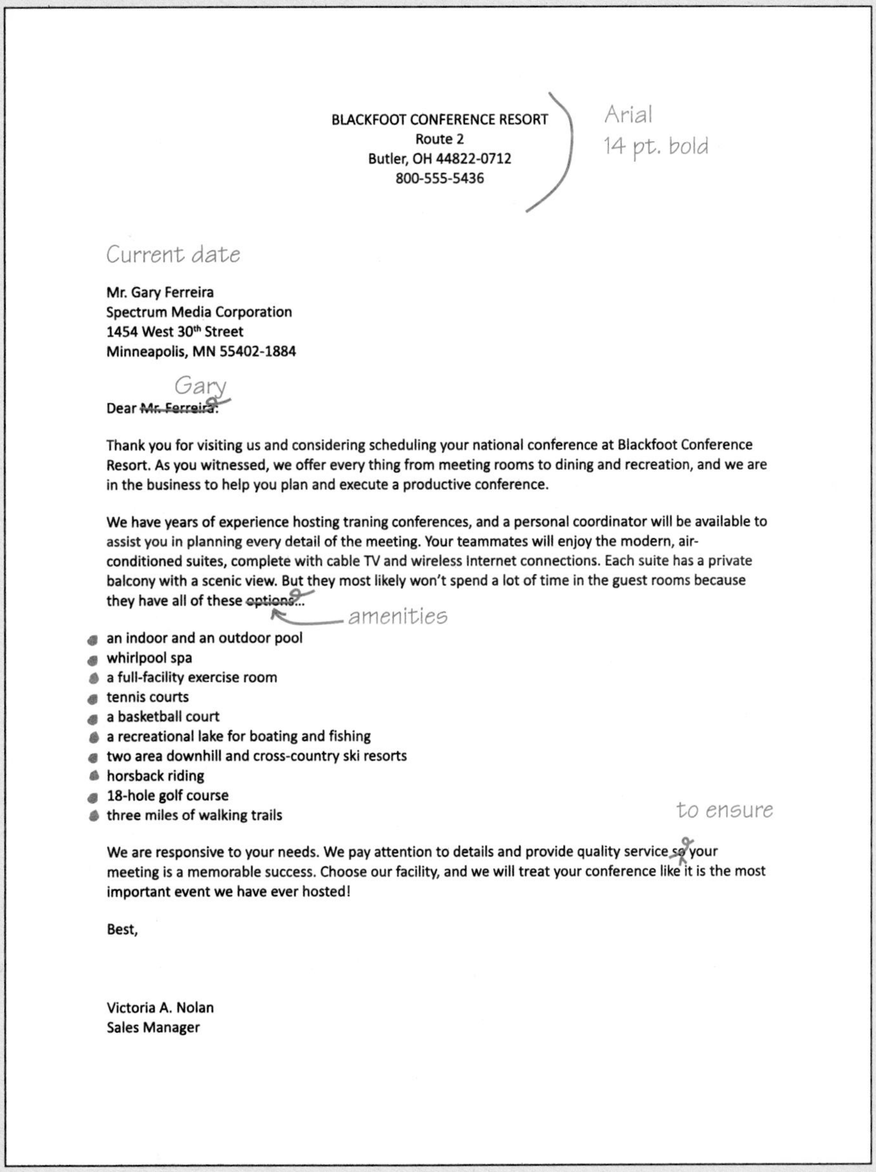

BLACKFOOT CONFERENCE RESORT
Route 2
Butler, OH 44822-0712
800-555-5436

Arial
14 pt. bold

Current date

Mr. Gary Ferreira
Spectrum Media Corporation
1454 West 30th Street
Minneapolis, MN 55402-1884

Gary

Dear ~~Mr. Ferreira~~:

Thank you for visiting us and considering scheduling your national conference at Blackfoot Conference Resort. As you witnessed, we offer every thing from meeting rooms to dining and recreation, and we are in the business to help you plan and execute a productive conference.

We have years of experience hosting traning conferences, and a personal coordinator will be available to assist you in planning every detail of the meeting. Your teammates will enjoy the modern, air-conditioned suites, complete with cable TV and wireless Internet connections. Each suite has a private balcony with a scenic view. But they most likely won't spend a lot of time in the guest rooms because they have all of these ~~options~~: *amenities*

- an indoor and an outdoor pool
- whirlpool spa
- a full-facility exercise room
- tennis courts
- a basketball court
- a recreational lake for boating and fishing
- two area downhill and cross-country ski resorts
- horsback riding
- 18-hole golf course
- three miles of walking trails

to ensure

We are responsive to your needs. We pay attention to details and provide quality service so your meeting is a memorable success. Choose our facility, and we will treat your conference like it is the most important event we have ever hosted!

Best,

Victoria A. Nolan
Sales Manager

FIGURE 1–9   Edits for the Word document in Project 1–1

SAM PROJECT 1-2

1. Launch PowerPoint and open a new presentation. Save the presentation as **Blackfoot Resort**, followed by your initials.

2. Create a slide show highlighting the guest amenities described in the Blackfoot Conference Resort letter in Project 1-1. This presentation will be distributed on the Internet to promote the resort.

3. Add pictures and graphics to help viewers visualize the amenities.

4. Add a creative title slide at the beginning of the presentation, and add a slide for closure at the end of the presentation.

5. Apply an appropriate design or background colors to the slides.

6. Add transitions to the slides, animations to the text, and objects on the slides to produce special effects and keep the viewer's attention.

7. Save the changes and exit PowerPoint.

PROJECT 1-3

1. If necessary, log onto the Internet and open your browser.

2. In the address bar, type **www.bing.com** and press Enter.

3. Enter the keywords **Conference Resorts Ohio** to search for Ohio-based conference resort sites that offer options for guests that are similar to the options described in the Blackfoot Conference Resort document you edited in Project 1-1.

4. When you find at least two Web sites promoting a conference center similar to the Blackfoot Conference Resort, save the sites to your Favorites list in a Conference Resort folder. *Hint*: Several hits may be sites that showcase multiple resorts, and you will need to navigate to the individual resort pages to get the required information.

5. Evaluate the Web sites and answer the following questions about each Web site.
   a. Were you able to find relevant information to compare resorts?
   b. Is the information at the site current?
   c. When was the site last updated?
   d. Is the site organized well, and is the information presented accurately and professionally?
   e. Does the site provide background information about the resort?
   f. Can you easily access information to contact the resort?
   g. Would you recommend this resort? Explain the reasons for your answer.

6. Close the browser.

PROJECT 1-4

1. Launch Excel and open the **January Sales.xlsx** file from the drive and folder where your Data Files are stored. Save the workbook as **First Qtr Sales**, followed by your initials.

2. In cell C1, type the column heading **February**. In cell D1, type the column heading **March**. In cell E1, type the column heading **Total**. In cell A7, type the row heading **Total**.

3. Enter the following data in the new columns.

	February	March
Byron Store	23112	42109
Fenton Store	38432	41002
Holly Store	31902	48111
Howell Store	27656	39202
Linden Store	29211	43007

4. Proofread the data entries to make sure you entered the numbers correctly.

5. Apply the Accounting number format to all the cells with numbers and remove the decimal places.

6. Enter a formula to calculate the sum of the cell range B2:D2 in cell E2, then fill the formula down through cell E6.

7. Enter a formula to calculate the sum of the cell range B2:B6 in cell B7, then fill the formula across through cell E7.

8. Create a 3-D column chart on the same sheet showing total sales by store. Apply a design of your choice.

9. Add a centered overlay title and type **First Qtr. Sales**. Turn off the legend options.

10. Reposition the chart on the sheet so you can see the sales data in the worksheet.

11. Save the changes and close the document.

PROJECT 1–5

1. Launch Access and open the **Clients.accdb** file from the drive and folder where your Data Files are stored. Save the database as **Updated Clients**, followed by your initials.

2. Open the CLIENTS table in Datasheet View.

3. Delete the record for Daniel Warner.

4. Update the address for Helen Sanderson. Her street address is now **709 Vienna Woods Drive, Cincinnati, OH 45211**.

5. In Design View, add a new field named **Mobile Phone**. Save the changes to the table and then switch back to Datasheet View.

6. Delete the home phone number for Paula Trobaugh and add her mobile phone number, **513-555-4465**.

7. Add two new clients:

   Penelope Rausch

   5074 Signal Hill

   Cincinnati, OH 45244

   Home Phone 513-555-0133

   Mobile Phone 513-555-0899

   Roger Williamson

   722 Red Bud Avenue

   Cincinnati, OH 45229

   Mobile Phone 513-555-1055

8. Save and close the database, then exit Access.

 # CRITICAL THINKING

ACTIVITY 1–1

Excel and Access have some similarities because both applications are used to organize data. If possible, look at two computer screens, side by side. On one computer, open an Excel worksheet. On the other computer, open an Access database table in Datasheet View. Compare the two screens, and create a list of similarities and differences between the worksheet and the database table. You should point out at least four similarities and four differences.

ACTIVITY 1–2

Open your browser and go to *www.bing.com*. Search for the keywords *Top Ten Search Engines*. Find the most current information available, and confirm that the sources are credible. Then, from the two sources, choose two search engines that you have never used and explore the features in each. Write a brief description of the features you like and why you would use them.

INTRODUCTORY UNIT

MICROSOFT POWERPOINT 2010

Estimated Time: 1.5 hours

LESSON 1

Microsoft PowerPoint Basics

OBJECTIVES

Upon completion of this lesson, you should be able to:

- Start PowerPoint, and understand the elements of the PowerPoint window.
- Open an existing presentation, and save it with a new name.
- Navigate a presentation and change views.
- Use the Slides and Outline tabs and the Slide and Notes panes.
- Change the layout on a slide.
- Delete a slide.
- Print a presentation.
- Exit PowerPoint.

VOCABULARY

animation
broadcasting
handouts
layout
Live Preview
Normal view
Notes Page view
Notes pane
Outline tab
PowerPoint presentation
Reading view
Slide pane
Slide Show view
Slide Sorter view
Slides tab
thumbnails
transition

Introduction to PowerPoint

▶ **VOCABULARY**

PowerPoint presentation

Microsoft PowerPoint 2010 is a Microsoft Office program that can help you create a professional, computerized slide show to use as part of a presentation. A *PowerPoint presentation* is an electronic slide show that allows you to present and deliver your message by using slides, outlines, speaker's notes, and audience handouts. PowerPoint presentations are viewed using a computer and monitor. Presentations are usually shown to an audience using a projector on a screen. A presentation can include text, drawn graphics, clip art, photographs, tables, charts, narration, and even video. Presentations can also include links to Web sites, so if you are connected to the Internet as you run the slide show, you can further enhance your presentation.

This lesson introduces you to some of the features available in PowerPoint 2010. You'll learn how to open and save a presentation, view the slide show, and switch views. You'll also learn how to delete a slide and print the presentation in a variety of ways.

Starting PowerPoint

Like other Office applications, you start PowerPoint by clicking the Start button, clicking All Programs, clicking Microsoft Office, and then clicking Microsoft PowerPoint 2010. If the Microsoft PowerPoint icon is on the desktop, you can double-click it to start PowerPoint rather than locating the command on the All Programs menu. The PowerPoint program opens, as shown in **Figure 1–1**.

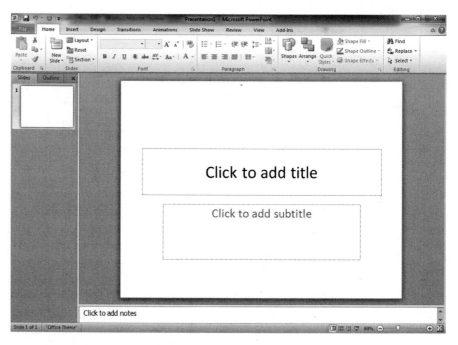

FIGURE 1–1   The PowerPoint window

Step-by-Step 1.1

1. On the taskbar, click the **Start** button 🌐 to open the Start menu.

2. Click **All Programs**, click **Microsoft Office**, and then click **Microsoft PowerPoint 2010**. The PowerPoint window opens with a new blank slide in the PowerPoint window. The new blank slide is a blank title slide. You will review the program window that is on the screen in the next Step-by-Step.

3. Leave the blank presentation open for the next Step-by-Step.

> **TIP**
>
> The first slide in a presentation is the title slide. The title slide provides a purpose similar to a title page in a report. The title slide introduces the presentation to your audience.

Reviewing the PowerPoint Window

The PowerPoint window shares several common elements and tools with other Office programs, such as Word, Excel, and Access. PowerPoint has several views that you will learn about. You work with these elements and tools in the different views to create presentations. Refer to **Figure 1–2**, which shows a simple presentation with two slides and identifies the elements in *Normal view*, which is a view of the presentation that allows you to add and delete slides, and add text and elements to slides.

▶ **VOCABULARY**
Normal view

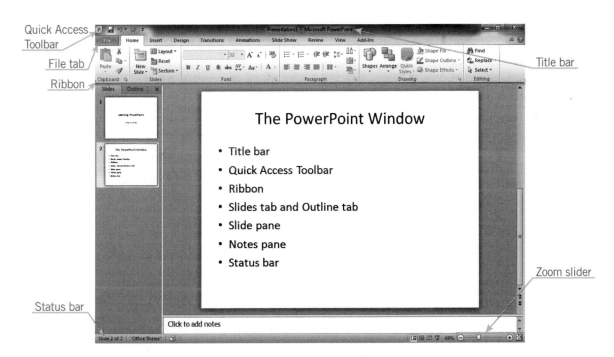

FIGURE 1–2   PowerPoint window in Normal view

The title bar, at the top of the window, identifies the window as a PowerPoint window and lists the name of the open presentation. For a new presentation, the name is simply Presentation followed by a number until you give it a name when you save the file.

The Quick Access Toolbar is on the left side of the title bar. You can add or remove buttons on the Quick Access Toolbar to meet your working style. For example, you might want to add the New, Open, or Spelling command.

Like other Office programs, the Ribbon contains the graphic collection of command buttons that are organized by tabs and in groups. The Home tab is the default tab on the Ribbon and includes many of the commands you will use most often when creating the slides. The File tab, which opens Backstage view, includes file management commands such as the Save, Save As, Open, Close, and Print commands.

The status bar appears at the bottom of your screen and provides information about the current presentation and slide. The area on the left side of the status bar shows which slide is displayed in the Slide pane and tells you the total number of slides in the presentation. On the right end of the status bar, you can click the View buttons to switch views, the way you view the presentation. As in other programs, the *Zoom slider* adjusts the zoom percentage of the window. To the right of the Zoom slider, the Fit slide to current window button is useful for quickly adjusting the selected slide to best fit in the current window.

TIP

Read more about Backstage view in the Microsoft Office 2010 Basics and the Internet lesson at the beginning of this book.

▶ VOCABULARY
Zoom slider

Step-by-Step 1.2

1. On the Ribbon, click the **Insert** tab to view the different commands. You can see that the buttons have images to show what each button does. The buttons are organized into the Tables, Images, Illustrations, Links, Text, Symbols, and Media groups.

2. On the Ribbon, click the **View** tab to view the different commands. PowerPoint has several views that you will learn about as you learn to create presentations.

3. On the Ribbon, click the **Design** tab to view the different commands. You can use buttons on this tab to add color and designs to your presentations.

4. On the status bar, click the **Zoom In** button ⊕ two times, and then click the **Zoom Out** button ⊖ four times so the Zoom percentage is 40%. Refer to **Figure 1–3**.

FIGURE 1–3
Zoom controls

5. On the status bar, click the **Fit slide to current window** button.

6. Leave the presentation open for the next Step-by-Step.

⊞ EXTRA FOR EXPERTS

The Zoom In and Zoom Out buttons increase or decrease the zoom level by values of 10. Drag the Zoom slider to change the zoom percentage as a sliding scale.

Opening an Existing Presentation and Viewing a Slide Show

When you want to open an existing presentation that you have recently viewed, you can choose the presentation from the Recent Presentations list in Backstage view. To view the Recent Presentations list, click the File tab on the Ribbon, and then click Recent on the navigation bar. If the presentation you want to work on or view is not on that list, click Open on the navigation bar, and then browse in the Open dialog box to locate the presentation file name. The Open dialog box is shown in **Figure 1–4**. The files and folders will differ for each computer system.

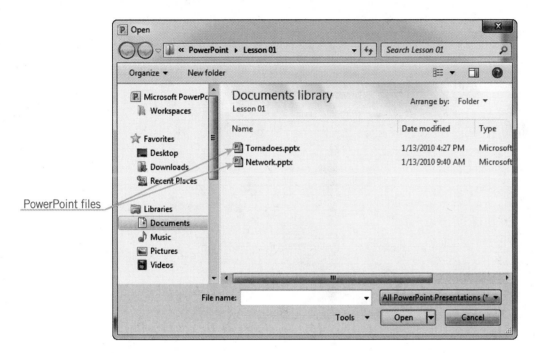

FIGURE 1–4   Open dialog box

Click the presentation you want to open, and then click Open. The presentation you selected appears on the screen in the PowerPoint window.

To view the presentation as a slide show, click the Slide Show button on the status bar. You can also click the Slide Show tab on the Ribbon, and then, in the Start Slide Show group, click the From Beginning or From Current Slide button. The slide show opens on the screen, and you can view it as it would appear if you were presenting it. You can press the right arrow key or the spacebar on the keyboard to advance the slides and the left arrow key to review a previous slide. You can also click the mouse button to advance a slide.

A slide show is a series of slides. *Transition* refers to the way each new slide appears on the screen. You can select from many exciting transition effects, such as checkerboards, swirls, dissolves, wipes, and cuts, to make your slide show fun to watch.

You can animate objects on a slide. An *animation* is an effect you can apply to text, objects, graphics, or pictures to make those objects move during a slide show. You can set up a slide to advance automatically through the animation or to pause and allow users to start the animation effect manually when it is most convenient.

As you view the presentation in Step-by-Step 1.3, press the right arrow key, Enter, or the spacebar, or click to advance to the next animation or slide.

▶ VOCABULARY
transition
animation

Step-by-Step 1.3

TIP

You can press the left arrow key or Page Up on the keyboard to view the previous slide or animation in the presentation.

1. On the Ribbon, click the **File** tab, and then on the navigation bar, click **Open**.

2. In the Open dialog box, navigate to the drive and folder where your Data Files are stored.

3. Click **Tornadoes.pptx**, and then click **Open**. The presentation file appears, as shown in **Figure 1–5**. The title slide is in the Slide pane.

FIGURE 1–5
Title slide for
Tornadoes
presentation

Title Slide
(Slide 1)

Identifies this
as Slide 1 of
14 total slides

Slide Show button

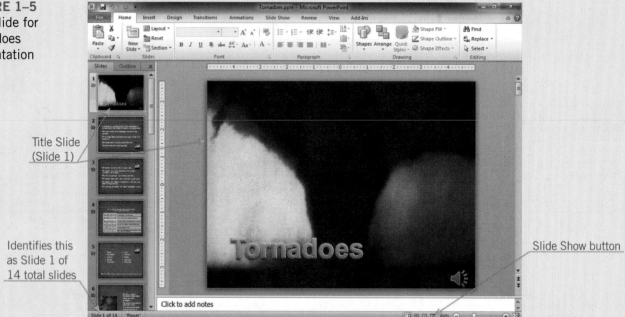

4. On the status bar, click the **Slide Show** button. The title slide fills the screen , as shown in **Figure 1-6**, and you see the word *Tornadoes* in the lower-left. Then, the background image flies onto the screen, and the word *Tornadoes* becomes animated. If your computer has a sound card and speakers, you also hear a thunderstorm.

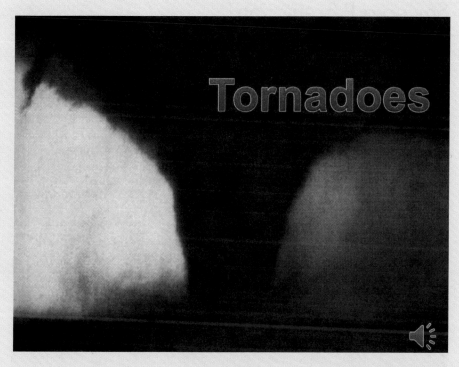

FIGURE 1–6
The slide fills the screen

5. Click the mouse to advance to the next slide. The transition makes Slide 1 look like it is shredding into pieces, and then Slide 2 is assembled from these pieces. The text animation on the slide advances automatically until five bulleted items appear.

6. Click the mouse again to advance to the next slide. Click the mouse as many times as necessary to display each bullet. The title of this slide appeared automatically. This slide show is set up so some text appears automatically, and some when you click the mouse.

7. Click the mouse as many times as necessary to advance the slides. As each slide in the presentation continues, notice the examples of animation. Some slides include pictures, and some of the pictures are animated. One of the slides includes an animated movie of a tornado. Slide 12, titled "Web Resources," contains several hyperlinks. If your computer is connected to the Internet, you can click one of those links to open the Web site in your browser. After you click the last slide, the Thank You on the last slide spins away.

8. Click the mouse again. The presentation ends with a black slide. The black slide lets you know the slide show is over.

9. Click the mouse one more time to end the slide show and return to Normal view.

10. Leave the presentation open for the next Step-by-Step.

TIP

There are many ways to advance through a slide show. Try pressing the right arrow key, the spacebar, the page up key, or using the scroll wheel on your mouse.

Saving a Presentation

To save a new presentation the first time, you use the Save As command. You can also use the Save As command to give an existing presentation a new name. If the presentation does not have a name, click the Save button on the Quick Access Toolbar to open the Save As dialog box, as shown in **Figure 1–7**. You can open the Save As dialog box by clicking the File tab on the Ribbon, and then clicking Save As. In the Save As dialog box, use the navigation pane to find the drive and folder where you will save your presentation. Click in the File name box to select the default name, such as Presentation1, type a new file name, and then click Save.

Presentation will be
saved with a pptx
file extension

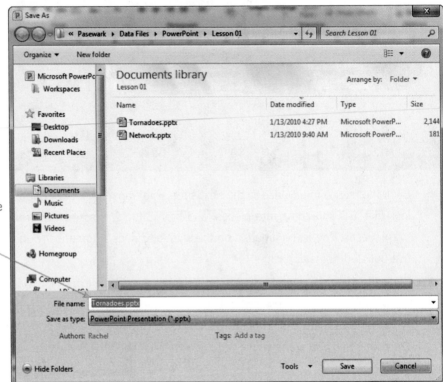

FIGURE 1–7   Save As dialog box

The next time you want to save changes to your presentation, click the Save button on the Quick Access Toolbar or press Ctrl+S. These commands save the file without opening the dialog box.

Step-by-Step 1.4

1. Click the **File** tab, and then on the navigation bar, click **Save As**. The Save As dialog box opens.

2. Navigate to the drive and folder where your Data Files are stored.

3. Click in the **File name** box, and then type **Tornado Report** followed by your initials.

4. Click **Save**. Leave the presentation open for the next Step-by-Step.

Changing Views

You can view a presentation four different ways using buttons found in the Presentation Views group of the View tab on the Ribbon: Normal, Slide Sorter, Notes Page, and Reading view. (See **Figure 1–8**.) You can also change to Normal view, Slide Sorter view, Reading view or start a slide show quickly by clicking one of the View Shortcut buttons on the status bar, shown in **Figure 1–9**.

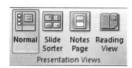

FIGURE 1–8   Presentation Views group on the View tab

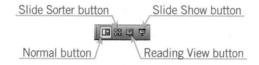

FIGURE 1–9   View shortcuts on the status bar

Normal View

You do most work creating slides in Normal view. This view can have up to four panes: the Slides tab and Outline tab, the Slide pane, the Notes pane, and the Task pane.

Using the Slides Tab and Outline Tab

When you are working with the slides in a presentation, PowerPoint displays all the slides in a pane on the left side of your screen. This pane has two tabs at the top, the Slides tab and the Outline tab. The *Slides tab* displays your slides as small pictures or *thumbnails*. The *Outline tab* displays all the text on your slides in outline

> **EXTRA FOR EXPERTS**
>
> Click and drag the pane borders to adjust the size of the different panes.

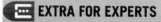

VOCABULARY

Slides tab

thumbnails

Outline tab

form. The Outline tab does not show you any graphics on a slide. See **Figure 1–10**. This pane lets you see the order of your slides and gives you a quick overview of the slides. It's a good way to see which slides come before and after other slides. Depending on the Zoom factor, you will see more slides (with smaller thumbnails) or less slides (with larger thumbnails). To switch between these modes, click the Slides tab or the Outline tab.

FIGURE 1–10   Slides tab

To select any slide in a presentation, click the thumbnail on the Slides tab or click the text on the Outline tab. You can use the Outline tab to add or edit text on the slide. You can reorder slides by dragging the thumbnail on the Slides or Outline tab. You can close the pane by clicking the Close button in the upper-right corner of the pane. Click the Normal button on the status bar to restore this pane.

Step-by-Step 1.5

1. Click the **Outline** tab. The slide number appears to the left of the text on the Outline tab.

2. On the Outline tab, drag the **scroll box** down in the scroll bar until you can see slide 8, and then click the **slide 8** slide icon ▣. Slide 8 appears in the Slide pane.

3. On the **Outline** tab, click anywhere on the selected text to deselect it.

4. On the Outline tab, in the second bullet point in Slide 8, double-click **75,000** to select the number, type **93,000**, and then press **spacebar**. Notice the number also changes on the slide in the Slide pane.

5. Click the **Slides** tab, and then click the **Save** button 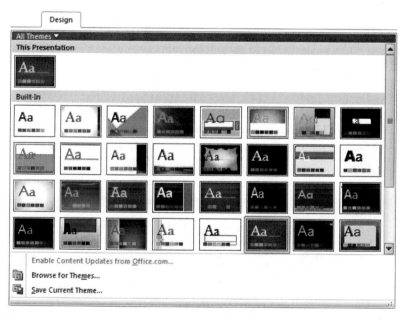 on the Quick Access toolbar.

6. Leave the presentation on the screen for the next Step-by-Step.

Using the Ribbon

The Ribbon on the top of the screen contains commands for the various tasks you will use when creating presentations. For example, on the Ribbon, you can click the Design tab to view themes, which are slide designs. You can then click the More button in the Themes group to open a gallery of themes and see all the thumbnails, as shown in **Figure 1–11**. The *Live Preview* feature lets you see the effect the theme will have on your slides before you apply it in your presentation. If you select a slide, you can see how the theme will change the background and text on the slide as you move the mouse pointer over each thumbnail.

▶ **VOCABULARY**
Live Preview

FIGURE 1–11   Themes gallery on the Design tab

Step-by-Step 1.6

1. On the Ribbon, click the **Design** tab.

2. On the Slides tab, drag the **scroll box** up to the top of the scroll bar, and then click the **slide 3** thumbnail. The slide number appears to the left of the slide thumbnail on the Slides tab.

EXTRA FOR EXPERTS

On the Ribbon, on the Design tab, in the Themes group, click the More button to open the Themes gallery and try out more themes for the slides.

3. On the Design tab, in the Themes group, move the pointer over each of the theme thumbnails to preview the different theme effects on the slide (but do not click the mouse button).

4. In the Themes group, click the **Colors** button to open the Built-in Theme Colors gallery, and then slowly move the pointer over each of the **Color Themes** thumbnails to preview the different color theme effects on the slide.

5. Press **Esc** to close the Colors menu without selecting anything.

6. In the Themes group, click the **Fonts** button to open the Built-in Fonts gallery, and then slowly move the pointer over each of the Font Themes thumbnails to preview the different font effects on the slide.

7. On the Ribbon, click the **Home** tab.

8. Leave the presentation on the screen for the next Step-by-Step.

Using the Slide Pane

VOCABULARY
Slide pane

The *Slide pane* is the workbench for PowerPoint presentations. It displays one slide at a time and is useful for adding and editing text, inserting and formatting illustrations or objects, or generally modifying a slide's appearance. The Slide pane displays your slides in an area large enough for you to easily work on a slide. You can select the slide to view in the Slide pane by clicking the thumbnail on the Slides tab, by scrolling the Slide pane, or by pressing Page Up or Page Down on the keyboard.

If you drag and select text, then move the mouse pointer back over the selected text, the Mini toolbar appears. The Mini toolbar has buttons for common formatting commands, such as font color, font style, font size, text alignment, and styling. Although buttons for these commands also appear in the Font group on the Ribbon, it is sometimes quicker to use the Mini toolbar. See **Figure 1–12**.

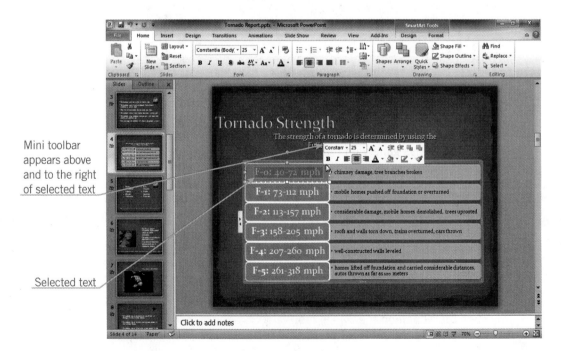

FIGURE 1–12   The Mini toolbar

Step-by-Step 1.7

1. On the Slides tab, click the **slide 5** thumbnail.

2. In the Slide pane, drag to select the text **Oklahoma City has been hit by more tornadoes than any other city since 1890** at the bottom of the slide.

3. In the Font group on the Home tab, click the **Font Color** button arrow [A▾]. A palette of colors opens.

4. In the first row of the palette in the Theme Colors section, click the sixth color box **Orange, Accent 2** (when you position the pointer on top of the box, a ScreenTip appears identifying the color). The text is formatted for the new color.

5. Save your work. Leave the presentation on the screen for the next Step-by-Step.

> **EXTRA FOR EXPERTS**
>
> When you drag to select text, the Mini toolbar appears, and you can use the buttons on it instead of the buttons on the Ribbon, if you wish.

Inserting a New Slide with a New Slide Layout

The slide *layout* is how objects are placed on a slide. Objects include text, images, illustrations, tables, media, and charts. When you create a slide, you determine the layout. The default layout includes placeholders for different objects on a slide. There are placeholders for slide titles, text, and content. When you insert a new slide, you can select the layout. You can also change the layout for a slide that already has content. On the Home tab, in the Slides group, click the Layout button to view the different default layouts. See **Figure 1–13**.

> **VOCABULARY**
> **layout**

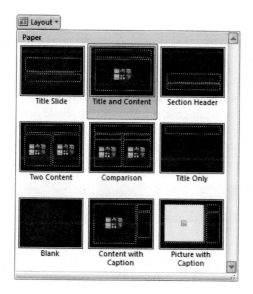

FIGURE 1–13   Default layouts

The Title and Content layout provides two placeholders, one for a title and one for content. Content can be text or any object. You click the placeholder and begin to type text, or you can click any one of the content icons to add an object. You will learn how to add text and content to slides in the next lesson.

Step-by-Step 1.8

1. On the Slides tab, scroll down until you can see slide 7, and then click the **slide 7** thumbnail.

2. On the Home tab, in the Slides group, click the lower part of the **New Slide** button. A gallery of layouts that you can choose for the new slide opens.

3. Click the **Title and Content** thumbnail on the Layout gallery. You added a new slide 8 with the Title and Content layout to the presentation.

4. Leave the presentation on the screen for the next Step-by-Step.

Notes Page View

> ▶ **VOCABULARY**
> **Notes Page view**
> **Notes pane**
> **Slide Sorter view**

The *Notes Page view* displays your slides on the top portion of the page, with any speaker notes that have been entered for each slide appearing in the *Notes pane* on the bottom of the page. You can use these notes to help you as you make a presentation. Notes are also helpful if you print a handout for your audience to guide them through your presentation. To add speaker notes, click in the Notes pane and begin typing. You can also enter notes in Notes Page view. To switch to Notes Page view, on the Ribbon, click the View tab, and then in the Presentation Views group, click the Notes Page button. To enter a note, click in the Click to add text placeholder below the image of the slide. You will learn more about the Notes pane and how to use it effectively in Lesson 2.

Using Slide Sorter View

Slide Sorter view displays thumbnails of the slides on the screen so that you can move and arrange slides easily by clicking and dragging. Slide Sorter view gives you an overview of the entire presentation. To switch to Slide Sorter view, on the status bar, click the View Shortcuts Slide Sorter button. You can also click the Slide Sorter button on the View tab in the Presentation Views group.

Step-by-Step 1.9

1. On the status bar, click the **Slide Sorter** button ▦. The screen appears, as shown in **Figure 1–14**.

FIGURE 1–14
Slide Sorter view

2. Click the **slide 11** thumbnail so that it is selected and outlined in gold. The slide number appears below and to the right of the thumbnail.

3. Drag the **slide 11** thumbnail to the left of slide 6. A line appears between the two slides. Release the mouse button. Slide 11 moves to become slide 6, and all other slides are moved forward and renumbered.

4. Click the **slide 1** thumbnail and then save your work.

5. Leave the presentation on the screen for the next Step-by-Step.

Using Slide Show View

In *Slide Show view*, you run your presentation on the computer as if it were a slide projector to preview how it will look to your audience. When you run the slide show, each slide fills the screen. Any animations, sounds, and videos will play in Slide Show view. To switch to this view, click the View tab on the Ribbon and then click the Slide Show button in the Presentation Views group, or click the Slide Show button on the status bar, or press F5.

▶ **VOCABULARY**
Slide Show view

INTERNET

Broadcasting a PowerPoint presentation to the Web allows others to watch your presentation as you give it from a remote location through a Web browser. Your audience does not have to have PowerPoint installed on their computer to view your broadcast presentation. To broadcast a presentation, click the File tab, click Save & Send, click the Broadcast Slide Show command, and sign in to your Windows Live account or to a SharePoint Server.

If you move the mouse pointer to the lower-left corner of the screen as the slide show runs, a Slide Show toolbar appears. This menu, which has four buttons, helps you control the slide show. You can also right-click (click the right mouse button) any slide to open the shortcut menu, which includes additional commands. See **Figure 1–15**. **Table 1–1** describes a few of the commonly used commands available on the toolbar and on the shortcut menu.

FIGURE 1–15   Slide Show shortcut menu

TABLE 1–1   Commonly used commands in Slide Show view

BUTTON	COMMAND ON SHORTCUT MENU	DESCRIPTION	NOTES
➡	Next	Advances to the next slide	
⬅	Previous	Displays the previous slide	
	Last Viewed	Displays the slide viewed immediately before the current slide	
✏	Pointer Options	Allow you to annotate a slide	Options include Arrow, Pen, Highlighter, Arrow options for Automatic, Hidden, Visible, and Ink Color options
	Screen	Changes the screen	Can display a black or white screen or switch to another open program
	Go to Slide	Displays a list of all slides in the presentation	Click to advance to any specific slide in the presentation
	End Show	Ends the slide show	

Step-by-Step 1.10

1. On the status bar, click the **Slide Show** button 📠. Slide 1 appears on the screen and you watch the animations on the slide.

2. Click the mouse to advance to slide 2.

3. Right-click anywhere on the slide. On the shortcut menu, point to **Go to Slide**, and then click **14 Stay SAFE**. Slide 14 appears on the screen.

4. Right-click anywhere on the slide, and then click **End Show** on the shortcut menu. The slide show ends and appears in Slide Sorter view again.

5. Leave the presentation open for the next Step-by-Step.

> **TIP**
>
> You can press Esc anytime during a presentation to return to the view displayed prior to viewing the show.

Using Reading View

In *Reading view*, you run your presentation very much like Slide Show view. The slide does not quite fill the screen and you can use navigation buttons on the status bar beneath the slide. **Figure 1–16** shows Slide 10 in Reading view.

> **▶ VOCABULARY**
> **Reading view**

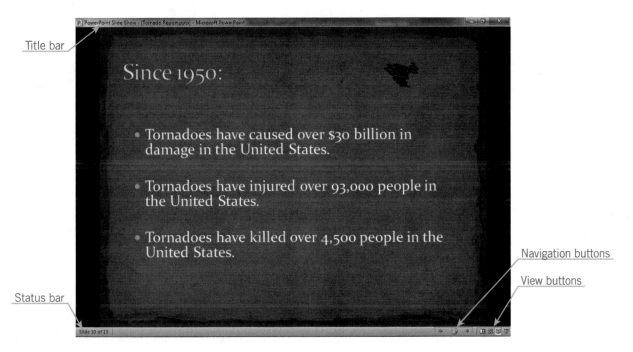

FIGURE 1–16   Slide in Reading view

Deleting Slides

If you decide that a slide does not fit your presentation, you can easily delete it. In Normal view, with the particular slide displayed, press Delete on the keyboard. You can also delete a slide, by right-clicking the slide, then cick Delete Slide on the shortcut menu. If you accidentally delete the wrong slide, immediately click the Undo Delete Slide button on the Quick Access Toolbar to restore the slide.

Step-by-Step 1.11

1. In Slide Sorter view, right-click the **slide 9** thumbnail, the new blank slide you inserted in a previous Step-by-Step. A shortcut menu opens.

2. On the shortcut menu, click **Delete Slide**. The slides renumber, and now there are 14 slides in the presentation.

3. Click the **slide 13** thumbnail.

4. Save the presentation and leave it open for the next Step-by-Step.

Printing a Presentation

▶ VOCABULARY
handouts

PowerPoint offers several print options that can enhance your presentation for an audience. You can print all the slides in the presentation, you can print *handouts* that contain small pictures or thumbnails of your slides, along with an area for taking notes. You can also print a text outline of the presentation. Click the File tab on the Ribbon, then click Print to view the Print options in Backstage view, as shown in **Figure 1–17**. You can choose to print your presentation using the various settings in the center pane. Using the Handouts option, you can print handouts with two, three, four, six, or nine slides per page and choose whether they are ordered horizontally or vertically. If you are printing multiple copies of your presentation, you can choose how you want the pages collated.

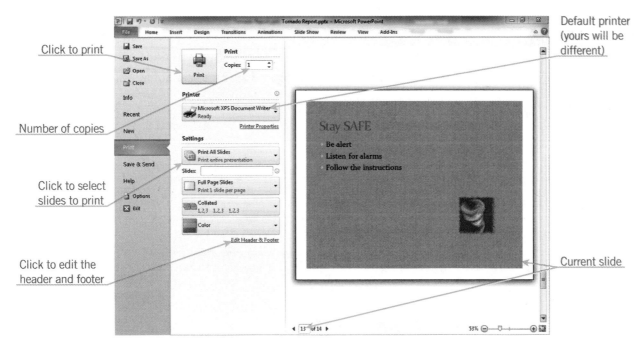

Click to print

Default printer (yours will be different)

Number of copies

Click to select slides to print

Click to edit the header and footer

Current slide

FIGURE 1–17   Print options

You can choose to print all the slides, only the current slide, or any combination of slides in your presentation. If you aren't printing your presentation in color, you can choose either the Grayscale or Pure black-and-white option. To make sure the slides print on the page correctly, there is a Scale to fit paper option. With the Frame slides option, you can choose whether the border of the slides appears when printed.

Step-by-Step 1.12

1. Click the **File** tab, and then on the navigation bar, click **Print**. The Print tab appears in Backstage View. (Refer again to Figure 1–17.)

2. In the first section, click the **Print All Slides** button, and then click **Print Current Slide**.

3. Make sure **1** appears in the Copies box. The selected slide, **slide 13**, appears in the right pane of Backstage view, as it would if you printed it.

4. To help distinguish your work from your classmates, enter your name in the presentation. At the bottom of the first section, click the **Edit Header and Footer** link to open the Header and Footer dialog box. Click the **Footer** check box, type your name in the Footer box, click the **Notes and Handouts** tab, click the **Footer** check box again, type your name in the Footer box, and then click **Apply to All**. Notice that your name appears at the bottom of slide 13 in the preview.

5. At the top of the first section, click the **Print** button, and then click **OK** in the Print dialog box to print the current slide.

> **TIP**
>
> You can preview what your presentation will look like when printed in black and white. On the Print tab in Backstage view, click the Color button, and then click Grayscale or Pure Black and White. You can also click the Grayscale or Black and White button in the Color/Grayscale group on the View tab on the Ribbon.

6. Click the **File** tab again, and then on the navigation bar, click **Print**. In the Settings section, click the **Print Current Slide** button, click **Print All Slides**, click the **Full Page Slides** button, and then click **Outline**.

7. Click the **Outline** button to open that menu again. See **Figure 1–18**.

FIGURE 1–18
Print Layout options

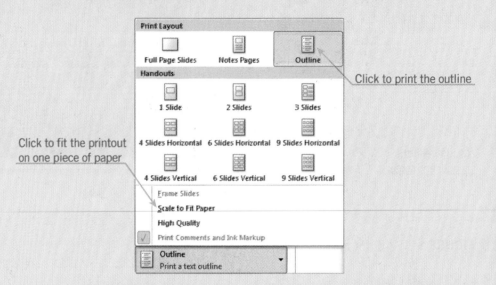

8. Click **Scale to Fit Paper**. Now the printout of the outline will fit on one piece of paper. The slide appears in the Print Preview tab window as an outline.

9. At the top of the first section, click the **Print** button, and then click **OK**. The presentation prints as an outline on one page.

10. Click the **File** tab, and then on the navigation bar, click **Print** again. In the center section, click the **Full Page Slides** button, and then in the Handouts section, click **9 Slides Horizontal**. This will print the first nine slides on one piece of paper, arranged horizontally, and the remaining five slides on another piece. Notice the right side of the Print tab changes to show this.

11. Click the **Print** button at the top of the center section. The presentation prints as a handout.

12. Click the **Home** tab on the Ribbon to leave Backstage view. Leave the presentation open for the next Step-by-Step.

Closing a Presentation and Exiting PowerPoint

When you want to close a presentation, click the File tab, and then on the navigation bar, click Exit, or click the presentation window Close button. If there are any unsaved changes to a presentation you have been working on, you will be asked if you want to save them before exiting.

Step-by-Step 1.13

1. Click the **File** tab, and then on the navigation bar, click **Exit** to close the presentation and exit PowerPoint.

2. Click **Yes** if prompted to save your changes.

SUMMARY

In this lesson, you learned:

- PowerPoint is an Office application that can help you create a professional presentation. When you start PowerPoint, you have the choice of opening an existing presentation or creating a new one.

- You can view your presentation in five different ways: Normal view, Slide Sorter view, Slide Show view, Reading view, and Notes Page view. Each view has its own advantages.

- You can insert slides, add text and objects to slides, and delete slides as you work to create the presentation.

- To view the presentation with animations and transitions, you use Slide Show or Reading view. A slide show can advance automatically or by clicking or pressing specific keys on the keyboard.

- You can print your presentation as slides using the Slides option, with notes using the Notes Pages option, or as an outline using the Outline View option. You can also choose to print handouts with two, three, four, six, or nine slides per page.

- To exit PowerPoint, click the File tab on the Ribbon, and then on the navigation bar, click Exit.

VOCABULARY REVIEW

Define the following terms:

animation	Notes Page view	Slide Show view
broadcasting	Notes pane	Slide Sorter view
handouts	Outline tab	Slides tab
layout	PowerPoint presentation	thumbnail
Live Preview	Reading view	transition
Normal view	Slide pane	Zoom slider

REVIEW QUESTIONS

MULTIPLE CHOICE

Select the best response for the following statements.

1. When you start PowerPoint, the first slide you see is the _____ slide.

    A.   main   C.   title

    B.   Slide Sorter   D.   animation

2. In which pane do you do most of the work creating and building slides?

    A.   Outline   C.   Notes

    B.   Slide   D.   Standard

3. Which of the following describes how objects are placed on a slide?

    A. Content   C. Animation

    B. Layout   D. Panes

4. How do you delete a selected slide?

    A. Click Delete Slide on the shortcut menu.

    B. Click the Erase Slide button.

    C. Click the New Slide button.

    D. Click the Zoom Out button.

5. Which of the following shows thumbnails of the slides?

    A. Notes pane   C. Outline tab

    B. Slide Show view   D. Slides tab

FILL IN THE BLANK

Complete the following sentences by writing the correct word or words in the blanks provided.

1. When you click the Title and Content thumbnail, you create a new slide from the _____ gallery.

2. The _____ tab in Normal view displays all of the text on your slides in the tab thumbnail.

3. The _____ shows only the text or words on the slides.

4. _____ are small images of the slides.

5. You can print _____ that contain small pictures or thumbnails of your slides.

MATCHING

Match the correct View in column 1 with the Description in column 2.

View	Description
_____ 1. Slide Sorter	A. Shows overview of all slides in the presentation
_____ 2. Normal	B. Displays each slide so that it fills the entire screen and so that you can see animations and transitions
_____ 3. Reading	C. Displays slides on the top portion of the page, with speaker notes on the bottom of the page
_____ 4. Slide Show	D. Full screen view of slides but with the title and status bar with navigation buttons
_____ 5. Notes Page	E. Use to add content to slides

■ PROJECTS

If you have a SAM 2010 user profile, your instructor may have assigned an autogradable version of the indicated project. If so, log into the SAM 2010 Web site at *www.cengage.com/sam2010* to download the instruction and start files.

PROJECT 1–1

1. Open the **Network.pptx** Data File.

2. Save the presentation as **Network Summary** followed by your initials.

3. Run the presentation as a slide show. Click to advance each slide, see the transitions and animations, and to display the bulleted items on each slide.

4. Leave the presentation open for the next project.

PROJECT 1–3

1. Search the Internet for a PowerPoint project about a subject that interests you.

2. Create a presentation with the list of your ideas on two slides.

3. Save the project to your computer.

4. Run the presentation as a slide show.

5. Print the presentation as audience handouts on one piece of paper.

6. Save and close the presentation. Exit PowerPoint.

PROJECT 1–2

1. View the **Network Summary** presentation in Slide Sorter view.

2. Select and move slide number 6 so that it is the second slide in the presentation.

3. Use the Font Color button in the Font group on the Home tab to change the color of any text on any slide.

4. Print the presentation as audience handouts with 9 Slides Vertical per page.

5. Switch to Reading view, and then run the presentation as a slide show.

6. Save and close the presentation. Exit PowerPoint.

CRITICAL THINKING

ACTIVITY 1–1

You can change the way that PowerPoint displays when you initially open the program. Open the PowerPoint Options dialog box by clicking the File tab, and then on the navigation bar, clicking Options. Review the General, Proofing, Save, and Advanced options that are available. Click Cancel to not save any changes.

ACTIVITY 1–2

It is helpful to plan a presentation before you actually create it on the computer. Sketch out ideas on paper for a presentation on one of the topics below, or make up your own. The presentation should have at least four slides. Include a title slide and indicate where you would put clip art, a video, and animation.

- Help start a community campaign to keep your city clean.
- Encourage people to donate blood in the blood drive campaign next week.
- Explain the procedure for some safety technique (performing CPR, fire prevention, how to baby-proof a house, performing first-aid).
- Offer the opportunity to be involved in a community project or volunteer organization.
- Explain the advantages of adopting an animal from the local shelter.
- Provide information about a new class that will be available in the fall.

LESSON 2

Creating and Enhancing PowerPoint Presentations

■ OBJECTIVES

Upon completion of this lesson, you should be able to:

- Create presentations and add slides.
- Insert headers and footers.
- Use the Slide Master and the Notes and Handout Master.
- Format slides, change layouts, and apply themes.
- Insert and edit text, then change alignment, spacing, case, and tabs.
- Check spelling, style, and usage.
- Add hyperlinks, clip art, and sounds.
- Apply custom animation and transitions.

■ VOCABULARY

align

animation

blank presentation

effect options

handout master

hyperlink

layout master

live preview

motion paths

notes master

placeholder

slide master

slide transitions

template

themes

Creating Presentations

When you start PowerPoint, a new *blank presentation* appears on the screen. You can begin a new presentation from a blank presentation, or you can use any of the built-in features to help you start a new presentation. There are different methods you can use to create a presentation. In this lesson, you will learn how to create a presentation from a template and how to enhance a presentation and make it your own. You will learn how to add different elements and features to create a presentation that communicates your ideas and interests your audience.

Starting to Create a Presentation

To create your presentation, you can start with a blank presentation, you can use slides from an existing presentation, you can use a template, or you can create a presentation from an existing theme. A *template* is simply a presentation that includes theme elements, text, and graphics predesigned for a presentation. Templates are often very useful to help you get started on your presentation. The templates that come with PowerPoint are already formatted with certain themes, graphics, colors, fonts, and layouts. Templates often include some text to help you get started.

Start PowerPoint, click the File tab, and then click New to view the Available Templates and Themes in Backstage view, as shown in **Figure 2–1**. Blank Presentation is the first option; however, you can select from Recent templates, Sample templates, Themes, My templates, and New from existing. The list of Recent Templates contains the template files that were last opened.

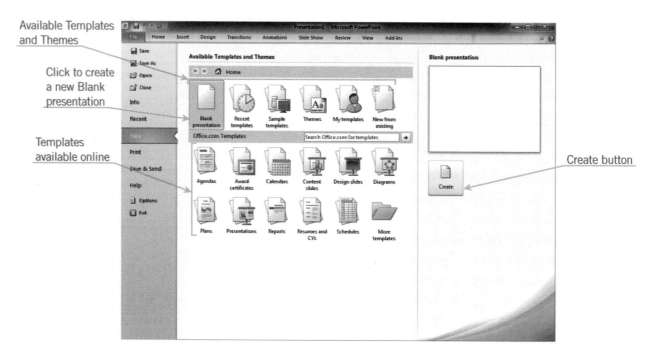

FIGURE 2–1   The New tab in Backstage view

The Blank Presentation option on the New tab in Backstage view lets you create a presentation from scratch, using the layout, format, colors, and graphics you prefer. If you decide to create a presentation using a template, you can choose a template that is right for the presentation you have planned. The Sample templates are shown in **Figure 2–2**.

EXTRA FOR EXPERTS

You can also create a presentation by opening an existing presentation, making changes, then saving with a new name. Click the File tab to open Backstage view, and then click New from existing to open an existing presentation. Search for templates on the computer. If you select an existing presentation, it opens with a temporary file name so you do not accidentally save changes to the original file.

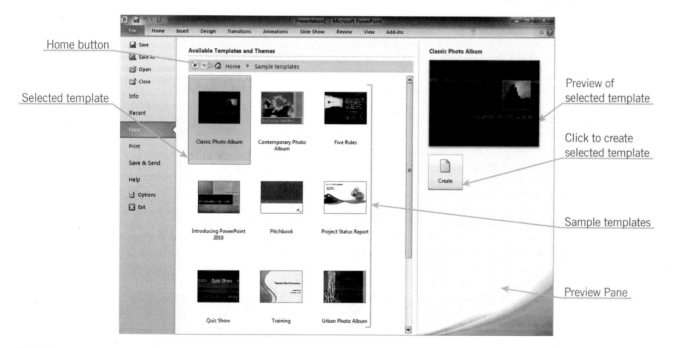

FIGURE 2–2   Sample templates on the New tab

When you select templates in Backstage view, you navigate through folders to find the template that you want. A navigation bar that works just like the Address bar in Windows Explorer appears above the list of templates in the center pane. Click the previous folder to back up a level, click Home to go to the first level showing all the templates, or click the Forward and Back buttons as needed to find the template to download.

If your computer is connected to the Internet, you can select from professional templates that are posted on Microsoft Office Online Web site at www.office.com. To choose a template from Microsoft's Web site, click the type of template you would like in the Office.com Online section, open a folder to display templates in that category, and then click any thumbnail. In Backstage view, the right pane is the *Preview pane* as it shows a preview of the selected template. Once you find the template you want, click Download, as shown in **Figure 2–3**.

Available Award Certificate templates at www.office.com

Selected template

Preview of selected template

Click to download selected template

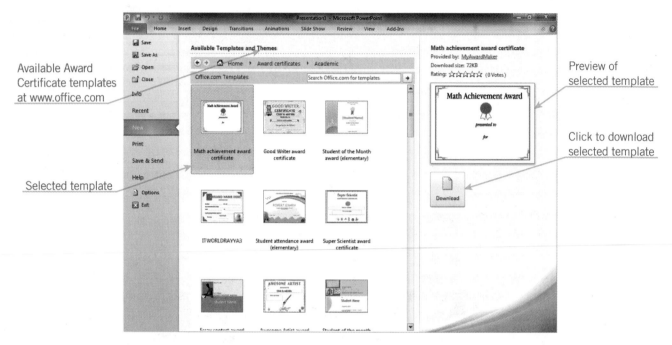

FIGURE 2–3 Award certificates category in the Available Templates and Themes section

Unless you have a particular reason for creating a presentation from a blank document, it is easier and less time consuming to use a template. You can always modify the presentation as you go along.

Step-by-Step 2.1

 WARNING

If the Introducing PowerPoint 2010 template is not available on your system, select any other template to complete these steps.

1. Start PowerPoint. Click the **File** tab, and then click **New**. Backstage view opens with options for templates, themes, or a new blank presentation.

2. In the top row, click **Sample templates**, scroll to view the available templates, and then click the **Introducing PowerPoint 2010** thumbnail.

3. Click the **Create** button in the Preview pane.

   A presentation that includes 20 slides, complete with sample content, is created, as shown in **Figure 2–4**. The text is formatted, and many of the slides include graphics. You can view, edit, and modify this presentation just as you would any presentation. You can add and delete slides as necessary for your purposes.

FIGURE 2–4
Presentation from template

4. On the Quick Access Toolbar, click the **Save** button, navigate to the drive and folder where your Data Files are stored, and then save the presentation as **PowerPoint2010 Tour**, followed by your initials.

5. On the status bar, click the **Slide Show** button and then press **spacebar** to advance through all of the slides in the presentation.

6. Click the **File** tab, and then click **Close** to close the presentation.

7. Leave PowerPoint open for the next Step-by-Step.

TIP

The Introducing PowerPoint 2010 presentation has useful information about PowerPoint 2010 and the new features in the program. At any point if you want to stop the show, press Esc.

Creating Presentations from Existing Templates

If you cannot find a template that you like on Office.com or that came with PowerPoint, you can use one created by yourself or a colleague.

EXTRA FOR EXPERTS

PowerPoint templates have a .potx file extension. PowerPoint presentations have a .pptx file extension.

Step-by-Step 2.2

1. Click the **File** tab, and then click **New**.

2. In the top row in the Available Templates and Themes section, click **New from existing**. The New from Existing Presentation dialog box opens.

3. Navigate to the drive and folder where your Data Files are stored, click **EMT.potx**, and then click **Create New**. EMT.potx is a template that was created for you. You created a new presentation from that template.

4. On the Quick Access Toolbar, click the **Save** button.

TIP

Be sure the file extension for the selected file is .potx.

5. Navigate to the drive and folder where your Data Files are stored, and then save the presentation as **EMT Rosewood**, followed by your initials.

6. On the vertical scroll bar, click the **Next Slide** button ⬇ as many times as needed to view the slides, and then press **Home** to return to the first slide. There are several slides in the presentation, but they do not have color, graphics, or any enhancements that would make a presentation fun and interesting to watch.

7. Leave the presentation open for the next Step-by-Step.

Inserting Headers and Footers

You can add text to every slide using the Header and Footer dialog box. You can also add the slide number, date, or time in a header or footer. Click the Insert tab on the Ribbon, and then in the Text group, click the Header & Footer button. This opens the Header and Footer dialog box, which has two tabs. You can add headers and footers to the slides or the notes and handouts.

Step-by-Step 2.3

1. On the Ribbon, click the **Insert** tab, and then in the Text group, click the **Header & Footer** button to open the Header and Footer dialog box. The **Slide** tab should be selected, as shown in **Figure 2–5**.

FIGURE 2–5
Header and Footer dialog box

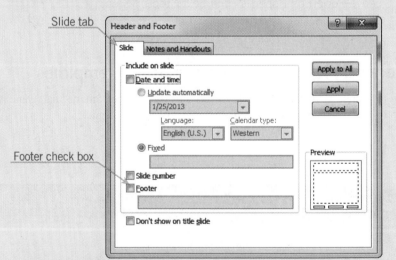

2. Click the **Footer** check box, and then, in the Footer box, type **This presentation is not intended as a substitute for professional medical training.**

3. Click **Apply to All**. The footer appears on all the slides in the presentation. See **Figure 2–6**.

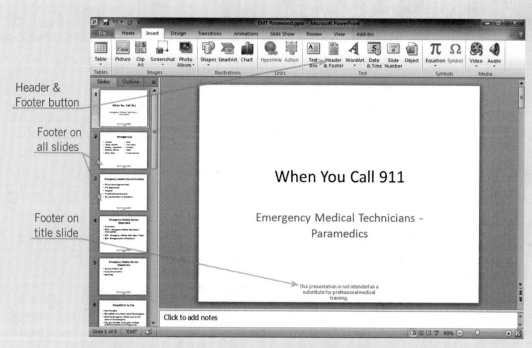

Header &
Footer button

Footer on
all slides

Footer on
title slide

FIGURE 2–6
Footer added to all slides

4. On the vertical scroll bar, click the **Next Slide** button ⬇ three times to view the next three slides, and then press **Home** to return to the first slide.

5. Leave the presentation open for the next Step-by-Step.

Applying Themes

You can use a theme to change the appearance of your slides without changing the content. *Themes* are predesigned graphic styles that you can apply to existing slides. Themes include fonts, colors, graphics and effects. After you apply a theme, you can change the color theme, font, formatting, and layout of your slides to create a different look.

Applying Themes to the Entire Presentation

To apply a theme to a presentation, first click the Design tab on the Ribbon. The Themes group on the Design tab displays all the available themes. Click the More button in the Themes group to open the Themes gallery. When you position the pointer over a theme, the name of the theme appears in a ScreenTip and the selected slide shows a Live Preview of the effect of the theme on the slide. Click the theme thumbnail to apply the theme to all the slides in the presentation.

▶ **VOCABULARY**

themes

📇 **EXTRA FOR EXPERTS**

To create a new presentation with a theme different from the default theme, click the File tab to open Backstage view, and then on the navigation bar, click New. In the top row in the Available Templates and Themes section, click Themes. Click the theme you want to use, and then click the Create button.

Step-by-Step 2.4

1. On the Ribbon, click the **Design** tab, and then in the Themes group click the **More** button to open the Themes gallery.

2. Move the mouse pointer over several of the themes to use Live Preview to see the effect on the slides.

3. Click the **Austin** theme (use the ScreenTips to help you identify this theme). PowerPoint applies the Austin theme to all of the slides in the presentation, as shown in **Figure 2–7**. The new theme caused some changes to be made to the format of some of the elements on the slides. The fonts changed, the footer moved to the right side of the title slide, and new graphics appear on the slides.

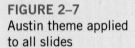

TIP

The themes in the gallery are organized in alphabetical order.

FIGURE 2–7
Austin theme applied to all slides

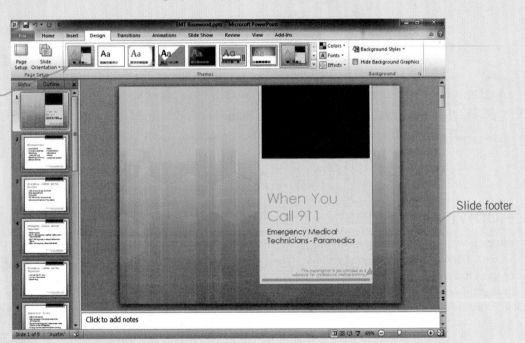

4. Save the presentation and leave it open for the next Step-by-Step.

Changing Theme Colors

All themes come with default theme fonts and theme colors. The styles of the fonts and the palette of colors help define the theme. You can change the theme fonts and colors at any time. Colors are assigned to specific elements in a presentation such as title or body text, background and accents. Themes create a unified look because the same colors are used for the same elements throughout a presentation. To apply different colors to your presentation, on the Ribbon, click the Design tab, and then in the Themes group, click the Colors button. A menu showing the list of the colors for each theme, as shown in **Figure 2–8**. You can use Live Preview with this menu. To apply a different set of theme colors to all of the slides without changing the theme, click the color scheme you want to use.

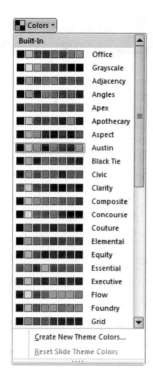

FIGURE 2–8   Colors gallery

You can apply a different color theme to all the slides by clicking the theme on the menu. You can also apply a color theme to selected slides. To select more than one slide, hold down Ctrl while you click the slides on the Slides tab. To apply color themes to only the selected slides, click the Colors button, right-click the Theme colors in the gallery, and then click Apply to Selected Slides on the shortcut menu.

> **TIP**
>
> You can use different colors to show a change of topics in your presentation.

Changing Theme Fonts

To apply a different set of theme fonts to your presentation, on the Ribbon, click the Design tab, and then in the Themes group, click the Fonts button. A menu opens listing the font sets for each theme. You can again use Live Preview to see the effect of applying each set of fonts. To apply a different set of fonts to the slides, simply click the set of fonts in the menu.

Applying a Theme to Individual Slides

You can use a theme to change the appearance of a single slide or several slides without changing the rest of the slides in the presentation. To select more than one slide, hold down Ctrl while you click the slides on the Slides tab. To view the themes, click the Design tab. If you right-click the theme thumbnail in the Themes group, the shortcut menu options let you apply the theme to all of the slides in your presentation or to only the select slides. To apply the new theme to these selected slides, click Apply to Selected Slide on the shortcut menu to apply the new theme to the selected slide rather than all the slides in the presentation.

> **TIP**
>
> Right-click the theme thumbnail to view options that you can use to set the default theme or add the Gallery to the Quick Access Toolbar.

Step-by-Step 2.5

1. On the Slides tab, click the **slide 6** thumbnail, *Dispatcher Duties*.
2. On the Design tab, click the **More** button ⊽ in the Themes group to open the Themes gallery.
3. In the Themes gallery, point to the **Apothecary** theme, see the effect on the slide, right-click the **Apothecary** theme, and then click **Apply to Selected Slides**. The theme of the current slide changes to the new theme.
4. In the Themes group, click the **Colors** button to open the Colors gallery, right-click **Flow**, and then click **Apply to Selected Slides**. The color of the text in the title as well as the color of the text in the body of the slide changed to dark teal. The bullets also changed from gray to blue to match the new theme colors.
5. Save the presentation and leave it open for the next Step-by-Step.

📧 EXTRA FOR EXPERTS

The Apply to Matching Slides option applies the selected theme to all slides in the presentation that have the same layout as the selected slide.

▶ VOCABULARY

slide master

placeholder

layout masters

📧 EXTRA FOR EXPERTS

Layouts also include placeholders for slide objects such as tables, charts, SmartArt graphics, movies, sounds, pictures, and clip art.

Using the Slide Master

The *slide master* controls the formatting for all the slides in the presentation. For each presentation the slide master stores information about the theme and slide layouts, including the background, color, fonts, effects, placeholder sizes and placement on the slides. *Placeholders* are the boxes in layouts that hold the content or slide objects such as body text and titles. Each slide master has several *layout masters*. There is a slide master and associated layouts for each theme in the presentation. You can use the slide master to change such items as the font, size, color, style, alignment, spacing, and background. Changing the slide master affects the appearance of all of the slides in a presentation associated with that master slide or layout, and gives all slides associated with the master a consistent look. You can add headers and footers to slides in the slide master. You can also place an object, such as a logo or graphic, on every slide by placing the object on the slide master.

To view the slide master and layouts, as shown in **Figure 2–9**, you need to switch to Slide Master view. Click the View tab on the Ribbon, and then in the Master Views group, click the Slide Master button. When you are in Slide Master view, the pane on the left displays the slide master as the first thumbnail and the layouts as thumbnails underneath it. The layouts are nested beneath each slide master. When you point to the slide master or to a layout, a ScreenTip displays the name of the master and the slide numbers of the slides in the presentation to which that layout is applied. To make changes to the slide master or a layout, click the master in the pane on the left to display it in the Slide pane.

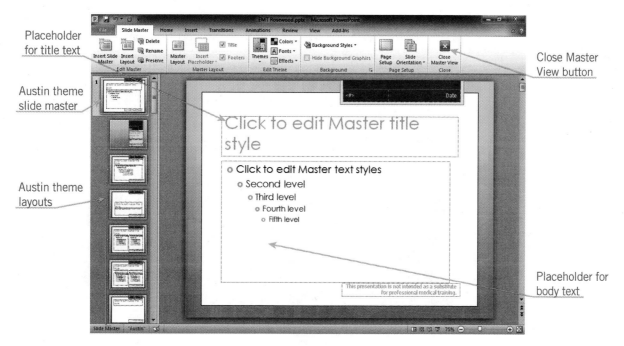

FIGURE 2–9   Slide Master view

In Slide Master view, the Slide Master tab appears on the Ribbon. Use the buttons in the Edit Master group to insert a new layout master or insert a new slide master. The Master Layout group buttons help you change the master layout, including headers and footers. The Edit Theme buttons change the theme characteristics for the entire slide show. The Background group buttons work to change the graphics behind the objects, and open the Format Background dialog box to change the Fill or Picture on the background of the selected layouts. The Page Setup group changes the slide orientation from Portrait to Landscape and changes margins for the entire slide show. Click the Close Master View button to return to Normal view.

TIP

You can override the formats applied to the presentation by the slide master by making changes directly to individual slides.

Step-by-Step 2.6

1. On the Ribbon, click the **View** tab, and then click the **Slide Master** button in the Presentation Views group to open Slide Master view. You see the Apothecary slide master.

2. Scroll to the top of the slide layout thumbnails, and then click the first thumbnail, the **Austin Slide Master**. Refer back to Figure 2–9.

EXTRA FOR EXPERTS

Display the slide master by pressing Shift and clicking the Normal button on the status bar in the lower-right corner of your screen. Press Shift and click the Slide Sorter button on the status bar in the lower-right corner of your screen to display the handout master.

3. In the pane on the left, click the **second thumbnail** to view the Title Slide Layout for the Austin master. Refer to **Figure 2–10**.

The Hide Background Graphics check box is selected for this layout. This is set by the theme. Later in these steps you will add a graphic to the slide master that will not appear on the title slide because this box is checked.

FIGURE 2–10
Austin Slide Master

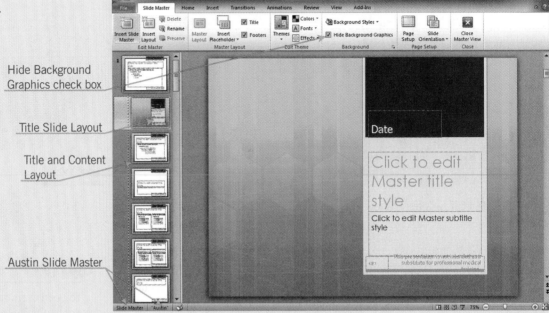

4. Point to the **third thumbnail**, the Title and Content Layout. The ScreenTip tells you which slides are used by the Title and Content Layout.

5. Click the **first thumbnail** to view the Austin Slide Master. On the Ribbon, click the **Insert** tab, and then in the Images group, click the **Picture** button to open the Insert Picture dialog box.

6. Navigate to the drive and folder where your Data Files are stored, click **FirstAid.jpg**, and then click **Insert**. The image of a red cross on a black background appears on the center of the slide master.

7. Click and drag the picture to the lower-left corner of the slide.

8. Position the pointer on top of the **upper-right sizing handle** so that it changes to ⟋, and then drag down and to the left to resize the picture smaller until the sizing handle is on top of the lower-left corner of the content placeholder. See **Figure 2–11**.

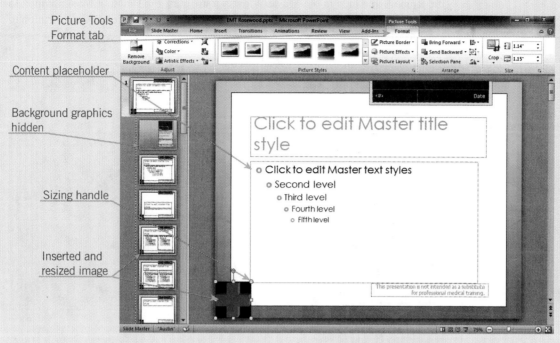

Picture Tools Format tab

Content placeholder

Background graphics hidden

Sizing handle

Inserted and resized image

FIGURE 2–11
Inserting a picture on the slide master

9. On the Ribbon, click the **Slide Master** tab, and then in the Close group, click the **Close Master View** button. Slide Master view closes and you see the presentation in Normal view again.

10. View the slides in the presentation. Slides 2–5 and 7–9, use the Austin theme, so they show the image of the red cross in the lower-left corner of the slide. Slide 6, which uses the Apothecary theme, does not show the image because it has its own slide master which does not include the image. The title slide does not show the image because the Hide Background Graphics check box is selected for the Title Slide Layout for this theme.

11. Save the presentation and leave it open for the next Step-by-Step.

Using the Notes Master and Handout Master

PowerPoint has other masters that are similar to the slide master. The *handout master* lets you add items that you want to appear on all your handouts, such as a logo, the date, the time, and page numbers. On the *notes master*, you include any text or formatting that you want to appear on all your speaker notes. Click the View tab on

▶ **VOCABULARY**
handout master

notes master

the Ribbon, and then in the Master Views group, click the Handout Master button to view the handout master, as shown in **Figure 2–12**. Click the Notes Master button to view the notes master, as shown in **Figure 2–13**.

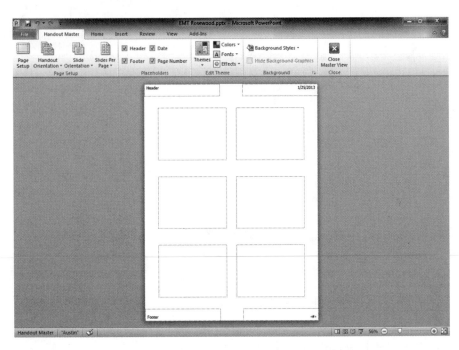

FIGURE 2–12   Handout master

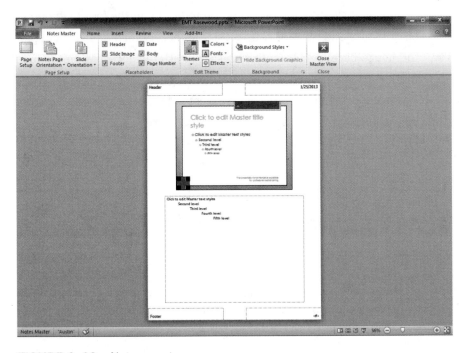

FIGURE 2–13   Notes master

Editing Pictures in PowerPoint

PowerPoint contains tools that allow you to edit, format, and stylize a picture to get the exact effect you need for a slide. Select the picture you want to edit to make the Picture Tools Format tab appear on the Ribbon. The Picture Tools Format tab includes buttons that allow you to adjust the picture's contrast, color and brightness, set a transparent color, or compress the picture. You can also apply a picture style and add a border. Use the Background Removal tool to remove the background of a picture so it blends in with the background of the slide. The picture editing tools include the ability to apply artistic effects. These are similar to effects you might find in picture editing programs, such as making the picture look like glass, appear cartoon-like, or seem to be painted using watercolors. You can arrange the picture to line up or *align* with the other objects on the slide. There are several align commands that place your object relative to other objects on the slide. Align commands include Left, Center, Right, Top, Middle, and Bottom. You can also crop, rotate, resize, or reposition the picture as needed to best fit the slide. The Reset Picture feature will undo all changes you made and display the picture as it originally appeared.

▶ **VOCABULARY**
align

Step-by-Step 2.7

1. On the Slides tab, click the **slide 1** thumbnail. On the Ribbon, click the **Insert** tab, and then in the Images group, click the **Picture** button to open the Insert Picture dialog box.

2. In the drive and folder where your Data Files are stored, click **Rose.jpg**, and then click **Insert**. A picture of a red rose appears in the center of the slide and fills the slide.

3. On the Picture Tools Format tab on the Ribbon, in the Size group, click in the **Shape Height** text box, type **2** and then press **Enter**. You don't need to change the width because it adjusted proportionally to 3" when you changed the shape height.

4. Drag the image of the rose to the center of the green panel so that it is positioned in a way that you find appropriate for the slide.

5. On the Format tab, in the Arrange group, click the **Align** button 🖺▾ to open the menu, and then click **Align Middle**. The photo is now in the middle of the green panel.

6. In the Picture Styles group, click the **More** button ▾ to open the Picture Styles gallery, and then slowly point to several picture styles to see the effect on the picture and read the ScreenTips identifying the name of each style.

7. In the Picture Styles gallery, click the **Metal Rounded Rectangle** style in the last row, second to last style.

8. In the Adjust group, click the **Artistic Effects** button. Move the mouse pointer over several of the thumbnails to see the effect on the photo and read the ScreenTips, and then click the **Glass** effect, the last effect in the third row.

9. In the Adjust group, click the **Color** button, and then in the Recolor section, click the **Green**, **Accent color 1 Dark** color box.

10. In the Adjust group, click the **Compress Pictures** button, make sure the **Apply only to this picture** check box is selected, and the **Use document resolution** option button is selected, and then click **OK**.

11. Click to deselect the picture and compare your slide to **Figure 2–14**.

FIGURE 2–14
Formatted picture
on the title slide

Formatted picture

12. Save the presentation and leave it open for the next Step-by-Step.

Understanding Layouts

When you want to change the arrangement of text or graphics on slides easily, you can use the theme's layouts. PowerPoint includes nine layouts that you can choose from to create a new slide or change the layout of an existing slide. The layouts include placeholders for text and content. Text includes paragraphs and bulleted lists. Content can be clip art, tables, organization charts, SmartArt graphics, objects, graphs, video, and media clips. Just click a placeholder icon and replace it with your own file or object. You can choose the layout that best fits the need of a particular slide.

Adding Slides

As you continue to create your presentation, you will want to add slides. On the Ribbon, on the Home tab, in the Slides group, click the New Slide button or right-click the slide thumbnail on the Slides tab or in Slide Sorter view, and click New Slide on the shortcut menu. You can also click the New Slide button arrow, then click Duplicate Selected Slides to insert a new slide that is the same as the selected slide or slides. In Normal view, PowerPoint places the new slide after the selected slide, using the same layout as the selected slide. Clicking the New Slide button arrow

 **EXTRA FOR EXPERTS**

You can reuse slides from other presentations. In the Slides group, click the New Slide button arrow, click the Reuse Slides command to open the Reuse Slides task pane, select the presentation that has the slides, and then select each slide you want to reuse.

opens the Slide Layout gallery, which allows you to choose a layout for the new slide. The Slide Layout gallery has the nine standard layouts based on the theme that has been applied. Click a layout to insert a new slide with that layout.

Step-by-Step 2.8

1. On the Slides tab, click the **slide 9** thumbnail, *Features of Emergency Departments*.

2. In the Slides group, click the **New Slide** button arrow to open the Slide Layout gallery. Because you applied a second theme to one of the slides in this presentation, there are two sets of layouts in the gallery labeled with the theme names: Austin and Apothecary.

3. In the Austin section, click the **Two Content** layout to insert a new slide with the Austin theme. The new slide 10 has a title placeholder and two content placeholders. Your slide should look similar to **Figure 2–15**.

> **TIP**
>
> The status bar tells you the slide number of the selected slide, total number of slides, and theme of the slide.

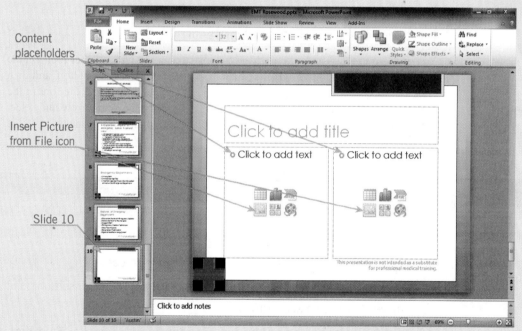

Content placeholders

Insert Picture from File icon

Slide 10

FIGURE 2–15
New slide with Two Content layout

4. In the right content placeholder, click the **Insert Picture from File** icon to open the Insert Picture dialog box. In the drive and folder where your Data Files are stored, click **FirstAid.jpg**, and then click **Insert**.

5. Use the buttons on the Picture Tools Format tab to apply your choice of picture effects to format the picture.

6. Save the presentation and leave it open for the next Step-by-Step.

Finding and Replacing Text on Slides

To find and replace text, on the Home tab of the Ribbon, in the Editing group, use the Find and Replace buttons. The Find what box is in the Find dialog box as well as the Replace dialog box. The Find command locates the word or phrase you type in the Find what box. The Replace command locates the word or phrase you type in the Find what box and replaces it as directed with the word or phrase you have typed in the Replace with box in the Replace dialog box. See **Figure 2–16**. Click Find Next to find the next occurrence, Replace to replace the next occurrence, and Replace All to replace all occurrences.

FIGURE 2–16   Replace dialog box

Finding and Replacing Fonts on Slides

You can also use the Replace command to replace one font with another font. On the Home tab in the Editing group, click the arrow next to the Replace button, and then click Replace Fonts. The Replace Font dialog box opens. You select the font in the presentation that you want to replace, and then you click the With arrow and select the font you want to replace it with. Click Replace and all the text formatted with the original font will be reformatted with the replacement font.

Step-by-Step 2.9

1. On the Home tab, in the Editing group, click the **Replace** button. The Replace dialog box opens at the bottom of the screen.

2. In the Find what box, type **Staff**, and then press **Tab**. The insertion point moves to the Replace with box.

3. In the Replace with text box, type **Personnel**, and then click **Find Next**. PowerPoint finds the word "Staff" on slide 9.

4. Click **Replace**. The word "Staff" is replaced on slide 9 with the word "Personnel" and PowerPoint searches for the next instance of the word "Staff." A dialog box opens telling you that PowerPoint has finished searching the presentation.

5. Click **OK** to close that dialog box, and then in the Replace dialog box, click **Close**.

6. Save the presentation and leave it open for the next Step-by-Step.

Adding Text to Slides

As you continue to work on your presentation, you may find that you need to add text to help explain a concept or introduce a new idea. Words should be used sparingly on a slide. However, you can always add text to existing slides to improve the presentation.

Working with Placeholders

The slide layouts create placeholders on the slides that reserve a space in the presentation for the type of information you want to insert. To replace a text placeholder, click the placeholder text. A box with a hashed-line border appears around the text. You can then type whatever you like. One way to enter text on a slide is to work in the Slide pane; this way you can see the text you enter, the formatting, and the placement on the slide.

TIP

You can also add a text box to a slide. A text box is created by clicking the Insert tab on the Ribbon, and then, in the Text group, clicking the Text box button.

Step-by-Step 2.10

1. On the Slides tab, click the **slide 10** thumbnail.

2. In the Slide pane, click the **Click to add title** placeholder, and then type **CPR**.

3. In the left content placeholder, click the **Click to add text** placeholder, type **Begin rescue breathing**, then press **Enter**. A new bullet appears for the second line in the content placeholder.

4. Type **Begin chest compressions**, press **Enter**, and then type **Call 911**. The slide has a slide title and a bulleted list with 3 lines of text in the left placeholder. The image you entered is in the right placeholder.

5. On the Ribbon, on the Home tab, click the **New Slide** button arrow in the Slides group, and then click the **Title and Content** layout to create a new slide 11.

6. In the Slide pane, click the **Click to add title** placeholder, and then type **Why Study First Aid?**.

7. Click the **Click to add text** placeholder, type **Injury and illness occur daily**, press **Enter**, type **Knowledge can help**, press **Enter**, and then type **Proper reaction may improve recovery**.

8. In the Slides group, click the **New Slide** button to insert a new slide 12 with a Title and Content layout.

9. In the Slide pane, click the **Click to add title** placeholder, and then type **Emergencies**.

10. Click the **Click to add text** placeholder. Type the following and press **Enter** after each line, and then click a blank area of the slide to deselect the placeholder. Compare your screen to **Figure 2–17** when you are finished.

- **Bleeding**
- **Shock**
- **Fractures**
- **Poisoning**
- **CPR**

FIGURE 2–17
New slides on Slides tab

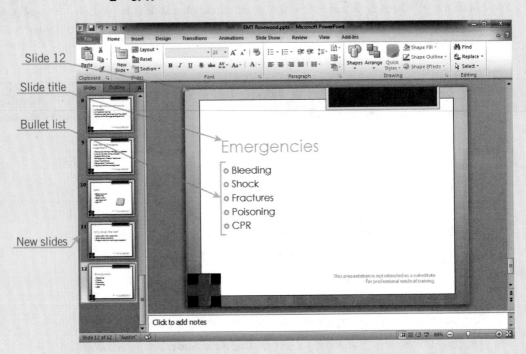

11. Save the presentation and leave it open for the next Step-by-Step.

Using the Outline Tab to Enter Text

You have learned how to enter text by typing it directly on the slide in the Slide pane. You can enter the rest of the presentation using the Outline tab. When you enter text using the Outline tab, pressing the Tab and Enter keys doesn't work the same way as when you work in the Slide pane.

Step-by-Step 2.11

1. In the left pane, click the **Outline** tab.

2. On the Ribbon, on the Home tab, click the **New Slide** button in the Slides group to insert a new slide 13 with a Title and Content layout.

3. On the Outline tab, type **Bleeding** as the title of the new slide 13. You did not have to click the title placeholder as you type on the Outline tab. The text appears in the placeholder on the Slide pane.

4. Press **Enter** and then press **Tab**. The insertion point is now after a new bullet that was created on the Bleeding slide.

5. Type the following as the content on the slide, pressing **Enter** after each line:

   - **Apply pressure**
   - **Use a clean bandage**
   - **Elevate injury**
   - **Slow bleeding**
   - **Call 911**

6. Press and hold **Ctrl**, and then press **Enter** to insert a new slide with a Title and content layout. Type **Shock** as the title for this slide.

7. Press **Enter** and then press **Tab** to move the insertion point the first bullet for this slide.

8. Type the following as the content on the slide, pressing **Enter** after each line:

   - **Lie down**
   - **Elevate legs**
   - **Maintain body temp**
   - **Monitor breathing**
   - **Provide air**
   - **Call 911**

9. Insert another new slide with the **Title and Content** layout using any method. Using either the Outline tab or the Slides tab, type **CPR ABC** as the title of this slide.

10. Type the following as the content on the slide:

    - **Airway**
    - **Breathing**
    - **Circulation**

TIP

If you press Tab, the text will become a bullet on the previous slide.

TIP

When the insertion point is in the slide title, you can also press and hold Ctrl, and then press Enter to move the insertion point into the content placeholder.

11. Compare your Outline tab and your slides with **Figure 2–18**. Save the presentation and leave it open for the next Step-by-Step.

FIGURE 2–18
New slides on the Outline tab

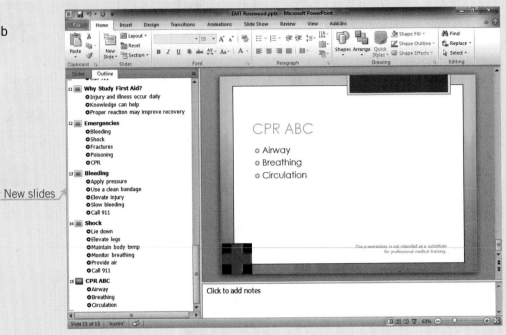

New slides

Entering Text in Text Boxes and Shapes

You have learned how to enter text by typing it directly on the slide in the Slide pane. You also learned that you can enter text using the Outline tab. These methods enter text into placeholders. There are times when you want to enter text on a slide where there is no placeholder. In this case, the text box or shape provides the perfect solution. You can use the Text Box tool to add text to a slide without using a content or text placeholder. On the Ribbon, on the Insert tab, in the Text group, click the Text Box button. To add a shape, on the Home tab click the Shapes button to open the Shapes gallery. The Shapes button is also on the Insert tab in the Illustrations group. Once you open the Shapes gallery, click to select a shape, then use the pointer to draw the shape on the slide. To add text to a shape, select the shape, then type the text in the shape.

Step-by-Step 2.12

1. In the pane on the left, click the **Slides** tab. **Slide 15**, *CPR ABC*, is selected and appears in the Slide pane.

2. On the Ribbon, click the **Insert** tab, and then in the Text group, click the **Text Box** button.

3. In the Slide pane, click in the middle of the slide. You created a text box on the slide.

4. Type **If the patient does not respond, call 911.**, and then click a blank area of the slide. Compare your screen to **Figure 2–19**. If your text box is in a different position than in the figure, click it, and then click drag the border of the text box (not a sizing handle) to move the text box to a new position on the slide.

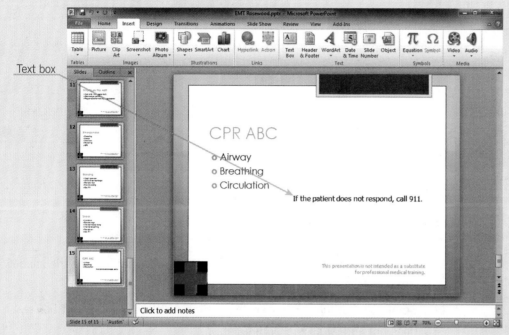

Text box

FIGURE 2–19
Text box on slide

5. On the Slides tab, click the **slide 3**, *Emergency Medical Service Providers* thumbnail.

6. On the Home tab on the Ribbon, in the Drawing group, click the **Shapes** button. The Shapes gallery opens. Use the Screen Tips in the Shapes gallery to identify the shapes you want.

7. In the Rectangles section, click the **Rounded Rectangle** shape ▢.

8. Click in the area of the slide just below and to the right of the word "above". A rectangle with rounded corners appears on the slide.

> **TIP**
>
> At higher resolutions, the Shapes button appears as a gallery on the Ribbon.

9. Type **EMS saves lives** as shown in **Figure 2–20**.

FIGURE 2–20
Text in a shape

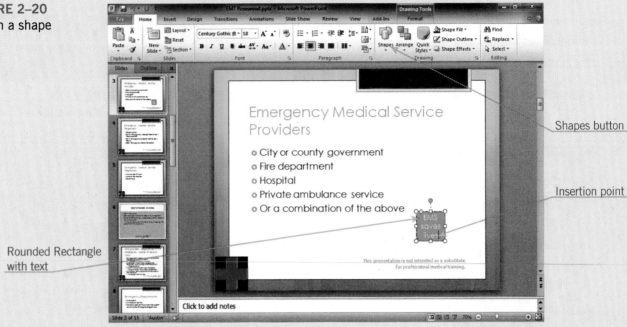

Shapes button

Insertion point

Rounded Rectangle
with text

10. Click the **Outline** tab. The outline for slide 3 does not include the shape with the text.

11. Scroll the Outline tab to view the outline for slide 15. The text box text does not appear on the Outline tab.

12. Save the presentation and leave it open for the next Step-by-Step.

Adding Notes to Slides

A good PowerPoint presentation generally contains brief, main points about the subject. You want your audience listening to you rather than reading large amounts of text on slides. Use the speaker notes to remind yourself of any additional information you need to include in your speech. To add speaker notes, click in the Notes pane below the Slide pane and begin typing, or switch to Notes Page view. If the text is too small to read in Notes Page view, you can increase the size by using the Zoom slider on the status bar.

Step-by-Step 2.13

1. In the pane on the left, click the **Slides** tab, and then click the **slide 10** thumbnail, *CPR*.

2. In the Notes pane, click the **Click to add notes** placeholder, and then type **Remember the ABCs of CPR: Airway, Breathing, Circulation**. See **Figure 2–21**.

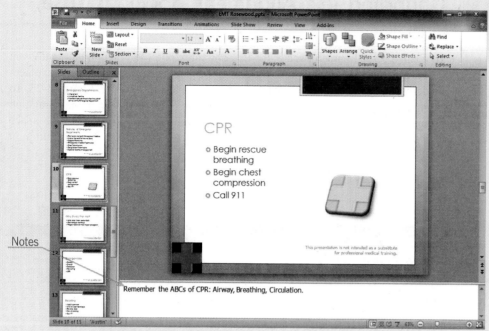

FIGURE 2–21
Note in Notes pane in
Normal view

3. On the Ribbon, click the **View** tab, and then in the Presentation Views
group, click the **Notes Page** button to see the Notes Page for slide 10.
See **Figure 2–22**.

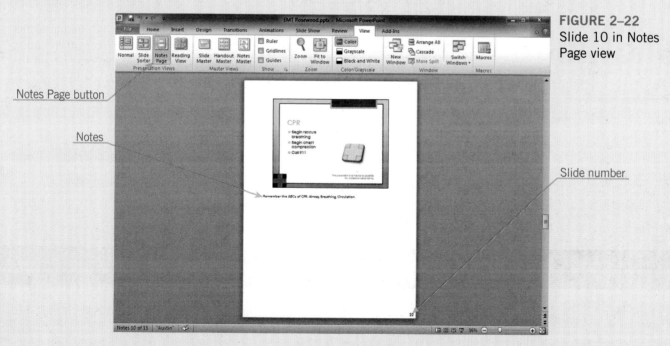

FIGURE 2–22
Slide 10 in Notes
Page view

4. Save the presentation and leave it open for the next Step-by-Step.

Changing Text Alignment, Spacing, Case, and Tabs

To change text alignment, select the text and click one of the alignment buttons in the Paragraph group on the Home tab on the Ribbon. Selected text in a content placeholder will also display the Drawing Tools Format tab as shown in **Figure 2–23**. To change line spacing, select the text, click the Line Spacing button in the Paragraph group, and then select the line spacing you want to use. To change the space between the characters or letters in your slide, use the Character Spacing button in the Font group.

Line Spacing button

Drawing Tools Format tab

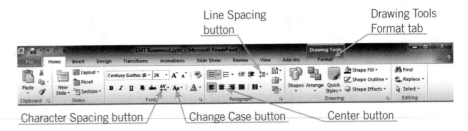

Character Spacing button   Change Case button   Center button

FIGURE 2–23   Drawing Tools Format tab

To change the case of text, first select the text. On the Ribbon, on the Home tab, in the Font group, click the Change Case button, and then choose one of the five options: Sentence case, lowercase, UPPERCASE, Capitalize Each Word, or tOGGLE cASE.

You can set a tab by selecting the text and clicking the Tab button at the left of the horizontal ruler. Clear a tab by dragging the tab marker off the ruler. See **Figure 2–24**. You turn the rulers on and off by clicking the View tab on the Ribbon, and then in the Show/Hide group, click the Ruler check box to select it.

Click to toggle through left, center, right, and decimal tabs

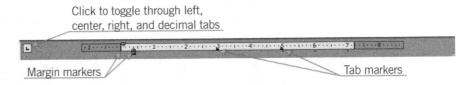

Margin markers   Tab markers

FIGURE 2–24   Tabs and margins on the ruler

Step-by-Step 2.14

1. On the status bar, click the **Normal** button ⊞ to switch back to Normal view.

2. On the Slides tab, click the **slide 15** thumbnail, *CPR*. Click the **Home** tab, and then in the Slides group, click the **New Slide** button. In the Slide pane, click the **Click to add title placeholder,** and then type **Web Resources** as the slide title.

3. Click in the content placeholder, type **American Red Cross** as the first bullet, press **Enter**, type **American Heart Association** as the second bullet, press **Enter**, and then type **KidsHealth** as the third bullet.

4. On the Home tab on the Ribbon, in the Paragraph group, click the **Center** button ≣. Because the insertion point was positioned in the third bullet, "KidsHealth," it is now centered on the slide.

5. Click directly on the **content placeholder border** so it becomes a solid line. Any formatting changes will now apply to all the text in the placeholder.

6. In the Paragraph group, click the **Line Spacing** button ‡≣▾ to display the Line Spacing options, and then click **2.0**. All of the bulleted text is now double-spaced.

7. Drag to select the text **American Red Cross**. In the Font group, click the **Change Case** button Aa▾, and then click **UPPERCASE**.

8. Click anywhere in the **American Heart Association** bullet, and then in the Paragraph group, click the **Align Text Right** button ≣. The text is right-aligned with the right margin of the content placeholder. Your slide should look similar to **Figure 2–25**.

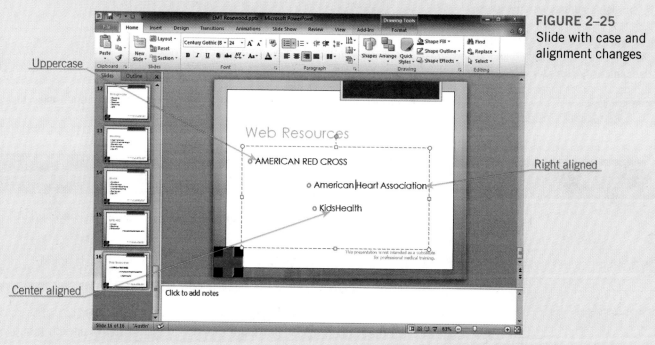

FIGURE 2–25
Slide with case and alignment changes

9. Save the presentation and leave it open for the next Step-by-Step.

Working with Bullets

Bullets define each new idea in the Content placeholder on a slide. Default bullets are determined by the theme. To change the formatting of bullets, selecting the text or placeholder, and then click the arrow next to the Bullets button in the Paragraph group on the Home tab to display the Bullets gallery. You cannot select a bullet to make changes; you must select the associated text. For more choices, click Bullets and Numbering to open the Bullets and Numbering dialog box, shown in **Figure 2–26**. On the Bulleted tab, you can select a bullet style or you can add a graphical bullet by clicking the Picture button. You can also change the bullet color or its size in relation to the text.

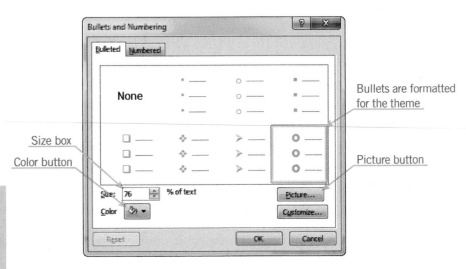

FIGURE 2–26   Bullets and Numbering dialog box

To change the appearance of the bullets throughout a presentation, make the changes on the slide master.

Step-by-Step 2.15

1. On the Ribbon, click the **View** tab, and then in the Master Views group, click the **Slide Master** button.

2. Click the **Austin slide master** (the first thumbnail in the left pane).

3. In the Slide pane, click the **Click to edit Master text styles** placeholder in the Content placeholder.

4. On the Ribbon, click the **Home** tab, and then, in the Paragraph group, click the **Bullets button arrow** to open the Bullets gallery and menu. Click **Bullets and Numbering**. The Bullets and Numbering dialog box opens with the Bulleted tab selected. (Refer back to Figure 2–26.)

5. Click the **Star Bullets** icon. In the Size box, double-click **76**, and then type **125**. Click **OK**. The dialog box closes and the bullet style and size changes for the first level bullet on the slide master, as shown in **Figure 2–27**.

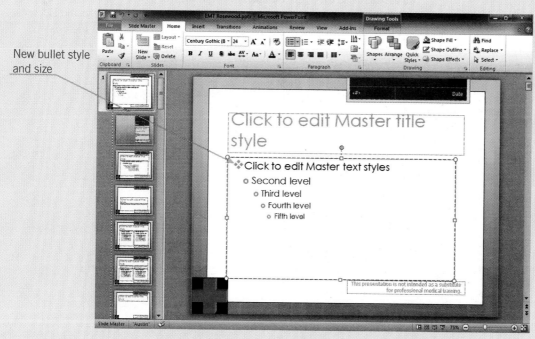

FIGURE 2–27
New bullet in the
Slide Master

New bullet style
and size

6. On the status bar, click the **Normal** button ⊞ to close Slide Master view. In the Slide pane, press **Home** to view slide 1, and then press **Page Down** to view slide 2 and see the changes to the first level bullets on the slide.

7. Save your work and leave the presentation open for the next Step-by-Step.

Changing Font Attributes

In a theme, the format of the text for body text, titles, and bullets on your slides is predetermined so that the layout, color theme, font, size, and style are consistent throughout the presentation. You can alter the format by making changes to individual slides. You change the font, style, size, effects, and color using the buttons on the Home tab in the Font group.

To make changes to words, first select the text. When you select text in a placeholder, the border of the placeholder is a dashed line. If you want to format all of the text in one placeholder, you can select the entire placeholder by clicking the border of the placeholder so it becomes a solid line. Any formatting to a selected placeholder will affect all of the text in the placeholder.

You can also use the Mini toolbar, shown in **Figure 2–28**, as a shortcut to changing the font, font size, font style, and font color. The Increase Font Size and Decrease Font Size buttons allow you to change the font size quickly in preset increments.

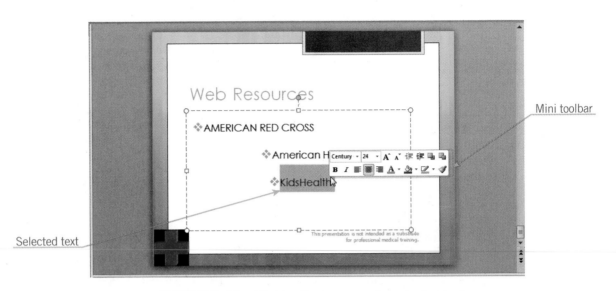

FIGURE 2–28   Mini toolbar appears for selected text

Step-by-Step 2.16

1. On the Slides tab, click the **slide 13** thumbnail, *Bleeding*, and then in the Slide pane, drag to select the text **clean**.

2. On the Ribbon, on the Home tab, in the Font group, click the **Font Color** button arrow . A palette of colors opens, organized into Theme colors and Standard colors.

3. Point to several colors and watch how the Live Preview shows the effect on the selected text, and then click any color.

4. In the Slide pane, double-click **injury**. In the Font group, click the **Font** button arrow Calibri (Body) to display a list of installed fonts.

5. Point to several of the fonts in the list and watch how the Live Preview shows the effect on the selected text, and then click any font.

6. In the Slide pane, double-click **911**. In the Font group, click **Font Size** button arrow 40 to display a list of font sizes.

7. Point to several of the sizes in the list and watch how the Live Preview shows you the effect on the selected text, and then click **36**. Click a blank area of the slide, and then compare your slide to **Figure 2–29**.

> **TIP**
>
> You can also click More colors to open the Colors palette.

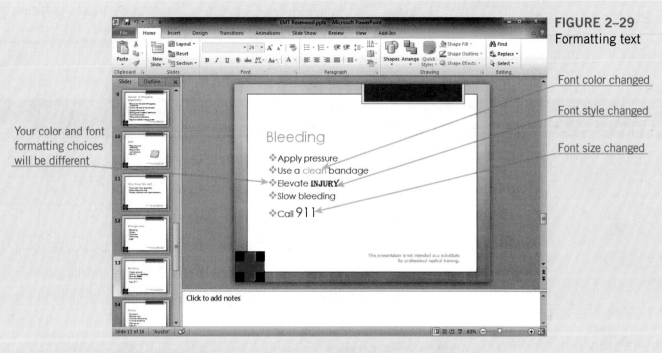

FIGURE 2-29
Formatting text

Font color changed

Font style changed

Font size changed

Your color and font formatting choices will be different

8. Save your work, and leave the presentation open for the next Step-by-Step.

Checking Spelling, Style, and Usage

Automatic spell checking identifies misspellings and words that are not in PowerPoint's dictionary by underlining them with a wavy red line immediately after you type them. To correct a misspelled word, right-click the underlined word. A shortcut menu appears with a list of suggested correctly spelled words. Click the suggestion that you want, and PowerPoint replaces the misspelled word. You can turn the automatic spell checker on or off, or change the way that it checks your document by clicking the File tab, clicking Options, and then clicking Proofing.

You can also check the spelling in a presentation after it is complete. Click the Review tab on the Ribbon, then, in the Proofing group, click the Spelling button. The Spelling dialog box contains options for ignoring words, making changes, or adding words to your own custom dictionary. When all spelling has been checked, a dialog box opens with the message "The Spelling Check is complete."

TECHNOLOGY CAREERS

An effective presentation should be consistent, error-free, and visually appealing. PowerPoint helps you determine if your presentation conforms to the standards of good style. For instance, title text size should be at least 36 points and the number of bullets on a slide should not exceed six. You should try to limit the number of words in each bullet to six. This is called the 6 by 6 rule, although sometimes you have to make exceptions.

Another useful PowerPoint tool is the Thesaurus. Click the Review tab on the Ribbon, and then click the Thesaurus button in the Proofing group. The Research task pane appears and offers a selection of alternative words with the same or similar meanings.

Step-by-Step 2.17

1. On the Slides tab, click the **slide 2** thumbnail, *Emergencies*, and then in the Slide pane double-click **Allergic**. The word is selected.

2. Type **Allrgic**, and then press **spacebar** to replace the selected word and enter a misspelled word in your presentation.

3. On the Slides tab, click the **slide 1** thumbnail. On the Ribbon, click the **Review** tab, and then in the Proofing group, click the **Spelling** button. Because there are spelling errors in the presentation, the Spelling dialog box opens, as shown in **Figure 2–30**.

FIGURE 2–30
Checking spelling

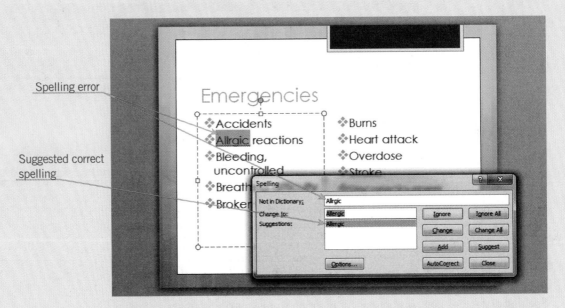

NOTE: Depending on how accurately you typed the text during these steps, you might have different words shown in the dialog box. You can choose to click Ignore to skip the words that are correct.

4. Review the suggestions in the dialog box. If the word in the Not in Dictionary box is "Allrgic" and the word in the Change to box is "Allergic," click **Change** to insert the correct spelling of Allergic. If another word appears as a misspelled word, select the correct spelling in the Suggestions list, and then click **Change**.

5. When the spell checker is finished, click **OK** in the spelling check is complete message box.

6. On the Slides tab, click the **slide 6** thumbnail, *Dispatcher Duties*, and then in the first bullet in the Slide pane, drag to select the word **Calm.**

7. On the Ribbon, click the **Review** tab, and then in the Proofing group, click the **Thesaurus** button.

8. Scroll down in the Research task pane to see the list of synonyms and antonyms under pacify (v.), point to the word **Soothe** until it is outlined with a box, click the **down arrow** next to the word, and then click **Insert.** The word *Soothe* replaces the word *Calm.*

9. In the upper-right corner of the Research task pane, click the **Close** button ⊠.

10. Save the presentation and leave it open for the next Step-by-Step.

Deleting Placeholders and Text from Slides

To change or delete text on an existing slide, scroll to display the slide you want to change. Then, select the text you want to change so that it is highlighted. Press Delete, Backspace, or type the new text to replace the selected text.

To delete a placeholder, click the placeholder box so that it is a solid line, and then press Delete. The text within the placeholder is replaced with the default placeholder text "Click to add text." Select the placeholder, then press Delete again to remove the placeholder from the slide.

Changing Slide Layouts

To change the layout for an existing slide, select the slide or slides. You can change more than one slide at a time by pressing and holding Ctrl, and then clicking slides on the Slides tab. On the Home tab, in the Slides group, click the Layout button, and then scroll to view the available layouts.

NET BUSINESS

Many businesses take place on the world stage. Being able to communicate in more than one language is essential if you want to conduct business among non-English speaking people. Sometimes, you might find you just need to include a word in a language other than English on a slide to make a point or reach an audience. PowerPoint provides a translation tool that gives you that power. You can use the Mini Translator to translate a word or a selected phrase when you point to it. Click the Review tab on the Ribbon, and then in the Language group, click the Translate button. To select the language you want to translate to, click Choose Translation Language, click the Translate to arrow, select the language, and then click OK. Next, click the Translate button again, and then click Mini Translator to turn it on. Now when you point to a word or select a phrase and then point to it, the Mini Translator appears displaying the translation of the word. The Mini Translator first appears faintly, and then darkens, similar to the Mini toolbar, when you move the mouse pointer onto it. Click the Translate button menu again, and then click Mini Translator to turn this feature off.

Step-by-Step 2.18

1. On the Slides tab, click the **slide 8** thumbnail, *Emergency Departments*. On the Ribbon, click the **Home** tab, and then in the Slides group, click the **Layout** button. The Layout gallery appears.

2. In the Slides group, click the **Layout** button, and then in the Austin section, click the **Picture with Caption** layout. The slide changes to the Picture with Caption layout. Click the **Undo** button [ ].

3. In the Slides group, click the **Layout** button again, and then in the Austin section, click the **Comparison** layout to apply it to the slide. See **Figure 2–31**.

FIGURE 2–31
Comparison layout
applied to slide 8

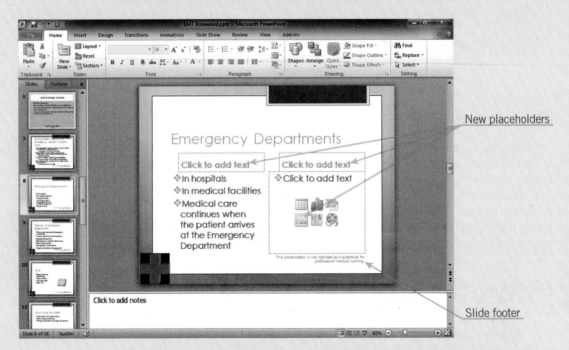

4. Save the presentation and leave it open for the next Step-by-Step.

Adding Clip Art and Sounds to Slides

If a content placeholder appears on a slide, you can choose from six objects: a table, a chart, a SmartArt graphic, a picture from file, clip art, and a media clip. You will work with tables, charts, media clips, and SmartArt graphic objects in Lesson 3.

Working with Clip Art

When you click the Insert Clip Art icon, the Clip Art task pane opens. See **Figure 2–32**. You find clips based on a keyword search. You can also import clips from other sources into the Clip Art Gallery and connect to the Web to access more clips. A keyword is a phrase or a word that describes the item you want in the Search text box. Click the Go button to show the results.

FIGURE 2–32 Results from search in the Clip Art task pane

If there is no content placeholder, you can still insert clip art on a slide. On the Ribbon, on the Insert tab, click the Clip Art button in the Images group. The Clip Art task pane opens. This task pane offers several options for finding the item you want to insert. To find an item, type one or more words into the Search for text box that might help identify the item. You can narrow your search by selecting from the Results should be options. In the Results should be box, you specify the media types you want to search for: Illustrations, Photographs, Video, and Audio. When the Include Office.com content check box is selected, the search includes clips on the Microsoft Office.com Web site as well as clip art that is on your computer.

The results appear in the task pane. You can click the clip thumbnail to insert the image or you can select from a menu of options. When you point to an icon in the task pane, an arrow for a drop-down menu appears to the right of the item. Click Insert to insert the image in the slide at the location of your insertion point. Click Preview/Properties to view the image and its properties without adding it to your document.

Step-by-Step 2.19

1. In the Slide pane on slide 8, in the Content placeholder, click the **Clip Art** icon to open the Clip Art task pane. Click the **Results should be** arrow, and then click the check boxes next to **Photographs**, **Videos**, and **Audio** to remove the check marks so that only the **Illustrations** check box is selected.

2. Click in the **Search for** box, type **Emergency 911**, and then click **Go**. Clip art that is associated with the phrase "Emergency 911" appears in the task pane. If you do not get results, try different keywords, such as "emergency", "rescue", or "911".

3. Review the results, and then click a thumbnail of the clip to insert the clip of your choice. The clip art you chose is inserted on the slide in the placeholder.

4. In the upper-right corner of the Clip Art task pane, click the **Close** button ⊠ to close the task pane.

5. Save the presentation and leave it open for the next Step-by-Step.

Adding Sound to Slides

You can add sound effects to any slide by inserting a sound. Click the Insert tab on the Ribbon, then, in the Media group, click the Audio button. You can insert a sound from a file that is stored on your computer or a disk, you can insert a sound using the Clip Art task pane or from a file stored on your computer, or you can record a sound for the presentation. Recorded sound is good for narration or you can create your own soundtrack. When a sound is on a slide, you will see the sound icon on the slide.

Step-by-Step 2.20

1. Display **slide 10**, *CPR*, in the Slide pane.

2. On the Ribbon, click the **Insert** tab, and then in the Media group, click the **Audio** button. The Insert Audio dialog box opens.

3. In the drive and folder where your Data Files are stored, click **911.wav**, and then click **Insert**. The dialog box closes and a sound icon and playback controls appear in the Slide pane as shown in **Figure 2–33**.

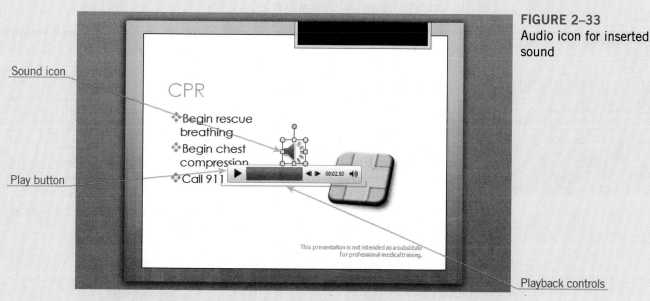

Sound icon

Play button

FIGURE 2–33
Audio icon for inserted sound

Playback controls

4. Click the **Play** button ▶ to hear the sound. (You will not hear the sound if your computer does not have speakers.) You can choose to have the sound play automatically or only when the sound icon is clicked during the slide show.

5. On the Ribbon, click the **Audio Tools Playback** tab. In the Audio Options group, click the **Start** arrow, click **Automatically** and then click the **Hide During Show** check box. See **Figure 2–34**. Now the sound will play automatically during the slide show and the sound icon will not be visible.

FIGURE 2–34
Audio Tools Playback tab on the Ribbon

Icon is not visible during the show

Sound plays automatically

6. On the status bar, click the **Reading View** button 📖. You hear the 911 sound file.

7. On the status bar, click the **Normal** button 🖵.

8. Save the presentation and leave it open for the next Step-by-Step.

Inserting Hyperlinks

▶ **VOCABULARY**

hyperlink

A *hyperlink* allows you to jump to another slide, a file, or to a Web site if you are connected to the Internet. You can also add a hyperlink that opens a message window for an e-mail address.

To insert a hyperlink in a presentation, select the text you want to make a hyperlink. On the Ribbon, click the Insert tab, and then in the Links group, click the Hyperlink button. The Insert Hyperlink dialog box opens, as shown in **Figure 2–35**. In the Link to section, choose where you want the link to go. The Look in section allows you to specify the Current Folder, Browsed Pages, or Recent files. You can also add the text for a ScreenTip to help the person using the slide show. When you click OK, the dialog box closes and the text you selected before opening the dialog box changes to a hyperlink is inserted in the document. The text you selected is formatted with a different color and underlined. The hyperlink color is one of the theme colors. Click it to go to the linked location.

TIP

You can also link to an Internet site by typing the Web address in the Address box in the Insert Hyperlink dialog box.

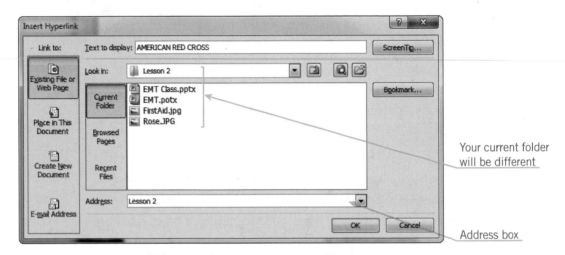

FIGURE 2–35   Insert Hyperlink dialog box

Step-by-Step 2.21

1. On the Slides tab, click the **slide 16** thumbnail, *Web Resources*.

2. In the Slide pane, select the **AMERICAN RED CROSS**. On the Ribbon, click the **Insert** tab, and then in the Links group, click the **Hyperlink** button. The Insert Hyperlink dialog box opens.

3. In the Address box, type **www.redcross.org**, and then click **OK**. The text is underlined in the slide and colored orange, indicating that it is a hyperlink. The program inserts http:// before www automatically.

4. Select the **American Heart Association**. In the Links group, click the **Hyperlink** button, type **www.americanheart.org** in the Address box, and then click **OK**.

5. Select **KidsHealth**, and then create a hyperlink to www.kidshealth.org.

6. On the status bar, click the **Reading View** button 📖. On the slide, point to the **American Heart Association** link, so that the pointer changes to 👆 indicating it is a hyperlink. See **Figure 2–36**.

FIGURE 2–36
Pointing to a hyperlink on a slide in Reading view

7. If you are connected to the Internet, click the **American Heart Association** hyperlink to open your Web browser and display the home page of the American Heart Association. Close the browser window.

8. On the status bar, click the **Normal view** button 🖥 and then click the **Slide Show** button. The Web Resources slide fills the screen in Slide Show view.

9. Close your Web browser, and then press **Esc** to exit the slide show.

10. Save the presentation and leave it open for the next Step-by-Step.

> **📧 EXTRA FOR EXPERTS**
>
> When you type an e-mail address on a slide, such as myaddress@ mailbox.com PowerPoint automatically creates a hyperlink that opens a new message window addressed to that e-mail address.

Using Animation

You can add select animation effects to any of the objects on a slide. *Animation* is what makes slide shows fun and interesting to watch. You can have a lot of fun creating animations on slides. When you animate an object, text, or slide, you add a visual effect. Animation enhances your presentation and increases audience interest.

On the Ribbon, click the Animations tab. You add Animations by clicking the Animation in the Animation group, or you can click the Add Animation button in the

> ▶ **VOCABULARY**
> **animation**

Advanced Animation group. See **Figure 2–37**. For more control over the way animations are displayed and played, you can click the Animation Pane button to open the Animation pane. Animations are organized into Entrance, Emphasis, Exit, and Motion Paths categories. Entrance and Exit animations define the animation for the entry and exit of an object. Emphasis defines the animation of an object that is showing on the slide. ***Motion Paths*** allow you to make an object move on the slide. As you point to each animation in the Animation gallery, a ***Live Preview*** will show you the effect on your object. You can click the More Effects option to display a dialog box containing all the animation features. Click the Start arrow to determine how the animation begins. Animations can start On Click, With Previous, or After Previous.

▶ **VOCABULARY**
Motion Paths
Live Preview

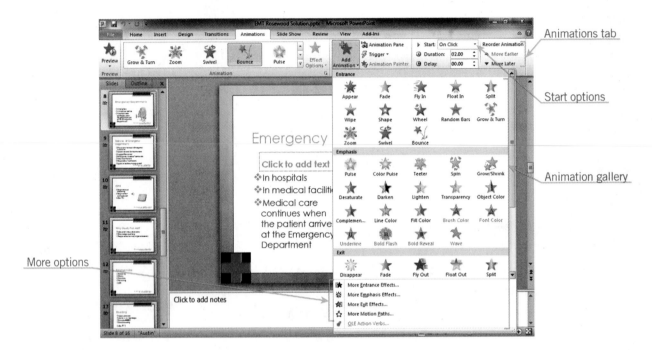

FIGURE 2–37   Animations gallery

Using the Animation Pane

On the Animations tab in the Advance Animation group, click the Animation pane button to open the Animation pane. This pane helps you track and organize the animations you set for each object. Each animated object is assigned a number on the slide, and the corresponding number is listed in the Animation pane. You can select how an object is animated, arrange animation order, determine whether to display the animation manually or automatically, and adjust the speed of the animation.

In the Animation pane, to the right of each animated object, an arrow opens the animation drop-down menu, which contains the commands that determine several animation settings for the object including the Start options, *Effect options*, and Timing options. To make adjustments to the effects, click the Effect Options button to open the Effect dialog box. In this dialog box, you can select enhancements for the animation. You can also choose a sound to accompany it. You have the option of dimming the object after it has been animated. If you are animating a text object, the text can appear all at once, by the word, or by the letter, and you can increase or decrease the delay percentage. The Timing tab allows you to adjust the timing of the animation and determine the trigger for the animation. When animating text, the Text Animation tab allows you to animate the text as a group or by individual levels.

Adding or Changing Slide Animation

You can apply an animation to the current (displayed) slide. Select the placeholder to apply animation to all text items on the placeholder. You can also individually animate text boxes, pictures, and transitions into the slide. After you apply an animation, the Preview button on the Animation tab allows you to preview the animation. Animations play in Slide Show and Reading view.

To copy an animation from one object to another, select the object with the animation you want to duplicate, click the Animation Painter button in the Advanced Animation group on the Animation tab, and then click the object you want to copy the animation to.

▶ **VOCABULARY**
Effect options

EXTRA FOR EXPERTS

The Show Advanced Timeline feature displays the time of the animation as a horizontal line graph. This allows you to easily see the timing of each object all at once.

Step-by-Step 2.22

1. On the Slides tab, click the **slide 8** thumbnail, *Emergency Departments*.

2. Select the **clip art** you inserted in a previous Step-by-Step.

3. On the Ribbon, click the **Animations** tab, and then in the Advanced Animations group, click the **Add Animation** button to open the Animation gallery. In the Entrance section, click the **Bounce** animation.

4. In the Advanced Animation group, click the **Animation Pane** button to open the Animation Pane. The object is listed in the task pane as Picture 2.

5. In the Advanced Animation group, click the **Add Animation** button to open the Animation gallery again. Click **More Entrance Effects** to open the Add Entrance Effect dialog box, and then scroll down the list of Entrance effects to the Exciting section. Click **Boomerang** in the Exciting section, and then click **OK**. A second animation has been added to the picture. See **Figure 2–38**.

FIGURE 2–38
Animation Pane

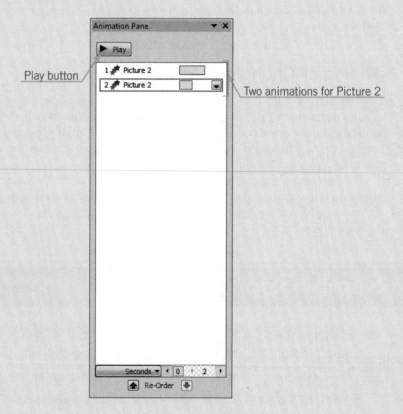

Play button
Two animations for Picture 2

6. In the Animation Pane, click **Play** to view the sequence of animations.

7. On the Animations tab on the Ribbon, click the **Animation Pane** button to close the Animation Pane.

8. Save the presentation and leave it open for the next Step-by-Step.

Using Slide Transitions

▶ **VOCABULARY**
slide transitions

When you run a presentation, *slide transitions* determine how one slide is removed from the screen and how the next one appears. You can set the transitions between slides. On the Ribbon, click the Transitions tab, then, in the Transition to This Slide group, click any of the transitions. You can click the More button to view additional transitions, as shown in **Figure 2–39**.

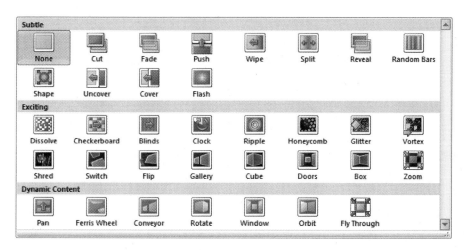

FIGURE 2–39   Transitions gallery

The Ribbon includes commands for a list of effects. The best view to use when you work on the transitions is Slide Sorter view. In the Timing slide section, you determine various aspects of speed and duration for the transition. You can set the duration of the transition—how long you actually view the transition. You can select the speed at which a slide displays before the next slide appears. You also determine whether to advance the slides manually or set the timing to advance slides automatically after a specified time. Click After and enter the number of seconds you want the slide to be displayed on the screen. If you click Apply to All, the selections you made affect all slides in the presentation. You can apply a transition to several slides by holding Ctrl down, and then clicking the slides on the Slides or Outline tab or in Slide Sorter view.

EXTRA FOR EXPERTS

If you choose Random Transition, PowerPoint randomly chooses a transition effect for each slide when you run the presentation.

Step-by-Step 2.23

1. On the status bar, click the **Slide Sorter** button, and then drag the Zoom slider to display 70% so that you can see all the slides.

2. Click the **slide 1** thumbnail. On the Ribbon, click the **Transitions** tab, and then in the Transition to this Slide group, click several of the **transitions** to see the transition on slide 1.

3. Click the transition that you like best. An icon beneath the slide thumbnail indicates that a transition is applied to the slide. On the Transitions tab, in the Timing group, notice that **On Mouse Click** has a check mark in the check box, and **No Sound** appears in the Sound box.

4. Click the **slide 2** thumbnail, *Emergencies*, press and hold **Shift**, scroll as needed, and then click the **slide 16** thumbnail, *Web Resources*. You selected slides 2–16.

TIP

Select the best zoom percentage for your screen so you can see all the slides in the window.

5. Click a transition of your choice for these slides. Watch the screen as the transition is applied to each slide. The ⭐ icon appears beneath each slide thumbnail. This transition icon is the same icon you saw when you added animations to the slide. Your screen should look similar to **Figure 2–40**.

FIGURE 2–40
Transitions in Slide Sorter view

Your transition selection will be different

Transition in progress

Transition icon

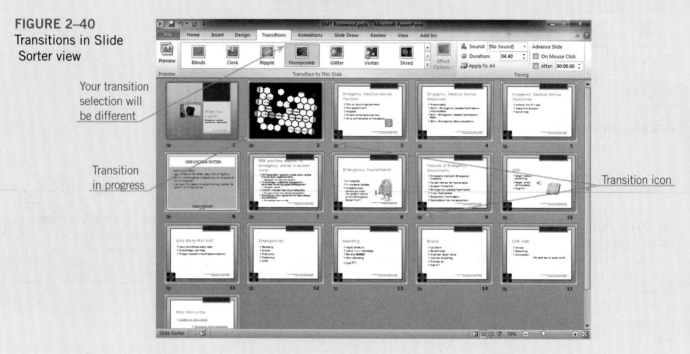

Preparing the Notes and Handouts

You want to be able to identify your presentation from among the others in your class. To personalize your presentation in a classroom or lab setting, add your name as a footer to the Notes and or Handouts pages. If you want to print the whole presentation, but don't want to use a lot of paper, you can print handouts or notes.

Step-by-Step 2.24

1. Click the **Insert** tab on the Ribbon, and then in the Text group, click the **Header & Footer** button to open the Header and Footer dialog box. Add your name as a footer to the Notes and Handouts, and then apply the footer to all slides.

2. Save the presentation, and then view the presentation in Slide Show or Reading view to see the final presentation.

3. Switch to Normal view when you are finished.

4. If your instructor wants a printout, click the **File** tab, and then on the navigation bar, click **Print** to open Backstage view.

5. In the Settings section, click the **Print All Slides** button to print the entire presentation, in the Slides section, click the **Full Page Slides** button to open the Print Layout gallery, in the Handouts section, click **9 Slides Horizontal**, and then click the **Print** button to print the handouts on two pages with nine slides per page.

6. Close the presentation, and then exit PowerPoint.

SUMMARY

In this lesson, you learned how to:

- Use PowerPoint to create new presentations using blank presentations or templates.
- Insert headers and footers in a presentation.
- Use the slide, notes, and handout masters.
- Enhance presentations in PowerPoint by applying slide layouts, themes, and color.

- Add slides to an existing PowerPoint presentation.
- Add text to slides and find and replace text.
- Change the appearance of text and bullets in PowerPoint.
- Check spelling, style, usage, and translate text.
- Add clip art, sounds, and hyperlinks.
- Apply animations and transitions to slides.

■ VOCABULARY REVIEW

Define the following terms:

align	hyperlink	placeholder
animation	layout master	slide master
blank presentation	Live Preview	slide transitions
effect options	motion paths	template
handout master	notes master	themes

■ REVIEW QUESTIONS

FILL IN THE BLANK

Fill in the best answer:

1. The _____ controls formatting for all the slides in a presentation.

2. Click the _____ button so that pictures in the presentation take up less disk space.

3. The slide _____ determines where content and objects are placed on a slide.

4. A(n) _____ is how one slide is removed from the screen and the next one appears.

5. Predesigned graphic styles that can be applied to your slides are called _____.

TRUE / FALSE

Circle T if the statement is true or F if the statement is false.

T   F   **1.**   You can change the appearance of the bullets—such as their shape, size, or color.

T   F   **2.**   The sound icon never appears during Slide Show.

T   F   **3.**   Graphics do not appear on the Outline tab.

T   F   **4.**   Automatic spell checking identifies misspellings and words not in PowerPoint's dictionary by highlighting them in yellow.

T   F   **5.**   You can select more than one slide by holding down the spacebar while clicking the slides.

WRITTEN QUESTIONS

Write a brief answer to each of the following questions.

1. How can you easily create a new presentation using the format, colors, and style you prefer without starting with a new, blank presentation? Explain why.

2. What types of content can you add to a Content placeholder using the icons?

3. How do you change colors and fonts on a slide?

4. How do you animate text or an object on a slide?

5. How do you insert a hyperlink?

PROJECTS

If you have a SAM 2010 user profile, your instructor may have assigned an autogradable version of the indicated project. If so, log into the SAM 2010 Web site at *www.cengage.com/sam2010* to download the instruction and start files.

PROJECT 2-1

1. Start PowerPoint.

2. Open the presentation **EMT Class.pptx** from the drive and folder where you store your Data Files.

3. Save the presentation as **EMT Class Spring Session**, followed by your initials.

4. View the presentation.

5. In Normal view on slide 2, change the slide layout to Two Content. Add relevant clip art or a photograph to the slide, using the Clip Art icon in the content placeholder.

6. Apply a new theme to all the slides in the presentation.

7. Apply a second theme only to the World Wide Web slide.

8. Using the Notes pane, enter the note **Be sure to connect to the Internet.** on slide 7. Enter notes on at least other two slides.

9. On slide 8 Cardiopulmonary Resuscitation, use the Outline tab to add two lines: **Saves lives** and **Improves recovery**.

10. Insert one new slide at the end of the presentation using the Comparison Layout. Add any text to the placeholders.

11. Add a hyperlink on slide 7 to the Web page address **www.cdc.gov**. Create the text CDC as the text that appears on the slide. Add two other links of your choice to the slide.

12. Add clip art, photographs, or any sounds that you find in the Clip Art task pane to several of the slides. Use image effects on the images you added.

13. Create at least two animations in the slide show; animate any objects or text.

14. Switch to Slide Sorter view and add at least two different transitions to the slide show.

15. Use the Thesaurus to replace at least one word with a synonym. Run the spelling checker.

16. Switch to Slide Show view and run the presentation.

17. Add your name as a footer to the Notes and Handouts pages, and then print the handouts as 6 slides per page.

18. Save the presentation, then exit PowerPoint.

SAM PROJECT 2-2

1. Start PowerPoint. Use the New from Existing Presentation command to create a new presentation from the EMT Class-Spring Session.pptx file you created in Project 2–1.

2. Save the presentation as **EMT Class-Spring Session – Copy** followed by your initials.

3. Open the Outline tab.

4. Insert a new slide after the last slide using the Title and Content layout.

5. On the last slide type **Prices** as the title of the slide.

6. Add the following in the content placeholder on the new slide:

Beginning Class — $200

Intermediate Class — $225

Advanced Class — $350

7. Format the text on slide 17 Circulation so that each line has a different font color, font style, and font size.

8. View the Slide Master and change the first level bullet to Hollow Square bullets using a Standard Red color.

9. Save your changes, print the slides as Handouts 9 slides per page. Exit PowerPoint.

PROJECT 2–3

1. Use the New from Existing Presentation feature to open the **EMT Class-Spring Session – Copy.pptx** presentation and save it as **EMT Class-Spring Session – Copy2** followed by your initials.

2. In Normal view, go to slide 1 and type the following in the Notes pane: **Be sure everyone has a handout.**

3. Print slide 1 using the Notes Pages print options.

4. Enhance the slide show, adding any additional objects or animations that you want. Check spelling. Save and print the entire presentation as handouts with 9 slides on a page.

5. Close the presentation and then exit PowerPoint.

■ CRITICAL THINKING

ACTIVITY 2–1

Use a template, either installed or from the Microsoft Office Web site, and the skills you learned in this lesson to create a presentation for an organization to which you belong. Be sure to check your presentation for correct spelling, punctuation, and grammar usage. Include clip art, at least one image from a file, and add animations and transitions to the slide show. Include one hyperlink to a favorite Web site. Save and print the entire presentation as handouts with six slides on a page.

ACTIVITY 2–2

Create a presentation using the ideas you organized in Critical Thinking Activity 1–2 in Lesson 1. Choose a theme. Add sound and clip art. Include slide transitions and animation. Run the presentation for your class.

LESSON 3

Working with Visual Elements

■ OBJECTIVES

Upon completion of this lesson, you will be able to:

- Insert, convert, and edit SmartArt graphics.
- Create and format WordArt.
- Build and format charts.
- Create and modify a table.
- Draw, edit, and format an object.
- Copy, move, order, and group objects.
- Create a text box on a shape.
- Animate shapes.
- Add a header or footer.

■ VOCABULARY

adjustment handle

category axis

cell

chart

column

datasheet

grouping

handle

organization chart

rotate handle

row

SmartArt graphic

table

value axis

WordArt

PowerPoint presentations provide a visual representation of your ideas and the concepts you want to present to your audience. With limited text on the slides, you can enhance your presentation with the many different graphic elements available within PowerPoint. Most people understand abstract ideas better if given visual clues and images. PowerPoint is an excellent teaching tool. Learning new skills is easy if graphics show you what you are supposed to do. In this lesson, you will learn how to create exciting and artistic presentations by using SmartArt graphics, WordArt, shapes, tables, and charts.

Working with SmartArt Graphics

When you have to present information to an audience, text is not always the best way to present content. Graphics are a more powerful way to visually convey information about flow, sequence, process, and organization. Graphics can simplify ideas. *SmartArt graphics*, which are dynamic diagrams and graphics, are available for you to use on your slides in PowerPoint.

> **VOCABULARY**
>
> **SmartArt graphics**

You can insert a SmartArt graphic on a slide by clicking the SmartArt icon on a content placeholder. To create a SmartArt graphic on a slide that does not have the SmartArt icon, click the Insert tab on the Ribbon. In the Illustrations group, click the SmartArt button to open the Choose a SmartArt Graphic dialog box gallery. You can also convert existing text into a SmartArt graphic by selecting the text object or text you want to convert, and then on the Home tab in the Paragraph group, click the Convert to SmartArt Graphic button and then select a SmartArt graphic from the gallery. PowerPoint includes over 80 basic styles of SmartArt graphics that are organized into eight categories: List, Process, Cycle, Hierarchy, Relationship, Matrix, Pyramid, and Picture. See **Figure 3–1**.

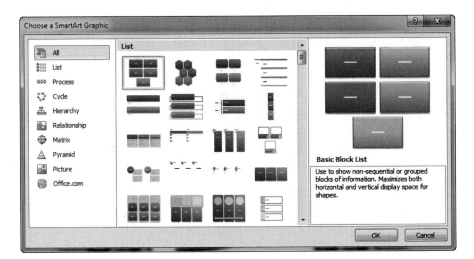

FIGURE 3–1   Choose a SmartArt graphic dialog box

Step-by-Step 3.1

1. Open the presentation file **History of Cotton.pptx** from the drive and folder where you store the Data Files for this lesson.

2. Save the presentation as **History of Cotton Report**, followed by your initials.

3. Click the **Home tab** on the Ribbon if it is not already selected, on the Slides tab click **slide 4**, *Types of Cotton*, to select the slide, click anywhere in the bullet list, and then in the Paragraph group, click the **Convert to SmartArt Graphic** button to open the SmartArt gallery.

4. Move the pointer slowly over the different **SmartArt thumbnails** in the gallery, view the Live Preview effect on the text, and then click the **Pyramid List SmartArt** style. See **Figure 3–2**.

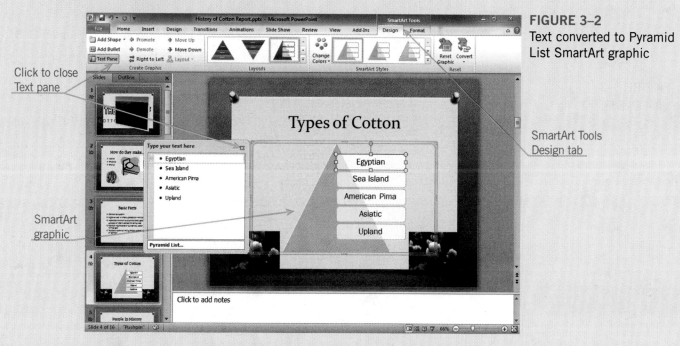

FIGURE 3–2
Text converted to Pyramid List SmartArt graphic

5. Save the presentation and then leave the presentation open for the next Step-by-Step.

Designing SmartArt Graphics

Each SmartArt graphic style can be altered in countless ways to give you artistic control over how the graphic looks on the slide. Work with the SmartArt Tools tab on the Ribbon to change layouts, styles, and colors. You can add additional shapes or bullets. Some SmartArt graphics include icons that you click to insert graphics and photographs. You can work using the features available through the buttons on the SmartArt Tools Format tab to change the way the text looks on each shape. You can use the Text pane to add text or edit and delete existing text. The Text pane provides an easy way to enter text in a SmartArt graphic. You can enter text either in the Text pane or directly in the SmartArt graphic.

Step-by-Step 3.2

1. Click the **Text pane close** button to close the Text pane.

2. Click the **SmartArt Tools Design** tab. In the SmartArt Styles group, click the **More** button ⬇ to open the gallery, move the pointer over the different SmartArt styles to see the Live Preview effect, and then in the 3-D group, click the **Bird's Eye Scene** icon.

3. In the SmartArt Styles group, click the **Change Colors** button, move the pointer over the different styles in the gallery, as shown in **Figure 3–3**, and then click **Gradient Range – Accent 2** in the Accent 2 section.

FIGURE 3–3
Changing colors

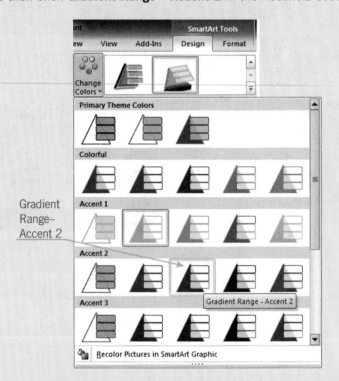

Gradient
Range–
Accent 2

4. Click the **triangle shape** in the SmartArt graphic, click the **SmartArt Tools Format** tab on the Ribbon, and then in the Shape Styles group click the **Shape Fill** button arrow. The Shape Fill colors palette opens.

5. In the Theme Colors section, click **Indigo, Text 2**. You have formatted the SmartArt graphic to present the different types of cotton in a very dramatic way.

6. Save the presentation and leave it open for the next Step-by-Step.

Working with Organization Charts

Organization charts are useful for showing the hierarchical structure and relationships within an organization. An organization chart is a way to graphically explain the structure of an organization in terms of rank. You can also use an organization chart to show relationships among objects, animals, or things that are related in a structured way. For a company or organization, the chart usually shows the managers and subordinates who make up its workforce. The graphics, such as boxes or ovals, contain the name of a person, position, or object. Vertical lines drawn between the graphics show the direct relationships among superior and subordinate items in the chart. A horizontal line shows a lateral or equal relationship on the same level.

To add an organization chart to a slide, you can apply a Content layout to a slide and then click the SmartArt Graphic icon in the content placeholder. The Hierarchy category of SmartArt Graphics provides many different layouts for you to use as you create the organization chart on the slide.

To fill in the chart, click in a text box and type the text. Use the SmartArt tools on the Ribbon to add more boxes to the organization chart. Graphic elements are grouped with the text boxes to enhance the chart. Graphics can include shapes as well as pictures or clip art.

> **VOCABULARY**
> **organization chart**

Step-by-Step 3.3

1. Scroll down the Slides pane, click **slide 14**, *Products and Byproducts of Cotton*, click the **Home** tab on the Ribbon. The slide displays a content placeholder with the six icons. An organization chart is a SmartArt graphic.

2. Click the **Insert SmartArt Graphic** icon ![icon] in the content placeholder. The Choose a SmartArt Graphic dialog box opens.

3. In the left pane, click **Hierarchy**, click the **Hierarchy** icon in the center pane, as shown in **Figure 3–4**, and then click **OK**. The Hierarchy chart appears on the slide with text placeholders, and the SmartArt Tools Design tab appears on the Ribbon. You can change the layout and style of the hierarchy chart at any time.

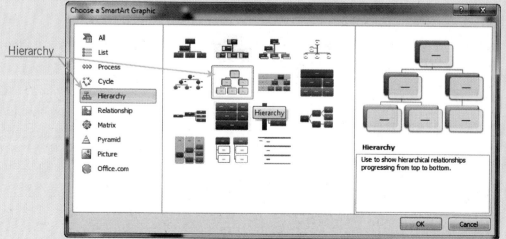

FIGURE 3–4
Choose a SmartArt Graphic dialog box

4. Save the presentation and leave it open for the next Step-by-Step.

NET BUSINESS

In many large companies the organization chart can be large and complicated, so companies often break the chart into several smaller charts for different departments. Using the tools available in PowerPoint, a manager can create a useful org chart (short for organization chart) to help explain the hierarchy of the business to all staff members and employees in the company.

Entering Text in a SmartArt Graphic

You can type text directly in the graphic or you can open the Text pane to the left of the SmartArt graphic to enter the text. Click the Text Pane button to open and close the Text pane. Each text box in a SmartArt graphic can be formatted to meet your needs for the slide. SmartArt graphics consist of text boxes and graphic elements that are grouped together. You can add and delete shapes and text boxes. You can promote and demote shapes and text boxes. As you enter text in the text box, the font size will adjust so the text is visible in the graphic. If at any time you want to go back to the original graphic, on the SmartArt Tools Design tab, click the Reset Graphic button. If at any time you want to change the SmartArt graphic to text, click the Convert button, then click Convert to text.

Step-by-Step 3.4

1. Click the top box **Text placeholder** if it is not already selected, and then type **Cotton**.

2. Click the left **Text placeholder** on the second level, and then type **Lint**.

3. On the second level, click in the right **Text placeholder**, and then type **Cotton Seed**.

4. On the third level, click the left **Text placeholder**, and then type **Fabric**.

5. On the third level, click the middle **Text placeholder** border so the shape has a solid line, and then press **Delete**. The third level now has two shapes.

6. On the third level, click the right **Text placeholder**, and then type **Cotton Seed Oil**.

7. Click the **SmartArt Tools Design** tab. In the Create Graphic group, click the **Add Shape** button arrow, click **Add Shape After**, and then type **Hulls**. There are two subordinate shapes for Cotton Seed and one subordinate shape for Lint. Refer to **Figure 3–5**.

TIP

If you make a mistake, you can press Ctrl+Z to undo your previous actions.

TIP

You can move boxes or shapes in a SmartArt Graphic once you create them if you find that categories or levels change. Use the Promote and Demote buttons in the Create Graphic group to move shapes in the SmartArt graphic to different levels.

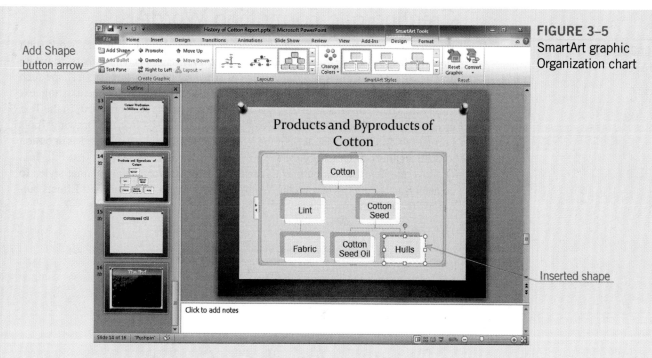

FIGURE 3–5
SmartArt graphic
Organization chart

Inserted shape

8. Save the presentation and leave it open for the next Step-by-Step.

You can animate a SmartArt graphic just as you do other slide objects. Click the Animations tab on the Ribbon, click the Custom Animation button, and then in the Custom Animation task pane, click the Add Effect button. Choose how you want to introduce the elements of the SmartArt graphic. You can select entry or exit animations, or have a segment animated for emphasis. If you want to add sound, click the Animation list arrow in the Custom Animation task pane, and then click Effect Options.

Creating and Formatting WordArt

WordArt is decorative text that you can insert on a slide. You can work with QuickStyles, predetermined combinations of color, fills, fonts, and effects, to create dramatic graphics from text. WordArt can also be shaped so the text fits a shape such as an arc, arrow, or oval. You can create new text as WordArt or change existing text into WordArt. To insert WordArt, click the Insert tab on the Ribbon. Next, in the Text group, click the WordArt button. If you have text selected, click the Drawing Tools Format tab on the Ribbon, and, in the WordArt Styles group, click the More button to open a gallery of QuickStyles, as shown in **Figure 3–6**, or click the Text Fill, Text Outline, and Text Effects buttons to create WordArt in your own personal style. To create a shape from the text, in the WordArt Styles group, click the Text Effects button, point to Transform, and then click the shape you want. See **Figure 3–7**.

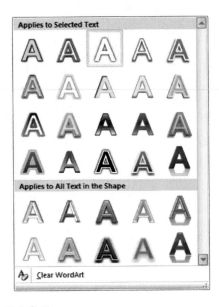

FIGURE 3–6   WordArt Gallery

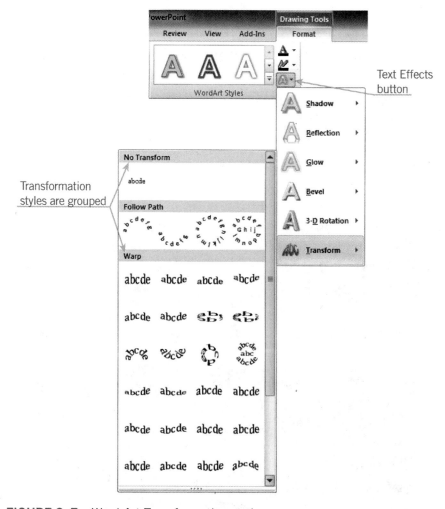

FIGURE 3–7   Word Art Transformation options

Step-by-Step 3.5

1. On the Slides tab, click **slide 11** (photograph of bales of cotton), and then click the **Insert** tab on the Ribbon.

2. In the Text group, click the **WordArt** button, click the **Fill – Red, Accent 2, Double Outline – Accent 2** icon (third row, last column), and then type **Wrapped for Protection.** The text you typed "Wrapped for Protection" replaces the default text and is styled in the text box.

3. On the **Drawing Tools Format** tab, click the **More** button ⊡ in the WordArt Styles group to open the WordArt Styles gallery, move the pointer over the styles to see the effect on the text, and then in the Applies to All Text in the Shape section, in the next to last row, click **Fill – Orange Accent 1, Plastic Bevel, Reflection.**

4. In the WordArt Styles group, click the **Text Effects** button A⁻, point to **Transform**, move the pointer over the styles to see the effect on the text, and then in the Warp section, click **Ring Outside**. If the text is a little difficult to read, you can resize it.

5. Using the **Resize Pointer**, drag the **lower-right sizing handle** to the left to shrink the box so you can read the words, and then use the **Move Pointer** ⁺↕₊ to drag the WordArt shape to the sky part of the photograph so that the WordArt on the slide looks like **Figure 3–8**.

FIGURE 3–8
WordArt formatted on a slide

WordArt

6. Save your work and then leave the presentation open for the next Step-by-Step.

Working with Charts

Charts, also called *graphs*, provide a visual way to display numerical data in a presentation. When you create a chart in PowerPoint, you are working in a program called Microsoft Excel. If you do not have Microsoft Excel installed, PowerPoint opens a program called Microsoft Graph to create and edit the chart. Microsoft Graph is much less powerful than Excel, but for simple graphing it does the job just fine. When you are building and modifying a chart, Microsoft Excel (or Graph) features, commands, and buttons become available to help you.

If you have an existing chart in an Excel worksheet, you can include that chart on a slide by linking or embedding the worksheet as an object in the slide. You will learn about linking and embedding objects in Lesson 4.

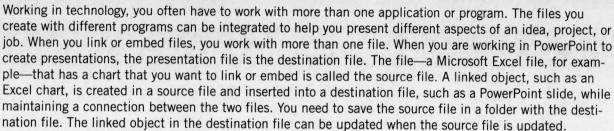

TECHNOLOGY CAREERS

Working in technology, you often have to work with more than one application or program. The files you create with different programs can be integrated to help you present different aspects of an idea, project, or job. When you link or embed files, you work with more than one file. When you are working in PowerPoint to create presentations, the presentation file is the destination file. The file—a Microsoft Excel file, for example—that has a chart that you want to link or embed is called the source file. A linked object, such as an Excel chart, is created in a source file and inserted into a destination file, such as a PowerPoint slide, while maintaining a connection between the two files. You need to save the source file in a folder with the destination file. The linked object in the destination file can be updated when the source file is updated.

The main difference between linking and embedding is where you store the data and how you update the data after you place it in the destination file. An embedded object can also be created in another application, such as Excel. An embedded object is inserted into a destination file. Once embedded, the object becomes part of the destination file. You do not need to save the source file or have the source file in the folder with the destination file. Changes you make to the embedded object are reflected in the destination file. The source file contains the information that is used to create the object. When you change information in a destination file, the information is not updated in the source file.

Building a Chart

To create a chart in a presentation, choose a slide layout that contains a content placeholder for a chart. Click the content placeholder Insert Chart icon to open the Insert Chart dialog box, as shown in **Figure 3–9**. To create a chart on a slide that does not have the Insert Chart icon on the Content Layout placeholder, on the Ribbon click the Insert tab, and in the Illustrations group click the Chart button. Once you select a chart type, the chart appears on the slide with default data. The screen splits in two, with PowerPoint and Excel windows open side by side. The data for the chart is in the Excel window. This is the *datasheet*, a worksheet that appears with the chart and has the numbers for the chart. You replace the sample data with your own. The chart changes to reflect the new data. When you are ready to return to the presentation, click the Close button to close the Excel window and you will see the chart on the PowerPoint slide.

▶ **VOCABULARY**
datasheet

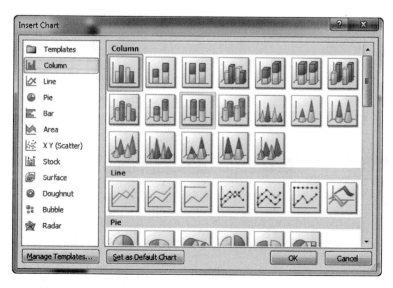

FIGURE 3–9   Insert Chart dialog box

A worksheet is made up of columns and rows. The intersection of each column and row is a cell. Cells are identified by their column letter and row number. The cell that is at the intersection of column C and row 3 would be cell C3.

Step-by-Step 3.6

1. Click **slide 7**, *Where Does Cotton Grow?* This slide has a Title and Content slide layout.

2. Click the **Insert Chart** icon on the content placeholder.

3. In the Insert Chart dialog box, **Column** is selected in the left pane, click the **Clustered Column** icon (first icon, first row), and then click **OK**.

The window splits so that you have PowerPoint open in a window on the left side of the screen and Excel open in a window on the right side of the screen. See **Figure 3–10**. The sample data in the Excel window is shown as a sample chart in the PowerPoint window. Excel displays the data in a worksheet. To enter data in an Excel worksheet, you click the cell and then type the numbers or text. You press Enter after you type the data in each cell. You can also press Tab to move from cell to cell. You have to replace the data with meaningful numbers for your chart. For this lesson, you can leave the numbers alone and simply enter the labels (the text) for the chart, to learn how charts work.

> **TIP**
>
> Press Enter to enter the text in cell A2 and move the insertion point to cell A3 and begin typing the next entry.

FIGURE 3–10
Creating a chart

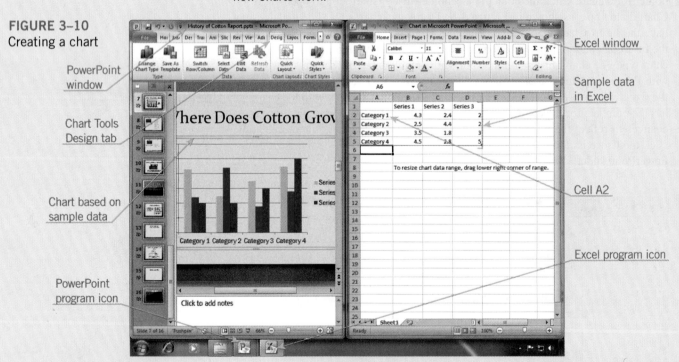

4. In the Excel window, click cell **A2**, and then type **Texas**.

5. Click cell **A3**, and then type **Missouri**.

6. Click cell **A4**, and then type **Virginia**.

7. Click cell **A5**, and then type **Alabama**.

8. Click cell **B1**, type **2010**, press **Tab**, type **2011**, press **Tab**, type **2012**, and then press **Enter**. The data is entered in the worksheet, as shown in **Figure 3–11**.

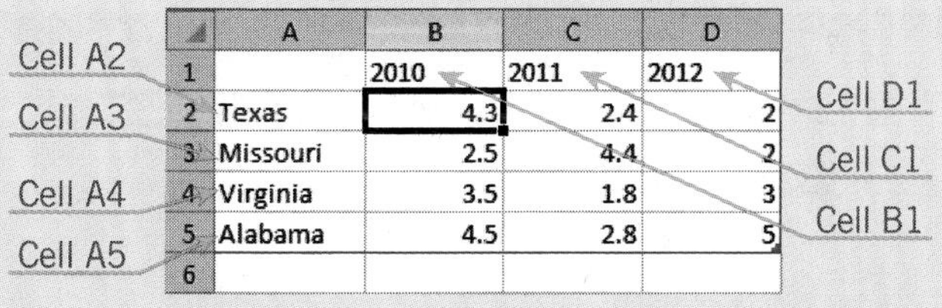

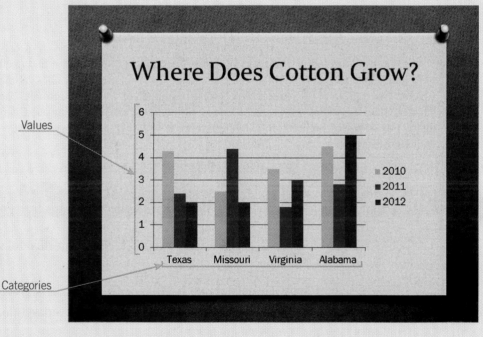

FIGURE 3–11
Data in Excel

The chart changes to reflect the new data. The states are listed on the horizontal axis. This is called the *category axis* or the x axis. The values in the worksheet are the numbers on the vertical axis. This is called the *value axis* or the y axis. and the legend shows each year in a different color for each column in the chart.

9. Click the Microsoft Excel **Close** button and return to the presentation, and then maximize the PowerPoint window if necessary. The chart looks like **Figure 3–12**.

FIGURE 3–12
Final Chart

10. Save the presentation and leave it open for the next Step-by-Step.

▶ **VOCABULARY**
category axis
value axis

Formatting a Chart

The chart gives a visual representation of numeric data. Any text you add to the chart helps your audience understand the data by identifying what each number refers to. A legend identifies the data series or bars in a column chart. A title gives the chart a name. To format and edit the chart, you can use the Ribbon commands on the Chart

Tools Design tab, the Chart Tools Layout tab, and the Chart Tools Format tab, as shown in **Figure 3–13**.

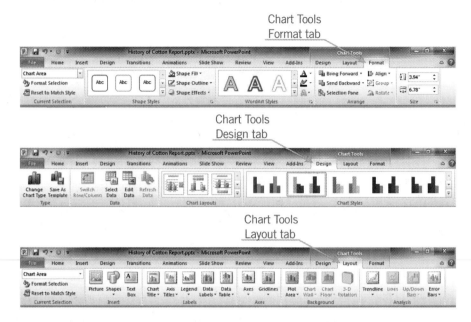

FIGURE 3–13   Chart Tools

If you need to modify a chart at any time, click the chart to select it and open the Chart Tools tab on the Ribbon. You can change the type of chart by clicking the Change Chart Type button in the Type group on the Chart Tools Design tab. The Change Chart Type dialog box that opens is basically the same as the Insert Chart dialog box shown in Figure 3–9. All you have to do is choose a chart type and then choose a subtype.

Step-by-Step 3.7

1. Click the **chart** to activate it and display the Chart Tools contextual tabs on the Ribbon.

2. Click the **Chart Tools Layout** tab on the Ribbon, in the Labels group click the **Chart Title** button, on the menu click **Centered Overlay Title**, and then type **Top Cotton Producing States**.

3. On the Chart Tools Layout tab on the Ribbon, in the Labels group, click the **Data Labels** button to open the menu, and then click **Inside End**.

4. Click the **Chart Tools Design** tab on the Ribbon, click the **More** button ⬛ in the Chart Styles group, and then click the **Style 45** icon. Your chart should look similar to **Figure 3–14**.

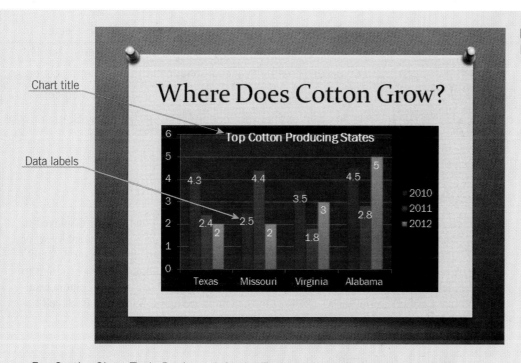

FIGURE 3–14
Formatted column chart

5. On the Chart Tools Design tab in the Type group, click the **Change Chart Type** button. In the Change Chart Type dialog box, in the left pane, click **Pie**. In the Pie section, click the **Pie in 3-D** icon (second pie icon), and then click **OK**. The chart is now a 3-D pie chart. See **Figure 3–15**.

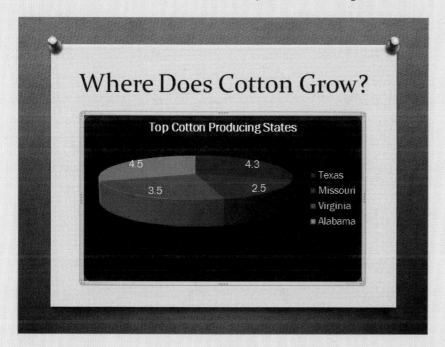

FIGURE 3–15
3-D Pie chart

6. Click the **Chart Tools Design** tab on the Ribbon, if not already selected. In the Type group, click the **Change Chart Type** button, and then in the left pane, click **Column**. Click the **Stacked Cone** icon in the Column section, and then click **OK**. The data is now charted in a series of stacked cones.

7. Save the presentation and leave it open for the next Step-by-Step.

Working with Tables

Tables are useful when you need to organize information that can be displayed in *rows* and *columns*. Each intersection of a row and column is a *cell*. You enter text or numbers in each cell. Tables can be formatted to enhance their appearance. A table can have column headings to identify each item in each column and row headings to identify the rows. A sample table for a club appears in **Table 3–1**. The column headings are the days of the week. The row headings are the assignments. Each cell has the name of a club member.

TABLE 3–1   A sample table

	MONDAY	TUESDAY	WEDNESDAY	THURSDAY	FRIDAY
Breakfast	Jennifer	Emily	Michael	David	Simon
Lunch	Emily	Michael	David	Simon	Jennifer
Dinner	Michael	David	Simon	Jennifer	Emily

Creating a Table

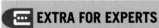

To include a table on a slide, you can use the Content slide layout and click the Insert Table icon to open the Insert Table dialog box. Type the number of columns and rows you want, and then click OK, and a table is inserted on the slide. Type the text in the table; you can move between cells by pressing the Tab key. If you prefer to use the Ribbon and you want to drag a table, click the Insert tab on the Ribbon, and then in the Tables group, click the Table icon. Drag to specify the number of rows and columns, as shown in **Figure 3–16**.

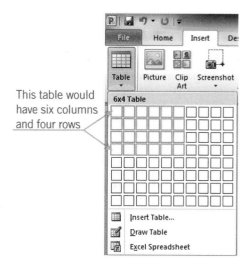

This table would
have six columns
and four rows

FIGURE 3–16 Dragging to create a table

Step-by-Step 3.8

1. Click **slide 13**, *Cotton Production in Millions of Bales*, in the Slides pane. Slide 13 is selected. The slide layout is Title and Content.

2. On the content placeholder, click the **Insert Table** icon ▦ to open the Insert Table dialog box.

3. In the Number of columns text box, type **4**, and then press **Tab**.

4. In the Number of rows text box, type **9**, as shown in **Figure 3–17**, and then click **OK**.

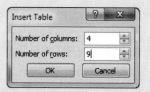

FIGURE 3–17
Insert Table Dialog Box

PowerPoint inserts a table with four columns and nine rows on the slide. The table is formatted according to the Pushpin theme. You can change the formatting at any time. The Table Tools contextual tabs appear on the Ribbon. The insertion point is in the first cell, ready for you to type the data. The table style applied by the theme on the slide includes a different style for column headings. You do not want column headings.

5. Click the **Table Tools Design** tab, if not already selected. In the Table Styles Options group, click the **Header Row** check box to remove the check mark.

6. Type the data as shown in **Figure 3–18**. Click each cell or press **Tab** to move from cell to cell. Do not worry if the text does not seem to fit or is not centered. You will format, align, and adjust the table data later.

FIGURE 3–18
Completed table

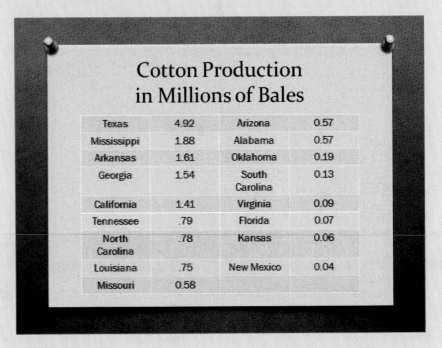

7. Save the presentation and leave it open for the next Step-by-Step.

Modifying Table Styles

To modify a table's borders, fill, or text boxes, select the table to open the Table Tools Design tab on the Ribbon, shown in **Figure 3–19**. You can apply a table style to format the table elements at once. If you want to work on individual elements, click the different buttons to change the shading, borders, and effects to give the table a unique look.

FIGURE 3–19   Table Tools Design Tab

Step-by-Step 3.9

1. Click the table to select it.

2. Click the **Table Tools Design** tab on the Ribbon, and then click the **More** button ⊡ in the Table Styles group to open the gallery, as shown in **Figure 3–20**. The Table Styles gallery is organized into sections: Best Match for Document, Light, Medium, and Dark.

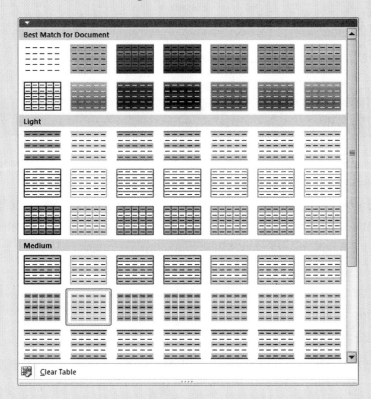

FIGURE 3–20
Table Styles gallery

3. Move the pointer over the different table styles in the gallery and watch as Live Preview shows the effect on the table.

4. Scroll down the gallery. In the Dark section, click **Dark Style 1 – Accent 5**.

5. Save the presentation and leave it open for the next Step-by-Step.

Modifying Table Layout

You can insert or delete columns and rows, merge or split cells, and change the alignment. You can add gridlines, distribute content among cells, rows, and columns, and even change the direction of text in a cell. You work using the Table Tools Layout tab on the Ribbon. See **Figure 3–21**. To change the width of a column or row, you can also click and drag a border.

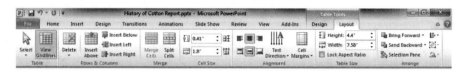

FIGURE 3–21   Table Tools Layout tab

Step-by-Step 3.10

1. On the Table Tools Layout tab, in the Alignment group, click the **Center Vertically** button 🔲.

2. Click the **Texas** cell. In the Rows & Columns group, click the **Insert Above** button, and then in the Merge group, click the **Merge Cells** button. A new row with one cell is in the top row of the table.

3. In the new top row, type **Data from US Department of Agriculture**, in the Cell Size group, click the **Table Row Height** text box, type **.75** and then press **Enter**.

4. Click the **Table Tools Design** tab on the Ribbon, and then in the Table Styles Options group, click the **Header Row** check box. The new row is now a header row and has header row formatting.

5. Place the pointer on the right middle sizing handle of the table border, drag ⟺ to the right to make the table slightly wider so that both North and South Carolina fit on one line in their cells and the table fits on the slide. Reposition the table as shown in **Figure 3–22**.

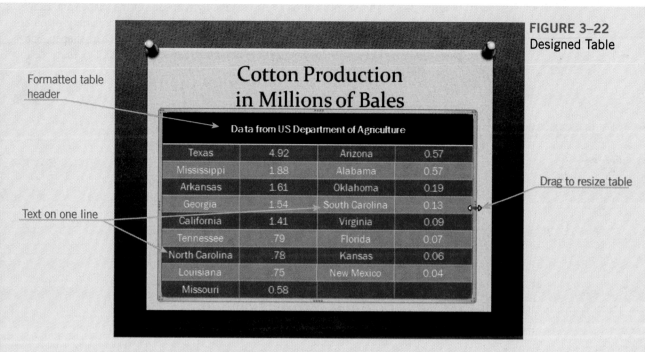

FIGURE 3–22
Designed Table

6. Save the presentation and leave it open for the next Step-by-Step.

Creating Shapes and Objects

You can add shapes and other drawing objects to your presentation to make it more interesting. Shapes include arrows, circles, cones, and stars. On the Insert tab, you can click the Shapes button to display a gallery of available shapes, as shown in

Figure 3–23. The Shapes button is also available by means of the shapes and drawing tools on the Home tab in the Drawing group. There are also a variety of other shapes you can add, including equation shapes, connectors, flow chart shapes, banners, and other kinds of objects that help draw the shape you want. Click the slide to insert the shape with a predefined size.

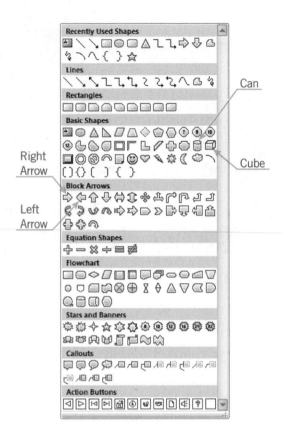

FIGURE 3–23   Shapes gallery

Drawing an Object

The Shapes gallery contains buttons for drawing objects such as lines, circles, arrows, and squares. Click the corresponding button to activate the tool. The Rectangle tools draw rectangles and squares. The Oval tool draws ovals and circles. To use a tool, click and hold the mouse button, and then drag to draw. To create a perfect circle or square, hold down the Shift key as you drag.

Selecting an Object

When you click an inserted object to select it, little squares appear at the edges of the graphic. These small squares are called *handles*. They indicate that the object is selected, and they allow you to manipulate the object. Drag these handles to resize the object. The yellow boxes are *adjustment handles*. The green circle is the *rotate handle*. You will learn more about selecting and manipulating objects later in the lesson.

▶ **VOCABULARY**
handle
adjustment handle
rotate handle

Step-by-Step 3.11

1. Click **slide 15**, *Cottonseed Oil*.

2. On the Home tab, in the Drawing group, click the **Shapes** button to open the Shapes gallery.

3. In the Basic Shapes section, click the **Cube** icon, as shown in Figure 3–23.

4. Click in the left side of the slide below the title text. A cube is drawn and handles appear on the object.

5. In the Drawing group, click the **Shapes** button to open the Shapes gallery. In the Recently Used Shapes section, click the **Cube** icon, and then click the right side of the slide below the title text to create another cube.

6. Create one more cube near the bottom of the slide, below the cube on the right side of the slide. Refer to **Figure 3–24** for placement.

 TIP

The Shapes button appears on the Home tab in the Drawing group on the Ribbon. It also appears on the Insert tab in the Illustrations group.

FIGURE 3–24
Six drawn objects

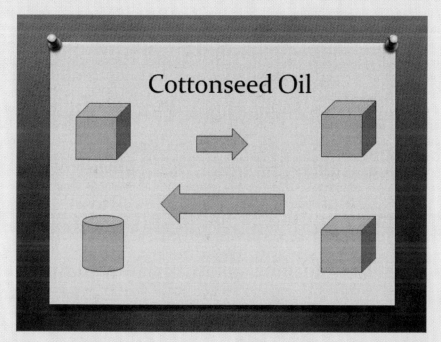

7. In the Drawing group, click the **Shapes** button to open the Shapes gallery. In the **Basic Shapes** section, click the **Can** icon, and then click near the bottom of the slide, below the left cube, to create a can similar to the one in Figure 3–24.

8. In the Drawing group, click the **Shapes** button to open the Shapes gallery. In the Block Arrows section, click the **Right Arrow** icon.

9. Click to the right of the left cube, and then drag to the right to draw an arrow to the right of the first cube you created.

10. In the Drawing group, click the **Shapes** button to open the Shapes gallery, in the Block Arrows section, click the **Left Arrow** icon, and then draw a left arrow in the middle of the screen, about twice as long as the arrow you drew in Step 9. Your slide should look similar to Figure 3–24.

11. Save the presentation and leave it open for the next Step-by-Step.

Manipulating Objects

Once you have created an object, there are many ways of manipulating it to achieve the final effect you want. You can rotate, fill, scale, or size an object, as well as change its color and position.

As you learned earlier in the lesson, to select an object, simply click it. To deselect an object, click another object or click any blank area on the slide. Handles do more than indicate that an object is selected. When you select an object, sizing handles surround it allowing you to manipulate it. They make it easy to resize an object that is too large or too small. Select the object to make the handles appear, and then drag one of the handles inward or outward to make the object smaller or larger.

You can move the object, resize the object, rotate the object, or change the key features of the shape. Corner sizing handles are round circles. Drag a corner handle outward to make an object wider and taller at the same time. Drag a corner handle inward to make an object shorter and narrower at the same time. Middle sizing handles are square boxes. Drag a square sizing handle to increase or decrease the size of the object in one dimension at a time. The yellow diamond is the adjustment handle and it changes the key features of an object. To scale an object, hold down Shift and drag a corner handle. This maintains an object's proportions. You scale and size clip-art graphics just as you do objects. Refer to **Figure 3–25**.

EXTRA FOR EXPERTS

You can size an object more precisely by using the height and width text boxes on the Drawing Tools Format tab in the Size group to specify a height and width.

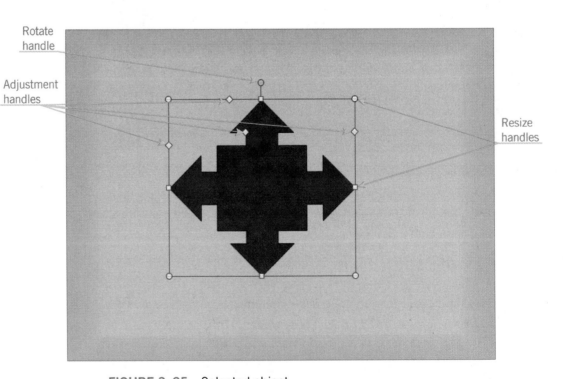

FIGURE 3–25   Selected object

Selecting More Than One Object

Sometimes you will want to select more than one object. PowerPoint gives you several ways to select more than one object using the mouse. One method is to shift-click; another is to draw a selection box around a group of objects. You can also click the Select button in the Editing group on the Home tab on the Ribbon to select all objects, or open the Selection and Visibility task pane.

Shift-Clicking

To shift-click, hold down the Shift key and click each of the objects you want to select. Use this method when you need to select objects that are not close to each other, or when the objects you need to select are near other objects you do not want to select. If you select an object by accident, click it again to deselect it, while still holding down the Shift key.

Drawing a Selection Box

Using the Select Objects tool, you can drag a selection box around a group of objects. On the Home tab on the Ribbon, in the Editing group, click the Select button and then click Select Objects. Use a selection box when all of the objects you want selected are near each other and can be surrounded with a box. Be sure your selection box is large enough to enclose all the selection handles of the various objects. If you miss a handle, the corresponding item will not be selected.

Combining Methods

You can also combine these two methods. First, use the selection box, and then shift-click to include objects that the selection box might have missed.

Rotating an Object

One way of modifying an object is to rotate it. When an object is selected, the Arrange commands appears in the Arrange group of the Drawing Tools Format tab. The Arrange button which opens a menu of commands including the Rotate commands, appears on the Home tab in the Drawing group. The rotate commands on the Arrange menu are Rotate Right 90°, Rotate Left 90°, Flip Vertical, Flip Horizontal, and More Rotation Options. The Rotate Right command moves a graphic in 90-degree increments to the right. The Rotate Left command rotates the graphic in

90-degree increments to the left. You can also drag the rotate handle, the green circle on a selected object, to rotate a graphic to any angle. You can flip an object by choosing the Flip Horizontal or Flip Vertical command. Refer to **Figure 3–26**.

FIGURE 3–26   Rotate commands

Using Guides and Gridlines

When you move objects on a slide, sometimes you want to be able to align and organize the objects along a grid. PowerPoint offers gridlines and guides to help you place objects exactly where you want them on the slide. Click the View tab on the Ribbon, then in the Show group, click the Guides check box to display a vertical and a horizontal guide on the slide. When you drag the guides, a measurement box appears to help you identify the exact location on the slide. Click the Grids check box to display a grid. When you move an object, it will snap to the nearest grid point. You can turn off the Snap to Grid feature. Right-click the slide and then click Grid and Guides or on the View tab, click the Show group launcher to open the Grid and Guides dialog box for other options. See **Figure 3–27**. The grid and guidelines help you place objects on the slide.

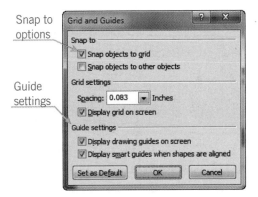

Snap to options

Guide settings

FIGURE 3–27 Grid and Guidelines dialog box

Step-by-Step 3.12

1. On the Ribbon, click the **View** tab. In the Show group, click the **Guides** check box, and then click the **Gridlines** check box. The grid and guidelines appear on the slide.

2. Drag the **horizontal guide** up until the measurement box displays 1.00.

3. Click the **left arrow** in the middle of the screen. Sizing handles appear around the perimeter of the shape, two adjustment handles appear at the prominent features—the arrow head and the arrow body—and a rotate handle appears near the top of the shape.

4. Drag the green **rotate handle** in a counterclockwise direction until the arrow is pointing from the upper-right cube to the can.

5. Click the **right arrow** you created on the slide, then drag it up so the point of the arrow is on the horizontal guide and the guide goes through the middle of the arrow.

6. On the Drawing Tools Format tab in the Arrange group, click the **Rotate** button, and then click **Rotate Left 90°**. The arrow is now pointing up. See **Figure 3–28**.

FIGURE 3–28
Positioning objects

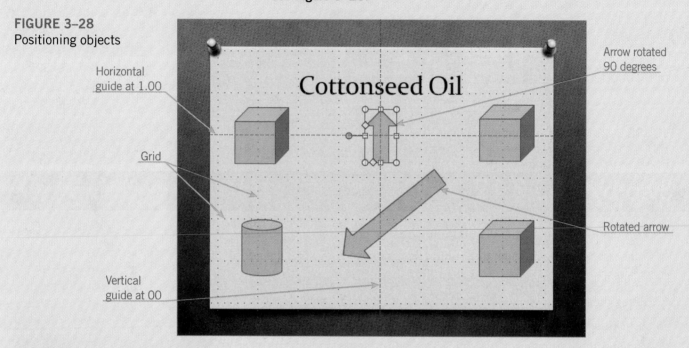

7. On the Ribbon, click the **View** tab. In the Show group, click the **Guides** check box, and then click the **Gridlines** check box to remove the check marks. The grid and guidelines no longer appear on the slide.

8. Save the presentation and leave it open for the next Step-by-Step.

TIP

As you rotate an object, the pointer will appear as a **rotate pointer**.

Applying Formatting

The Drawing Tools Format tab on the Ribbon contains tools you can use to apply formatting to visual elements in a presentation. You can change the fill, line, or font color. You can apply Shape Styles or WordArt Styles, or arrange objects for added effects.

Filling a Shape and Changing Shape Effects

Filling an object can help add interest to your drawing objects. Select the object you want to fill and click the Shape Fill button in the Shape Styles group on the Drawing Tools Format tab. See **Figure 3–29**. You can fill a shape with theme or standard colors, or click More Fill Colors to open a full color palette in the Colors dialog box. You can also use a picture, gradient, or texture to fill a shape.

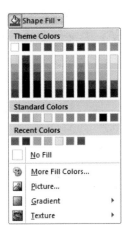

FIGURE 3–29   Shape Fill options

Changing Line Color

Another way to apply formatting to a drawing object is to change the line color. Click the Shape Outline button in the Shape Styles group on the Drawing Tools Format tab. See **Figure 3–30**. Click to select a theme or standard color in the palette, or click More Outline Colors to open a full color palette in the Colors dialog box. Other Outline options include changing the weight or thickness of the outline or creating dashes or a designed line.

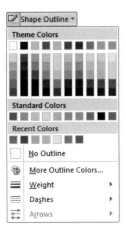

FIGURE 3–30   Shape Outline options

Changing Shape Effects

Another way to apply formatting to a drawing object is to change the shape effects. Click the Shape Effects button in the Shape Styles group on the Drawing Tools Format tab. Shape effects include Shadow, Reflection, Glow, Soft Edges, Bevel, and 3-D Rotation.

To work on the shape, or design your shape, you can use the Format Shape dialog box, shown in **Figure 3–31**. To open the Format Shape dialog box, click the Shape Styles dialog box launcher in the Shape Styles group.

FIGURE 3–31   Format Shape dialog box

Step-by-Step 3.13

1. Click the **upper-left cube object**. On the Drawing Tools Format tab, in the Shape Styles group, click the **Shape Fill** button arrow, and then click **Picture**. The Insert Picture dialog box opens.

2. Locate the folder that contains the Data Files for this lesson, click the **Cotton Gin.jpg** picture file, and then click **Insert**. The picture of the cotton gin appears on the cube.

3. Click the **lower-right cube object**. On the Drawing Tools Format tab, in the Shape Styles group, click the **Shape Fill** button arrow, and then click **Picture**. The Insert Picture dialog box opens.

4. Click **Potato Chip Plant.jpg**, and then click **Insert**. The picture of the potato chip plant appears on the face of the cube.

5. Click the **can object**. On the Drawing Tools Format tab, in the Shape Styles group, click the **Shape Fill** button arrow, and then click **Green Accent 4** in the Theme Colors section.

6. Click the **upper-right cube object**. On the Drawing Tools Format tab, in the Shape Styles group, click the **Shape Effects** button, point to **Glow**, and then in the Glow Variations section, click **Red, 18 pt glow Accent color 2**, in the last row.

7. The **upper-right cube** should still be selected. On the Drawing Tools Format tab, in the Shape Styles group, click the **Shape Outline** button. In the Theme Colors section, click **Orange Accent 5**, click the **Shape Outline** button arrow, point to **Dashes**, and then click **Long Dash**. Click a blank area on the slide. Your shapes should look similar to **Figure 3–32**.

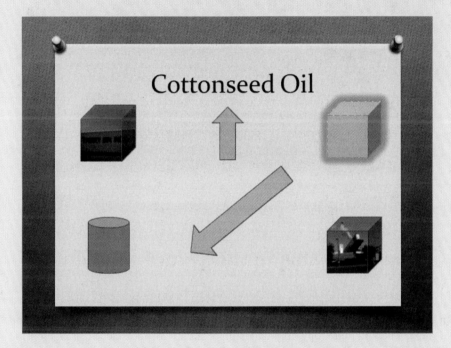

FIGURE 3–32
Formatted shapes

8. Save the presentation and leave it open for the next Step-by-Step.

Applying Artistic Effects

Formatting images or photographs can be fun and provide professional appeal to your slides. PowerPoint includes a collection of artistic effects that can be applied to pictures. Use the artistic effects to make an image look as though it is a watercolor painting, broken glass, wrapped in plastic, or even cast in cement! You should use these effects sparingly as they can overwhelm the slide and take the focus away from your message. To open the Artistic Effects gallery, select the picture to display the Picture Tools Format tab. In the Adjust group, click Artistic Effects. You can see the effect on the picture using Live Preview. See **Figure 3–33**.

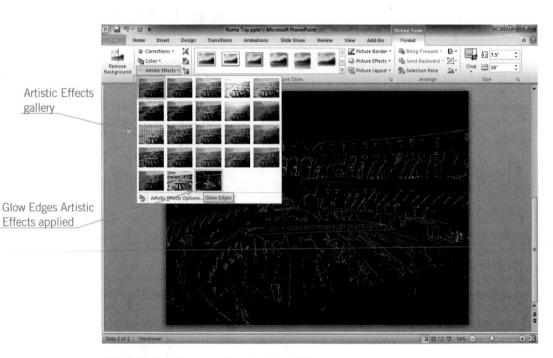

Artistic Effects gallery

Glow Edges Artistic Effects applied

FIGURE 3–33   Applying Artistic Effects to a picture

Copying or Moving an Object

When you create an object on a slide, you might decide that the object is not in the correct place. You can move text or graphic objects. To move an object, first select it and then drag it into place. You can cut, copy, and paste objects the same way you do text. The Cut and Copy commands place a copy of the selected image on the Office Clipboard. Pasting an object from the Office Clipboard places the object in your drawing. Paste Options include being able to retain the objects formatting based on the original theme. You can also paste an object as a picture. Once you paste an object, you can then move it into position.

Grouping Objects

As your drawing becomes more complex, you might find it necessary to "glue" objects together into groups. *Grouping* allows you to work with several items as if they were one object. To group objects, select the objects you want to group, and then on the Home tab on the Ribbon, in the Drawing group, click the Arrange button to open the menu shown in **Figure 3–34**, and then click Group. You can ungroup objects using the Ungroup command.

▶ **VOCABULARY**
grouping

FIGURE 3–34   Arrange commands

Step-by-Step 3.14

1. Click the **upper-left cube**, press and hold **Ctrl**, click the **upper-right cube,** click the **lower-right cube**, and then release **Ctrl**. The three cube objects are selected.

2. On the Drawing Tools Format tab, in the Arrange group, click the **Group** button, and then click **Group**. The three cubes are now grouped into one object. Sizing handles and the rotate handle affect all three objects at once. Any formatting changes or resizing will affect all objects in the group.

3. Move the pointer over the **upper-left sizing handle** until it becomes a diagonal double arrow pointer.

4. Click and drag the **pointer** up and to the left so that the slide title is inside the group frame and you enlarge the three cubes.

5. Click the **Drawing Tools Format** tab. In the Arrange group, click the **Align** button and then click **Align Center**. The objects are larger and centered on the slide, as shown in **Figure 3–35**.

FIGURE 3–35
Grouping objects

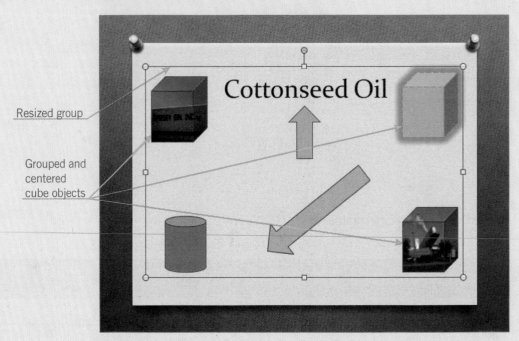

Resized group

Grouped and centered cube objects

6. Click the **can object**, and then drag the yellow **adjustment handle** down slightly so it is even with the two middle sizing handles. You changed a feature of the object by dragging the yellow adjustment handle.

7. Click the **top arrow object** between the two top cubes, use the **rotate handle** pointer ↻ to rotate the arrow to the right 90 degrees so the arrow faces the orange cube. Right-click the border of the arrow. Drag the arrow slightly down and to the right, release the right mouse button, and then click **Copy Here**. A copy of the arrow is pasted below the original arrow, offset from the original arrow.

8. Use the Move pointer ✥ to drag the **arrow object** to a new position between the can and the lower-right cube, to the right of the longer arrow.

9. Click the **can object**. On the Home tab, in the Clipboard group, click the **Copy** button 📋, and then right-click a blank area of the slide, in the Paste Options section. Click the **Use Destination Theme** Paste button 📋, right-click a blank area of the slide, and then click the **Use Destination Theme** Paste button 📋 again to add two new cans to the slide.

10. Move the **arrows** as needed, and then arrange the **cans** as shown in **Figure 3–36**.

TIP

Paste Options include the option of pasting the object as a picture. If the object was copied using another theme, you can paste with the original theme.

TIP

If any of the cans appears to go behind another and you want to bring it forward, click the Arrange button, and then click Bring to Front.

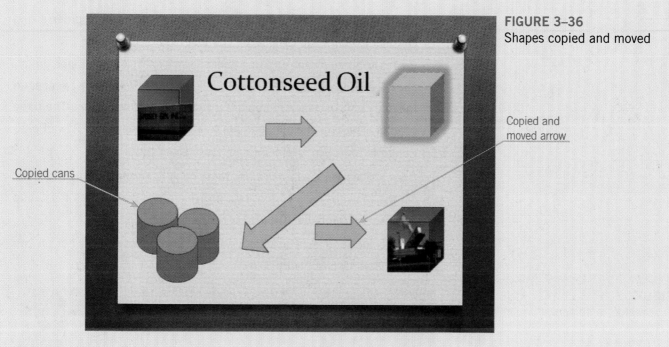

FIGURE 3–36
Shapes copied and moved

11.   Save the presentation and leave it open for the next Step-by-Step.

Create a Text Box on a Shape

To place text inside a shape, simply click the shape and then begin to type. A text box will appear on the shape. You can wrap text or change the alignment of text in a shape by working in the Format Shape dialog box. Right-click any shape, and then click Format Shape to open the Format Shape dialog box. You cannot type text on an object that is part of a group. You can ungroup the object to add special formatting or text, and then regroup it to make it part of the original group again.

Step-by-Step 3.15

1.   Click any **cube** to select the cube group. On the Home tab on the Ribbon, in the Drawing group, click the **Arrange** button, and then click **Ungroup**. The three cubes are no longer grouped.

2.   Click a blank area of the slide to deselect the three cubes, and then click the **upper-right cube** that does not have a picture.

3.   Type **Cottonseed Oil Mill** inside the text box. The text wraps in the shape.

4.   Drag to select the text **Cottonseed Oil Mill** you just typed in the cube. On the Ribbon, click the **Drawing Tools Format** tab, click the **More** button ⬇ in the WordArt Styles group, move the pointer over the different WordArt styles to see the effects, and then click **Gradient Fill – Gray, Outline - Gray** in the third row.

5. If the shape is not big enough to fit the text, drag the corner sizing handles to resize the cube so all the text fits on two lines.

6. On the Ribbon, on the Drawing Tools Format tab, in the Arrange group, click the **Group** button, and then click **Regroup.** You made changes to the one cube, and then regrouped it with the other two cubes. The three objects are grouped again, and are treated as one object by PowerPoint.

7. Click the front **can**, and then type **Cottonseed Oil**.

8. Drag a **selection box** around the three cans to select the three objects. On the Drawing Tools Format tab, in the Arrange group, click the **Group** button, and then click **Group.**

9. Resize the grouped can object so the text Cottonseed Oil fits on two lines, as shown in **Figure 3–37**.

FIGURE 3–37
Text added to objects

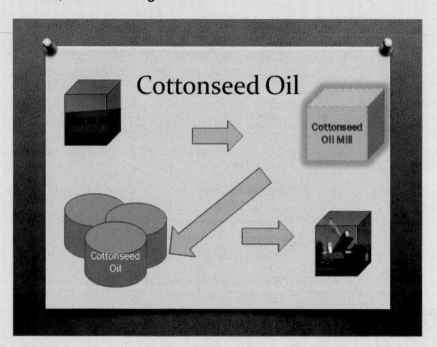

10. Save the presentation and leave it open for the next Step-by-Step.

Animating Shapes

When you create shapes on a slide, often you want to add animation to the shapes to help the slide to tell a story. Grouped objects will animate as a single object. If you want the individual objects in a group to animate separately, you have to ungroup them. If you take the time to create an animation that includes several effects and you want that same sequence of effects applied to another object, you can use the Animation Painter. Select the object with the animation effects you want to copy, click the Animation tab on the Ribbon, then in the Advanced Animation group, click the Animation Painter. To apply the same animation to more than one object, double-click the Animation Painter button. The Animation Pointer ⊾ 🖌 is 'sticky' and any objects you click will have that animation applied to it.

Step-by-Step 3.16

1. Click any **cube** on the slide, and then click the **Drawing Tools Format** tab. In the Arrange group, click **Group**, click **Ungroup**, and then click a blank area on the slide.

2. Click the **upper-right cube**, click the **Animations** tab on the Ribbon, click the **Add Animation** button to open the Animation gallery, and then in the Entrance section, click **Swivel**. The effect is set to start On Click.

3. Click the **upper-right cube**, click the **Animations** tab on the Ribbon, click the **Add Animation** button to open the Animation gallery, and then in the Emphasis section, click **Color Pulse**. The cube has two animation tags.

4. Click the **upper-right cube**, in the Advanced Animation group, click the **Animation Painter button**, and then use the Animation Pointer ⊾ 🖌 to click the **upper-left cube** with the picture on it. The same animations are applied to the second cube and animation tags 3 and 4 appear next to that cube.

5. Click the **upper-right cube**, in the Advanced Animation group, click the **Animation Painter button**, and then use the Animation Pointer to click the **lower-right cube** with the picture on it. The same animations are applied to the third cube and animation tags 5 and 6 appear next to that cube. See **Figure 3–38**.

FIGURE 3–38
Using the Animation Painter

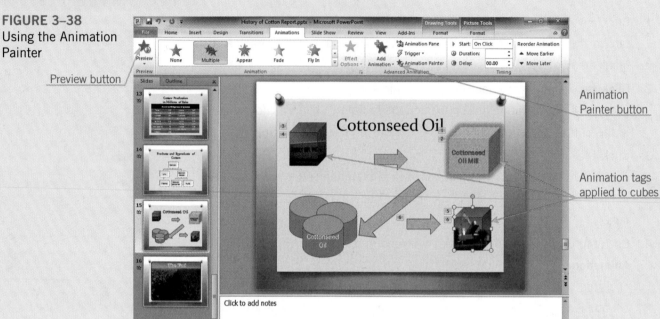

Preview button

Animation Painter button

Animation tags applied to cubes

Using the Animation Pane

As you build the animations in a slide, it is often helpful to get an overall picture of the sequence and timings of the animations. The Animation Pane provides that feature. Click the Animations tab on the Ribbon, then in the Advance Animation group, click the Animation Pane button. Use the Animation Pane in the next step-by-step to finish animating this slide. If you use the Add Animation button, animations build upon each other. If you use the Animations gallery that is what is applied to the object.

Step-by-Step 3.17

1. On the Animations tab, in the Advanced Animation group, click the **Animation Pane** button. The Animation Pane opens. You see the six animations currently applied to the cubes on the slide.

2. Click the **top arrow** between the two cubes, click the **Add Animation** button, click **More Entrance Effects**, in the Add Entrance Effect dialog box, scroll to the Exciting group, click **Boomerang**, and then click **OK**. This effect is currently set to start On Click.

3. In the Timing Group, click the **Start** list arrow, and then click **After Previous**. The animation for the arrow will begin after the cube animations.

4. Select the **left arrow** that points to the cans in the middle of the slide, click the **More** button in the Animation group to open the Animations gallery, and then in the Emphasis section, click **Object Color.**

5. Click **left arrow** again, in the Animation group click the **Effect Options** button, on the palette in the Theme Colors section, click the **blue box** in the first row, fourth column. In the Timing group, click the **Duration** box, type **.75**, and then set the animation to start **After Previous.**

6. Click the **cans group**, click the **More** button in the Animation group to open the Animations gallery, scroll to the Exit section, click **Shrink & Turn**, click the **Start** list arrow in the Timing section, and then click **After Previous**.

7. Click the **bottom arrow**, click the **More** button in the Animation group to open the Animations gallery, scroll to the Exit section, click Zoom, click the **Start** list arrow, and then click **After Previous**.

The slide should look similar to **Figure 3–39**, although the numbers for your objects may be different.

> **TIP**
>
> Animation is one of the most interesting, fun, and creative features in PowerPoint. You should continue to experiment with animating objects until you get the effects you want for a slide.

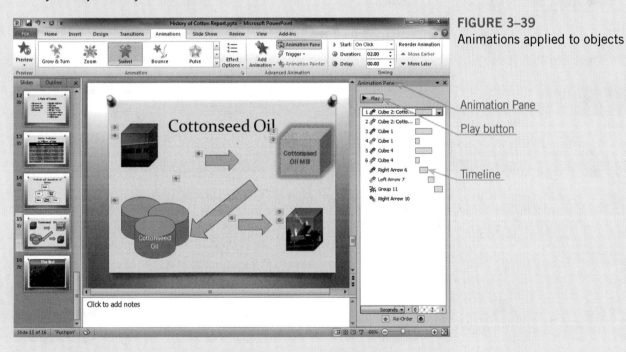

FIGURE 3–39
Animations applied to objects

8. Click **Cube 2:Cotton..** in the first animation in the Animation Pane, click the **Play** button in the Animation Pane, and then watch the timeline and animations for the slide.

9. Close the Animation Pane, save the presentation, and then leave it open for the next Step-by-Step.

Ordering Visual Elements

If you add an object to a slide that already contains other objects, the last object is stacked on top of the other objects. To bring an object forward or send it backward, select the object you want to move, and click the Bring to Front, Send to Back, Bring Forward, or Send Backward command in the Arrange group on the Drawing Tools Format tab. These commands are also available on the Picture Tools Format tab on the Ribbon. You can also access this feature by right-clicking the object, then making a selection from the shortcut menu. When you insert a picture, you might find that the picture has a background color. Often you can remove the background color, so the picture looks integrated with the total image you are trying to create. PowerPoint has powerful image editing tools that help you edit pictures to achieve these visual effects. To remove background color, click the picture, then on the Picture Tools Format tab, click the Remove Background button.

Step-by-Step 3.18

1. Click **slide 15**, *Cottonseed Oil*, click the **Home** tab on the Ribbon, in the Slides group click the **New Slide** button arrow, and then click the **Blank** layout.

2. Click the **Insert** tab on the Ribbon, and then, in the Images group, click the **Picture** button to open the Insert Picture dialog box.

3. Locate the folder that has the Data Files for this lesson, click the file **Sky.jpg**, and then click **Insert**. The picture of a blue sky appears on the slide.

4. Click the **Design** tab on the Ribbon, in the Background group click the **Hide Background Graphics** check box, click the **Background Styles** button, click **Style 1** to remove any graphics from the background, and then drag the **corner sizing handles** so that the picture fills the entire slide.

5. Click the **Insert** tab on the Ribbon, and then, in the Images group, click the **Picture** button to open the Insert Picture dialog box.

6. Locate and insert the picture **Truck.jpg** on the slide, and then move the truck down to the lower portion of the slide.

7. Click the **Insert** tab on the Ribbon, and then, in the Images group, click the **Picture** button to open the Insert Picture dialog box, insert the picture **Highway.jpg** on the slide, and then resize and position the **Highway.jpg** picture so that it covers the bottom half of the slide and covers the Truck.jpg picture.

8. On the Picture Tools Format tab, in the Arrange group, click **Send Backward**. The truck appears again. The stacking order of the pictures should be sky, highway, and then truck. You should see all three images.

9. Click the **Truck.jpg** picture on the slide and resize the picture so that it is proportional to the cars in the Highway.jpg picture, and then move the **Truck.jpg** picture so that it is positioned on the left side of the overpass, slightly off the slide (see **Figure 3–40**).

FIGURE 3–40
Pictures inserted on a slide

10. Click the **Truck.jpg** picture so it is selected. On the Picture Tools Format tab on the Ribbon, in the Adjust group, click the **Remove Background** button. The Background Removal tab appears and the image is marked for changes. The purple areas will be discarded. See **Figure 3–41**.

TIP

If you make a mistake coloring a picture, click the Reset Picture button.

FIGURE 3–41
Background Removal tool

TIP

If parts of the truck are purple or marked to discard, in the Refine group, click the Mark Areas to Keep button, and then click those areas on the image to be sure to include the whole truck.

FIGURE 3–42
Background removed

11. Carefully drag the selection handles as needed to include the entire truck image inside the dashed lines, and then click the **Keep Changes** button on the Background Removal tab. The white background is gone and the truck should blend in with the sky above it and the overpass below it. See **Figure 3–42**.

12. Drag the truck image so the truck appears to be on the overpass but is still off the slide to the left.

13. With the **Truck.jpg** picture selected, click the **Animations** tab on the Ribbon, click the **More Animations** button ⊟ to open the gallery, scroll to Motion Paths, click **Lines**, click the **Effect Options** button in the Animation group, and then click **Right**. The truck should move to the right along the overpass in the picture.

TIP

You can tell the direction of a motion path. The green side of the path is the start point, the red side is the end point.

14. Click the **Motion Path** on the slide, drag the red side of the path to extend it off the slide on the right side of the overpass. See **Figure 3–43**.

FIGURE 3–43
Motion path extended

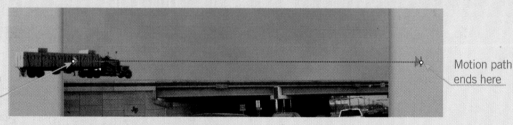

Motion path starts here

Motion path ends here

15. Verify that the animation is set to start On Click, click the **Duration** text box, and then type **5.00**.

16. Click the **Preview** button. The truck appears to travel along the motion path on the slide for five seconds.

17. Save the presentation and leave it open for the next Step-by-Step.

Inserting Objects on a Slide

Objects can include Excel charts, media clips, video, bitmaps, or almost any other media file that can be embedded into a PowerPoint presentation. To insert an object on a slide, click the Insert tab on the Ribbon. To insert a picture of any program that is not minimized on the taskbar, click the Screenshot button in the Images group. A menu of available images appears and you can click to insert on a slide. See **Figure 3–44**.

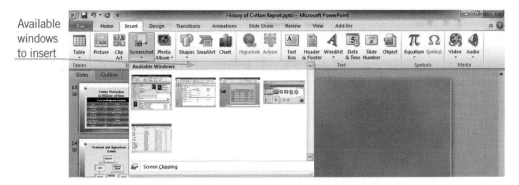

FIGURE 3–44   Inserting a screenshot

To insert an object, click the Object button in the Text group. The Insert Object dialog box opens, as shown in **Figure 3–45**. Scroll through the list of objects that are compatible with PowerPoint, and click the type of object you want to insert. If you are inserting an object that has already been created, click Create from file. The dialog box changes to allow you to locate the file you want to insert. Click OK to close the Browse dialog box, and click OK again to embed the file. You will learn more about embedding files in the next lesson.

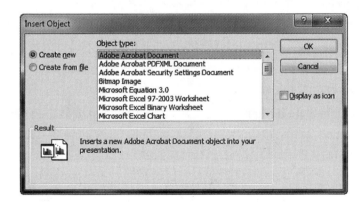

FIGURE 3–45   Insert Object dialog box

Inserting a video helps bring concepts to life. Video is an excellent medium to transmit ideas. PowerPoint video editing tools make it possible for you to create the perfect video for your presentation. To insert a video, click the Video button in the Media group. To insert a sound, click the Audio button in the Media group.

Video can be formatted just as a picture can. The Video Tools Format tab is shown in **Figure 3–46**. Video can be edited to play in any way that best suits your presentation. See **Figure 3–47**.

FIGURE 3–46   Video Tools Format tab

FIGURE 3–47   Video Tools Playback tab

Step-by-Step 3.19

1. Select **slide 2**, *How do they make...?*, click the **clipart** of a bed, then press **Delete**. Click the **Insert** tab on the Ribbon, in the Media group, click the **Video button arrow** and then click **Video from File**.

2. In the Insert Video dialog box, locate and click **cribbedding.mpg** from the Data Files for this lesson, then click **Insert**. The video is inserted in the center of the slide with video editing controls selected and the Video Tools Format tab selected.

3. Click the **More** button ⊡ in the Video Styles group, and then click **Metal Rounded Rectangle** in the Intense section. See **Figure 3–48**.

FIGURE 3–48
Video formatted

4. Click the **Video Tools Playback** tab, if not already selected, in the Video Options group, click the **Start** list arrow, and then click **Automatically**.

5. Click the **Play button** in the Preview section, and then view the short video.

6. Save the presentation and leave it open for the next Step-by-Step.

> **TIP**
>
> In the Preview section, the Play button is a Pause button while the video is playing. Click it to stop the video.

Adding a Header or Footer

You add a header or footer to the slides or notes pages by using the Header and Footer dialog box. Click the Insert tab on the Ribbon; in the Text group, click the Header & Footer button. The Header and Footer dialog box opens on the screen, as shown in **Figure 3–49**. Slides have footers. You can add the date and time, slide number, and any text you want to the footer of the slide. Although a footer is often defined as text that appears on the bottom of a page or slide, some themes place the footer in different places on the slide. When you click the Notes and Handouts tab, you have the option of creating a header as well as a footer. The header appears at the top of the notes page, the footer at the bottom of the page. Some items that you might include in a header or footer are the presenter's name, e-mail address, Web site address, or phone number.

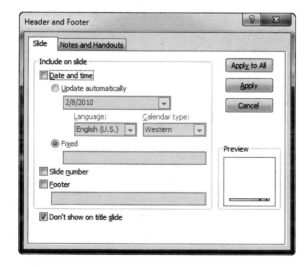

FIGURE 3–49   Header and Footer dialog box

Step-by-Step 3.20

1. Click the **Insert** tab on the Ribbon, and then, in the Text group, click the **Header & Footer** button. The Header and Footer dialog box opens.

2. Click the **Notes and Handouts** tab in the Header and Footer dialog box.

3. Click the **Footer** check box, and then type **The Story of Cotton**.

4. Click the **Date and time** check box, if it is not already selected. It is set to Update automatically.

5. Click the **Header** check box. In the Header text box, type your name.

6. Click **Apply to All**.

7. Click the **File tab**, review the Print options, and then print the slide show as directed by your teacher.

8. Save and close the presentation, and then exit PowerPoint.

SUMMARY

In this lesson, you learned:

- How to insert and modify SmartArt graphics to give special effects to text and graphics on a slide.

- How to create and format WordArt.

- How to build and format charts in a presentation using Microsoft Excel.

- How to create, format, and modify a table.

- How to add shapes and objects to your presentation to add effects to the text.

- How to rotate, fill, scale, or size an object as well as change its fill or line color.

- How to copy, move, order, and group objects on a slide.

- How to animate shapes and use the animation painter to copy animation.

- How to order visual elements, create a motion path, and make and remove a background from a picture.

- How to insert objects on slides, including worksheets, sounds, and videos.

- How to add a header or a footer to slides in a presentation.

VOCABULARY REVIEW

Define the following terms:

adjustment handle	datasheet	row
category axis	grouping	SmartArt graphic
cell	handle	table
chart	organization chart	value axis
column	rotate handle	WordArt

REVIEW QUESTIONS

TRUE / FALSE

Circle T if the statement is true or F if the statement is false.

T   F   **1.**   Organization charts are useful for showing the hierarchical structure and relationships within an organization.

T   F   **2.**   After you insert a table on a slide, you can convert it to a pie chart to better understand the data.

T   F   **3.**   When an object is selected, the yellow boxes are adjustment handles.

T   F   **4.**   Grouping allows you to work with several items as if they were one object.

T   F   **5.**   Video cannot be formatted using the same styles as Pictures.

MULTIPLE CHOICE

Select the best response for the following statements.

1. To apply the same animation to more than one object, it is suggested that you use the _____.

   A. Animation Painter   **C.** Format Painter

   B. SmartArt Graphics   **D.** Animation Pane

2. Use the _____ feature to make an image look as though it is a watercolor painting, broken glass, wrapped in plastic, or even cast in cement!

   A. Animation Painter   **C.** Artistic Effects

   B. SmartArt Graphics   **D.** Picture Styles

3. Which command do you use to turn a graphic, such as an arrow, from facing right to facing down?

   A. Rotate Left 90°   **C.** Flip Vertical

   B. Rotate Right 90°   **D.** Flip Horizontal

4. Which feature makes it possible for you to delete unwanted portions of a picture to make it look as though it is part of another image on the slide?

   A. Motion Paths   **C.** Swipe Animation

   B. Insert Texture   **D.** Background Removal

5. If you want to create a SmartArt graphic from a bullet list on a slide, you click the _____ button.

   A. Insert SmartArt   **C.** Convert to WordArt

   B. Convert to SmartArt   **D.** Insert WordArt

FILL IN THE BLANK

Complete the following sentences by writing the correct word or words in the blanks provided.

1. On the View tab, in the Show group, click the _____ check box to display a vertical and a horizontal line on the slide to help you place objects.

2. The _____ is a worksheet that appears with the chart and has the numbers for the chart.

3. You can type text directly in the graphic or you can open the _____ to the left of the SmartArt graphic to enter text.

4. An object will follow a(n) _____ on a slide; the green side is the starting and the red side is the ending position.

5. _____ are useful when you need to organize information that can be displayed in rows and columns.

■ PROJECTS

If you have a SAM 2010 user profile, your instructor may have assigned an autogradable version of the indicated project. If so, log into the SAM 2010 Web site at *www.cengage.com/sam2010* to download the instruction and start files.

PROJECT 3–1

1. Start PowerPoint, open the **Shelter.pptx** presentation from the drive and folder where you store your Data Files, and then save it as **Animal Shelter**, followed by your initials.

2. Display slide 4, and then convert the text to a SmartArt graphic of your choice.

3. Insert a new slide after slide 4 with the blank layout, draw five different objects on the slide, and then enter text on at least three of the objects. Group two of the objects. Format the objects using fills and styles.

4. Display the gridlines and guides. Move the horizontal guide to a new position. Add an object to the slide you created in Step 4 using the guide. Remove the gridlines and guides from view.

5. Create a table on a slide. Create a header row. Enter the text of your choice. Format text in the table. Format the table using a style.

6. Create a chart on a slide with the title **Funds Raised This Year**. Enter data for at least four rows and four columns in the data sheet.

7. Add your name to the handouts as a footer on all slides, print the presentation handouts, and then save the presentation.

SÁM PROJECT 3–2

1. Open the **DogsAndCats.pptx** presentation from the drive and folder where you store your Data Files, and then save it as **DogsAndCats Palace**, followed by your initials.

2. Display the slide with the chart. On the Chart Tools Design tab, in the Type group, click the Change Chart Type button and then choose a Chart Type. Apply a new chart type to the chart. Add data labels to the chart.

3. Change two of the data points. Add a chart title to the chart.

4. Insert a new slide after slide 8, and then add two pictures of your choice, from your own files or search the Internet for images you like. You can also use Clip Art.

5. Use the Background Removal tool on one of the pictures.

6. Order the photos on the slide in a way that makes sense to you, and then animate one of the photos using a motion path.

7. Animate the SmartArt graphic. Use the Animation Painter to copy an animation from one object to another object in the presentation.

8. Open another window and any program you choose on your computer. Use the ScreenShot tool to add that screen to a new slide in the presentation after slide 9.

9. Add your name as a footer on the notes page. Save the presentation. View the presentation and then note any changes you want to make.

10. Save the presentation, print the handouts with four slides per page, and then exit PowerPoint.

CRITICAL THINKING

ACTIVITY 3–1

Use the Internet to research a company. Use the information you find to create a presentation about the company that includes an organization chart, a SmartArt graphic, a chart, a table, and at least one other SmartArt object. Be sure to include an animated object.

- Apply a theme to the presentation.
- Include your name in the header of the handouts.
- Use the spelling checker to make sure you have no spelling errors in the presentation.
- Save the presentation using the name of the company.

ACTIVITY 3–3

Think about a company that you want to start. Use a template from Microsoft Office Online to create several slides in a new presentation to let people know about your company. The presentation should include at least four slides:

- A title slide with the name of your company
- A slide with a chart
- A slide with two drawn objects
- A slide with a SmartArt graphic
- A slide with a formatted table
- Include your name in the slides footer
- Save the presentation as MyCompany followed by your initials

ACTIVITY 3–2

You want to make some changes to some graphics on several slides. Use the Microsoft Office PowerPoint Help system to find out how to do the following:

- Change the shape of any drawn object, such as a star or arrow, on a slide.
- Display text vertically instead of horizontally in a table cell.
- Change the various features in a chart.

LESSON 4

Expanding on PowerPoint Basics

■ OBJECTIVES

Upon completion of this lesson, you should be able to:

- Integrate PowerPoint with other Office programs.
- Create new slide masters.
- Create Action buttons.
- Insert comments and work collaboratively with others.
- Create custom slide shows, organize slides into sections, and hide slides for specific audiences.
- Rehearse timings, set up a slide show, and use on-screen annotation tools.
- Send a presentation using email, package a presentation for CD, and broadcast a presentation option.
- Save a presentation as a video.

■ VOCABULARY

Action button

comment

custom show

destination file

Document Inspector

document properties

embed

Format Painter

grid

guidelines

import

link

linked object

Package for CD

Presenter view

Snap to

source file

A presentation is meant to be shared with other people as a tool for teaching or viewed by audiences to share ideas and concepts. Often a presentation includes information from other programs. Rather than recreating the chart, document, graphic, or video created in another program, you can easily include this information in a slide show. Once you have completed a presentation, you have several options for preparing it so it can be viewed by others. Slide shows do not always have to follow the same order of slides. You can create action buttons to create a show that displays specific slides in any order as needed. You can create custom shows, sections, and hide slides to use the same series of slides in different ways for different audiences. You can add comments and collaborate with others about the slides to help you create the perfect presentation. During a slide show, you can use pens and highlighters to make notes and then save the notes in the presentation for later use. PowerPoint provides many different ways for you to deliver a presentation including broadcasting it on the Web for people who are not in the same room as you, saving the presentation as a video, and e-mailing it in different formats to meet the needs of your audience. In this lesson, you will learn how all these features work together to help you create and deliver quality slide shows to your audience.

Integrating PowerPoint with Other Office Programs

As you learn to work with the different computer programs, you will develop preferences for using certain programs for various tasks. You may find that you created a chart or have data in Microsoft Excel, for example, that you want to include as part of your PowerPoint presentation. You may also have a document that you created in Microsoft Word, and you want to include that text in the presentation. You do not have to recreate that work to use it in a presentation. You can easily insert objects and link or embed text or data from other programs into slides.

Inserting Text from a Word Outline

If you have a lot of text that you want to use in a presentation, you may find it easier to type the text using Microsoft Word. You can then import text from Word to create a new presentation or add slides to an existing presentation. *Import* means to bring a file or part of a file into the presentation. A Word outline is the easiest kind of document to import because it is formatted with styles, and each heading level is translated into a corresponding level of text in PowerPoint. For example, Heading 1 text is converted to slide titles. If the Word document does not have heading styles applied, PowerPoint uses the Tabs that create paragraph indentations to create the slides. If a paragraph begins at the margin without a tab, the paragraph becomes the slide title. Each tab creates a new level text in bulleted lists on the slide.

▶ **VOCABULARY**
import

Step-by-Step 4.1

1. Click the Start button 🪟 on the taskbar, type **Microsoft Word** in the Search box, and then click **Microsoft Word 2010** on the Programs menu to start Microsoft Word.

2. Click the **File** tab on the Ribbon, click **Open**, locate the drive and folder where you store your Data files, click **Planet Facts.docx** and then click **Open** to open the document file. Notice that the Planet Facts document is formatted as an outline. Each planet name is a Level 1 head.

3. Click the **File** tab on the Ribbon, and then click **Exit** to close the file and exit Word.

4. Start PowerPoint to open a new blank presentation.

5. In the new presentation title slide, click the **Click to add title** place-holder, type **Our Solar System**, click the **Click to add subtitle** place-holder, and then type **Planet Facts**.

6. On the Home tab, in the Slides group, click the **New Slide** button arrow, and then click **Slides from Outline** at the bottom of the Layout gallery. The Insert Outline dialog box opens.

7. In the Insert Outline dialog box, navigate to the Data Files for this lesson, click the document file **Planet Facts.docx**, and then click **Insert**.

PowerPoint imports the Word document text into the presentation and formats it as slides. Nine new slides appear. There is one slide for each Level 1 head. The way the outline was created set up the slide show so that the planet name is the title of each slide. See **Figure 4–1**.

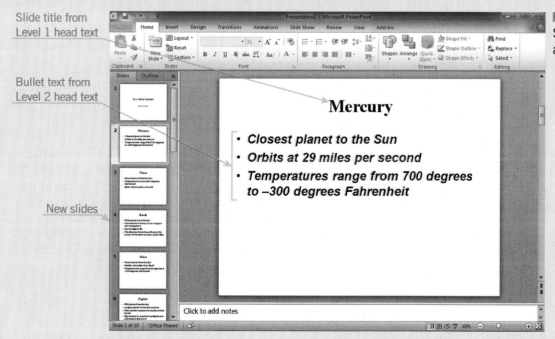

Slide title from Level 1 head text

Bullet text from Level 2 head text

New slides

FIGURE 4–1
Slides inserted from a Word outline

8. Click the **Save** button 🖫 on the Quick Access toolbar, locate the folder where you store the Data Files for this lesson, and then save the presentation as **Our Solar System**, followed by your initials. Leave the presentation open for the next Step-by-Step.

Applying a Theme

The outline was inserted into a new blank presentation. The Office theme is applied to the slides in the presentation by default. Now that you have the text in the slides, you can begin to work on the design and graphics to enhance the presentation.

Step-by-Step 4.2

> **TIP**
>
> Themes are in alphabetical order in the Themes gallery.

1. Click the **Design** tab on the Ribbon. In the Themes group, click the **More** button 🔽 to open the Themes gallery, and then in the gallery click the **Newsprint** theme. This theme adds a gray background to the slides, puts a red bar at the top of the slides, and places the slide title at the bottom of the slide above a thin red line.

2. Click **slide 1** on the Slides tab, click the **Slide Show** button 🖵 on the status bar, and then click to advance the slides and view the slide show. The presentation includes 10 slides.

3. Press **Esc** after you view the last slide, to return to Normal view.

4. Save the presentation and leave it open for the next Step-by-Step.

Understanding Embedding, Linking, and Paste Special

> ▶ **VOCABULARY**
> **destination file**
> **source file**
> **embed**

When you work with more than one file, it is often convenient to refer to the files as source or destination files. Since you are creating a presentation in PowerPoint, the presentation file is the ***destination file***. The ***source file*** is where you have the text, chart, numbers, or whatever data it is you want to bring into the presentation.

Remember that the main difference between linking and embedding is where you store the data and how you update the data after you place it in the destination file.

When you move data among applications by cutting or copying and pasting, Microsoft Office changes the format of the data you are moving so that it can be used in the destination file. When it is easier to edit the information using the original application, you can ***embed*** the data as an object using the Insert Object dialog box. You have two options: create a new object or insert an existing file as an object. To create a new object, click the Insert tab on the Ribbon, in the Text group, click the Object button to open the Insert Object dialog box. See **Figure 4–2**.

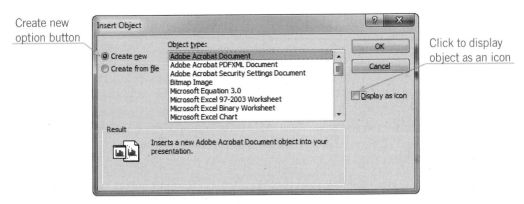

FIGURE 4–2   Insert Object dialog box—Create new option

If you have already created the object and saved it as a file, you can insert an object from an existing file. Click the Insert tab on the Ribbon, in the Text group click the Object button to open the Insert Object dialog box, and then click the Create from file option button. See **Figure 4–3**.

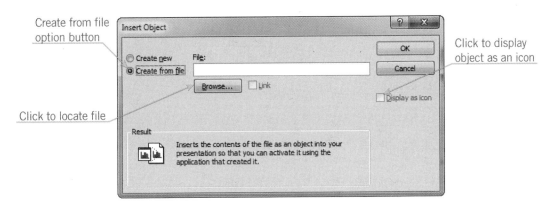

FIGURE 4–3   Insert Object dialog box—Create from file option

The embedded information becomes part of the new file, but as a separate object that can be edited using the application that created it. For example, if a table from a Word document is embedded into a PowerPoint presentation, PowerPoint enables the table to be edited using Word. If you insert an object from a file, you can choose to link the object. If you *link* the object, a connection is retained between the source and destination files. With a linked object, if you update the source file, the data in the destination file is also updated. It is a way to always have the most recent data on the slides.

▶ **VOCABULARY**
link

📼 **EXTRA FOR EXPERTS**

If you click the Display as icon check box in the Insert Object dialog box, the program's icon will be displayed in the slide. The icon is a clue as to the originating program.

Using Paste Special

Data from one application can be embedded into another application, using the copy and paste commands. PowerPoint offers Paste option buttons when you click the Paste button arrow, see **Figure 4–4**, to help you copy and paste data either from within the presentation or among programs. Using Excel data as an example:

- Click the Keep Source Formatting button to copy the data as a PowerPoint table but keep the appearance of the original worksheet.

- Click the Use Destination Styles button to copy the Excel data as a PowerPoint table and use the theme to create a PowerPoint table.

- Click the Embed button to copy the Excel data as a worksheet that can be edited in Excel.

- Click the Picture button to copy the Excel data as a graphic or picture that cannot be edited.

- Click the Keep Text Only button to copy the Excel data text in a text box.

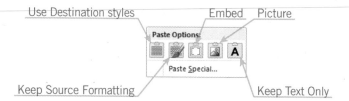

FIGURE 4–4   Paste Options buttons

The Paste Special command has several options that provide flexibility in how data is copied from a source file to a destination file. The Paste Special dialog box has different options depending on the source of the object. **Figure 4–5** shows the Paste Special dialog box options for data that was copied from an Excel worksheet.

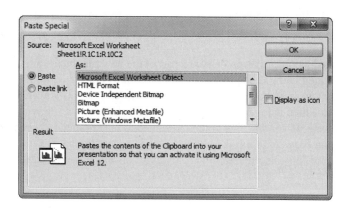

FIGURE 4–5   Paste Special options for Excel data

Figure 4–6 shows the Paste Special dialog box for text that was copied from a Word document. If you choose to paste a link, you will link rather than embed the data, so you will retain the connection between the source and destination files.

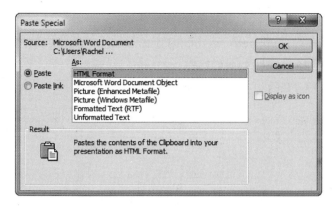

FIGURE 4–6 Paste Special options for Word text

Table 4–1 explains the different Paste Special options.

TABLE 4–1 Paste Special options

OPTION	PASTES THE CONTENTS OF THE CLIPBOARD INTO THE PRESENTATION AS
HTML Format	HTML format; HTML is the format that can be read by a browser, the format of Web pages
Microsoft Office Word	A document that can be edited using Microsoft Word Document Object
Picture (Enhanced Metafile)	An enhanced metafile picture, to edit the contents using Picture Tools
Picture (Windows Metafile)	A metafile picture, to edit the contents using Picture Tools
Formatted Text (RTF)	Formatted text in Rich Text Format, retaining coding and formatting
Unformatted Text	Unformatted text, with all coding removed

Step-by-Step 4.3

1. Click **slide 6**, *Jupiter*, on the Slides tab. Click the **Home** tab on the Ribbon, in the Slides group, click the **New Slide** button arrow, and then click the **Blank** slide layout.

2. Click the **Start** button on the taskbar, click **Microsoft Word 2010** to start Word. Click the **File tab**, click **Open**, locate the drive and folder where you store the Data Files for this lesson, and then open the document file **The Moons of Jupiter.docx**. Notice that the document is one page.

3. Click the **Enable Editing** button, if necessary. In the Editing group on the Ribbon, click the **Select** button, and then click **Select All**. All of the text in the Word document is selected.

4. In the Clipboard group on the Ribbon, click the **Copy** button 🖹 to copy the text to the Clipboard.

5. Click the **File** tab, and then click **Exit** to close the file and exit Word. Slide 7, a blank slide, should be in the PowerPoint window on your screen.

6. In the Clipboard group on the Ribbon, click the **Paste** button arrow, and then click **Paste Special**.

7. In the Paste Special dialog box, click **Microsoft Word Document Object**, and then click **OK**. Your slide should look similar to **Figure 4–7**.

FIGURE 4–7
Word text pasted as an object on a slide

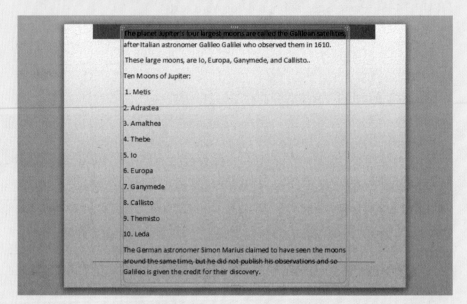

8. Save the presentation and leave it open for the next Step-by-Step.

Editing Embedded Data

To make changes to the Word file embedded in the PowerPoint presentation, double-click the text you want to edit. Word, the program in which the file was created, opens so that you can edit the text. When you finish and return to PowerPoint, the presentation includes the changes you made to the text. You can also resize and reposition the borders of the object box to place the pasted object as you want on a slide.

Step-by-Step 4.4

1. Display **slide 7**, if it is not already displayed in the Slide pane.

2. Double-click inside the **Word object box** anywhere on the text, to activate Word for editing the text. The Word Home tab on the Ribbon appears above the slide. You have full access to all the Word editing features. See **Figure 4–8**.

Word Home tab

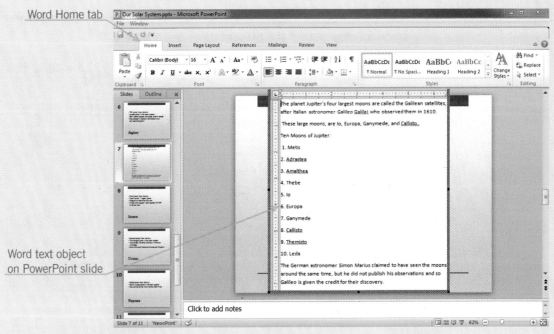

Word text object
on PowerPoint slide

FIGURE 4–8
Editing the Word
text in Word

3. In the first paragraph, add a comma after "Galileo Galilei". In the second paragraph, click to the right of the second period after the word Callisto, press **Backspace** to delete the extra period, and then delete the **comma** after "large moons".

4. Click to the right of the word **Ten** just above the list of moons, and then type **of the**.

5. In the list of moons double-click **Io**, press and hold **Ctrl**, double-click **Europa**, double-click **Ganymede**, and then release **Ctrl** so that all three moons are selected.

6. On the Home tab, in the Font group, click the **Font Color** list arrow, and then click **Dark Blue, Text 2** in the Theme Colors palette.

7. Drag to select from **1. Metis** to **10. Leda** to select the entire list of moons. On the Ribbon, click the **Page Layout** tab, in the Page Setup group, click the **Columns** button, and then click **Three**.

8. Click outside the Word object to exit Word. Notice that the changes you made are now part of the presentation. See **Figure 4–9**.

FIGURE 4–9
Formatted Word object

Text edited

Font color changed

List in three columns

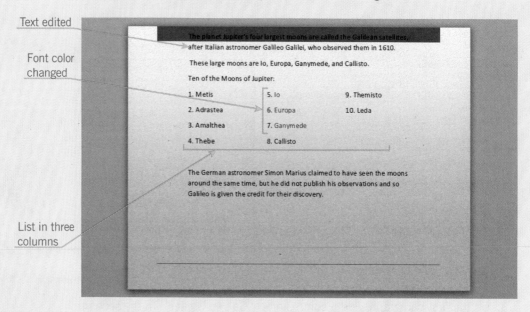

9. Save the presentation and leave it open for the next Step-by-Step.

EXTRA FOR EXPERTS

To place the Word object on the slide so all text is visible, you can move or resize the Word object. Select the object and drag a corner to make the object larger or smaller.

Importing an Excel Worksheet into a Presentation

You learned how to build and modify a chart on a slide and use Excel to edit and change the chart and data on the slide. Excel offers powerful tools for creating worksheets and charts. Therefore, you may want to create the worksheet in Excel and then import data from the existing Excel worksheet.

Step-by-Step 4.5

1. Click **slide 11**, *Pluto*, on the Slides tab. In the Slides group, click the **New Slide** button arrow, and then click the **Blank** slide layout to insert a new slide with a blank layout. The new slide 12 is selected.

2. On the Ribbon, click the **Insert** tab, and then in the Text group, click **Object** to open the Insert Object dialog box.

3. Click the **Create from file** option button, click **Browse**, locate the folder where you store the Data Files for this lesson, click the Excel file **Planets.xlsx**, click **OK**, and then click **OK** to close the Insert Object dialog box and insert the Planets.xlsx worksheet file.

4. Use the diagonal resize pointers ↖ and ↗ to drag the corners of the Excel worksheet object so the object is as wide as the red bar and fits between the red bar and the red line on the slide. Use the move pointer ✛ to position the object in the center of the slide. Your screen should look similar to **Figure 4–10**.

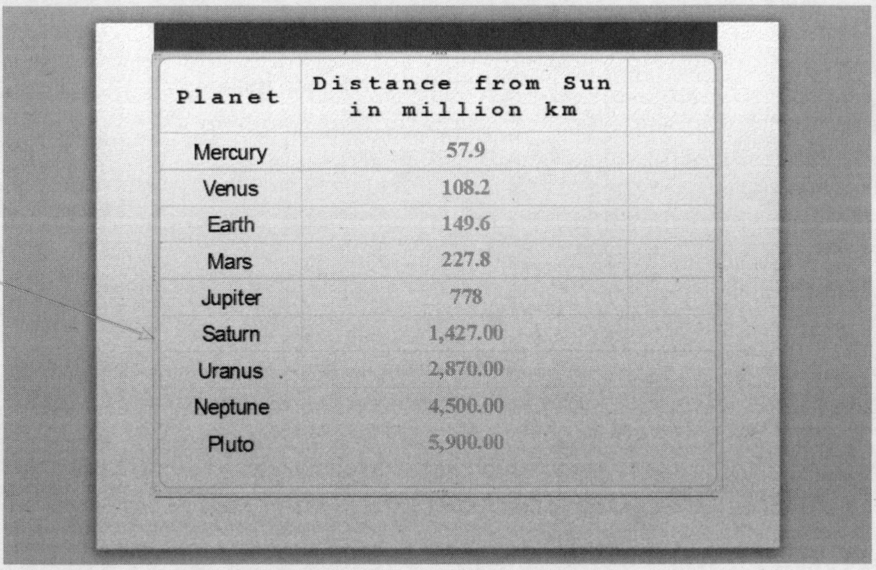

FIGURE 4–10
Excel worksheet inserted in PowerPoint slide

Object resized and placed on the slide

Planet	Distance from Sun in million km
Mercury	57.9
Venus	108.2
Earth	149.6
Mars	227.8
Jupiter	778
Saturn	1,427.00
Uranus	2,870.00
Neptune	4,500.00
Pluto	5,900.00

5. Double-click the **Excel worksheet object** to open it for editing in Microsoft Excel. The Excel Home tab appears on the Ribbon.

6. Click **cell A1** and drag to **cell B10**. You selected the cells from A1 to B10.

7. Click the **Insert** tab on the Excel Ribbon. In the Charts group, click the **Bar** button, and then click the **Clustered Bar in 3-D** chart type button. A chart is created in Excel. See **Figure 4–11**. You can continue to use the Excel chart-formatting features to enhance and resize the chart, or you can change the data in the worksheet using the Excel features.

FIGURE 4–11
Chart created in Excel on a PowerPoint slide

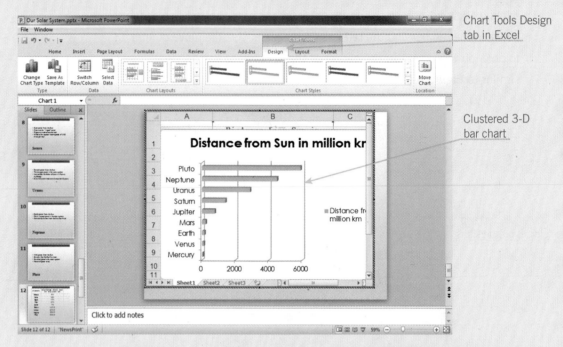

Chart Tools Design tab in Excel

Clustered 3-D bar chart

8. Click a blank area of the slide to exit Excel and return to the slide in PowerPoint.

9. Save the presentation and leave it open for the next Step-by-Step.

Reusing Slides from Other Presentations

Slides often take time to create. If you have presentations with slides that work well, you can certainly use them in more than one presentation. There are different methods for reusing slides. You can copy and paste slides from one presentation to another. Open the presentation that has the slides you want to copy. Switch to Slide Sorter view. Click to select the slides you want to reuse, and then on the Home tab on the Ribbon, in the Clipboard group, click the Copy button. Open the new presentation or the presentation in which you want to paste the slides, switch to Slide Sorter view, and then click after the slide that you want the new slides to follow. On the Ribbon, in the Clipboard group, click Paste.

You can also use a Slide Library to store favorite slides that you want to reuse again and again. To use the Reuse Slides task pane, click the New Slide button, and then click Reuse Slides. You browse to find the PowerPoint file that has the slides or the Slide Library.

EXTRA FOR EXPERTS

To duplicate one or more slides, click to select the slides you want to duplicate, click the Copy button arrow, and then click Duplicate. Or, click the New Slide button arrow and then click Duplicate Selected slides.

Step-by-Step 4.6

1. Click **slide 12**, the last slide in the presentation, if it is not already selected, and then click the **Slide Sorter** button on the status bar.

2. Click the **Home** tab on the Ribbon. In the Slides group, click the **New Slide** button arrow, and then click **Reuse Slides** at the bottom of the gallery. The Reuse Slides task pane opens.

3. In the Reuse Slides task pane, click **Browse**, and then click **Browse File** to open the Browse dialog box.

4. Locate the folder where your Data Files are stored for this lesson, click the presentation file **Sun Facts.pptx**, and then click **Open**. Five slides appear in the Reuse Slides task pane.

5. In the Reuse Slides task pane, point to each slide to see an enlarged version of each of the slides from the Sun Facts presentation. See **Figure 4–12**.

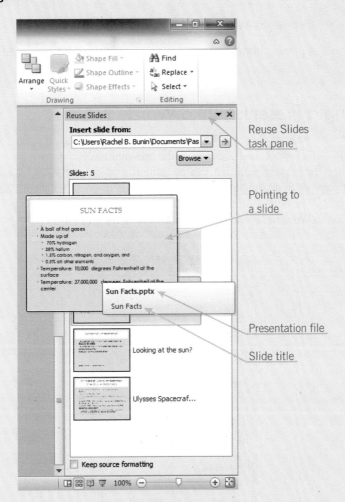

FIGURE 4–12
Reusing slides from another presentation

Reuse Slides task pane

Pointing to a slide

Presentation file

Slide title

6. In the Reuse Slides task pane, click each of the five slides, and then click the Reuse Slides task pane **Close** button to close the task pane. Each slide is inserted into the current presentation. The slides have taken on the NewsPrint theme of the current presentation. See **Figure 4–13**.

FIGURE 4–13
Slides inserted
in current
presentation

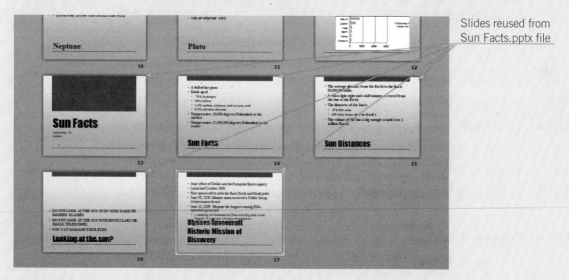

Slides reused from
Sun Facts.pptx file

7. Save the presentation and leave it open for the next Step-by-Step.

Sending a Presentation to Word

You can save a presentation as a Word document to use as a handout, or create other documents using the text and slides from the presentation.

To save the presentation that can be edited in Microsoft Word, click the File tab, click Save & Send, click Create Handouts, and then click Create Handouts in the right pane. The options in the Send To Microsoft Word dialog box can send your presentation to Word in several different formats. See **Figure 4–14**.

FIGURE 4–14   Send To Microsoft Word

Step-by-Step 4.7

1. Click the **File** tab, click **Save & Send**, in the center pane click **Create Handouts,** and then in the right pane click **Create Handouts**. The Send To Microsoft Word dialog box opens.

2. Click the **Blank lines next to slides** option button in the dialog box.

3. Click **OK**. The presentation is exported into Word and formatted as a document.

4. Click the **Document1 Word** button on the taskbar, close the Navigation pane if it is open, and then scroll through the document to view all the pages. See **Figure 4–15**.

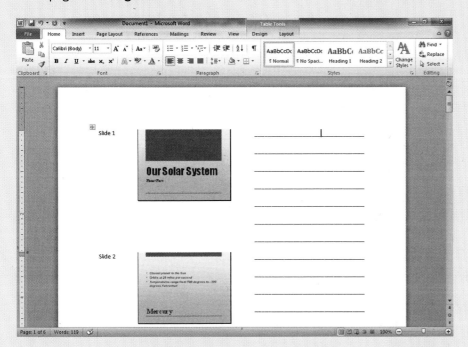

FIGURE 4–15
Presentation handouts saved as a Word file

5. Type your name on the first page of the document on the lines next to slide 1, Our Solar System, click the **Save** button ![save icon] on the Quick Access toolbar, and then save the document as **Solar System Handouts**, followed by your initials.

6. Click the **File** tab, click **Print**, click **the Print All Pages** button, click **Print Current Page**, and then click **Print** to print the first page of the document.

7. Click the **File** tab, and then click **Exit** to close the document and exit Word. The presentation file is on the screen in a PowerPoint window in Slide Sorter view.

WARNING

You have to delete same number of underlines as characters in your name so the document does not create a new page.

Creating New Masters

PowerPoint allows you to apply more than one slide master to a presentation. This is useful if your presentation contains slides with more than one theme or any other features that are controlled by the slide master. This saves time as you are creating presentations, because you can choose which master to apply to each slide.

There are several ways that you can create a new master. Display the slide masters by clicking the View tab on the Ribbon, and then clicking the Slide Master button. In the Edit Master group, click the Insert Slide Master button. See **Figure 4–16**.

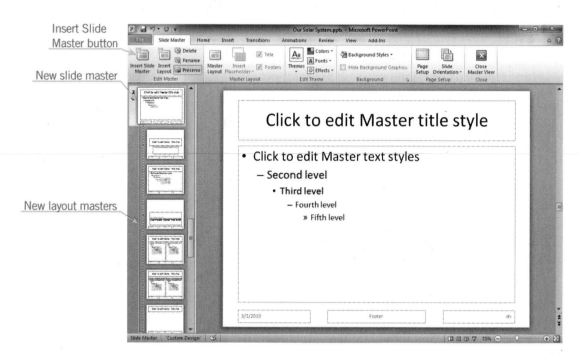

Insert Slide Master button

New slide master

New layout masters

FIGURE 4–16   Inserting a new slide master

Another way to create a slide master is to apply a new theme. Each theme will generate a new slide master and the corresponding layout masters.

Creating New Layout Masters

PowerPoint allows you to create a new layout master for any slide master. When you click the New Slide button, you are presented with a series of layouts for that slide master. There may be times when you want to place objects and text on a slide and the existing masters do not quite work for you. PowerPoint allows you to create a custom slide layout and then add the placeholders as needed. The placeholders available on the Insert Placeholder menu are: Content, Text, Picture, Chart, table, SmartArt, Media, and Clip Art.

Step-by-Step 4.8

1. Click **slide 1**, *Our Solar System*, in Slide Sorter view to select the first slide.

2. Click the **View** tab on the Ribbon. In the Master Views group, click the **Slide Master** button to switch to Slide Master view.

3. Point to the **Slide Master** thumbnail in the left pane. The ScreenTip tells you that the NewsPrint slide master is used by all 17 slides in the presentation.

4. On the Slide Master tab on the Ribbon, in the Edit Master group, click the **Insert Layout** button. A new layout is added to the bottom of the left pane as part of the NewsPrint slide master. It has a Title placeholder, a Date, Footer, and Slide number placeholder.

5. On the Slide Master tab on the Ribbon, in the Master Layout group, click the **Insert Placeholder** button arrow. You can select from a list of placeholders and place them anywhere on the layout master.

6. Click **SmartArt**, point to the upper-left corner of the slide below the lower-left corner of the red bar, press and hold the left mouse button, and then drag to draw a box in the center of the slide to just above the Master title style placeholder as shown in **Figure 4–17**.

FIGURE 4–17
Inserting a new layout master

7. Release the mouse button. A SmartArt graphic placeholder appears centered on the slide.

TIP

You can name custom layouts with descriptive titles.

8. Click the **Close Master View** button in the Close group to return to Slide Sorter view with the **Home** tab selected on the Ribbon. In the Slides group, click the **New Slide** button arrow to open the Layout gallery, and then click the **Custom Layout thumbnail**. A new slide is inserted with the new custom layout that you just created.

9. Double-click the new **slide 2** to open it in Normal view, and then click the **Click icon to add SmartArt Graphic** icon in the new slide to open the Choose a SmartArt Graphic dialog box.

10. Click **List** in the left pane, click the **Vertical Box List** icon, and then click **OK**. You added a Vertical Box List SmartArt graphic.

11. Type **The Sun** to add the text to the first **Text** placeholder, click the second **Text** placeholder, type **The Planets**, click the third **Text** placeholder, and then type **The Moons**.

12. Click **Click to add title**, and then type **Overview** as the title for the slide. Your completed slide should look like **Figure 4–18**.

FIGURE 4–18
New slide using custom layout

13. View the presentation as a slide show.

14. Save the presentation and leave it open for the next Step-by-Step.

Formatting Text and Objects

You have learned the basics of formatting text and objects. Formatting enhances the presentation giving you the freedom to change colors, fonts, and effects in both text and objects. PowerPoint has several helpful features to make formatting easier.

Replacing Text Fonts

You can replace a font throughout your presentation to another font. On the Home tab on the Ribbon, in the Editing group, click the Replace list arrow, and then click Replace Fonts. The Replace Font dialog box opens, as shown in **Figure 4–19**. In the Replace box, choose the font you want to replace. In the With box, choose the font you want to use as a replacement, and then click Replace. Any text in the presentation that has the Replace font will now have the font you designated in the With box.

FIGURE 4–19   Replace Fonts dialog box

Step-by-Step 4.9

1. Click **slide 3**, *Mercury*, and then click **miles** in the body text.

2. On the Home tab on the Ribbon, in the Editing group, click the **Replace** list arrow, and then click **Replace Fonts**.

   The Replace Font dialog box opens. The body text on the slides is in the Arial font. In the Replace box, Arial is selected.

3. Click the **With** list arrow, scroll the font list, click **Cambria**, and then click **Replace**. All the text in Arial font throughout the presentation is replaced with the Cambria font.

4. Click **Close** to close the Replace Fonts dialog box. Save the presentation. Leave the presentation open for the next Step-By-Step.

Using the Format Painter

If you format an object with certain attributes, such as fill color and line color, and then want to format another object the same way, use the *Format Painter*. Select the object whose attributes you want to copy, click the Format Painter button, and then click the object you want to format. You can use the same process to copy text attributes, such as font, size, color, or style, to other text. To copy attributes to more than one object or section of text, select the object whose attributes you want to copy, double-click the Format Painter button, and then click each of the objects or sections of text you want to format. When you are finished, click the Format Painter button. The Format Painter button is located on the Mini toolbar, as well as on the Home tab on the Ribbon in the Clipboard group.

▶ **VOCABULARY**
Format Painter

Step-by-Step 4.10

1. Click **slide 4**, *Venus*, and then click and drag to select the words **900 degrees Fahrenheit** in the second bullet.

2. In the Font group, click the **Font Color** list arrow ![A] , and then click the **Orange** color swatch in the Standard Colors palette.

3. With **900 degrees Fahrenheit** still selected, in the Clipboard group, click the **Format Painter** button ![icon].

4. The pointer changes to ![icon].

5. On the Slides tab, click **slide 3**, *Mercury*, and then click and drag the pointer over the words **700 degrees to –300 degrees Fahrenheit**.

   You have painted the formatting. The format of the text changed so it is the same as 900 degrees Fahrenheit in the second bullet point on the Venus slide.

6. Save the presentation and leave it open for the next Step-by-Step.

> **TIP**
>
> Format painting can be used to copy several formats such as text that is a specific font, style, size, and color at one time.

Using the Grid, Guides, and Rulers to Align Objects

A good presentation uses short phrases, pictures, and graphs to convey its point. Out-of- alignment text or pictures can distract from the point of a presentation. Use the *grid*, *guidelines*, and ruler in concert to place objects on a slide. To align a text box or picture, you can display the grid and guidelines on the slide pane; the ruler identifies the exact placement on the slide. As you learned in Lesson 3, to turn on the grid and to display the guidelines, click the View tab on the Ribbon, and then, in the Show group, click the Guide or Gridlines check boxes. Alternatively, to turn on Grids and Guide lines, you can right-click any blank area of a slide (do not click inside a placeholder) and click Grid and Guides to open the Grid and Guides dialog box. The *Snap to* option "Snap objects to grid" moves an object to the closest intersection of the grid on a slide. The grid appears to be "magnetic," which is very useful when you want to place objects exactly in position. The Grid settings section sets the spacing between the intersections of the gridlines. You can also choose to display the grid by clicking the check box. The Guide settings area displays a set of crosshairs on the screen to help you align an object in the center, left, right, top, or bottom of the slide. The Ruler option displays a vertical and horizontal ruler on the slide pane to identify the exact placement of objects. Click the Ruler check box in the Show group to display the ruler.

> **TIP**
>
> If you click a guide and begin to drag it, a ScreenTip appears with the location of the guide on the ruler so you can place the guide exactly where you want it on the slide.

> ▶ **VOCABULARY**
>
> **Snap to**
>
> **grid**
>
> **guidelines**

Step-by-Step 4.11

1. Click **slide 5**, *Earth*, on the Slides tab to select the slide, right-click any blank area of the slide, and then, on the shortcut menu, click **Grid and Guides**. The Grid and Guides dialog box opens.

2. Click the **Display grid on screen** check box to insert a check mark, click the **Display drawing guides on screen** check box to insert a check mark, verify that the **Snap objects to grid** check box has a checkmark, and then click **OK**.

3. Click the **View** tab on the Ribbon, notice the check marks in the **Gridlines** and **Guides** check boxes, then click the **Ruler** check box to insert a check mark and display the vertical and horizontal rulers.

4. Click the **Insert** tab on the Ribbon, and then, in the Text group, click the **Text Box** button. To the right of the vertical guide and below the horizontal guide, click in a blank area of the slide, and then type **Our home planet**.

5. Use the Move pointer to drag the **Our home planet** text box so that the top sizing handles are at the **−1"** position on the vertical ruler and the green rotation handle and the middle sizing handles are on the vertical guide at the **0"** position on the horizontal ruler. See **Figure 4–20**.

TIP

To temporarily disable the snap to feature, press and hold ALT while dragging the object.

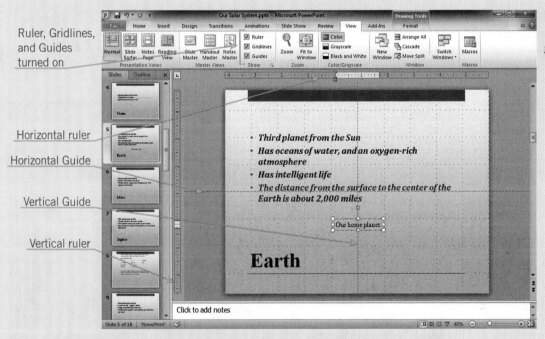

FIGURE 4–20
Using the gridlines, guides, and ruler

6. Click the **View** tab, if it is not already selected, in the Show group, click the **Ruler** check box to remove the check mark, click the **Gridlines** check box to remove the check mark, and then click the **Guides** check box to remove the check mark.

7. Save the presentation and leave it open for the next Step-by-Step.

Inserting Comments

Working with friends or coworkers to collaborate on a project is sometimes the way to get the best presentation. You may have a question about the content or design of a particular slide, or you may have a comment about the entire presentation. You do not have to be present with the slide show to pass along comments. You can insert *comments* in the slide for others to see. You can use the Comment features on the Review tab on the Ribbon, in the Comments group. You can insert, review, and edit comments. Each user's comment will have a different color or initial, so you can identify who originated each comment.

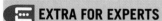

VOCABULARY

comment

EXTRA FOR EXPERTS

Click the Show Markup button to display comments and changes in the presentation.

Step-by-Step 4.12

TIP

The letters or name identifying the source of the note will vary, depending on whom the computer is registered to.

1. Click **slide 6**, *Mars*, click the **Review** tab on the Ribbon, and then, in the Comments group, click the **New Comment** button. A new comment opens.

2. Type **This slide needs clip art.** in the comment box. See **Figure 4–21**.

FIGURE 4–21
Inserting a comment

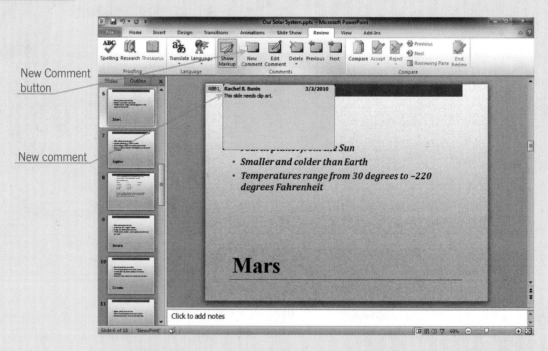

3. Click **slide 8**, *Jupiter Moons*. In the Comments group, click the **New Comment** button, and then type **This slide needs a title and a new layout.** in the comment box.

4. In the Comments group, click the **Previous** button to review the last comment, click the **Next** button to review the next comment, and then click the **Next** button to review the last comment. You can click the Previous and Next buttons to review all the comments in a presentation.

5. Save the presentation and leave it open for the next Step-by-Step.

TIP

In the Comments group, click the Delete button arrow to open a menu to delete the current comment, Delete all Markup on the Current Slide, or Delete All Markup in this Presentation.

Using the Compare Tool

Rather than just commenting on each other's work, sometimes group members working on a presentation will make changes to the presentation. Being able to compare ideas and see the changes that each member contributes is possible by using the Compare tool. The Compare tool makes it possible to see which changes have been made by each contributor and create one presentation file that includes all the changes. By merging all versions of a presentation, you are able to work with the latest version of the shared file. The compared view shows the changes made among the versions. You can use the Revisions panel to see the changes that were made. To use the Compare tool, click the Review tab on the Ribbon, in the Compare group, click the Compare button. In the Choose File to Merge with Current Presentation dialog box, select the file you wish to merge, and then click Open. The Reviewing pane displays the changes to the Presentation and a popup box identifies all changes that you can accept or reject. See **Figure 4–22**.

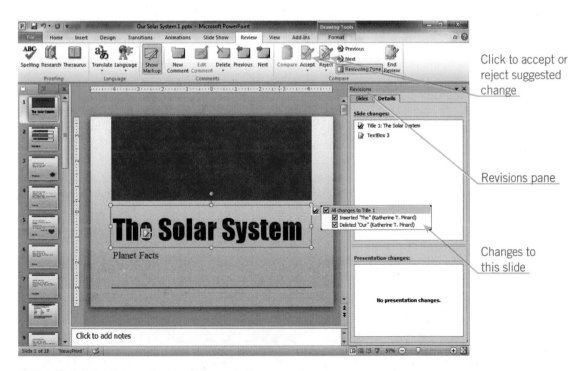

FIGURE 4–22   Comparing two presentations

Delivering a Presentation

To start a slide show, click the Slide Show button on the status bar. You can start the slide show at any slide by displaying or selecting the slide you want to begin with before clicking the Slide Show button. You can also set up and then begin to view the slide show by clicking the buttons using the Slide Show tab on the Ribbon. See **Figure 4–23**.

Buttons for starting the slide show   Buttons for setting up the slide show

FIGURE 4–23   Slide Show tab

Adding Sections to Your Presentation

A well-organized document is always better than a disorganized one. If your presentation has a lot of slides, you might find it helpful to break the presentation into sections. Working with sections helps you organize long presentations making it easier to work with them as you create and edit the slides. Sections are also helpful when you deliver a presentation. How you organize your presentation is up to you. You can create sections based on content, on type of slide, or on some other presentation feature. For example, a presentation on teaching a skill may include background information on the skill, hands-on activities, video presentations, and then a recap. If you have organized your presentation in sections, you can easily jump to the relevant section of the presentation as needed. To add a section, click the first slide in the section you want to create, on the Home tab, in the Slides group, click Section, and then click Add Section. A section marker appears on the Slides tab. Sections have the "untitled" name by default. The Section menu includes options to rename, collapse, expand, and remove sections easily. Sections are easily viewed in both Normal view and Slide Sorter view, see **Figure 4–24**.

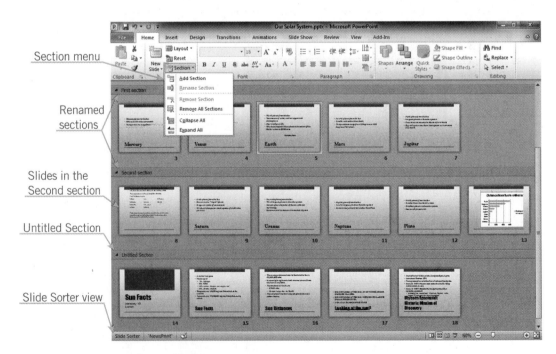

Section menu

Renamed
sections

Slides in the
Second section

Untitled Section

Slide Sorter view

FIGURE 4–24   Adding sections

Creating Custom Shows

A *custom show* is a way to limit the slides in any slide show for a particular audience. Click the Slide Show tab on the Ribbon, click the Custom Slide Show button in the Start Slide Show group, and then click Custom Shows. The Custom Shows dialog box allows you to select an existing custom show or create a new one. Click New to open the Define Custom Show dialog box in which you select the slides you want in a show and then name the show. See **Figure 4–25**.

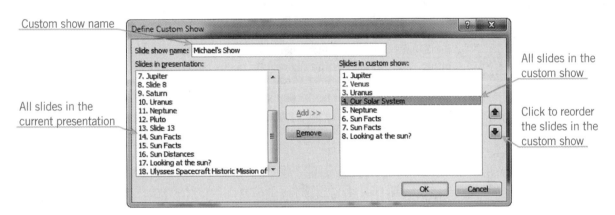

Custom show name

All slides in the current presentation

All slides in the custom show

Click to reorder the slides in the custom show

FIGURE 4–25   Define Custom Show dialog box

Using On-Screen Tools

There are on-screen navigation tools you can use to control a presentation while presenting it. When you run the presentation, buttons appear in the lower-left corner of the screen. Click the Menu button and a Slide show menu is displayed, as shown in **Figure 4–26**.

FIGURE 4–26   Slide show menu

When you click the mouse, the slides advance in order. You can choose the Previous or Next button to display the slide before or after the current one. To go to another slide, choose Go to Slide from the menu that is displayed and Slide Navigator from the submenu. Click the slide you want to display. To exit the slide show, choose End Show from the menu.

The Slide show menu (also available if you right-click the screen in Slide Show view) has many useful features. To make the screen appear blank, point to Screen, and then click Black Screen or White Screen. Switch Programs displays the Windows toolbar to give you access to other programs that you may want to display during a presentation.

Creating Action Buttons

▶ **VOCABULARY**
Action button

Another on-screen tool is the Action button. *Action buttons* are buttons that are inserted on a slide. They enable you to jump from slide to slide, even to slides in another slide show, or to other documents. Action buttons are assigned hyperlinks to direct the actions. You can insert an Action button using one of two methods. Click the Shapes button, and then click the Action button you want in the Action Buttons group. The Action Setting dialog box opens automatically. You can also insert an Action button using a custom shape. Open the Shapes gallery, and then draw the shape that you want to be the button. With the shape selected, click the Insert tab on the Ribbon, and then, in the Links group, click the Action button. Create the Action button using the Action Settings dialog box, as shown in **Figure 4–27**.

FIGURE 4–27   Action Settings dialog box

Step-by-Step 4.13

─┴─ **WARNING**

If the Shapes button is expanded, you don't have to click the Shapes button. Just click the Sun icon in the Basic Shapes section.

1. Click **slide 3**, *Mercury*, on the Slides tab to display it in the Slide pane.

2. On the Home tab in the Drawing group, click the **Shapes** button. In the Basic Shapes section, click the **Sun** icon, and then drag to draw a sun shape on the lower-right corner of the slide.

3. Click the **Insert** tab on the Ribbon, and then click the **Action** button in the Links group. The Action Settings dialog box opens. The Sun shape is selected. You will apply an action to this drawn shape.

4. Click the **Hyperlink to** option button, and then click the **Hyperlink to** list arrow, scroll down, and then click **Slide**. The Hyperlink to Slide dialog box opens.

5. Click **slide 14**, *Sun Facts*, click **OK**, and then click **OK** again. The Action button on slide 3 is hyperlinked to slide 14.

6. Click **slide 14**, *Sun Facts*, on the Slides tab to display it, click the **Insert** tab, click the **Shapes** button in the Illustrations group, click the **Action Button: Back or Previous** icon in the Action Buttons section (the first icon, last row), and then drag to draw a **box** on the lower-right corner of the slide below the red line. The Action Settings dialog box opens, the Hyperlink to option button is selected, and Previous Slide is selected.

7. Click the **Hyperlink to** list arrow, scroll down, click **Last Slide Viewed**, refer to **Figure 4–28**, and then click **OK**.

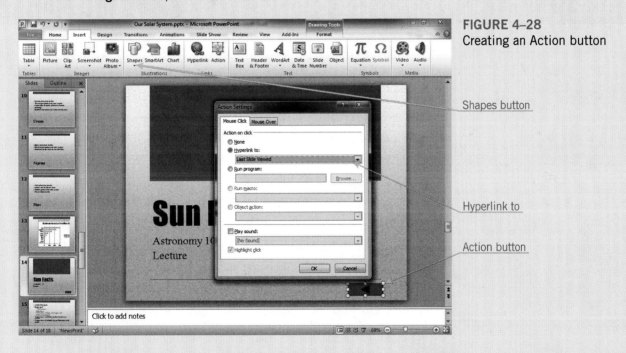

FIGURE 4–28
Creating an Action button

Shapes button

Hyperlink to

Action button

You have created a return button in the lower-right corner of the slide that hyperlinks back to the last viewed slide. If you view slide 14 by clicking the hyperlink on slide 3, and then click the Action button on slide 14, you will return to slide 3.

8. Click the **Slide Show** tab on the Ribbon, click the **From Beginning** button in the Start Slide Show group, and then press the **spacebar** two times. View slide 1 and slide 2.

9. When you get to slide 3, click the **sun** action button. The presentation jumps to slide 14, *Sun Facts*.

10. Click the **return** Action button that you drew to return to **slide 3**, *Mercury*.

11. Finish viewing the presentation.

12. Save the presentation and leave it open for the next Step-by-Step.

Hiding Slides

EXTRA FOR EXPERTS

You display a hidden slide by choosing it in the Slide Navigator dialog box. Parentheses around the slide number indicate that it is hidden.

If you need to limit the number of slides you are showing to a particular audience, you can quickly hide slides. You can hide a slide and then quickly unhide a slide by clicking the Hide Slide button in the Set Up group on the Slide Show tab. If you just need to hide a slide for one show, using this feature is faster than creating a custom show.

Step-by-Step 4.14

1. Click the **Slide Sorter** button ⊞ on the status bar to switch to Slide Sorter view, and then click **slide 13**, *Distance from Sun in Million km* chart.

2. On the Ribbon, click the **Slide Show** tab, and then, in the Set Up group, click the **Hide Slide** button.

3. Click **slide 18**, the last slide, and then, in the Set Up group, click the **Hide Slide** button.

   Notice that the slide number in the lower-right corner of the hidden slides has a box and a slash through it, showing that it is a hidden slide.

4. Click **slide 11**, *Neptune*, on the Slide Show tab on the Ribbon, and then, in the Start Slide Show group, click the **From Current Slide** button. The presentation begins on slide 11.

5. Click to advance through the slide show. Notice that you did not see slide 13 or slide 18 during the show.

6. Click **slide 13**, *Distance from Sun in Million km* chart. In the Set Up group, click the **Hide Slide** button, click **slide 18**, *the last slide*, and then, in the Set Up group, click the **Hide Slide** button. These slides are no longer hidden.

7. Save the presentation and leave it open for the next Step-by-Step.

Annotating a Show

As you are presenting the slide show to the audience, you can use the on-screen annotation tools to emphasize specific text or graphics on a slide. You have several pointer options. When you move your mouse during the slide show, an arrow appears so that you can point out parts of the slide. Right-click the screen, point to Pointer Options, point to Arrow Options, and then select from: Automatic, Visible, and Hidden. Automatic displays the arrow as you move it around a slide, but hides it if you do not move the mouse for a short period of time. Visible displays the arrow all of the time during a presentation, and Hidden hides the arrow during a presentation. The Pen and Highlighter are tools that allow you to write or highlight features on the screen. You can choose the colors from the Ink Color menu. The Eraser tool erases any ink it touches, and Erase All Ink on Slide deletes all ink marks.

Step-by-Step 4.15

1. Click **slide 1**, *Our Solar System*. On the Slide Show tab on the Ribbon in the Start Slide Show group, click the **From Current Slide** button. The presentation begins on slide 1. Press the **spacebar** to advance the show to slide 2, *Overview*.

2. Right-click the **slide** on the screen, point to **Pointer Options** on the on-screen navigation tools menu, and then click **Highlighter**.

3. Right-click the **slide** on the screen again, point to **Pointer Options**, point to **Ink Color**, and then click the **Light Blue** color swatch in the Standard Colors section of the palette.

4. Press the **spacebar** to advance the show to **slide 2**, *Overview*, and then drag the pointer to highlight the words The Sun. See **Figure 4–29**.

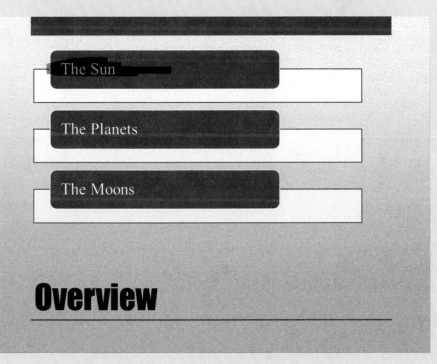

FIGURE 4–29
Annotating a slide show

5. Right-click the **slide** on the screen, point to **Pointer Options** on the on-screen navigation tools menu, and then click **Arrow**. The pen changes to a pointer.

6. Right-click the **slide** on the screen, and then click **End Show** from the menu to exit the slide show. You will be prompted by a message box asking if you want to keep or discard your ink annotations.

7. Click **Discard**.

8. Save your work and then leave the presentation on the screen for the next Step-by-Step.

Setting Up a Slide Show

PowerPoint has many features to help you make a presentation interesting and effective. There are several options for delivering a presentation. A presentation can be set up to be self-running, for viewing at a trade show booth, for example. You can also broadcast a presentation for remote viewers who view the show using a browser over the Internet. However, the most common method is to run a presentation with a speaker who directs the show.

To set up the slide show, on the Slide Show tab on the Ribbon, click the Set Up Slide Show button. The Set Up Show dialog box opens (**Figure 4–30**). It has six sections. See **Table 4–2**.

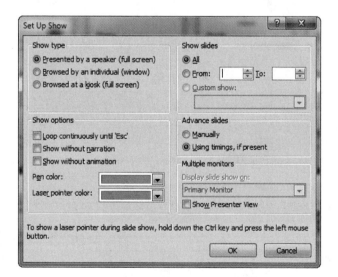

FIGURE 4–30   Set Up Show dialog box

TABLE 4-2   Understanding Set Up Show

OPTION	DESCRIPTION
Show type	Determines how the show will be viewed
Show slides	Allows you to choose which slides you are showing
Show options	Allows you to choose features that you want to include when making your presentation
Advance slides	Determines whether you advance the slides manually or automatically
Multiple monitors	Sets up your computer when you are using a secondary monitor or projector. Allow you to select Presenter View
Pen Color	Lets you determine pen and laser pointer colors

Presenter View

If you create numerous notes for your presentation using the Notes pane, *Presenter view* offers a way for you to view your presentation with the speaker notes showing on one computer screen, while an audience views the presentation without viewing the speaker notes on another computer screen. This feature is useful if you are presenting to an audience and want to be able to track your presentation and use your notes as a script. It offers you a way to deliver a professional presentation. When you work in Presenter view you can use thumbnails to select slides to show your audience without them seeing you actually select specific slides. Presenter view only works if your computer is set up with two or more monitors.

> **VOCABULARY**
> **Presenter view**

Step-by-Step 4.16

1. Click the **Slide Show** tab on the Ribbon, and then click the **Set Up Slide Show** button. The Set Up Show dialog box opens.

2. In the Show type section, click the **Presented by a speaker option** button, if it is not already selected.

3. In the Show slides section, click **From**. The first box should be 1. Press **Tab**, and then type **18** in the To text box.

4. In the Advance slides section, click **Using timings, if present**, if it is not already selected.

5. Click **OK**.

6. Save your work and then leave the presentation on the screen for the next Step-by-Step.

Rehearsing Timing

PowerPoint can automatically advance the slides in your presentation at preset time intervals. This is helpful in the case of an unattended presentation at a kiosk or sales booth, or if you must make a presentation within a specific time limit.

To rehearse timing for a presentation, on the Slide Show tab in the Set Up group, click the Rehearse Timings button. The slide show automatically starts, and the Rehearsal toolbar (See **Figure 4–31**), with a timer for the slide and a timer for the presentation, appears on the screen. When you think enough time has passed for a slide to appear on the screen, click the Next button. The presentation advances to the next slide, and the slide timer starts over. You can pause the timer by clicking the Pause button. The Repeat button resets the slide timer back to zero and the presentation timer back to the time that has elapsed, through the previous slide. When you get to the end of the show, a dialog box appears, asking if you want to keep the slide timings for the presentation.

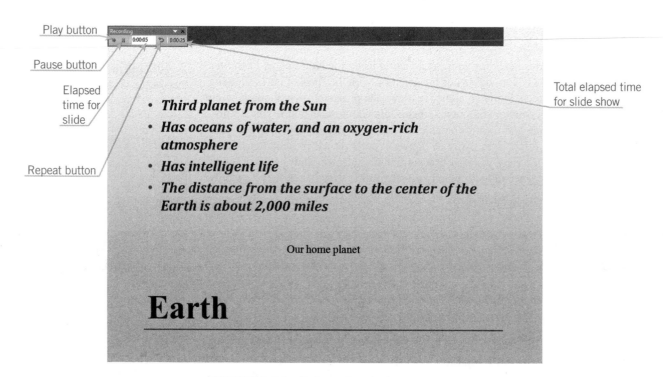

FIGURE 4–31   Rehearsing timings

To view rehearsal times for each slide, view the presentation in Slide Sorter view. The time allotted to each slide is listed at the lower-left corner of each slide. You can further edit the timing of each slide by opening the Slide Transition dialog box and changing the time below the Advance slide area of the dialog box.

Step-by-Step 4.17

1. Switch to **Slide Sorter view** if it is not the current view.

2. Click the **Slide Show** tab on the Ribbon, and then, in the Set Up group, click the **Rehearse Timings** button. The slide show starts, and the timers for the slide and the slide show begin.

3. Click the **Next** button every three to four seconds. Don't worry if you click in slightly less or more time.

   When you reach the end of the slide show, a message box opens, shows you the total time for the slide show, and asks if you want to keep the timings.

4. Click **Yes**. The presentation returns to Slide Sorter view.

5. Click the **Transitions** tab on the Ribbon. In the Timing group, in the Advance Slide section, click the **After up arrow** to add 2 seconds to the first slide.

   You can continue to adjust the time for each slide using the Advance slide section in the Timing group.

6. Click the **Slide Show button** on the status bar. The slides will automatically advance at the rate you set for each slide.

7. Save the changes to the presentation and then leave the presentation open on the screen for the next Step-by-Step.

> **TIP**
>
> Use the Transitions tab to apply different transition effects to each slide.

NET BUSINESS

Not everyone has PowerPoint installed on their computers nor will everyone be able to attend your presentation. In a world where many people work remotely from home or different offices around the world, PowerPoint 2010 lets you broadcast a presentation to others at remote locations whether or not they have PowerPoint installed on their computers. The Broadcast Slide Show feature works with SharePoint Server 2010 or Windows Live. To broadcast your presentation, click the Slide Show tab, in the Start Slide Show group, click the Broadcast Slide Show button, and then click Start Broadcast. In order for the people you want to view the broadcast to have access to the link to the show, they have to create a Windows Live ID and then log into Windows Live ID. To do so, go to www.login.live.com. The broadcast service will e-mail the link to your presentation to the people you designate, so that they can log in using their Windows Live account and be a part of the presentation. The broadcast displays the PowerPoint slide show; it will not transmit the audio from your presentation. If you want the remote audience to hear your presentation, you can set up a conference call using the phone system or voice over IP so that participants can hear your narration, ask questions, and participate in the presentation.

Inspecting a Document and Viewing Document Properties

Before you send a presentation out for review, or even submit it as final, it is a good idea to inspect the document for personal information or anything that you might not want to "travel" with the presentation file. The *Document Inspector* is a feature that can get this job done easily. To use the Document Inspector, click the File tab, click Info, click Check for Issues, and then click Inspect Document. The Document Inspector dialog box gives you choices as to what you want to look for. See **Figure 4–32**.

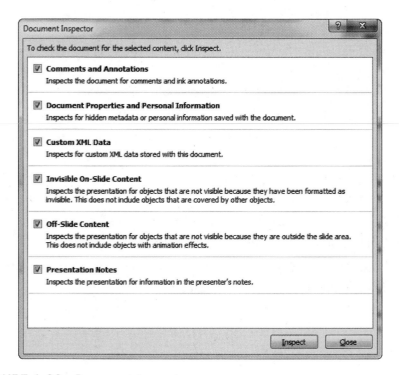

FIGURE 4–32   Document Inspector

The Document Properties Panel stores information about the document, the *document properties*, that can be helpful as you develop the presentation. Document properties include the author name, document title, subject, keywords, category, and status. You may choose to remove this information before you pass a file along. You may also choose to modify the default information that is added when you create a document. To view the Document Properties pane, click the File tab, click Info, click Properties, and then click Show Document Panel. See **Figure 4–33**.

FIGURE 4–33   Document Properties Panel

Step-by-Step 4.18

1. Click the **File** tab, click **Info**, click **Check for Issues**, and then click **Inspect Document**.

   The Document Inspector dialog box opens.

2. Verify that all the boxes have check marks, and then click **Inspect**.

   Review the inspection results. The document should have comments and personal information.

3. Click **Remove All** to remove the Comments and Annotations.

4. Click **Remove All** to remove the Document Properties and Personal Information.

5. Click **Reinspect**, click **Inspect**, and then click **Close** to close the Document Inspector.

Embedding Fonts

Not all computers have every font style installed on them. If you are giving your presentation on a computer other than your own, your presentation text might not look exactly as it did when you created it. PowerPoint can embed fonts into your presentation so that your text appears exactly as you originally created it.

TIP

You do not have to embed common fonts, such as Times New Roman, Arial, or Courier New, that are installed with Windows.

To embed fonts in your presentation, click the File tab, and then click Options to open the PowerPoint Options dialog box. Click Save in the left pane. The Customize how documents are saved pane appears, as shown in **Figure 4–34**. Click the Embed fonts in the file option button, and then click Embed only the characters used in the presentation option button. Click OK to close the PowerPoint options dialog box.

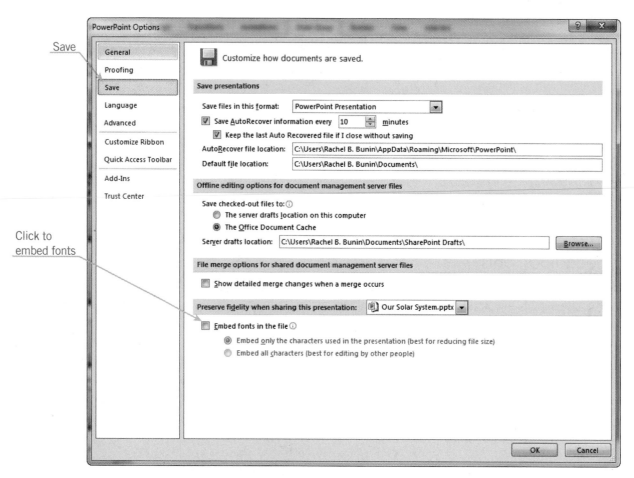

FIGURE 4–34 PowerPoint Save options

Step-by-Step 4.19

1. Click the **File** tab, and then click **Options** to open the PowerPoint Options dialog box.

2. Click **Save** in the left pane. The Customize how documents are saved pane opens.

3. Click the **Embed fonts in the file** option button, and then click **Embed only the characters used in the presentation (best for reducing file size)** option button.

4. Click **OK** to close the PowerPoint Options dialog box.

5. Click the **Save** button on the Quick Access toolbar to save the file. Notice the green progress bar on the status bar indicating that the fonts are being embedded in the file.

6. Leave the presentation open on the screen for the next Step-by-Step.

Using Package Presentation for CD and Copying Presentations to Folders

Some presentations can be quite large. Once you add images, video, and photographs, the files can exceed the limits of a disc or small flash drive. If you are giving your presentation on another computer, you can use *Package for CD* to compact all your presentation files into a single, compressed file that fits on a CD. You can then unpack the files when you reach your destination computer.

To use this feature, click the File tab, click Save & Send, click Package Presentation for CD and then click Package for CD. The Package for CD dialog box is shown in **Figure 4–35**. The dialog box gives several options for preparing your presentation. The Add button selects the presentation you want to package. The Copy to Folder button allows you to choose the destination folder for your files. The Options button opens another dialog box where you can choose the linked files and fonts you want to package. If the computer on which you are giving your presentation does not have PowerPoint installed, you can download a PowerPoint Viewer. This dialog box will also allow you to include a password on your PowerPoint file.

VOCABULARY
Package for CD

WARNING

You must have a CD burner installed on your computer and a blank CD to complete this exercise. If you do not have a CD burner, read but do not complete the steps in this section, and continue with the next section, "Sending a Presentation via E-mail".

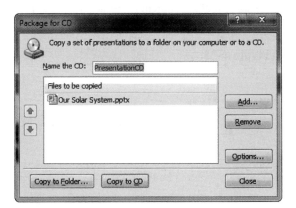

FIGURE 4–35   Package for CD dialog box

Step-by-Step 4.20

1. Click the **File** tab, click **Save & Send**, click **Package Presentation for CD** and then click **Package for CD**.

2. In the Package for CD dialog box, in the Name the CD box, type **Solar System** followed by **your initials**, and then click the **Copy to Folder** button. The Copy to Folder dialog box opens.

3. Click the **Browse** button, locate the folder where you store your Data Files, click **New Folder** in the Choose Location dialog box, type **Package Solar System – Your Name**, and then click **Select** twice. The folder location appears in the Location section of the Copy to Folder dialog box.

4. Click **OK**, and then click **Yes** to copy the linked files to the package. The files are copied to the folder. Close any open dialog boxes.

5. Click the **Options** button. The Options dialog box opens. This presentation does not include any linked files, and you embedded the fonts and checked for private information in the previous Step-by-Step.

6. Deselect both the **Linked files** and **Embedded TrueType fonts** check boxes.

7. Click **Viewer Package** in the Package type section, if it is not already selected, and then click **OK**.

8. Insert a blank CD in the CD burner of your computer.

9. Click **Copy to CD**, and the files are copied to the destination CD burner.

10. Save the presentation and leave it on the screen for the next Step-by-Step.

Sending a Presentation via E-mail

There are several ways you can use e-mail in conjunction with PowerPoint. You can send a presentation as an e-mail attachment or e-mail it to a recipient for review.

Open the presentation you want to send, click the File tab, click Save & Send, and then click Send Using E-mail. The Send Using E-Mail options in Backstage view are shown in **Figure 4–36**.

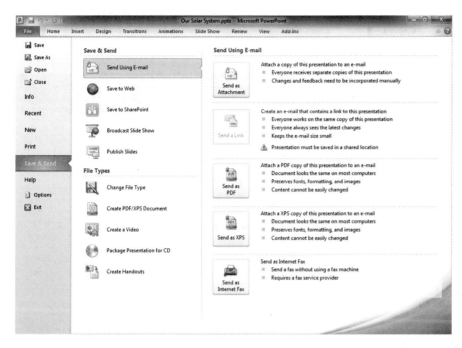

FIGURE 4–36   Send Using E-mail options

If you click Send as Attachment, if you have the Outlook e-mail program installed on your computer, a new blank message will open with the presentation attached. See **Figure 4–37**. Fill in the recipient information, type a message, and click Send. A copy of the presentation is e-mailed, but the original stays open so you can continue working on it.

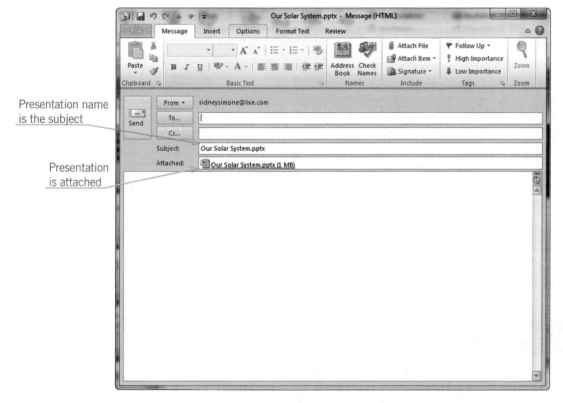

FIGURE 4–37   New e-mail message

To complete this next Step-by-Step, arrange with a friend to exchange presentations via e-mail.

Step-by-Step 4.21

EXTRA FOR EXPERTS

You can mark a presentation as final so other people can look at the presentation but cannot make any changes to it. Click the File tab, click Info, click Protect Presentation, and then click Mark as Final. You can also password-protect your presentation file if you want to safeguard who can and cannot look at the slide show. Click the File tab, click Info, click Protect Presentation, and then click Encrypt with Password. You will be asked to create a password and then confirm the password. Be sure you remember the password or write it down in a safe place. If you forget the password, you will not be able to open the presentation again.

1. Click the **File** tab, click **Save & Send**, click **Send Using E-mail** and then click **Send as Attachment.** The Microsoft Outlook e-mail program opens a new message window with the presentation as an attachment.

2. Enter the e-mail address of a friend, click in the **message body**, type **This is the presentation I told you about**, and then click **Send** to exchange your presentations.

3. Close the Microsoft Outlook e-mail program if it is open.

Setting Up the Pages

You can alter the output format of your presentation by working in the Page Setup dialog box. You can change the orientation of your slides or notes, handouts, and outline. Before you print or share a presentation, you should check spelling, review the design of each slide, and run the show to check timings.

Step-by-Step 4.22

1. Click the **Design** tab, and then in the Page Setup group, click the **Page Setup** button. See **Figure 4–38**.

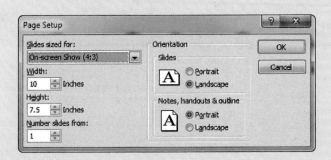

FIGURE 4–38
Page Setup dialog box

2. Click the **Slides sized for** list arrow, review the options, click **On-screen Show 4:3** and then click **OK**.

3. Click the **Insert** tab, in the Text group, click **Header & Footer**, click the **Notes and Handouts** tab, click the **Header** check box, type **your name** in the Notes and Handouts Header text box, and then click **Apply to All**.

4. Click the **Review** tab, and then in the Proofing group, click the **Spelling** button, and check for any spelling errors.

5. If your teacher wants a printout, click the **File** tab, click **Print**, and then print your presentation as **Handouts (6 Slides Per Page)**.

6. Save and close the presentation.

7. Exit PowerPoint.

EXTRA FOR EXPERTS

We live in a world where video is a common medium. Students learn by watching videos; people are entertained by watching videos. To engage your audience, you can save your presentation as a video. Click the File tab, click Save & Send, and then click Create a Video. Refer to **Figure 4–39**. You can specify the settings and then click Create Video.

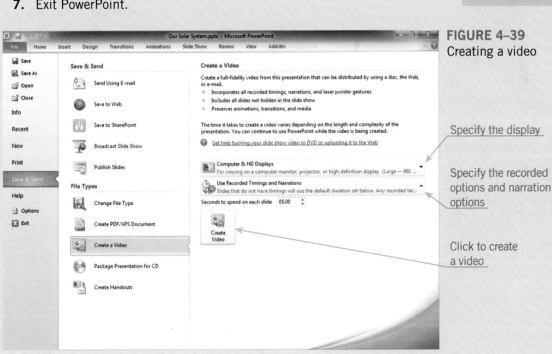

FIGURE 4–39
Creating a video

Specify the display

Specify the recorded options and narration options

Click to create a video

SUMMARY

In this lesson, you learned:

- To embed or link data from other applications such as Microsoft Excel and Microsoft Word into PowerPoint presentations. Embedded information can be edited using the original application. To make changes to an embedded object, double-click on it to open the application that created it. Changes made when editing are reflected in the destination file.

- Text can be imported from Word to create a new presentation or add slides. It is easiest for PowerPoint to convert the text to slides when the Word document is in outline form.

- Slides can be copied and pasted from one presentation to another. You can also use a Slide Library to store favorite slides that you want to reuse again and again. You can also save a presentation as a Word document to use as a handout, or create other documents using the text and slides from the presentation.

- To apply multiple slide masters to a presentation. This can help you save time if you are creating a presentation containing slides with more than one theme or any other features that are controlled by the slide master.

- PowerPoint allows you to create a new layout master for any theme or slide master. You can also create custom slide layouts and then add the placeholders as needed.

- To replace fonts throughout an entire presentation, use the Replace Font dialog box.

- To copy the formatting of an object or text by clicking the Format Painter button. Use the Format Painter to apply the same format to another object or text.

- To align a text box or picture, you can add grid lines, the ruler, and guides to slides.

- Comments can be inserted in a slide for others to see. You can use the Compare feature to work collaboratively with others.

- A custom show can be created to limit the slides displayed in any slide show for particular audiences. You can hide slides for certain audiences.

- Action buttons are the buttons inserted on a slide that enable you to jump from slide to slide, even to slides in another slide show, or to other documents.

- When presenting a slide show, you can use on-screen annotation tools to emphasize specific text or graphics on a slide. The Pen, and Highlighter tools allow you to write or highlight features on the screen. The Eraser tool erases any ink it touches, and Erase All Ink on Slide deletes all ink marks.

- A presentation can be set up to be self-running, so that it automatically advances the slides at preset time intervals.

- To inspect a presentation for personal information or anything that you might not want to "travel" with the presentation file, using the Document Inspector.

- If you are giving your presentation on another computer, you can use Package for CD to compact all your presentation files into a single, compressed file that fits on a CD. You can then unpack the files when you reach your destination computer.

- PowerPoint helps you easily broadcast a presentation for remote users to view on the Internet.

- To send a presentation as an e-mail attachment to a recipient for review.

- To alter a presentation's output format depending on the target audience.

■ VOCABULARY REVIEW

Define the following terms:

Action button	embed	linked object
comment	Format Painter	Package for CD
custom show	grid	Presenter view
destination file	guidelines	Snap to
Document Inspector	import	source file
document properties	link	

REVIEW QUESTIONS

FILL IN THE BLANK

Complete the following sentences by writing the correct word or words in the blanks provided.

1. A Word _____ is the easiest kind of document to import because it is formatted with styles, and each heading level is translated into a corresponding level of text in PowerPoint.

2. If you format an object with certain attributes, such as fill color and line color, and then want to format another object the same way, use the Format _____ .

3. The Paste _____ command has several options that provide you with flexibility in how you copy data from a source file to a destination file.

4. In order to be sure the Excel chart in the slide always has the most up-to-date numbers, you should link it rather than _____ it in the presentation.

5. The placeholders available on the Insert Placeholder menu are: Content, Text, Picture, Chart, table, _____, Media, and Clip Art.

TRUE / FALSE

Circle T if the statement is true or F if the statement is false.

T   F   **1.**   Being able to compare ideas and see the changes that each member contributes to the presentation is possible by using the Compare tool.

T   F   **2.**   A broadcast show is a way to limit the slides in any slide show for a particular audience.

T   F   **3.**   Action buttons enable you to jump from slide to slide, even to slides in another slide show, or to other documents.

T   F   **4.**   The Document Inspector is a feature that checks to see if all slides have correct spelling and grammar and the transitions and timings are appropriate for the show.

T   F   **5.**   If you are giving your presentation over the Internet, you can use Package for CD to compact all your presentation files into a single, compressed file that can be posted on a Web site.

MATCHING

Write the letter of the term or phrase from Column 2 that best matches the description in Column 1.

Column 1

_____ 1. Helps you organize long presentations so that you can work with them when creating and editing your work.

_____ 2. A way for you to view your presentation with the speaker's notes showing on one computer screen, while an audience views the presentation without viewing the speaker notes on another computer screen.

_____ 3. Where you have the text, chart, numbers, or whatever data it is you want to bring into the presentation.

_____ 4. Used when you want a presentation to contain only certain slides.

_____ 5. Moves an object to the closest intersection of the grid on a slide.

Column 2

A.   Presenter View

B.   Custom Show

C.   Snap to

D.   source file

E.   sections

F.   Slide Navigator

G.   Exit show

■ PROJECTS

If you have a SAM 2010 user profile, your instructor may have assigned an autogradable version of the indicated project. If so, log into the SAM 2010 Web site at *www.cengage.com/sam2010* to download the instruction and start files.

PROJECT 4–1

For an astronomy club meeting, you need to create a custom slide show presentation about the solar system. After the presentation, the club members ask you for a file so that they can post the presentation to their Web site.

1. Start PowerPoint and open the The Solar System presentation file you worked on earlier in this lesson. Save the presentation as **Astronomy Club**, followed by your initials.

2. Change the theme to a new theme of your choice.

3. Replace the current font for the slide titles throughout the presentation with a font of your choice.

4. Select the title Our Solar System on slide 1, change the font to 60-point Aharoni.

5. Add a comment to the second slide.

6. Insert a text box on slide 7 with a new fact about Jupiter, format the text box using a new font, fill, and color. You can also apply a shape effect. Use grids and guidelines to place the box on the slide.

7. Insert a new text box on slide 9, Saturn, with a new fact about Saturn. Use the Format Painter to apply the same format as the text box on slide 7 to the text box on slide 9.

8. Add an action button on a slide, the action button can link to any other slide in the presentation.

9. Inspect the document, and then view the document properties.

10. Add your name to the notes and handout footer. Save, print the presentation as handouts with four slides per page, and then close the presentation.

PROJECT 4–2

You decide to create another presentation about the moons around each planet.

1. Open a new blank presentation. Enter the title on the title Slide as **Many Moons**, and then type **By Your name** as the subtitle.

2. Save the presentation as **Many Moons.pptx**.

3. Insert a new slide with a blank layout.

4. Start Word and view the Planet Number of Moons.docx Data File that has a Word table containing the following information:

Planet	Number of Moons
Mercury	0
Venus	0
Earth	1
Mars	2
Jupiter	16
Saturn	18
Uranus	15
Neptune	8
Pluto	1

5. Embed the Word table in the Many Moons presentation file that is open.

6. Center the text box on the slide. Open the file in Word and format the text as you see fit.

7. View the presentation.

8. Create a custom layout using a SmartArt graphic and a clip art placeholder.

9. Create a slide using the new custom layout.

10. Add another slide using this text, and format the text:

Planet	Time to Rotate Around Sun
Mercury	88 Earth days
Venus	224.7 Earth days
Earth	365.3 days
Mars	687 Earth days
Jupiter	12 Earth years
Saturn	29.5 Earth years
Uranus	84 Earth years
Neptune	165 Earth years
Pluto	248 Earth years

11. Add as many slides as you want to create the presentation. Apply a theme and use graphics and design elements to enhance the presentation.

12. Inspect the file, and then check the document properties.

13. Save, print the presentation as handouts with two slides per page, and then close the presentation.

CRITICAL THINKING

ACTIVITY 4–1

Your supervisor wants you to insert a chart into the presentation you are editing for him. You decide to use a Microsoft Excel chart that you will create on your own. Use the Excel Help system to find out how to enter data in a worksheet, and then create a chart using Excel. Use the features on the Chart Tools Layout tab to add titles, gridlines, and data labels. Embed the chart in a new presentation.

ACTIVITY 4–2

Create an outline in Word using heading styles. Use at least three Heading 1 styles so your presentation has at least three slides. Import the text into PowerPoint to create a new presentation. Email the presentation to a friend. If you have access to a LiveID, broadcast the presentation, and send a link to a friend to view the presentation.

UNIT REVIEW

Introduction to Microsoft PowerPoint

 REVIEW QUESTIONS

TRUE / FALSE

Circle T if the statement is true or F if the statement is false.

T   F   **1.**   To add text and graphics to a slide, it is best to work in Normal view.

T   F   **2.**   A transition is an effect you can apply to text, objects, graphics, or pictures to make those objects move during a slide show.

T   F   **3.**   The Zoom Slider adjusts the font size on the slide.

T   F   **4.**   There are many ways to advance slides in a slide show; you can click, press Enter, press the arrow keys, press Page Down or Page Up, or press Spacebar.

T   F   **5.**   You cannot change colors or fonts in a theme.

MULTIPLE CHOICE

Select the best response for the following statements.

1. In Normal view, you can:

   A.   View each slide on a full screen.

   B.   See an overview of all the slides in the presentation.

   C.   Add text, graphics, charts, sounds, and other objects to a slide.

   D.   View each slide as a thumbnail with notes next to the slide.

2. What reserves space on a slide for text, graphics, or an object?

   A.   Master   C.   Placeholder

   B.   Template   D.   Object box

3. An organization chart is an example of _____ .

   A.   SmartArt   C.   animation

   B.   text box   D.   theme

4. Which PowerPoint feature should you use to organize data in rows and columns on a slide?

A. Text box   C. Placeholder

B. SmartArt   D. Table

5. You can apply formatting or design changes to all the slides in the presentation using the _____

A. Notes master   C. Header and Footer dialog box

B. Slide master   D. Handout master

FILL IN THE BLANK

Complete the following sentences by writing the correct word or words in the blanks provided.

1. Title and Content, Comparison, and Two Content are examples of slide _____.

2. Create _____ if you want to show some slides to one audience and other slides to another audience, and reorder slides for yet another audience from the same presentation.

3. Use the _____ to copy the Fly In and Swivel effects from one object to another.

4. Apply a(n) _____ such as Austin to change the overall design of all the slides in the presentation.

5. The _____ includes information about the presentation such as Author, Title, Subject, Keywords, Category, and Status.

■ PROJECTS

PROJECT PPT 1

1. Use the Angles installed theme to create a new presentation.

2. Type **My Favorite States** as the slide title, then type by your name as the subtitle.

3. Save the presentation as **States Project 1.pptx**, followed by your initials.

4. Insert a new slide with a Title and Content layout.

5. Type the name of the state you live in as the title of the slide. (*Note*: If you do not live in the United States, type the name of a state you want to learn more about.)

6. Type four facts about your state in the content placeholder.

7. Insert a third slide with a Title and Content layout.

8. Type the name of a state you want to visit as the title of the third slide. Enter three facts about that state in the content placeholder.

9. Use the Outline tab to add two more slides to the presentation. Enter state names as the title and three facts for each state.

10. Change the font color for the facts on slides 3, 4, and 5 to different colors of your choice.

11. View the presentation in Slide Sorter view.

12. Add transitions and timings to the title slide in the presentation.

13. Add clip art to the title slide.

Figure UR–1 shows an example of what your presentation might look like.

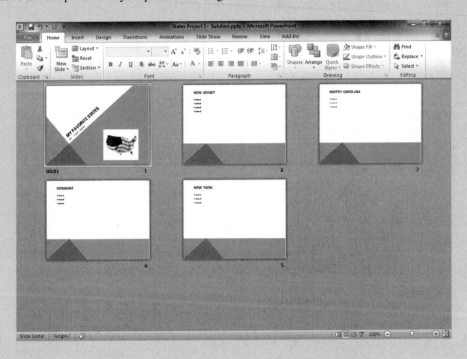

FIGURE UR–1

14. Add your name to the handouts header. Print the presentation as handouts with four slides per page.

15. View the presentation as a slide show. Save and close the presentation.

PROJECT PPT 2

1. Open the **States Project 1.pptx** presentation file you created in Project 1, and then save the presentation as **States Project 2.pptx**, followed by your initials.

2. Add at least two more slides, choose two more states, adding content for each of them.

3. Change the theme of the presentation.

4. Change the clip art on the title slide and then apply an effect to the clip art on the title slide. Add another clip to the slide and remove the background color if necessary to make the clip blend in with the slide.

5. Change the layout of the third slide to Two Content.

6. Replace the right placeholder with a picture that is relevant to the state you chose.

7. Add a speaker's note to slide 4: **Remember to show the flags for all states.**

8. Change the style of the bullets for all slides in the presentation to a different color and style.

9. Add a small graphic object to the slide master so it appears on all slides.

10. Change the font attributes for the Title and Content slide layout to a different color and font style.

11. Draw a different shape on at least three slides of your choice. Add effects to the shapes.

12. Insert a last slide with hyperlinks to www.usa.gov and www.whitehouse.gov. Give the slide a meaningful title. Format and design the slide as necessary.

13. Apply animation effects to at least two slides. Use the Animation Painter to copy the animation to another object in the presentation.

14. Apply slide transitions to all the slides.

15. Check the spelling. Refer to **Figure UR–2** for a sample of what the final presentation might look like.

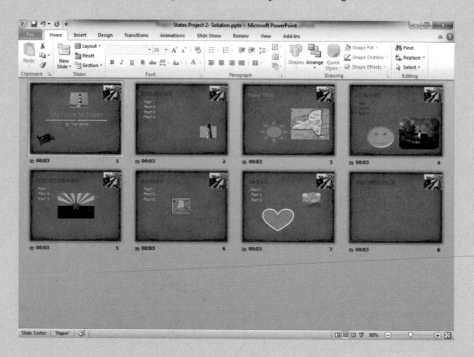

FIGURE UR–2

16. Print the presentation as audience handouts with six slides per page.

17. Save and close the presentation.

PROJECT PPT 3

1. Create a new presentation file from a template (you can use an installed template or one from Microsoft Office Online). Templates include content, so you can select a template with a topic that is of interest to you. Save the presentation as **Project 3 Template Presentation.pptx**, followed by your initials.

2. Insert a SmartArt graphic on one slide, and then convert any existing text on another slide to a SmartArt graphic. If the template does not have enough slides to complete the following steps, add additional slides.

3. Create and format WordArt on two slides.

4. Create a line chart on a slide, then format the chart. Add an appropriate slide title.

5. Create a table with three columns and three rows. Enter text in all the cells. You can enter any text that is relevant to the presentation topic.

6. Use a Table Style to modify the table's style and layout.

7. Insert a new slide, give the slide a meaningful title, draw and format a star and an arrow shape, then scale and size the shapes. Group the shapes into one object.

8. On a new slide, draw five shapes. Format the shapes with colors and fills. Enter a descriptive title on the slide.

9. Insert an oval object on the slide with five shapes, then type **This is an oval.** to create a text box on the oval shape.

10. Animate the drawn objects.

11. Add a footer with your name and the current date to all slides.

12. Apply transition effects and timings to the slides.

13. Create and save one custom show in the presentation. Add your name to the Document Properties Panel.

14. Save your work. View the slide show, and then print the presentation in any view.

15. Refer to **Figure UR–3** for a sample of what the presentation might look like in Slide Sorter view.

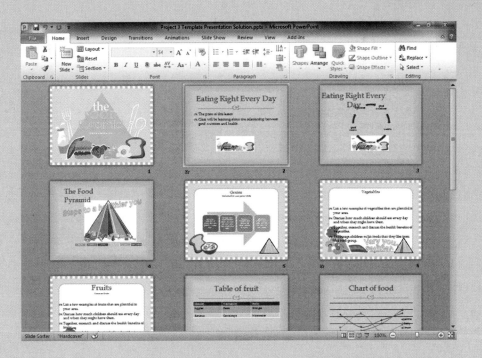

FIGURE UR–3

16. Save and close the presentation.

PROJECT PPT 4

1. Open the **Project 3 Template Presentation.pptx** presentation that you created in Project 3, and then save the presentation as **Project 4 Template Presentation.pptx**, followed by your initials.

2. Switch to Slide Master view, then create a new layout master that includes a picture placeholder, a media placeholder, and text placeholder. Refer to **Figure UR–4** for a sample of what the new layout might look like. You can format the text or change the bullets. Create one slide that uses the new custom layout.

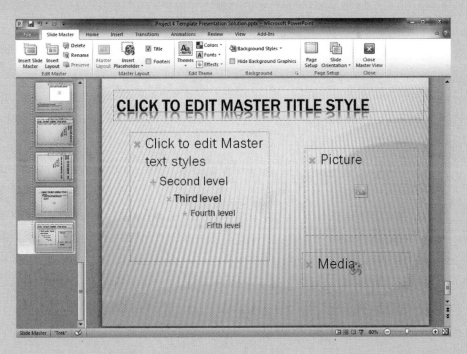

FIGURE UR–4

3. Change the theme of the presentation. Work the design and objects until you are happy with the design of the presentation.

4. Align text and pictures on any of the slides using the Arrange commands.

5. Insert comments on three of the slides.

6. Use the Rehearsal toolbar to set up the timing for the slide show.

7. Send the presentation via e-mail to a friend or colleague.

8. View the presentation, return to Slide Sorter view, hide a slide, then view the presentation again.

9. Save and print the presentation as handouts with four slides per page.

10. Save the presentation as a Video, preview it in Media Player or whatever the default video player is on your computer.

11. Save and close the presentation.

12. Exit PowerPoint.

SIMULATION

JOB PPT 1

The Java Internet café is working to increase the number of members who visit the café. They also want to find a way to ensure that customers stay longer and order more food and drinks once they come to the café. The manager asks you to create a presentation to show to all new members so they can learn about all the benefits of coming to the Java Internet cafe.

1. Start PowerPoint and open the **Java Cafe.pptx** presentation from the drive and folder where you store your Data Files. Save the presentation as **Java Cafe Info.pptx**, followed by your initials.

2. Apply a theme to the presentation.

3. Convert the text on slide 2: *Welcome* into a SmartArt graphic. You can change the formatting as you see fit.

4. Change the layout of slide 3: *Introduction* to Two Content layout and insert a clip art picture relevant to the slide.

5. Create WordArt on slide 4: *Agenda* using the text **Have Fun!**

6. On slide 5: *Overview*, draw and format three shapes, then insert the text **Good for you!** onto one shape. Animate the shapes.

7. Insert a new slide after slide 2 with a Title Only layout. Type **Sample Coffee Pricing** as the title. Insert the Microsoft Excel worksheet Data File, **Coffee Prices.xlsx**, as an embedded object. Search for two clip art objects using the keyword **coffee**. Insert both appropriate clips on the slide and then group the two clips.

8. On slide 8: *Vocabulary*, add a hyperlink on the text **Google** to www.google.com. Preview the page and test the hyperlink.

9. Add clip art images as needed to other slides.

10. Insert a sound file for clapping from the Clip Organizer to the last slide. It should play automatically and loop until stopped.

11. Add transitions and timings to all the slides.

12. Add your name as a footer to the handout master.

13. View the slide show. Save and print the presentation as handouts with nine slides per page.

14. Close the presentation and then exit PowerPoint.

ADVANCED

MICROSOFT POWERPOINT UNIT

LESSON 5

Editing and Formatting Slide Content

■ OBJECTIVES

Upon completion of this lesson, you should be able to:

- Customize the AutoCorrect list.
- Create a custom dictionary.
- Insert symbols and adjust character height.
- Number paragraphs and customize bullets.
- Format items for progressive disclosure.
- Create an interactive text box.
- Modify SmartArt graphics.
- Organize slide content and create a summary slide.

■ VOCABULARY

hot spot

image map

progressive disclosure

summary slide

ADVANCED   Microsoft PowerPoint Unit

Your first impression of a PowerPoint slide is probably the graphical elements, such as colors, background pattern, and layout. However, text is also an important element, and the text formatting can help you create a very impressive presentation. In this lesson, you will learn how to edit and manipulate text on slides.

Editing and Proofing the Text

Words can be very powerful when the right ones are used effectively. Correct spelling is also important because when your audience notices a misspelled word, you quickly lose credibility. Even when we know how to correctly spell a word, we sometimes type it incorrectly. PowerPoint offers several features to help you proof the text you add to slides. The proofing tools not only check spelling and grammar, but they also check capitalization and formats.

Customizing the AutoCorrect List

PowerPoint's AutoCorrect feature will automatically correct commonly misspelled words, without prompting you, so you may not even realize the correction was made. To ensure you don't misspell words that you commonly use, you can add the words to the AutoCorrect list. You can also customize the AutoCorrect list to include terms and phrases with unique spelling and/or capitalization that you don't want PowerPoint to automatically correct.

In the next Step-by-Step, you will add a new entry to the AutoCorrect list and create an AutoCorrect exception. However, because you may be sharing a computer, you will delete the new entry and the exception at the end of the Step-by-Step.

Step-by-Step 5.1

1. Launch PowerPoint. Open the **Coasting** file from the drive and folder where your Data Files are stored. Save the presentation as **Revised Coasting 1**, followed by your initials.

2. Click the **File** tab, and then click **Options**. In the left pane of the PowerPoint Options dialog box, click **Proofing**.

3. Under AutoCorrect options, click **AutoCorrect Options**. The AutoCorrect dialog box opens, as shown in **Figure 5–1**. (If necessary, click the AutoCorrect tab.) Text shown in the left column (Replace) is automatically replaced with the text shown in the right column (With).

FIGURE 5–1
AutoCorrect dialog box

4. Scroll through the list of frequently misspelled words until you see *acheive*. Note that PowerPoint will automatically correct this misspelling and change the word to *achieve*.

5. In the Replace text box, type **aep**. In the With text box, type **Aventura EXtreme PlayLand**. Click **Add**.

6. In the AutoCorrect dialog box, click **Exceptions** to open the AutoCorrect Exceptions dialog box, as shown in **Figure 5–2**. Click the **INitial CAps** tab. Your dialog box may include a list of exceptions.

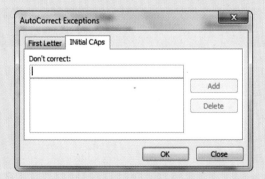

FIGURE 5–2
AutoCorrect Exceptions dialog box

7. In the Don't correct text box, type **EXtreme** and then click **Add**. Normally, PowerPoint would automatically change the second capital letter in the word EXtreme to lowercase, but this exception will prevent PowerPoint from making that AutoCorrect change.

8. Add the following words to the list: **EXperience**, **EXciting**, and **EXhilarating**. Click **OK** three times to close the dialog boxes.

9. On slide 1, click the **Click to add subtitle** placeholder. Type **aep** and then press the **spacebar**. When you press the spacebar, the text you typed is automatically altered to show the park name *Aventura EXtreme PlayLand*.

10. On slide 2, change *Experience* in the title to **EXperience**. In the Click to add text placeholder, type the following three bulleted items:

    EXtreme

    EXciting

    EXhilarating

11. Click the **File** tab, and then click **Options**. In the left pane of the PowerPoint Options dialog box, click **Proofing** and then click **AutoCorrect Options**. In the Replace text box, type **aep**. The entry in the list is selected. Click **Delete**.

12. Click **Exceptions**, and then click the **INitial CAps** tab. Select each of the four entries (EXciting, EXhilarating, EXperience, and EXtreme) and click **Delete**.

13. Click **OK** three times to close the dialog boxes and the PowerPoint options.

14. Save the changes and leave the presentation open for the next Step-by-Step.

Creating a Custom Dictionary

If you frequently use proper names and acronyms that are not in Word's standard dictionary, you will find that adding those words to a custom dictionary is helpful so they aren't flagged as unknown or misspelled words during a spell check. Creating a custom dictionary in PowerPoint is the same as creating a custom dictionary in other Office applications. When you add words to a dictionary, the new words are saved in the dictionary designated as the default dictionary.

Step-by-Step 5.2

1. If necessary, open the **Revised Coasting 1** file from your solution files. Save the presentation as **Revised Coasting 2**, followed by your initials.

2. Go to slide 2. If your Proofing settings are set to check spelling as you type, a wavy red line appears below the unknown words, such as those beginning with *EX*.

3. Click the **File** tab, and then click **Options**. In the left pane of the PowerPoint Options dialog box, click **Proofing**. Under When correcting spelling in Microsoft Office programs, click **Custom Dictionaries** to open the Custom Dictionaries dialog box, as shown in **Figure 5–3**. Your list of available dictionaries may differ. The CUSTOM.DIC default dictionary appears in the Dictionary List.

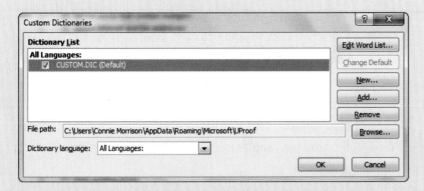

FIGURE 5–3
Custom Dictionaries dialog box

4. In the dialog box, click **New** to open the Create Custom Dictionary dialog box. Navigate to the drive and folder where you save your solution files. In the File name box, type **AEP**, followed by your initials. Do not change the file type. Word will add the .dic extension to the filename. Click **Save**. Now there are two dictionaries in the Dictionary List; the check marks indicate that both dictionaries are active.

5. In the Custom Dictionaries dialog box, select the AEP dictionary if necessary. Click **Edit Word List**. A dialog box for the new AEP dictionary opens. Currently, the Dictionary List contains no words. In the Word(s) text box, type **EXtreme**, click **Add**, and then click **OK**. The new word is added to the Dictionary List.

6. In the Custom Dictionaries dialog box, the AEP dictionary should still be selected. (Be sure not to uncheck it.) Click **Change Default**. In the Dictionary List, the order of the dictionaries is rearranged, and the AEP dictionary is now the default dictionary. When you save a word to the dictionary during a spell check, the word will be saved in the AEP dictionary.

7. Click **OK** twice to close the dialog boxes. Check slides 1 and 2 and note that the wavy red line no longer appears under the word EXtreme.

8. In slide 2, right-click the word **EXperience**. In the shortcut menu, click **Add to Dictionary**. The word is added to the AEP dictionary because that is the default dictionary.

9. Using the same right-click method, add the words *EXciting* and *EXhilarating* to the default dictionary. There are no more red wavy lines on slide 2.

10. Go to slide 1. Add the word *PlayLand* to the dictionary.

11. Click the **Review** tab. In the Proofing group, click the **Spelling** button to start the spell checker. The word *clickety* is flagged as an unknown spelling. Click **Add**. A prompt appears indicating that the spelling check is complete. Click **OK** to close the prompt. Note that the red wavy line no longer displays below the word *clickety*.

12. Click the **File** tab, and then click **Options**. In the left pane of the PowerPoint Options dialog box, click **Proofing**. Click **Custom Dictionaries**. The AEP dictionary is already selected. Click **Edit Word List**. Note that the custom dictionary now lists six words. Click **OK** to close the AEP.dic dialog box.

13. In the Custom Dictionaries dialog box, select **CUSTOM.DIC**, and then click **Change Default**. Click the **AEP** dictionary, and then click **Remove**. Close the dialog box, and then click **OK** again to close the PowerPoint Options dialog box.

14. Save the changes and leave the presentation open for the next Step-by-Step.

Improving the Readability of Slide Content

Using symbols and characters instead of words can help to explain the content in a presentation and also make the text easier to read. Adjusting the height of the font characters can also improve readability. To further clarify the content, you can number lists to indicate a sequence or a ranking of content.

Inserting Symbols and Adjusting Character Height

Sometimes you can improve the readability of the slide content and also reduce the number of words on a slide by inserting special characters and symbols. For example, you can you can use the symbol ≥ instead of *greater than or equal to*. You are not limited to the symbols shown for the current font (called *normal text* in the dialog box). Fonts such as Webdings and Wingdings supply many different types of symbols, shapes, arrows, and numbers.

The Repeat button on the Quick Access Toolbar is useful when inserting the same symbol in different locations throughout the presentation. If you frequently use the Quick Access Toolbar, you can reposition it below the Ribbon for ease of use.

Depending on the font style, the height of numbers and letters may be significantly different. You can easily adjust the character height to make the text easier to read. When you apply the Equalize Character Height option, the selected characters are expanded to fill the height of the line of text. The newly formatted text often appears taller than the surrounding characters, making this format useful when formatting the height of numbers or whole words.

Step-by-Step 5.3

1. If necessary, open the **Revised Coasting 2** file from your solution files. Save the presentation as **Revised Coasting 3**, followed by your initials.

2. On the right side of the Quick Access Toolbar, click the **Customize Quick Access Toolbar** button. At the bottom of the menu, click **Show Below the Ribbon**.

3. Go to slide 8. In the second bulleted item, select the words **of greater than or equal to**. Click the **Insert** tab. In the Symbols group, click the

Symbol button to open the Symbol dialog box, as shown in **Figure 5–4**. Your settings will be different.

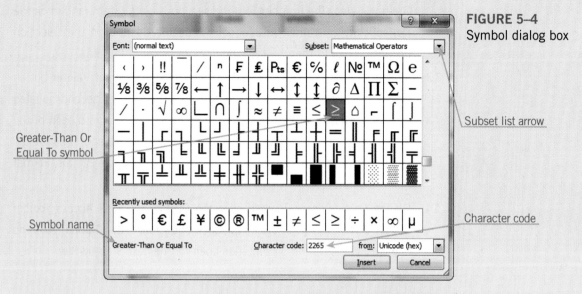

Greater-Than Or Equal To symbol

Subset list arrow

Symbol name

Character code

FIGURE 5–4
Symbol dialog box

4. Click the **Subset** list arrow, scroll down and select **Mathematical Operators**, and then click the **Greater-Than Or Equal To** symbol. The name of the symbol displays in the lower-left corner of the dialog box.

5. Click **Insert** and then close the dialog box. The symbol replaces the selected text.

6. Go to slide 5. Position the insertion point in front of the word *Pro*. Click the **Symbol** button to reopen the Symbol dialog box.

7. Click the **Font** list arrow, scroll down to the bottom of the list, and then select **Wingdings**. Find and select a **thumbs-up** symbol. Click **Insert** and then close the dialog box.

8. Go to slide 4. Position the insertion point in front of the word *Pro*. Click the **Repeat** button 🔄 on the Quick Access Toolbar to insert the thumbs-up symbol.

9. Position the insertion point in front of the word *Con*. Click the **Symbol** button. The Symbol dialog box opens, displaying the Wingdings symbols. Find and select a **thumbs-down** symbol. Click **Insert** and then close the dialog box. Go to slide 5. Position the insertion point in front of the word *Con* and repeat the edit.

10. Go to slide 8. In the first bulleted item, select the number **1**. Click the **Home** tab, and then in the Font group, click the **Dialog Box Launcher** to open the Font dialog box.

11. Under Effects, enable the **Equalize Character Height** option and then click **OK**. The height of the selected text is adjusted to a size comparable to the surrounding text.

12. In the second bulleted item, select the **Greater-Than Or Equal To** symbol and the number **3**. Then click the **Repeat** button on the Quick Access Toolbar. Select the number **5** in the second bulleted item, and click the **Repeat** button again. You cannot include the decimal in the selection because it would then be the same height as the numbers.

13. With the number 5 still selected, double-click the **Format Painter** button in the Clipboard group. Then click the word **scary** in the second bulleted item to apply the font format. Drag the mouse pointer across each of the numbers in the third bulleted item to copy the format and equalize the height for each of those characters. Press **Esc** to toggle off the Format Painter feature.

14. On the Quick Access Toolbar, click the **Customize Quick Access Toolbar** button. At the bottom of the menu, click **Show Above the Ribbon**. Save the changes and leave the presentation open for the next Step-by-Step.

Formatting Bulleted and Numbered Lists

Many of the slide layouts help you organize text data into bulleted lists. To "jazz up" the bulleted list, you can customize the bullets using a symbol. If a list of items indicates a specific sequence or a ranking, you can replace the bullets with numbers. When applying the numbering format, the items are automatically numbered. If you edit the list and add, delete, or rearrange the order of the items, the numbers are automatically updated. If you want to continue the numbered list on a successive slide, you can specify a starting number.

Step-by-Step 5.4

1. If necessary, open the **Revised Coasting 3** file from your solution files. Save the presentation as **Revised Coasting 4**, followed by your initials.

2. Go to slide 11. Select all the items in the bulleted list. If necessary, click the Home tab. In the Paragraph group, click the **Numbering** button. The paragraphs are formatted with numbers 1, 2, 3, and 4.

3. Go to slide 12 and select all the items in the bulleted list. Click the **Numbering** button arrow. At the bottom of the menu, click **Bullets and Numbering** to open the Numbered tab in the Bullets and Numbering dialog box, as shown in **Figure 5–5**. Your settings will differ.

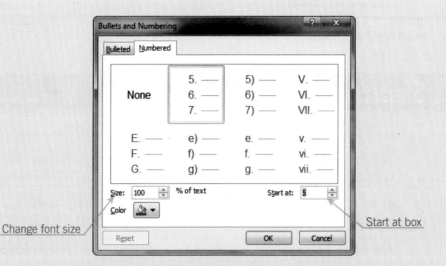

FIGURE 5–5
Numbered tab in the Bullets and
Numbering dialog box

4. Select the **1., 2., 3.** number format. Change the setting in the Start at box to **5**. Your settings should match those in Figure 5–5. Note that you can change the font size for the number as a percentage of text. Click **OK**.

5. With the numbered list still selected, click the **Numbering** button arrow, click **Bullets and Numbering**, and then click the **Bulleted** tab. Click **Customize** to open the Symbol dialog box.

6. Click the **Font** list arrow, scroll down, and select **Wingdings**. Then select a symbol showing a check mark inside a box. Click **OK**. The new bullet option is added to the Bulleted tab. Click **OK** again. The bullets are updated to show the new symbol.

7. Go to slide 11. Select the numbered list, and then click the **Repeat** button on the Quick Access Toolbar.

8. Deselect the bulleted list.

9. Save the changes and leave the presentation open for the next Step-by-Step.

Formatting Progressive Disclosure

When delivering a presentation, you can format the titles, subtitles, bulleted and numbered lists, and graphics for progressive disclosure. *Progressive disclosure* is a technique that reveals slide content in increments. By using progressive disclosure, the objects will appear one at a time, as opposed to all the objects appearing at the same time, allowing the audience to focus on a single item. To format slide content for progressive disclosure, you apply customized animations. PowerPoint provides numerous animations for entrance, emphasis, exit, and motion path effects. Commonly used and recently used effects appear in the Animation group on the Animations tab. To view all the effects available, click the More button in the Animation group and then select one of the More Effects commands at the bottom of the menu. When formatting animations, you can control the direction from which objects enter or exit the slide and you can also adjust settings to reveal text in specified increments, such as one word at a time, one paragraph at a time, or all paragraphs at once.

▶ **VOCABULARY**
progressive disclosure

In the next Step-by-Step you will customize the animation for text, but keep in mind that you can also create custom animations for objects such as clip art, charts, and SmartArt graphics.

Step-by-Step 5.5

1. If necessary, open the **Revised Coasting 4** file from your solution files. Save the presentation as **Revised Coasting 5**, followed by your initials.

2. If necessary, go to slide 11. Click anywhere within the bulleted list to select the placeholder. (Do not select all the text in the bulleted list.)

3. Click the **Animations** tab. In the Advanced Animation group, click the **Add Animation** button. At the bottom of the submenu, click **More Entrance Effects**. Under Basic, click the **Peek In** entrance effect. A live preview appears in the Slide pane. Click **OK**. Note that in the Slide pane, each of the items in the bulleted list is assigned a number indicating the sequence of the animated objects.

4. On the Animations tab, in the Advanced Animation group, click the **Animation Pane** button. In the Animation Pane, click the **list arrow** to the right of the #1 animation object *Content Place*. The submenu for the animation object opens, as shown in **Figure 5–6**. Note that the option *Start On Click* is already selected.

FIGURE 5–6
Animation Pane

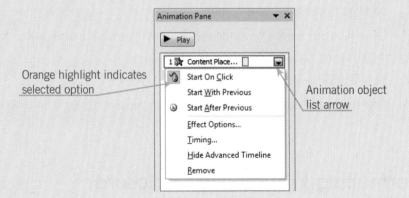

Orange highlight indicates selected option

Animation object list arrow

5. In the submenu, click Effect Options. The Peek In dialog box opens, as shown in **Figure 5–7**. Your settings will differ.

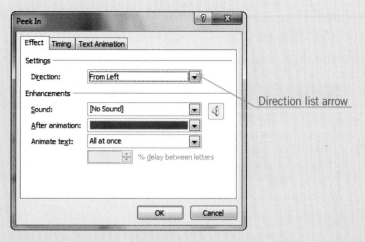

FIGURE 5–7
Effect tab in the Peek In dialog box

6. Under Settings, click the **Direction** list arrow and then click **From Right**. Click the **Text Animation** tab. Click the **Group text** list arrow and then click **All Paragraphs At Once**. Click **OK**. The animation previews on the slide.

7. In the Animation Pane, click the **list arrow** to the right of the #1 animation object **Content Place** and then click **Effect Options**. Click the **Text Animation** tab. Click the **Group text** list arrow and then click **By 1ˢᵗ Level Paragraphs**. Click the **Effect** tab. Under Settings, click the **Direction** list arrow and then click **From Left**. Click the **After animation** list arrow, and then select the **dark red** color in the color grid. When your settings match those shown in Figure 5–7, click **OK**.

8. In the Slide pane, click anywhere within the bulleted list placeholder. (Do not select all the text in the bulleted list.) In the Advanced Animation group, double-click the **Animation Painter** button.

9. Go to slide 12 and click anywhere within the bulleted list to copy the animation formats. Then go to slide 10 and click anywhere within the bulleted list. Click the **Animation Painter** button to toggle off the feature. Note that all the items in the second level paragraphs of the bulleted list are assigned the number 2 in the animation sequence, which means all the items will appear at the same time.

10. In the Animation Pane, click the **Expand** button 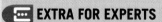 to show all the animation objects. In the Slide pane, select all the second level bulleted paragraphs. Note that the items are also selected in the

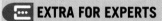

EXTRA FOR EXPERTS

When customizing animations, you can also use the setting to hide the object following the animation. In the Animation Pane, select the object list arrow, click Effect Options, and then click the After animation list arrow. Click Hide After Animation, and then click OK.

EXTRA FOR EXPERTS

To change the order of the animated objects, drag and drop the objects in the Animation Pane.

Animation Pane. In the Animation Pane, click the **list arrow** for the last item. Then click **Timing** to open the Peek In dialog box, as shown in **Figure 5–8**. Your settings will be different.

FIGURE 5–8
Timing tab in the Peek In dialog box

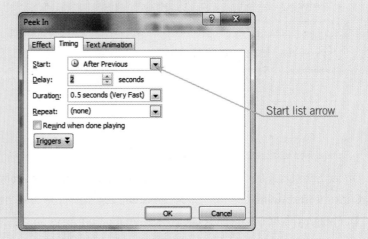

11. Click the **Start** list arrow, and then click **After Previous**. Change the Delay setting to **2**. When your settings match those in Figure 5–8, click **OK** and then close the Animation Pane.

12. Click the **Slide Show** tab. In the Start Slide Show group, click the **From Current Slide** button. Click to advance to the first two bulleted items on the slide. Then wait patiently as the second level paragraph bulleted items automatically appear.

13. Click to advance to the next slide and continue to click through the progressive disclosure for all the bulleted items on the last two slides.

14. Press **Esc** to return to Normal view. Save the changes and leave the presentation open for the next Step-by-Step.

Adding Interactive Features to the Slide Content

Adding an interactive feature can help to make a slide show more interesting and a presentation more practical. For example, you can add content to the slides while delivering the presentation, and you can create links to other slides and documents to provide access to additional information.

TECHNOLOGY CAREERS

Workplace communication skills are essential in today's workplace. Today's employees need to organize, analyze, and communicate information in both verbal and written formats. Moreover, the ability to formally present information logically, clearly, and in an engaging fashion is an increasingly important skill. For example, a supervisor may recommend strategies to management, or an accountant may be called upon to make a proposal to the board of directors. The audience may be as small as one or two coworkers, or it may be a much larger group of people. In most cases, technology is used to deliver the message. For example, the message may be submitted in a report or discussed in person using a slide show; or the message may be broadcast in a video conference or published on the Web. To communicate the message effectively, all methods of delivery require oral, written, and technical skills.

Adding ActiveX Controls to the Slide

The ActiveX controls on the Developer tab enable you to create interactive objects on a slide. For example, you can insert a text box, adjust the text box size as needed, and access the Properties pane to apply additional formats to the text box such as the font style or size. Then, as you deliver the presentation in Slide Show view, you can type text in the box to update the content on the slide. For example, during a presentation, you ask the audience about their preferences for wooden or steel roller coasters, and then you tally the responses and type the numbers on the slide. When you use this interactive feature, the new content is automatically saved with the presentation.

Step-by-Step 5.6

1. If necessary, open the **Revised Coasting 5** file from your solution files. Save the presentation as **Revised Coasting 6**, followed by your initials.

2. If the Developer tab already appears on the Ribbon, go to Step 3. If the Developer tab does not appear on the Ribbon, click **File** and then click **Options**. In the left pane of the PowerPoint Options dialog box, click **Customize Ribbon**. In the pane on the right, enable the **Developer** option and then click **OK**.

3. Go to slide 6. Click the **Developer** tab. In the Controls group, click the **Text Box (ActiveX Control)** button [abl]. The mouse pointer changes to a cross-hair $+$.

4. In the Click to add text placeholder on the left, under *Wooden*, drag the mouse pointer to create a text box approximately 1 inch high and 1 inch wide. (*Hint*: Show the Ruler.) Center the new text box under the word *Wooden*.

5. Right-click the **text box**, and then click **Properties**. The Properties pane, similar to the one shown in **Figure 5–9**, opens.

FIGURE 5–9
TextBox1 Properties pane

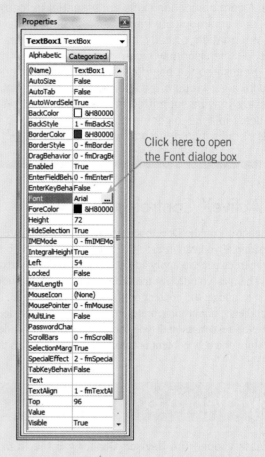

Click here to open the Font dialog box

6. In the left column, click **Font**, and then click the **ellipsis** button (...) in the right column to open the Font dialog box. Change the font size to **36** and then click **OK**. Close the Properties pane.

7. Copy and paste the text box, then reposition the second text box so it is centered under the word *Steel* in the Click to add text placeholder on the right. (*Hint*: Drag and drop the text box, or use the arrow keys.)

8. Save the changes to the presentation.

9. Switch to Slide Show view, showing the current slide. Click the **text box** under *Wooden* and type the number **15**. Click the **text box** under *Steel* and type the number **36**.

10. Press **Esc** to switch to Normal view. Note that the numbers still appear in the interactive boxes.

11. Save the changes and leave the presentation open for the next Step-by-Step.

Modifying SmartArt Graphics

You can easily reorder and resize the shapes in a SmartArt graphic. To work with the shapes individually, you can convert a SmartArt graphic to shapes. For example, you can reposition one or more of the shapes without affecting the other shapes. However, there is no command available for converting the shapes back to a SmartArt graphic.

An *image map* a graphic that contains multiple hyperlinks on various parts of the image without dividing the graphic into separate objects. Typically, image maps are used for hyperlinks on Web pages, but you can also create them for PowerPoint slide graphics such as charts and SmartArt graphics.

In the next Step-by-Step, you will format a transparent (invisible) shape on top of a SmartArt shape to identify a *hot spot*, which is a hyperlink created for a part of the image map. You can have multiple hot spots on a graphic, each mapped to a target. By adding ScreenTips, you can make the user aware of the hot spots.

▶ **VOCABULARY**

image map

hot spot

Step-by-Step 5.7

1. If necessary, open the **Revised Coasting 6** file from your solution files. Save the presentation as **Revised Coasting 7**, followed by your initials.

2. Launch Word, and then navigate to the drive and folder where your Data Files are stored and open the **Terms.docx** document. Save the document as **Coaster Terms**, followed by your initials, and then close the document. Exit Word.

3. In PowerPoint, go to slide 9. Right-click anywhere within the bulleted list placeholder, point to **Convert to SmartArt**, and then click **More SmartArt Graphics**. In the left pane, click **Cycle**. In the center pane, click the **Nondirectional Cycle** option, as shown in **Figure 5–10**. Click **OK**.

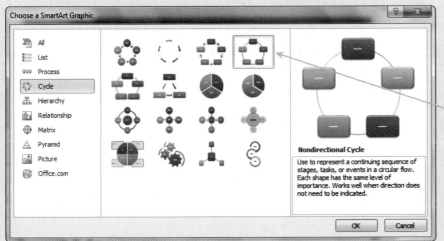

FIGURE 5–10
Cycle category in the Choose a SmartArt Graphic dialog box

Nondirectional Cycle option

4. Maximize the SmartArt graphic by dragging the borders so that the object fills the lower portion of the slide. Then resize and reorder the SmartArt graphic objects:

   a. Click the SmartArt graphic object containing the text *corkscrew* to select it. Press and hold **Ctrl** and select each of the other rounded rectangle objects in the circle. Make sure the selection handles appear around each of the rounded rectangles.

   b. Click the **SmartArt Tools Format tab**. In the Shapes group, click the **Larger** button three times to increase the size of the rounded rectangles. Then click the **Smaller** button once to reduce the size of the rounded rectangles. Deselect the rounded rectangles.

   c. Select the **corkscrew** SmartArt graphic object. Click the **SmartArt Tools Design tab**. In the Create Graphic group, click the **Move Down** button. The *corkscrew* object exchanges positions with the *inverted* object. Click the **Move Up** button to restore the original positions.

   d. The **corkscrew** SmartArt graphic object should be selected. Drag it to the center of the circle. Note that as you move the rounded rectangle, the lines on both sides of the rounded rectangle move with it. Click the **Undo** button on the Quick Access Toolbar to restore the original position of the corkscrew object.

5. Click in a blank area of the SmartArt graphic to select it and to deselect the corkscrew object. Click the **SmartArt Tools Design tab**. In the Reset group, click the **Convert** button and then click **Convert to Shapes**. The shapes look very similar and are arranged the same.

6. Select the **corkscrew** shape and drag the shape to the center of the circle. The connecting lines do not move. Click **Undo** on the Quick Access Toolbar twice to undo moving the shape and to undo converting the SmartArt graphic to shapes.

7. Click the **Insert** tab. In the Illustrations group, click the **Shapes** button. Under Rectangles, click the **Rounded Rectangle** shape. The mouse pointer changes to a cross-hair. Click and drag the mouse pointer over the G-force rounded rectangle in the SmartArt graphic to create a new rectangle shape. Drag the corner shape handles to resize the new rectangle shape as needed so it fits within the G-force SmartArt graphic object, as shown in **Figure 5–11**.

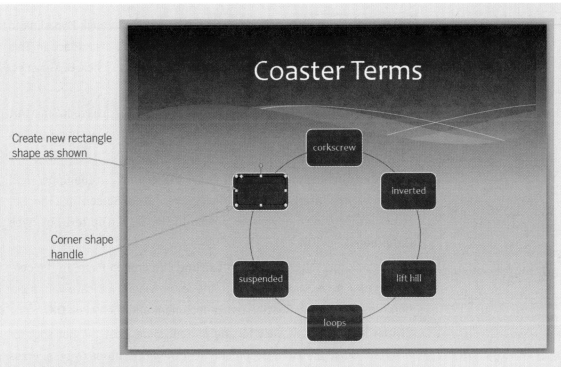

FIGURE 5–11
New shape
positioned over
the G-force
SmartArt graphic
object

8. Right-click the new **rounded rectangle** shape and then click **Format Shape** to open the Format Shape dialog box, as shown in **Figure 5–12**. Your settings will differ. Format the shape:

    a. Drag the **Transparency** slider to the right to change the transparency setting to **100%**.

    b. In the left pane, click **Line Color**. In the right pane, click the **No line** option.

    c. Click **Close**. The new shape is still selected, and the text in the G-force SmartArt graphic object is again visible.

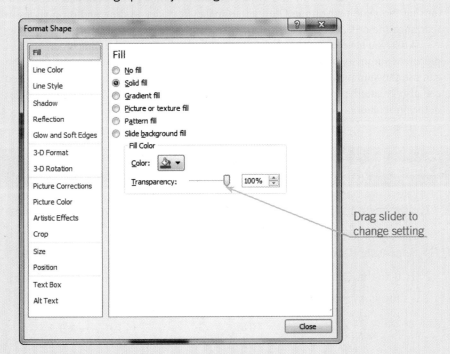

FIGURE 5–12
Format Shape dialog box

9. Right-click the **transparent rectangle** shape, and then click **Hyperlink** to open the Insert Hyperlink dialog box. Under Link to, click **Place in This Document**. Under Select a place in this document:, click **8. G-forces**. Click **OK** to close the dialog box.

10. Create a rounded rectangle shape to cover the **inverted** SmartArt graphic object. Repeat steps 6 and 7 to format the new shape so it is 100% transparent, with no line color.

11. Right-click the new shape, and then click **Hyperlink**. In the upper-right corner of the Insert Hyperlink dialog box, click **ScreenTip**. The Set Hyperlink ScreenTip dialog box opens. In the ScreenTip text box, type **Definition**. Click **OK**.

12. Under Link to:, select the option **Existing File or Web Page**. In the center pane, if necessary, navigate to the folder where you save your solution files. Select the **Coaster Terms** document and then click **OK**.

13. Switch to Slide Show view for the current slide. Test the hot spot for *inverted*. Close the Word document. Test the hot spot for *G-force*. Press **Esc** to switch to Normal view.

14. Save the changes and leave the presentation open for the next Step-by-Step.

Organizing the Presentation Content

Working with a presentation outline is similar to working with an outline in Word. The Outline tab enables you to organize slides and edit the slide text. On the Outline tab, you can add new slides to a presentation, and you can also add new text to a slide. However, you cannot add or edit graphics. Although it is not necessary, collapsing the slide text on the Outline tab makes it easier to drag and drop slides to rearrange the order.

After you have completed the slide content and confirmed the slide order, you can prepare a summary slide. A *summary slide* reviews the topics in a presentation. You can use the summary slide as an introduction to or a review of the presentation. You can also create hyperlinks and use the summary slide to help navigate to other slides in the presentation.

▶ VOCABULARY
summary slide

Step-by-Step 5.8

1. If necessary, open the **Revised Coasting 7** file from your solution files. Save the presentation as **Revised Coasting 8**, followed by your initials. If necessary, switch to Normal view.

2. Click the **Outline** tab. All slides appear on the Outline tab, and each slide is numbered. The text for each slide is also displayed.

3. On the Outline tab, edit the text on slide 7 so that each word begins with a capital letter. Note that as you make the change on the Outline tab, the edit is also applied to the text in the Slide pane.

4. On the Outline tab, right-click anywhere in the slide 12 text. In the shortcut menu, click **Collapse**. The bulleted text for the slide is hidden, but the title is still visible on the Outline tab.

5. Click the **slide 6** slide icon ▦ to select the slide. Click the **Repeat** button on the Quick Access Toolbar to collapse the slide text.

6. With the insertion point positioned anywhere on the Outline tab, press **Ctrl+A** to select all the slides. Right-click the **selection** and then click **Collapse**. Click anywhere outside the list to deselect the slides.

7. Click the **slide 6** slide icon, and then drag the slide to the position between slides 3 and 4. The slide numbers are adjusted for the new order.

8. Right-click in the slide 9 text. In the shortcut menu, click **Move Up**. Press the **F4** key to repeat the edit and move the slide up one more position.

9. Click the **slide 2** slide icon to select it. Press and hold **Ctrl**, and then click the **slide icons** for slides 7, 8, 9, 10, and 11. Then copy the selection to the Clipboard.

10. On the Outline tab, right-click in the slide 12 text and then click **New Slide**. In the Slide pane, click the **Click to add title** placeholder and type **Summary**. Then click the **Click to add text** placeholder and paste the copied slides from the Clipboard. If necessary, reposition the place-holder so that all the text fits on the slide.

11. Select all the text in the first bulleted item, and then right-click the selection. In the shortcut menu, click **Hyperlink**. If necessary, select Place in This Document. Under Select a place in this document, select **2. The Ultimate EXperience**. Then click **OK**.

12. Create hyperlinks to the corresponding slides for all other items in the bulleted list.

13. Switch to Slide Show view and test the hyperlinks. *(Hint*: Press **End** after testing each link to return to the summary slide.) Press **Esc** to switch to Normal view.

14. Save the changes and close the presentation.

SUMMARY

In this lesson, you learned:

■ To ensure that commonly used words are spelled correctly, you can customize the AutoCorrect list and add words to a custom dictionary.

■ Special characters can help to make your text more accurate and easier to read.

■ You can automatically number paragraphs in a placeholder.

■ You can use symbols to customize bullets.

■ Animation features enable you to format progressive disclosure to control both when and how slide content appears.

■ To make a presentation more engaging, you can add ActiveX controls to the slide content to make the presentation interactive.

■ You can easily reorder and resize the shapes in a SmartArt graphic, and to work with the shapes individually, you can convert a SmartArt graphic to shapes.

■ You can divide an image into sections and create links for additional information using other types of resources, such as other slides in your presentation or other files on your computer or server.

■ The Outline tab enables you to reorganize slides and edit slide text.

■ You can create a summary slide from the titles of slides in a presentation.

 ## VOCABULARY REVIEW

Define the following terms:

hot spot	progressive disclosure
image map	summary slide

 ## REVIEW QUESTIONS

TRUE / FALSE

Circle T if the statement is true or F if the statement is false.

T   F   **1.**   When you open the Symbols dialog box, the available symbols are limited to the current font style.

T   F   **2.**   You can copy animation formats from one object to another and from one slide to another.

T   F   **3.**   Both graphics and text appear on the Outline tab.

T   F   **4.**   You can only create custom animations for text.

T   F   **5.**   To rearrange the order of slides on the Outline tab, you must first collapse the text on the slides you want to move.

MULTIPLE CHOICE

Select the best response for the following statements.

1. Using symbols in slide content _____.

   A.   can help to clarify the message   C.   can make the text easier to read

   B.   can reduce the number of words   D.   all of the above

2. If you frequently use a word or acronym with a unique spelling and you want to save time typing the term or phrase in a document, you should _____.

   A.   add the term or phrase to a custom dictionary   C.   add the term or phrase to the AutoCorrect list

   B.   add the term or phrase to the standard dictionary   D.   any of the above

3. When you add a word to the dictionary during a spell check, the word is saved in _____.

   A.   the standard dictionary   C.   the document template

   B.   the default dictionary   D.   none of the above

4. On the Outline tab, you can _____.

   A.   change the order of slides   C.   add graphics

   B.   edit text formats   D.   all of the above

5. Hyperlinks are used to _____.

   A.   link to a Web page   C.   open a document in another Office application

   B.   move to a place in the same document   D.   all of the above

WRITTEN QUESTIONS

Write a brief answer to the following questions.

1. Describe how to control the font style and size in an interactive text box.

2. Explain how to quickly adjust the size of numbers, symbols, and text characters so the height is comparable to surrounding text.

3. What are the benefits of creating and using a custom dictionary?

4. What is the purpose of progressive disclosure?

5. Describe how to create a summary slide.

■ PROJECTS

If you have a SAM 2010 user profile, your instructor may have assigned an autogradable version of the indicated project. If so, log into the SAM 2010 Web site at *www.cengage.com/sam2010* to download the instruction and start files.

PROJECT 5–1

1. Open the **Lightning** file from the drive and folder where your Data Files are stored. Save the presentation as **Revised Lightning**, followed by your initials.

2. Scroll through the slides to become familiar with the content.

3. Go to slide 3. Convert the bulleted list to a numbered list, applying the **1., 2., 3.** format.

4. Format all the bulleted items in slides 2, 4, 5, and 6 for progressive disclosure. Apply the **Fade** entrance effect. Set the trigger for the animation to **Start On Click**. Apply an effect option so that when you advance to the next animation, the previous item changes to a dark blue-gray color.

5. Go to slide 3 and create an ActiveX text box approximately 1-¼ inch wide by ½ inch tall. Position the interactive text box over the line at the beginning of item #1. Format the text box font size as **24** point.

6. Create three more interactive text boxes, and position the text boxes over the lines in items # 2, 3, and 4. (*Hint:* You can copy and paste the text boxes.)

7. Move slide 3 to the end of the presentation.

8. Save the changes.

9. Switch to Slide Show view, showing the current slide. Enter the following numbers in the interactive text boxes:

Item #1	**2000**
Item #2	**100**
Item #3	**40,000**
Item #4	**80,000**

10. Switch to Normal view. Then save the changes and close the presentation.

SAM PROJECT 5–2

1. Open the **Employee Manual** file from the drive and folder where your Data Files are stored. Save the presentation as **Revised Employee Manual**, followed by your initials.

2. Scroll through the slides in Normal view to review the information in the manual. Note that the company name *ExperTech* is not a known word in the standard dictionary.

3. Create a custom dictionary. Name the dictionary **ET**, followed by your initials, and be sure to save the dictionary in the folder where you save your solution files. Add the word *ExperTech* to the dictionary. Set the new *ET* dictionary as the default dictionary.

4. Add a new entry to the AutoCorrect list so that *Expertech* is automatically replaced with *ExperTech*.

5. Go to slide 2. In the second bulleted item, position the insertion point after *client base* and type **at Expertech**, then press the **spacebar**. The capitalization of the word should automatically be corrected.

6. Equalize the character height for all the numbers throughout all the slides. (*Hint:* You can use the Repeat button or Format Painter.)

7. Go to slide 1. The company name *ExperTech* is a registered trademark. Insert the registered symbol (®) after the company name (and before ", Inc."). (*Hint:* Look in the Normal text font, Latin-1 Supplement subset.) Also add the registered symbol to the company name on slide 15.

8. In the text box on the yellow graphic on slide 1, position the insertion point below the word *Revised:* and type the current date using the XX/XX/XXXX format.

9. Go to slide 6. Replace the bullets with a custom symbol. Search through the Wingdings font symbols and apply a clock symbol. Increase the size of the symbol as needed.

10. Move slides 8–12 to the end of the presentation so they are positioned just before the last slide.

11. Insert a Title and Content slide at the end of the presentation to create a summary slide. Change the title of the summary slide to **Contents**, and use slides 2, 3, 4, 8, 9, and 10 for the bulleted list. Move the new summary slide so it is the second slide in the presentation. Then create hyperlinks to the corresponding slides for each item in the summary slide.

12. Run a spell check. Add the words *ExperTech's*, *Tashia*, and *Weingartner* to the dictionary.

13. Change the settings so the CUSTOM.dic is the default dictionary. Remove the ET dictionary from the list. Also, delete the entry *Expertech* from the AutoCorrect list.

14. Save the changes. Run the slide show and test the hyperlinks. Make any necessary changes, save the changes, and close the presentation.

PROJECT 5–3

1. In Word, open the **1950 Paint.docx** file from the drive and folder where your Data Files are stored. Save the document as **Before 1950**, followed by your initials. Close the file.

2. Open the **RRP.docx** file from the drive and folder where your Data Files are stored. Save the document as **RRP Rule**, followed by your initials. Close the file and close Word.

3. In PowerPoint, open the **Lead Poisoning.pptx** file from the drive and folder where your Data Files are stored. Save the presentation as **Final Lead Poisoning**, followed by your initials. Scroll through the slides to become familiar with the content.

4. Go to slide 10. Add some symbols to make the blood lead levels easier to read and understand:
   a. Replace the letter *u* with the micro sign symbol, the small Greek letter *mu* (μ). (*Hint:* Look in Normal text font, Basic Latin subset.) Repeat the edit to replace the second occurrence of the letter *u* with the micro sign symbol.
   b. Replace the words *Less than* with the Less-Than Sign symbol (<).
   c. The numbers *10* and *19* are a range. Number ranges are usually indicated using en dashes (–). Insert the En Dash symbol (–) and delete the blank space between the two sets of numbers. (*Hint:* Look in the Normal text font, General Punctuation subset.)

5. Add a new entry to the AutoCorrect list to replace *ug* with **μg/dL**.

6. Add the following two items at the end of the bulleted list on slide 10. Copy and paste the En Dash symbol to indicate the ranges.

   20–44 ug/dL moderate lead poisoning

   45–69 ug/dL severe lead poisoning

7. Go to slide 6. Create a hot spot for the *Built before 1950* section of the pie chart. When you format the transparency for the shape, you will also need to remove the line color. Link the hot spot to the *Before 1950* Word document. Add a ScreenTip to display *Paint before 1950*.

8. Create a second hot spot for the *Built before 1978* section of the pie chart. Link the hot spot to the *RRP Rule* Word document. Add a ScreenTip to display *EPA rule*.

9. Run the slide show and test the hyperlinks. Make any necessary corrections.

10. Delete the *ug* entry from the AutoCorrect list.

11. Save the changes and close the presentation.

CRITICAL THINKING

ACTIVITY 5–1

In this lesson, you learned how to rearrange slides and edit text on the Outline tab. Now that you are familiar with the Outline tab features, do you think you will first create an outline and then add graphic and other elements to the slides, or do you think you will create the slides first and then rearrange them as needed? Explain the reasons for your preference.

ACTIVITY 5–2

You created a presentation containing a number of hyperlinks to documents on your intranet. During a cleanup operation, you moved some of the documents to new folders. Now your hyperlinks don't work. What happened and how can you fix the problem?

Use the PowerPoint Help screens to identify the cause of the problem and how to resolve it. Write a brief summary of your findings.

LESSON 6

Working with Tables and Charts

■ OBJECTIVES

Upon completion of this lesson, you should be able to:

- Change the table structure.
- Use the drawing tools to modify a table and create a new table.
- Apply a custom table style.
- Use multiple slides to build a table.
- Choose the correct chart type and identify data to be represented in a chart.
- Link to data in an Excel chart.
- Animate chart data.
- Modify and animate an organization chart.

■ VOCABULARY

axis

axis title

data label

data series

embedded object

legend

linked object

plot area

Tables and charts are useful for presenting a large collection of text or numbers in a meaningful way. This lesson explores features for customizing table and chart formats.

Working with Tables

Table structures and formats are rarely perfect the first time around. It often takes some adjustment to make a table look good on a slide. You can use design and layout tools on the Table Tools tab to modify the table's structure and format.

Changing the Table Structure

If the table contents need to be rearranged, you can drag and drop the data to a new location in the table. However, if you drag and drop data into a cell that already contains data, the data in the destination cell will be replaced with the data you are moving. Therefore, if you want to retain all of the data in a table, you need to add new columns and rows and then drag and drop the data to an empty cell.

To combine the content of two or more cells into a single cell, you can merge the cells by using the Table Eraser tool to remove the cell boundaries. To create a new border within a cell, you can split the cell. You can also create a diagonal border, which enables you to insert two different kinds of information into one table cell.

Remember that slides use large font sizes for ease of reading. Text and numbers you enter in a table should also appear in a large font size. To fit the text and numbers within a cell, you can adjust the font size or the column width. To change column width and row height, you can use the AutoFit command, the Distribute Rows command, or the Distribute Columns command. You can also manually set the spacing, or you simply drag a row or column boundary line to a new position.

Step-by-Step 6.1

1. Open the **Coaster History** file from the drive and folder where your Data Files are stored. Save the presentation as **Revised Coaster History 1**, followed by your initials.

2. Go to slide 2. In the last row of the table, select **6 mph**, and then drag and drop the selected text to the empty cell to the right in the *1800s* column.

3. Position the insertion point anywhere in the *Drop* row. Click the **Table Tools Layout** tab. In the Rows & Columns group, click the **Insert Above** button. Select all the cells in the *Speed* row, and then drag and drop the content in the first cell in the new blank row. Right-click anywhere in the last row, which is now blank, and click **Delete Rows**.

4. Select all the cells in the last three rows of the table. Click the **Table Tools Layout** tab. In the Cell Size group, click the **Distribute Rows** button ⊞. The height of the selected rows is distributed equally.

5. Click anywhere in the table to deselect the last three rows. Position the mouse pointer over the right border of the *1800s* column. When the mouse pointer changes to a double-headed arrow, as shown in **Figure 6–1**, double-click to AutoFit the column width to the content.

TIP

If the content does not fit in the destination row, undo the edit and repeat the step. As you drop the selected content, make sure the insertion point is positioned in the first cell of the new row.

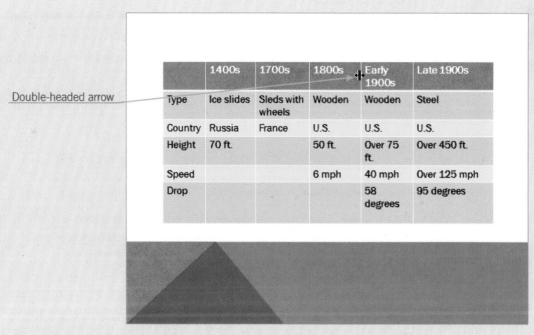

FIGURE 6–1
AutoFit cell boundary

Double-headed arrow

6. Repeat Step 5 to AutoFit the column width for the *Early 1900s* and *Late 1900s* columns.

7. If necessary, click anywhere in the table to select it. On the Table Tools Design tab, in the Draw Borders group, click the **Table Eraser** button. The mouse pointer changes to an eraser ✐. Click the border between the *Type* and *Country* cells, as shown in **Figure 6–2**. The boundary is removed and the two cells are merged.

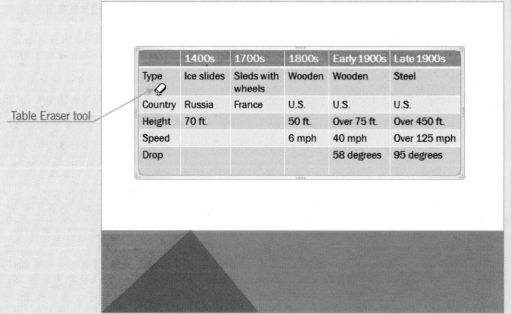

FIGURE 6–2
Erase cell boundary

Table Eraser tool

8. Click the remaining cell boundaries below all the cells in the *Type* row. When you are done, all the cells in the *Type* and *Country* rows are merged, as shown in **Figure 6–3**. Click anywhere outside the table to toggle off the Table Eraser tool.

FIGURE 6–3
Merged cells in the Type and Country rows

	1400s	1700s	1800s	Early 1900s	Late 1900s
Type Country	Ice slides Russia	Sleds with wheels France	Wooden U.S.	Wooden U.S.	Steel U.S.
Height	70 ft.		50 ft.	Over 75 ft.	Over 450 ft.
Speed			6 mph	40 mph	Over 125 mph
Drop				58 degrees	95 degrees

9. Click the **Type Country** cell. Click the **Table Tools Layout** tab, and in the Merge Group, click the **Split Cells** button. In the Split Cells dialog box, change the Columns setting to **1** and change the Rows setting to **2**. Click **OK**. The cell is split, but all the text appears in the top cell. Click **Undo**.

10. Click the **Type Country** cell. Click the **Table Tools Design** tab, and in the Table Styles group, click the **Borders** button arrow ⬚▾. At the bottom of the drop-down menu, click **Diagonal Up Border**. A diagonal border is added to the active cell. Select the remaining cells in the *Type/Country* row. Click the **Diagonal Up Border** button to apply the diagonal border.

11. In the *Type Country* cell, position the insertion point in front of the word *Country* and press **Enter** twice. Add additional space before the country names in the remaining cells in the first row. You need to press Enter only once before the word *France*.

12. Right-click the table, and then click **Select Table**. Click the **Home** tab. In the Font group, change the font size to **15** point.

13. In the *Type/Country* cell, click anywhere in the word *Country*. In the Paragraph group, click the **Align Text Right** button ▤. Repeat to right-align the country information in the remaining cells in the second row.

14. Select the last three rows of cells. Click the **Table Tools Layout** tab, and in the Alignment group, click the **Center Vertically** button ▤. The selected content is centered vertically within each cell.

15. Save the changes and leave the presentation open for the next Step-by-Step.

Creating a Table Using the Draw Table Tool

The Draw Table tool gives you considerable flexibility in creating a table. If, for example, some rows of the table need to be a different height or some rows need to contain more columns than others, the Draw Table tool may be the best tool because you won't have to spend time splitting and merging cells individually. The Draw Table tool also enables you to size cells precisely within the table, and you can show gridlines to help you align the cell borders.

> You can rotate the text within a table cell so that it appears vertical or stacked. When the text is rotated, the spacing between characters changes. To adjust this, you can use the Kerning option in the Font dialog box.

TIP

Choosing the line styles and weights before drawing a table can save formatting time later.

Step-by-Step 6.2

1. If necessary, open the **Revised Coaster History 1** presentation from your solution files. Save the presentation as **Revised Coaster History 2**, followed by your initials. If necessary, click the View tab and show the Ruler.

2. Go to slide 2. If necessary, click the Home tab. In the Slides group, click the **New Slide** button arrow, and then click **Blank**.

3. Click the **Insert** tab. In the Tables group, click the **Table** button, and then click **Draw Table**. The mouse pointer will change to show a pencil .

4. In the white area of the slide, draw a box approximately 8 inches wide by 4½ inches high. (Use the rulers to estimate the box size.) The Table Tools contextual tabs will display on the Ribbon.

5. Click the **Table Tools Layout** tab. In the Arrange group, click the **Align** button, and then click **View Gridlines**. Make adjustments to the size of the table as needed.

6. On the Table Tools Design tab, in the Draw Borders group, click the **Draw Table** button.

TIP

The Draw Table tool stays active until you click the Draw Table button to toggle it off, or once you begin typing text. As soon as you begin typing text, the tool is automatically toggled off.

TIP

You can also show or hide gridlines by clicking the View tab and then enabling or disabling the Gridlines option in the Show group.

7. Use the Draw Table tool to create the cell boundaries shown in **Figure 6–4**. The approximate cell widths and heights are indicated in the figure, and you can show the Ruler and then use the gridlines as a guide. To adjust the cell, you can drag the boundary lines or you can format the cell sizes manually using the settings in the Cell Size group. In the Arrange group, click the **Align** button and then click **View Gridlines** to toggle off the feature.

FIGURE 6–4
Cell boundaries for new table

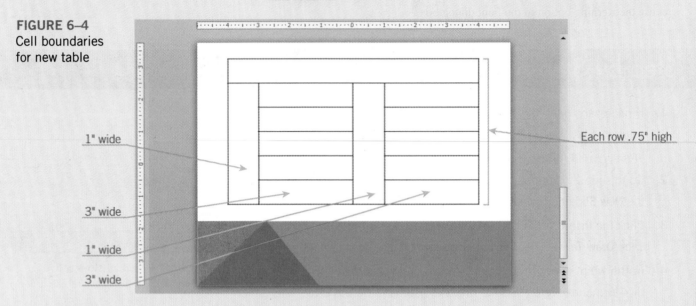

8. Type the table content shown in **Figure 6–5**.

FIGURE 6–5
Table content

Among the Favorites			
Track Layout	Corkscrew	Train Type	Floorless
	Dueling		Inverted
	Figure 8		Launched
	Twister		Stand-up
	Vertical drop		Suspended

9. Click anywhere in the *Track Layout* cell. Click the **Table Tools Layout** tab, and in the Alignment group, click the **Text Direction** button. Click **Stacked**. Repeat the formatting for the *Train Type* cell.

10. Select all the text in the *Track Layout* cell. Click the **Home** tab. In the Font group, click the **Dialog Box Launcher**. In the Font dialog box, click the **Character Spacing** tab. Click the **Spacing** list arrow, and then select **Condensed**. In the By text box, select the text and then type **6**. When your settings match those shown in **Figure 6–6**, click **OK**.

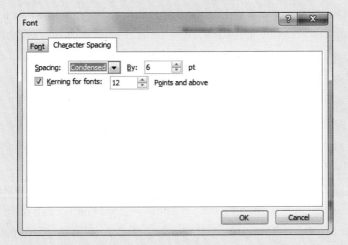

FIGURE 6–6
Character Spacing tab in the Font dialog box

11. Click anywhere in the first row (*Among the Favorites*). Click the **Table Tools Layout** tab. In the Alignment group, click the **Center** button ▤.

12. Select the entire table. In the Alignment group, click the **Center Vertically** button.

13. Click the **Table Tools Design** tab. In the Table Styles group, click the **More** button. Under Best Match for Document, click the third option in the first row, the **Themed Style 1 – Accent 2** table style. If necessary, drag a table corner to position the table in the center of the white area on the slide.

14. Save the changes and leave the presentation open for the next Step-by-Step.

Applying a Custom Table Style

When you create a new table in PowerPoint, a style is applied to the table. A table style provides formats for shading, borders, and effects. The colors used in the style are based on the theme colors of the presentation. You can change the style by applying a different style, or you can modify the existing style by changing some of the formats, such as the shading or border colors. To apply a custom style, you must first remove any existing style. Then you can apply new shading, border, and effect formats. However, you will not be able to save the custom style settings for use in another presentation.

Step-by-Step 6.3

1. If necessary, open the **Revised Coaster History 2** presentation from your solution files. Save the presentation as **Revised Coaster History 3**, followed by your initials. If necessary, go to slide 2.

2. Click anywhere inside the table to display the Table Tools contextual tabs. If necessary, click the Table Tools Design tab. In the Table Styles group, click the **More** button. At the bottom of the menu, click **Clear Table**. All the shading and border colors are removed, including the diagonal borders in the first row.

3. Select all the cells in the second row (*Type/Country*). In the Table Styles group, click the **Borders** button arrow, and then click **Diagonal Up Border**.

4. Right-click the table, and then click **Select Table**. In the Table Styles group, click the **Shading** button arrow. At the bottom of the menu, point to **Table Background**. Under Theme Colors, in the third row, select the **Turquoise, Accent 3, Lighter 60%** color. The color is added to all the table cells.

5. Select all the cells in the first row. Click the **Shading** button arrow. Under Theme Colors, in the first row, select the **Orange, Accent 2** color.

6. All the cells in the first row should still be selected. In the Table Styles group, click the **Effects** button arrow and then point to **Cell Bevel**. Under Bevel, select the last option, the **Art Deco** effect.

7. All the cells in the first row should still be selected. Click the **Home** tab. In the Font group, click the **Font Color** button arrow, and then select the **White, Background 1** font color.

8. Format the first column for consistency with the header row.

9. In the *Type/Country* cell, click the word **Country**. In the Paragraph group, click the **Align Text Right** button.

10. Select all the cells in the first row. In the Paragraph group, click the **Center** button.

11. Click anywhere in the *Type/Country* cell. To change the diagonal border format:

    a. Click the **Table Tools Design** tab.

    b. In the Draw Borders group, click the **Pen Style** list arrow and then select the last option in the drop-down menu.

    c. Click the **Pen Weight** list arrow, and then select **1 ½ pt**.

    d. Click the **Pen Color** button, and then select the **White, Background 1** color.

    e. Click the diagonal border in the Type/Country cell to apply the style.

12. Click the **Pen Color** button, and then select the **Orange, Accent 2** color. Then click each of the remaining diagonal borders in the Type/Country row.

13. Click anywhere outside the table to toggle off the Pen tool. Click anywhere within the table to make the table active. In the Table Styles group, click the **Effects** button arrow and then point to **Shadow**. Under Outer, click the last option, the **Offset Diagonal Top Left** effect. Click anywhere outside the table to see the effect.

14. Save the changes and leave the presentation open for the next Step-by-Step.

Using Multiple Slides to Build a Table in a Presentation

Showing all the information in a table all at once can be overwhelming for your audience. You can introduce parts of a table in segments, emphasizing each point individually, and building the table as you progress through the slides. For example, if the table has six columns of information, you can introduce one column at a time on six separate slides.

The Duplicate Slides command enables you to quickly copy and paste one or more selected slides. In the previous Step-by-Steps, you formatted the table about roller coaster history. In the next Step-by-Step, you will duplicate a slide of the *Coaster History* table and create multiple copies of the slide. Then, in reverse order, you will deconstruct the table on each slide, which will allow you to build the table point-by-point when you advance through the slides in Slide Show view.

Step-by-Step 6.4

1. If necessary, open the **Revised Coaster History 3** presentation from your solution files. Save the presentation as **Revised Coaster History 4**, followed by your initials.

2. If necessary, switch to Normal view. On the Slides tab, click the **slide 3** thumbnail. In the Slide pane, select the table.

3. Click the **Table Tools Layout** tab. In the Arrange group, click the **Align** button, and then click **Align Center**. You may not see much change because the table is already centered between the left and right borders. Click the **Align** button again, and then click **Align Middle**. The table is aligned vertically between the top and bottom borders of the slide (not the white area on the slide).

4. Go to slide 2. If necessary, click the Home tab. In the Slides group, click the **New Slide** button arrow, and then click **Duplicate Selected Slides**. A copy of the selected slide is inserted above the active slide (slide 2). On the Quick Access Toolbar, click the **Repeat** button three times to create three more copies of the slide.

5. Go to slide 5. Right-click anywhere in the *Late 1900s* column, and then click **Delete Columns**.

6. Go to slide 4. Select the **Early 1900s** and **Late 1900s** columns. Right-click the selection, and then click **Delete Columns**.

7. Click anywhere outside the table to deselect it, then right-click anywhere in the *Drop* row. Select **Delete Rows**.

8. Go to slide 3. Select and delete the **1800s**, **Early 1900s**, and **Late 1900s** columns. Also select and delete the **Drop** and **Speed** rows.

9. Go to slide 2. Select and delete the **1700s**, **1800s**, **Early 1900s**, and **Late 1900s** columns. Also delete the **Speed** and **Drop** rows.

10. Go to slide 6. Select the table. Click the **Animations** tab. In the Animation group, click the **More** button. At the bottom of the menu, click **More Exit Effects**. Scroll down to the Exciting category and then click the **Pinwheel** exit effect. Click **OK**.

11. Go to Slide 7. Select the table. In the Animation group, click the **More** button. At the bottom of the menu click **More Motion Paths**. Scroll down to the Special category and then click the **Loop de Loop** motion path. Click **OK**. In the Preview group, click the **Preview** button.

12. Select the table. In the Animation group, click the **Custom Path** effect. The mouse pointer changes to a cross-hair. Beginning in the lower-left corner of the slide, drag the mouse pointer to the right and up and down (the path of a roller coaster). When you reach the right side of the slide, drag the pointer back to the center of the slide and then double-click to end the path. The motion path will preview and a line will appear on the slide showing the custom motion path.

13. Go to slide 1, then switch to Slide Show view. Advance through the slides to watch the table progressively develop throughout the presentation and to view the exit and motion path animations.

14. Switch to Normal view. Save the changes and close the presentation.

Working with Charts

A chart provides a graphic representation of data. The first step in creating a chart is to choose a chart type that presents the data in the clearest way possible. To understand the differences in chart types, you must first understand the elements in a chart. **Figure 6–7** identifies the chart elements. **Table 6–1** provides definitions for several of the chart elements.

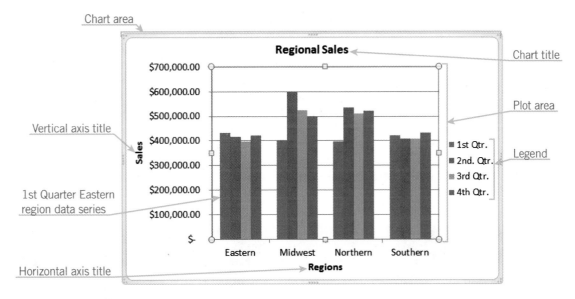

FIGURE 6–7   Chart elements

TABLE 6–1   Definitions of chart elements

CHART ELEMENT	DEFINITION
axis	A line bordering the chart plot area used as a frame of reference for measurement. The y-axis is the vertical axis and usually contains data. The x-axis is the horizontal axis and usually contains categories.
axis title	A label that clarifies what is being measured, such as dollars, number of units, or time spans.
data label	Text or numbers that provide additional information about a value in the data series.
data series	Related data points that are plotted in a chart; each data series in a chart has a unique color or pattern.
legend	A list that identifies the data series indicated by the colors or patterns used in the chart.
plot area	A rectangular border that encloses the two axes and the data series. Depending on the chart formats, the plot area may also include category names, data labels, and axes titles.

▶ **VOCABULARY**
axis
axis title
data label
data series
legend
plot area

Choosing the Right Chart Type

Charts help to summarize, clarify, and highlight data. An attractive chart can get attention, but it is only useful when the data and values are represented correctly. PowerPoint offers many different types of charts, from the familiar line and pie charts to specialized types such as bubble and radar charts.

PowerPoint also provides several different slide layouts and color schemes for each chart type. The slide layouts include background settings, which can be altered to further enhance the appearance. You can also apply quick styles and borders.

The chart type you choose will depend on the data you want to represent. **Table 6–2** describes the chart types available in PowerPoint.

TABLE 6–2   Chart types

CHART TYPE	DESCRIPTION
Column	Each column in the chart shows the value of one item of data. Effective in making comparisons among individual items or showing changes over a period of time. *Sample use*: Compare company sales by regions.
Line	Each line in the chart shows the changes in the value of one item of data. Effective for showing trends over time. *Sample use*: Show the change in temperatures over a period of time.
Pie	Each portion, or slice, of the pie shows the value of one item and how it relates to a whole unit; the portions total 100 percent. Effective for showing how parts relate to a whole; shows only one data series at a time, such as one column of data. *Sample use*: Show marketing expenses as a percentage of the entire company budget.
Bar	Each bar in the chart shows the value of one item of data. Useful when you want to make comparisons among individual items. *Sample use*: Compare the progress of sales reps achieving sales goals.
Area	Illustrates the magnitude of change over time, displaying the sum of plotted values. Effective for emphasizing trends in total values over time.
X Y (Scatter)	Data points are plotted using two value axes, and are displayed in uneven intervals or clusters. Effective for showing trends in numeric data, especially when there are a large number of data points. *Sample use*: Show scientific data from experiments. If desired, you can draw a "best fit" line where the data points are close together, indicating a stronger correlation.
Stock	Illustrates fluctuation of stocks (or other data) over a period of time; data must be carefully structured to match specific type of chart. *Sample use*: Show the high, low, and close figures for a stock.
Surface	A 3-D surface uses colors and patterns to indicate areas that are in the same value range. Effective in finding combinations between two sets of data.
Doughnut	Illustrates parts as they relate to a whole, like a pie chart, but can be used for more than one data series.
Bubble	Displays sets of values, represented by bubbles. The relative size of each bubble represents another data set. Effective for representing three sets of data.
Radar	A line connects a value axis from the center for each category to all values in the same series. Effective in comparing the collected values of several data series.

Step-by-Step 6.5

1. Open the **Deer Creek Inn** presentation from the drive and folder where your Data Files are stored. Save the presentation as **Updated Deer Creek Inn 1**, followed by your initials.

2. Go to slide 2. Note that a column chart shows a data series representing revenues from lodge rooms, lodge suites, and cabins. The chart makes it easy to compare revenues for the Winter, Spring, Summer, and Fall seasons. Click in the blank area above the legend to select the chart.

3. Click the **Chart Tools Design** tab, and in the Type group, click the **Change Chart Type** button. The Change Chart Type dialog box opens, as shown in **Figure 6–8**.

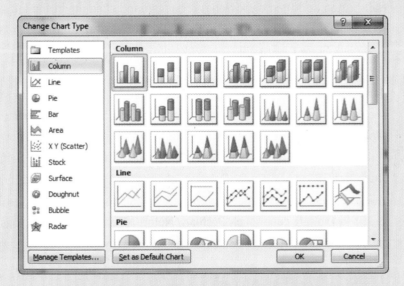

FIGURE 6–8
Change Chart Type dialog box

4. In the right pane of the Change Chart Type dialog box, in the second row under Column, click the second option, the **Stacked Cylinder** chart sub-type. Click **OK**. The revenues for all three types of lodging are combined in a single column for each season, and each column reflects total revenue. The vertical axis adjusts to reflect the change as well.

5. Click the **Change Chart Type** button. In the right pane of the dialog box, in the second row under Column, click the third option, the **100% Stacked Cylinder** chart subtype. Click **OK**. Each column in the chart now shows the percentage of revenue generated from each type of lodging for each season. The vertical axis changes again to show percentages.

6. Click the **Change Chart Type** button. In the right pane of the dialog box, in the second row under Column, click the fourth option, the **3-D Cylinder** chart subtype. Click **OK**. Each type of lodging is represented by a separate column for each season.

> **TIP**
>
> A 100% Stacked Cylinder column chart combines the comparison features of a column chart with the proportional features of a pie chart because each cylinder shows the relationship of items to the whole.

7. Click the **Change Chart Type** button. In the left pane of the dialog box, click **Line**. In the right pane, under Line, click the first option, the **Line** chart subtype. Click **OK**. The lines overlap in the chart, and it's not as easy to compare the values for the seasons.

8. Click the **Change Chart Type** button. In the left pane of the dialog box, click **Column**. In the right pane, in the second row under Column, click the first option, the **Clustered Cylinder** chart subtype. Click **OK**.

9. In the Chart Layouts group, click the **More** button. Ten layout options are available. Click the **Layout 10** chart layout.

10. In the Chart Styles group, click the **More** button. Numerous color options are available. In the fifth row, click the second option, the **Style 34** chart style.

11. Click the **Chart Tools Layout** tab. In the Background group, click the **Chart Wall** button and then click **None**. A background shading on the left and back walls of the chart is removed. Click the **Chart Wall** button again and then click **Show Chart Wall**. The background effect is reapplied.

12. In the Background group, click the **Chart Floor** button, and then click **None**. The background shading at the bottom of the chart is removed. Click the **Chart Floor** button again and then click **Show Chart Floor**. The background effect is reapplied.

13. In the Background group, click the **3-D Rotation** button to open the Format Chart Area dialog box. Under Rotation, change the Y setting to **0**, as shown in **Figure 6–9**. Note the change in the chart rotation. Restore the Y setting to **15**. In the left pane, click **Position**. Note that you can alter settings to position the chart precisely. Click **Close**.

FIGURE 6–9
Format Chart Area dialog box

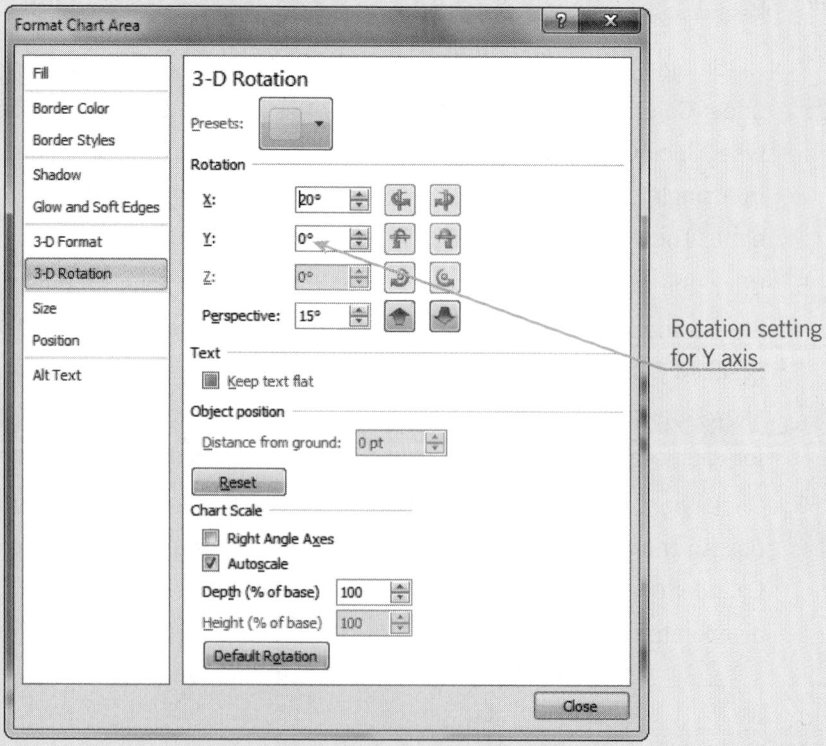

14. Save the changes and leave the presentation open for the next Step-by-Step.

Identifying the Data to be Represented in a Chart

Often the Excel worksheet contains much more data than you want to represent in the chart. You can specify the data that you want to include in the chart. You can also change the direction in which PowerPoint plots data.

> **TIP**
>
> If you do not have Excel installed on your computer, when you create a new chart on a slide, a second window with a datasheet will open.

Step-by-Step 6.6

1. If necessary, open the **Updated Deer Creek Inn 1** presentation from your solution files. Save the presentation as **Updated Deer Creek Inn 2**, followed by your initials.

2. On the Slides tab, right-click the **slide 2** thumbnail, and then click **Duplicate Slide**. On the new slide 3, click in a blank area of the chart to select it. Click the **Chart Tools Design** tab. In the Type group, click the **Change Chart Type** button.

3. In the left pane of the Change Chart Type dialog box, click **Pie**. In the right pane, under Pie, click the second option, the **Pie in 3-D** chart subtype. Click **OK**. Roll over the chart to display the ScreenTips identifying the data series for each slice. Notice that the chart shows data only for one of the data series, *Lodge rooms*. That's because a pie chart represents only one data series.

> **EXTRA FOR EXPERTS**
>
> To use pie charts to compare data, you can insert more than one pie chart on a slide.

4. In the Data group, click the **Select Data** button. The Select Data Source dialog box and an Excel worksheet open. Under Legend Entries (Series), click **Cabins**. Your dialog box should match the one shown in **Figure 6–10**. The chart data range is cells A1 through E4.

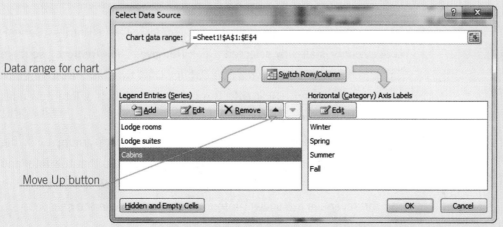

FIGURE 6–10
Select Data Source
dialog box

5. Click the **Move Up** button twice to move the *Cabins* data series to the top of the list. A note appears below the Chart data range indicating that the data range is too complex to be displayed. Because of the chart type, not all of the data will appear in the chart.

6. Click **OK**. The chart changes and now represents the values for the revenues for Cabins. Close the worksheet.

7. On the Slides tab, copy slide 2 and paste the copied slide between slides 1 and 2. In the Slide pane on the new slide 2, click in a blank area of the chart to select it. Click the **Chart Tools Design** tab. In the Data group, click the **Select Data** button. The Select Data Source dialog box and an Excel worksheet open.

8. If necessary, reposition the dialog box so you can see the worksheet. The marquee surrounding the cells in the worksheet also indicates the chart data range. Only rows 1 through 4 are included in the chart data range.

9. Drag the mouse pointer across all the data in the worksheet to change the selection. The data range will change in the Chart data range box. The Chart data range box now shows *=Table1[#All]*.

10. Under Legend Entries (Series), the list of data series changes, as shown in **Figure 6–11**.

FIGURE 6–11
New legend entries in
Select Source dialog box

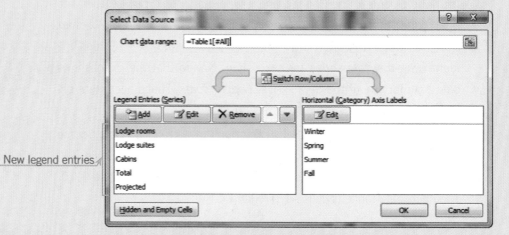

New legend entries

11. In the Select Data Source dialog box, under Legend Entries (Series), *Lodge rooms* is already selected. Click **Remove**. Click **Remove** two more times to remove *Lodge suites* and *Cabins*. Only two data series will now appear in the chart. Click **OK**. The chart compares the Total revenues with the Projected revenues.

12. Switch to the PowerPoint presentation. In the Data group, click the **Switch Row/Column** button. The data is rearranged so that the Total and Projected revenues are represented in the horizontal axis of the chart and the revenues are shown in four columns based on the seasons.

13. Click the **Switch Row/Column** button again to return to the original arrangement of data.

14. Save the changes. Exit Excel. Leave the presentation open for the next Step-by-Step.

Customizing a Data Chart

You can customize a chart by modifying the chart elements. For example, you can add a title to the chart and each axis, position the legend, and choose data labels. The chart elements consist of graphics and text boxes. Just as you select other objects on slides, you can click an element within the chart area to select it. Then you can rearrange the elements in the chart area or use the sizing handles to resize them, and you can show gridlines to help you place the chart elements.

Pie charts give you some unique opportunities for displaying information. You can apply a style from the gallery to create an exploded slice on a pie chart to make it more obvious, or you can manually create the exploded slice by dragging a slice away from the pie chart. Also, 3-D effects enable you to present certain types of data effectively and make your charts more compelling.

> **EXTRA FOR EXPERTS**
>
> If you plan to use a customized chart in the future, you can save the chart as a template. After finalizing the chart, click the Chart Tools Design tab. In the Type group, click the Save As Template button. Enter a filename. The document is saved with the file extension *.crtx*.

Step-by-Step 6.7

1. If necessary, open the **Updated Deer Creek Inn 2** presentation from your solution files. Save the presentation as **Updated Deer Creek Inn 3**, followed by your initials.

2. Go to slide 2. Select the chart, and, if necessary, click the Chart Tools Design tab. In the Type group, click the **Change Chart Type** button. In the left pane of the Change Chart Type dialog box, click **Bar**. In the right pane, under Bar, select the first option, the **Clustered Bar** chart subtype, and then click **OK**.

3. Click the **Chart Tools Layout** tab. In the Labels group, click the **Chart Title** button. Then click **Above Chart** and type **Projected Revenue**.

4. Click the **Axis Titles** button, point to **Primary Vertical Axis Title**, and then click **Rotated Title**. Type **Seasons**.

5. Click the **Axis Titles** button, point to **Primary Vertical Axis Title**, and then click **More Primary Vertical Axis Title Options**. In the right pane, enable the option **Solid fill**. Click the **Color** button, and then click the **Olive Green, Accent 3** theme color. In the left pane, click **Border Color**. In the right pane, enable the option **Solid line**. Click the **Color** button, and then click the **Olive Green, Accent 3** theme color. Click **Close**.

6. Click the **Data Labels** button, and then click **Inside End**. The data values are added to the bars in the chart. Click the horizontal axis values below the chart. When the text box is selected, press **Delete**.

7. Go to slide 4. Select the chart. Click the **Chart Tools Layout** tab. In the Labels group, click the **Legend** button, and then click **Show Legend at Left**. Click to select the **legend** chart object. Click the **Home** tab. In the Font group, change the font size to **24** point.

8. Click the **Chart Tools Format tab**. In the Arrange group, click the **Align** button, and then click **Grid Settings**. In the Grid and Guides dialog box, under Guide settings, click to enable the **Display drawing guides on screen** option, then click **OK**. Click the **legend** chart object to select it, and then using the drawing guides as a guide, align the top of the legend chart object with the horizontal drawing guide.

9. Click the **Chart Tools Layout** tab. In the Labels group, click the **Data Labels** button, and then click **More Data Label Options** to open the Format Data Labels dialog box. See **Figure 6–12**.

FIGURE 6–12
Format Data Labels dalog box

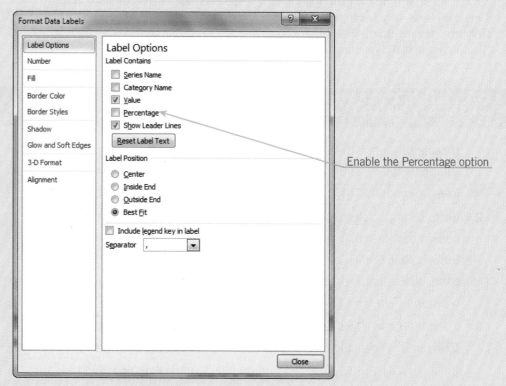

Enable the Percentage option

10. In the right pane of the Format Data Labels dialog box, under Label Contains, enable the **Percentage** option. The Value option and the Show Leader Lines option should already be enabled. Click **Close**. The values and the percentages appear in the portions of the pie chart. When the data cannot fit within the portion, a leader line connects the data information.

11. Click the **Data Labels** button, and then click **More Data Label Options**. Disable the **Value** option. Click **Close**.

12. All four percentages should be selected. Right-click one of the percentages to show the Mini toolbar. Change the font size to **24** point. Click the **Chart Title** button, and then click **Centered Overlay Title**. Type **Cabin Revenues**. Select the new text and change the font size to **32** point.

13. Click the **Summer** data series (slice) of the pie chart. Drag it down slightly to pull it away from the rest of the chart, as shown in **Figure 6–13**. (*Hint:* If the other portions separate from the chart, you can drag them back to the center to reconnect them.)

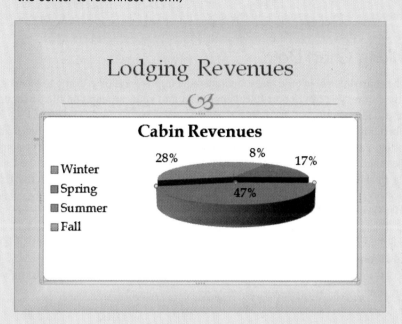

FIGURE 6–13
Exploded slice in pie chart

14. Right-click the pie chart, and then click **3-D Rotation**. The Format Chart Area dialog box opens. In the right pane, under Rotation, change the Y setting to **40**. When your dialog box matches **Figure 6–14**, click **Close**.

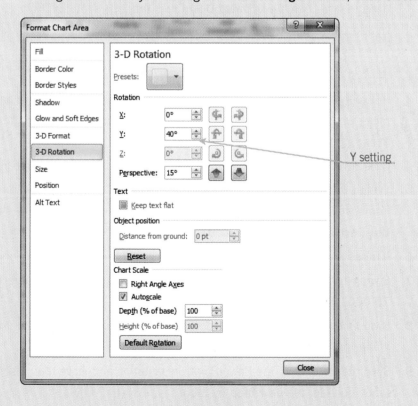

FIGURE 6–14
Format Chart Area dialog box

15. Click the **Chart Tools Format** tab. In the Arrange group, click the **Align** button and then click **Grid Settings**. Under Guide settings, click to disable the **Display drawing guides on screen** option, then click **OK**. Save the changes and leave the presentation open for the next Step-by-Step.

Linking Chart Data

If the chart data you would like to include in your presentation is going to be updated in the future, you can import Excel chart data into your presentation file as either an embedded object or a linked object. You may already be familiar with linking and embedding from other units. An *embedded object* becomes part of the destination file and can be edited in the destination file. A *linked object* is inserted as a static object and accesses data stored in the source file, so you cannot update the linked data in the destination file. You edit linked data by editing the data in the Excel worksheet. When linked data is modified in the source file, the data is automatically updated on the slide when both files are open or when you reopen the destination file. To create linked or embedded objects, you can use the Paste options, which also enable you to use the destination theme (the theme applied to the current slide) or source formatting (the formatting applied to the chart in the source file).

To complete the following Step-by-Step, you must have Excel installed on your computer.

Step-by-Step 6.8

1. If necessary, open the **Updated Deer Creek Inn 3** presentation from your solution files. Save the presentation as **Updated Deer Creek Inn 4**, followed by your initials.

2. Go to slide 5.

3. In Excel, navigate to and open the **Next Year.xlsx** file from the drive and folder where your Data Files are stored. Save the worksheet as **The Year Ahead**, followed by your initials.

4. Click anywhere within the chart to select it. Copy the chart to the Clipboard.

5. Switch to the PowerPoint presentation. Right-click under the heading *The Year Ahead*. In the shortcut menu, under Paste Options, click the **Use Destination Theme & Link Data** button 🖼.

6. If necessary, position the chart below the horizontal line under the slide title.

7. Switch to the Excel worksheet. Click cell **B4** and change the value to **75,000**. Click cell **B5** and change the value to **45,000**.

8. Switch to the PowerPoint presentation. Note that the values for the Winter projected revenues are updated.

9. Save the changes to the PowerPoint presentation and leave the presentation open for the next Step-by-Step.

10. Save the changes to the Excel worksheet. Close the file and exit Excel.

Animating Chart Data

You can apply animation effects to create progressive disclosure and control when the chart objects appear. PowerPoint offers several effect options to animate the chart elements. For example, you can animate the chart to appear as one object, to appear by series or category, or to appear by elements in a series or elements in a category. By revealing parts of the chart individually, you can help your audience focus on specific data represented in the chart.

You can also create hyperlinks for an object in a chart. For example, you can create a link to a Web site or to another slide in the presentation.

Step-by-Step 6.9

1. If necessary, open the **Updated Deer Creek Inn 4** presentation from your solution files. Save the presentation as **Updated Deer Creek Inn 5**, followed by your initials.

2. Go to slide 2. Select the chart. Click the **Animations** tab. In the Animation group, click the **Appear** button.

3. In the Advanced Animation group, click the **Animation Pane** button. In the Animation Pane, click the **Content Placeholder** list arrow. In the drop-down menu, click **Effect Options**. The Appear dialog box opens. Click the **Chart Animation** tab.

4. Click the **Group chart** list arrow, and then click **By Element in Category**.

5. Disable the option **Start animation by drawing the chart background**. When the settings in your dialog box match those in **Figure 6–15**, click **OK**.

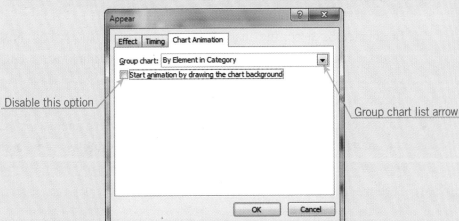

FIGURE 6–15
Appear dialog box with custom settings

6. Click the **Slide Show** tab. In the Start Slide Show group, click the **From Current Slide** button. Click to progressively disclose the elements in each category (season) in the chart. When the chart is fully displayed, press **Esc** to return to Normal view.

7. Go to slide 3. Select the chart. Click the **Animations** tab. In the Animation group, click the **More** button. Under Entrance, click the **Float In** option.

8. In the Animation group, click the **Effect Options** button. The Float Up option is already selected. Under Sequence, click **By Category**.

9. Go to slide 4. Select the chart. In the Animation group, click the **More** button. At the bottom of the menu, click **More Entrance Effects**. The Change Entrance Effect dialog box opens.

10. Under Subtle, click **Expand**, as shown in **Figure 6–16**. Click **OK**.

FIGURE 6–16
Change Entrance Effect dialog box with custom animation selected

Select this option

11. In the Animation group, click the **Effect Options** button, and then click **By Category**.

12. Go to slide 5. Select the chart. Click the **Insert** tab, and in the Links group, click the **Hyperlink** button. In the Insert Hyperlink dialog box, under Link, click **Place in This Document**. Under Select a place in this document, click **2. Lodging Revenues**. Click **OK**.

13. Go to slide 3, and switch to Slide Show view. Review the animations for the charts on slides 3 and 4. Test the hyperlink on the last slide, and then switch back to Normal view.

14. Save the changes and close the presentation.

Modifying an Organization Chart

Organization charts are most commonly used to show the structure of personnel in a company. Over time, employees get promoted and/or the structure of the organization changes. It is easy to add and delete text boxes in an organization chart, but you need to be careful because it can affect the hierarchy of the related text boxes. For example, when you delete a text box, a subordinate text box is automatically moved up in the hierarchy. To promote and demote objects in the hierarchy, you can also use the Promote and Demote buttons on the SmartArt Tools Design tab.

To further enhance the presentation of the organization chart, you can animate the SmartArt graphic and format the elements so that they appear in segments.

After finalizing the organization chart, you can convert the SmartArt graphic to text and the content can be presented in a bulleted list on the slide. You can also copy the text to the Clipboard and use the text in other documents.

Step-by-Step 6.10

1. Open the **Organization** presentation from the drive and folder where your Data Files are stored. Save the presentation as **Revised Organization 1**, followed by your initials.

2. Note that the Engineering Manager reports to the Co-Director on the right. Select the **Co-Director** text box on the right. Be sure to select the white text box and not the blue background box. Then press **Delete**. The Engineering Manager is promoted to the Co-Director level and the Engineering Staff is also promoted to a higher level. On the Quick Access Toolbar, click the **Undo** button.

3. The Co-Director text box should still be selected. Click the **SmartArt Tools Design** tab. In the Create Graphic group, click the **Demote** button. The Co-Director text box is moved down a level.

4. The Co-Director text box is still selected. Press **Delete**. The position is removed without changing the hierarchy. Edit the text in the Co-Director text box at the top of the chart so the title reads **Director**.

5. Click the **Advertising Manager** text box. In the Create Graphic group, click the **Add Shape** button arrow, and then click **Add Shape Below**. In the new text box, type **E-Marketing Manager**.

6. The E-Marketing Manager text box should still be selected. In the Create Graphic group, click the **Promote** button. The text box is moved to the next level above.

7. On the SmartArt Tools Design tab, in the SmartArt Styles group, click the **More** button. Under 3-D, select the second option, the **Inset** SmartArt style.

8. To emphasize the two new staff positions, format the boxes and text with a different color. Select the **Director** text box. Press and hold **Shift** and then click the **E-Marketing Manager** text box. Click the **SmartArt Tools Format** tab. In the Shape Styles group, click the **Shape Fill** button arrow. Under Theme Colors, click the **Red, Accent 2** color.

TIP

You can also promote and demote the organization chart objects by selecting and moving the object text in the Text pane.

TIP

You can also access the Effect Options by clicking the Effect Options button in the Animation group.

TIP

For a quick preview of the animations, click Play in the Animation Pane.

9. Click in a blank area to select the whole chart. Click the **Animations** tab. In the Animation group, click the **More** button. At the bottom of the menu, click **More Entrance Effects**. Under Subtle, click **Zoom**, and then click **OK**.

10. If necessary, in the Advanced Animation group, click the Animation Pane button. In the Animation Pane, click the **SmartArt Placeholder** list arrow. Click **Effect Options**, and then click the **SmartArt Animation** tab.

11. Click the **Group graphic** list arrow, and then click **By branch one by one**. Click **OK**.

12. Switch to Slide Show view and review the animations in the organization chart. Switch back to Normal view.

13. Save the changes. Then save the presentation as **Revised Organization 2**, followed by your initials.

14. If necessary, select the SmartArt object. Click the **SmartArt Tools Design** tab. In the Reset group, click the **Convert** button, and then click **Convert to Text**.

15. Save the changes and close the presentation.

SUMMARY

In this lesson, you learned:

- After creating a table on a slide, you can easily rearrange the content. You can also adjust the font size, AutoFit the columns, and distribute the rows and columns for equal spacing.

- The Draw Table tools are useful for creating or modifying a table, especially for merging and splitting cells.

- PowerPoint provides several features for modifying table styles.

- It is important to choose the correct chart type so that the data and values are represented correctly and for maximum effect.

- You can introduce parts of a table in segments, emphasizing each point individually, and building the table as you progress through the slides.

- You can specify the data that is represented in a chart.

- You can modify the chart elements to clarify the information represented in the chart.

- A linked object must be edited in the source application. The edits will appear in the linked object automatically if the destination document is already open, or the updates will appear when the destination document is reopened.

- You can animate chart objects for progressive disclosure.

- PowerPoint offers many features to help you modify the structure of an organization chart as well as change the chart formats.

■ VOCABULARY REVIEW

Define the following terms:

axis	data series	linked object
axis title	embedded object	plot area
data label	legend	

REVIEW QUESTIONS

TRUE / FALSE

Circle T if the statement is true or F if the statement is false.

T   F   **1.**   A table style provides formats for shading, borders, and effects.

T   F   **2.**   Column and bar charts are useful in making comparisons among individual items.

T   F   **3.**   New columns and rows are automatically added to a table when you drag and drop table data to cells that already have content.

T   F   **4.**   A pie chart can show up to three data series, such as three rows of data.

T   F   **5.**   You can rotate the text within a table cell so that it appears vertical or stacked.

MULTIPLE CHOICE

Select the best response for the following statements.

1. A _____ chart is useful in showing trends over time.

   A.   column

   B.   bar

   C.   line

   D.   scatter

2. To adjust the column width and row height, you can _____.

   A.   drag the cell boundaries

   B.   use the AutoFit command

   C.   use the Distribute Rows and Distribute Columns commands

   D.   all of the above

3. The Table Eraser tool can be used to _____.

   A.   split cells

   B.   merge cells

   C.   remove cell content

   D.   all of the above

4. To adjust the spacing between characters, _____.

   A.   use the Kerning option

   B.   distribute the columns evenly

   C.   drag the cell boundaries

   D.   change the text alignment

5. If the chart data you would like to include in your presentation is going to be updated in the future, you should consider _____.

   A.   embedding the data in the presentation file

   B.   creating an embedded object

   C.   linking to the data in the destination file

   D.   linking to the data in the source file

MATCHING

Match the correct term in Column 2 to its description in Column 1.

Column 1

_____ 1. encloses the two axes and the data series

_____ 2. text or numbers that provide additional information about a value in the data series

_____ 3. a list that identifies the data series indicated by colors or patterns

_____ 4. a line bordering the chart plot area used as a frame of reference for measurement

_____ 5. related data points that are plotted in a chart

Column 2

A. axis

B. data label

C. data series

D. legend

E. plot area

■ PROJECTS

If you have a SAM 2010 user profile, your instructor may have assigned an autogradable version of the indicated project. If so, log into the SAM 2010 Web site at *www.cengage.com/sam2010* to download the instruction and start files.

PROJECT 6–1

1. Open the **Financial Review** file from the drive and folder where your Data Files are stored. Save the presentation as **Updated Financial Review**, followed by your initials.

2. Go to slide 5. In Excel, open the **Expenses.xlsx** file from the drive and folder where your Data Files are stored. Save the spreadsheet as **Q1 Expenses**, followed by your initials.

3. Copy the chart in the Expenses worksheet. Switch to the presentation and with the **Use Destination Theme & Embed Workbook** paste option, paste the chart on slide 5.

4. Change the chart data range so that the Total is not included in the chart. Apply a chart layout and/or style.

5. Add the chart title **Departmental Travel Expenses**. Move the legend as desired. Add the vertical axis title **Dollars**. Change the font size and attributes of the labels as desired. Resize the chart to fill the slide.

6. Animate the parts of the chart to appear by category, triggered by a click. Apply an appropriate entrance effect for the chart type.

7. Copy slide 5 and paste the copied slide at the end of the presentation.

8. In the new slide 6, change the chart to a 3-D pie chart. Change the chart data range so that the chart shows only the Total data. (*Hint*: Press Ctrl and drag to select the first column and the Total column.) Switch the row/column. Apply a chart layout and/or style if desired.

9. Apply 3-D rotation effects and drag the Airfare portion of the chart from the rest of the chart to explode that slice of the pie.

10. Change the slide title to **Q1 Departmental Travel Expenses**.

11. Add labels to show only percentages in the portions of the pie chart. Resize the chart if necessary so the labels fit within portions of the pie chart.

12. When you copied the chart, the animation effects remained with the new chart. Change the entrance for the animation using an entrance effect appropriate for the chart type.

13. Switch to Slide Show view and test the animations. Make any necessary corrections.

14. Save the changes, close Excel, and close the presentation.

SAM PROJECT 6–2

1. Open the **Wetlands** file from the drive and folder where your Data Files are stored. Save the presentation as **Revised Wetlands**, followed by your initials.

2. Scroll through the slides to become familiar with the content.

3. Go to slide 4. Modify the table as necessary to fit all the information on the slide without overcrowding.

4. Move the content in the last row so that it appears in the first row below the headings.

5. Go to slide 10. Use the Draw Borders tools to create the table shown in **Figure 6–17**. Apply formatting as necessary.

Native Mammals		
Monotremes	**Marsupials**	**Placental Mammals**
Platypus	Planigales Kangaroos Koalas Wombats	Rodents (rats) Bats
Introduced Mammals		
Cows, foxes, goats, foxes, and sheep		

FIGURE 6–17   Table content for Step 5

6. Go to slide 12. Apply a new column chart style. Insert the vertical axis label **In 1,000s of Acres**. If desired, reposition the legend and format the fonts for the legend and the axis title.

7. Copy slide 12 and paste the new slide immediately after slide 12. On the new slide 13, change the chart type to a pie chart. Then select the data for the pie chart to show the 1780 loss. (*Hint*: Select chart data range B1:D2.) Switch the row/column.

8. Add percentage labels and a chart title, **Wetland Loss in 1780**, to make the data clear.

9. Go to slide 14. In Excel, open the **Loss Rate.xlsx** file from the drive and folder where your Data Files are stored. Save the worksheet as **Rate of Loss**, followed by your initials.

10. Copy the chart in the Rate of Loss worksheet. Switch to the presentation and paste the chart as a link, using destination formatting, on slide 14. Close Excel.

11. Add the vertical axis title: **Land Loss in Sq Mi/Yr.**. Resize the chart as needed to fill the slide area. Format and size the axis labels, axis title, and legend for legibility and to fit the theme.

12. Add animations to the charts on slides 12, 13, and 14.

13. Review the chart animations in Slide Show view, then switch back to Normal view.

14. Save the changes and close the presentation.

PROJECT 6–3

1. Open the **Byron Chart** file from the drive and folder where your Data Files are stored. Save the presentation as **Revised Byron Chart**, followed by your initials.

2. Move the *City Attorney* text box so the box is the same level as the *City Manager* and *City Clerk* text boxes.

3. Add a new text box after the *Accounting* text box, with the label **Finance**.

4. Add a new text box below the *Building Inspection* text box, with the label **Planning**. Promote the new text box so it is the same level as the *Building Inspection* text box.

5. Move the *Wastewater Treatment* text box so that it appears one level down from the *Water Utility* text box.

6. Animate the objects in the chart with the **Zoom** entrance effect. Group the objects so that they appear by branch, one by one.

7. Switch to Slide Show view and review the animations.

8. Save the changes and close the presentation.

■ CRITICAL THINKING

ACTIVITY 6–1

You work for a company whose stock is traded on a local exchange. Your boss has asked you to prepare a chart showing the performance of stock investments over the past month. What kind of information do you need to gather to create such a chart? What kind of chart would you use for this task? Create some hypothetical data and create the necessary chart on a PowerPoint slide.

ACTIVITY 6–2

Typically, an organization chart shows the structure of a company by identifying the various levels of management and job positions. The information does not have to show job titles and people within an organization. Think about other types of information that can be provided in an organization chart. Describe at least one type of information (other than a company's structure) that can effectively be presented in an organization chart.

LESSON 7

Working with Visual and Sound Objects

■ OBJECTIVES

Upon completion of this lesson, you should be able to:

- Crop, resize, reposition, and change graphics.
- Recolor graphics and shapes.
- Insert animated clip art.
- Modify pictures and digital images.
- Convert objects to SmartArt graphics.
- Create a photo album.
- Save a presentation as a video.
- Insert video and sound clips and record a narration.

■ VOCABULARY

aspect ratio

bitmap

bits

crop

nudging

outcrop

pixels

raster graphics

scaling

streaming video

vector graphics

Using visuals and sounds in a presentation helps the audience focus on and comprehend the points in a presentation, making a presentation even more effective. Just as text, tables, and charts are inserted on slides as objects, so are visuals and sounds. All objects can be animated, arranged, and formatted to further enhance the appearance and effectiveness of the slide content.

Working with Graphics

You can access graphics such as digital pictures or clip art from a number of sources, including the Clip Art task pane, the Internet, servers, CD-ROMs, digital cameras, and phones.

After inserting a picture or clip art, you might find that the graphic you choose isn't quite right for the slide. Perhaps the image isn't the right size or you need only part of it, or the colors don't go well with the current design theme. Fortunately, you can modify clip art and pictures so that they complement the presentation and effectively illustrate relevant points in the presentation.

Cropping Graphics

▶ **VOCABULARY**

crop

outcrop

aspect ratio

If you want to display only a portion of a graphic on a slide, you can *crop* the graphic to trim one or more edges of the graphic. To crop, you drag a border to the center of the graphic. Even though a portion of the graphic is hidden, the graphic remains unchanged and you can restore a cropped graphic to its original size by dragging the border away from the center or by using the Reset Picture command. To add blank space around the graphic, you can *outcrop* a graphic by dragging a border away from the center of the graphic.

You can crop a graphic to fit or fill a specific shape, or you can crop it to a common picture *aspect ratio*, which is the ratio between the width and height. The ratio is calculated by dividing the width of the graphic by its height.

Step-by-Step 7.1

1. Open the **Happy Tails** file from the drive and folder where your Data Files are stored. Save the presentation as **Revised Happy Tails 1**, followed by your initials. Scroll through the slides to become familiar with the content.

2. Go to slide 2. In the content placeholder, click the **Clip Art** icon 🖿 to open the Clip Art task pane.

3. In the Search for text box on the Clip Art task pane, type **dog**. Click the **Results should be** list arrow. Enable the option **Illustrations** and disable all the other options. When your options match those shown in **Figure 7–1**, click the **list arrow** again to collapse the list.

▶ **TIP**

If there is no content placeholder on the slide, you can access the Clip Art command in the Images group on the Insert tab.

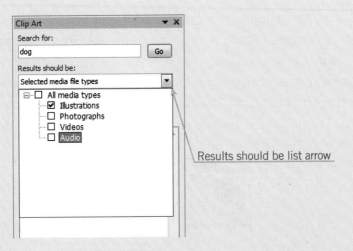

FIGURE 7–1
Media file type options for a clip art search

4. If necessary, enable the Include Office.com content option in the Clip Art task pane, as shown in **Figure 7–2**. Click **Go**. (If you have a current Internet connection, PowerPoint automatically searches for clip art at the Microsoft Office Clip Art and Media Library Web site.)

FIGURE 7–2
Options for clip art search

5. Scroll through the search results in the Clip Art task pane and select an illustration of a dog, such as the one shown in **Figure 7–3**. When you select the clip art thumbnail in the Clip Art task pane, the clip art object is inserted in the center of the content placeholder on the slide. Close the Clip Art task pane.

FIGURE 7–3
Sample clip art illustration of a dog

6. With the clip art object selected on the slide, the Picture Tools Format tab appears. In the Size group, click the **Crop** button. The sizing handles surrounding the image on the slide change to thick black lines, as shown in **Figure 7–4**.

FIGURE 7–4
Sizing handles with cropping feature enabled

7. Position the mouse pointer over the lower-right corner until you see the pointer change to the shape of the corner ⌐. Then drag the border upward to remove a portion of the image. As you drag the border, the mouse pointer changes to a cross-hair. When you release the mouse button, you will see the new cropped border as well as the original border. A portion of the image is removed, as shown in **Figure 7–5**.

FIGURE 7–5
Cropped image with bottom portion removed

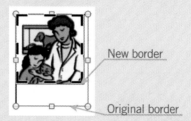

8. In the Adjust group, click the **Reset Picture** button arrow and then click **Reset Picture & Size** to restore the graphic to its original size.

9. With the cropping feature still enabled, position the mouse pointer on the sizing handle in the middle of the top border and then drag the border upward to add more space above the image. Click the **Undo** button on the Quick Access Toolbar.

10. With the clip art object still selected, click the **Crop** button arrow and then point to **Crop to Shape**. Under Basic Shapes, click the **Oval** shape. The image is trimmed to fit within the selected shape. However, depending on the clip art you chose, you may not notice a change. Experiment with cropping to other shapes.

11. Click the **Undo** button arrow and undo all Change Shape edits.

12. In the Size group, note the graphic dimensions for height and width. With the clip art object still selected:

    a. Click the **Crop** button arrow, and then point to **Aspect Ratio**. Under Square, click **1:1**. When you change aspect ratio, the image height and width dimensions change.

    b. With the clip art object still selected, click the **Crop** button arrow and then click **Fit**. The image is adjusted to fit within the new dimensions. However, depending on the clip art you chose, you may not see a change.

13. Use your new understanding of the tools to experiment with various aspect ratio settings, fitting and filling, and new shapes to find a format that works with your clip art. Use the Reset Picture & Size command to start over. When you are satisfied with the results, click the **Crop** button to toggle off the cropping feature.

14. Save the changes and leave the presentation open for the next Step-by-Step.

EXTRA FOR EXPERTS

To crop or outcrop two sides equally at the same time, press and hold CTRL as you drag one of the center cropping handles. The opposite side will also be cropped. To crop or outcrop all four sides equally at the same time, press and hold CTRL as you drag a corner cropping handle.

Resizing, Repositioning, and Changing Graphics

You have several options for resizing a graphic such as a clip art illustration or a picture. The simplest way is to drag one of the selection handles in the direction you want to resize. When resized this way, the graphic does not necessarily maintain its original proportions. You can distort the graphic using this method—which you might want to do to make a particular point. You can enable a setting so that when you adjust the graphic size using a corner sizing handle, the aspect ratio of the graphic is maintained. Sizing a graphic to exact proportions is referred to as *scaling*. You can enter a specific height or width for the graphic, or you can specify a percentage reduction or enlargement for the graphic.

To reposition an object on a slide, you can drag the object to a new location. To achieve a more precise location for the graphic, you can nudge the object. *Nudging* is moving an object vertically or horizontally in small increments. With the object selected, you press one of the arrow keys to move the object. To move in even smaller increments, hold down the Ctrl key as you press the arrow keys.

If you are not satisfied with a picture that was inserted from a file, you can easily replace the picture using the Change Picture button.

▶ **VOCABULARY**

scaling

nudging

Step-by-Step 7.2

1. If necessary, open the **Revised Happy Tails 1** file from your solution files. Save the presentation as **Revised Happy Tails 2**, followed by your initials.

2. If necessary, go to slide 2 and select the clip art object. Position the mouse pointer over the upper-right corner handle. When the pointer changes to a diagonal double-arrow ⤢ , drag the corner handle upward and to the right to enlarge the graphic. Then drag the upper-left corner downward and to the right to reduce the graphic size. When you drag a corner handle, the image is resized proportionally.

3. Position the mouse pointer over the middle handle on the top border and drag the border down. Notice that as you drag the border, the height of the picture changes but the width remains the same. The image is no longer proportional. Click the **Undo** button.

4. In the Size group, click the **Dialog Box Launcher** to open the Format Picture dialog box, as shown in **Figure 7–6**. Your settings will differ, depending on the clip art you chose and how you resized the image.

FIGURE 7–6
Format Picture dialog box

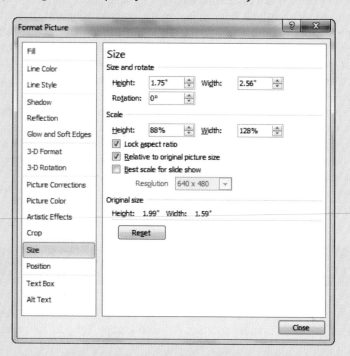

5. Under Scale, make sure the option Lock aspect ratio is enabled. Under Size and rotate, increase the height settings a few increments. Note that as you change the height setting, the width setting automatically adjusts to keep the original proportion of the image. Click **Close**.

6. In the Adjust group, click the **Reset Picture** button arrow and then click **Reset Picture & Size**.

7. Right-click the **clip art** object, and then click **Size and Position** to open the Format Picture dialog box.

8. Disable the option **Lock aspect ratio**. Under Scale, change the Height setting to **75%**. The height size and scale settings both change, but the width settings do not change. Then enable the option **Lock aspect ratio**. Under Original Size, click **Reset**. Close the dialog box. No changes are made to the clip art. Center the clip art object.

9. Go to slide 3. In the placeholder on the right, click the **Insert Picture from File** icon [icon]. The Insert Picture dialog box opens. Navigate to the drive and folder where your Data Files are stored. Select the **Taffy.jpg** file, and then click **Insert**.

10. The picture is inserted on the slide. The picture object is selected and the Picture Tools Format tab appears. In the Size group, change the Shape Height to **3"**, as shown in **Figure 7–7**. Because the aspect ratio is locked, the width will automatically adjust.

FIGURE 7–7
Size group on the Picture Tools
Format tab

11. Drag the picture object upward to align it with the top border of the placeholder on the left. With the picture object still selected, press the **right arrow** key a few times to nudge the object. Then press and hold **Ctrl** and press the **right arrow** key a few times. The image moves in smaller increments.

12. In the placeholder on the left, click the **Insert Picture from File** icon. If necessary, navigate to the drive and folder where your Data Files are stored. Select the **Charlie.jpg** file, and then click **Insert**. You realize you inserted the wrong picture. The Ribbon already displays the Picture Tools Format tab. In the Adjust group, click the **Change Picture** button ![icon]. Select the **Cuddles.jpg** file, and then click **Insert**. The Charlie picture is replaced with the Cuddles picture.

13. The Cuddles picture is wider than the Taffy picture. Resize and reposition the picture:

    a. Crop the left and right edges of the picture so that the image is approximately 3.6" wide.

    b. With the image selected, in the Size group, click the **Dialog Box Launcher**. Disable the **Lock aspect ratio** option, and then click **Close**.

    c. In the Size group, change the dimensions so that the height is **3"** and the width is **3.48"** (the exact dimensions of the Taffy picture).

    d. Click the **Crop** button to toggle off the cropping feature.

    e. Reposition the cat and dog images side by side on the slide.

14. Save the changes and leave the presentation open for the next Step-by-Step.

EXTRA FOR EXPERTS

To crop or outcrop a graphic to exact dimensions, click the Format Picture Tools tab, and then click the Size group Dialog Box Launcher. In the Format Picture dialog box, click Crop in the left pane, and then enter exact dimensions.

Recoloring Graphics and Shapes

You are not limited to the original colors of a clip art or picture. You can customize a graphic by changing the image colors to match the other colors in the current design theme. You can choose from a large palette of colors or even create your own custom color scheme.

When you add shapes to a slide, you can customize the shape formats with fills, outlines, and effects. After applying custom formats, you can set the shape formatting as the default, so that the next time you insert a shape in the presentation, all of the custom formats will be applied to the new shape. The settings for a default shape are only saved with the current presentation.

Step-by-Step 7.3

1. If necessary, open the **Revised Happy Tails 2** file from your solution files. Save the presentation as **Revised Happy Tails 3**, followed by your initials.

2. Click the **Design** tab. In the Themes group, click the **More** button and then select the **Technic** theme. (*Hint*: The themes are arranged in alphabetical order, and Technic is a built-in theme.)

3. If necessary, go to slide 3. Select the **Taffy (dog) picture** object. Click the **Picture Tools Format** tab. In the Adjust group, click the **Color** button to show the color options, as shown in **Figure 7–8**. (When the image has a background color, such as the Taffy picture, you see more options.)

FIGURE 7–8
Color options for picture

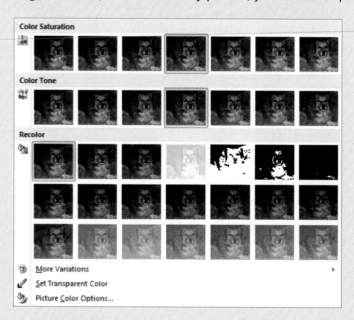

4. Under Recolor, hover the mouse pointer over the options to preview the different colors. The colors offered for recoloring are consistent with those in the current color scheme.

5. Point to the menu option **More Variations** to show the color palette. Move the mouse pointer over the colors to preview some of the theme colors. (You'll be able to see part of the picture behind the palette.) Select any color in the palette to change the image color.

6. In the Adjust group, click the **Reset Picture** button to restore the original picture colors.

7. Go to slide 4. Click the **Clip Art** icon in the placeholder on the right. In the Clip Art task pane, search for another illustration of a dog. Choose an image that shows a background color, such as the image shown in **Figure 7–9**. Close the Clip Art task pane.

FIGURE 7–9
Clip art illustration with
background color

8. With the clip art object selected on the slide, in the Adjust group, click the **Color** button. At the bottom of the menu, click **Set Transparent Color**. The mouse pointer changes to a pen ✐. Click anywhere in the color background. The background is no longer visible. (If the image has more than one background color, only one of the colors will become transparent.)

9. In the placeholder on the left, click the **Clip Art** icon. Search for and insert an illustration of a cat. Remove the color background, if necessary. Close the Clip Art task pane.

10. Adjust the height of both images so that the images are about the same size. Because of the image backgrounds, the heights may differ. Position the images side by side in the center of the slide. Recolor the images applying the **Aqua, Accent color 1 Dark** color.

11. Go to slide 3. Click the **Insert** tab. In the Illustrations group, click **Shapes**, and then under Callouts, click the **Cloud Callout** shape. Insert a callout shape in the upper-right corner of the slide (connected to the top of the dog's head), and then, in the callout shape, type **Woof!**.

12. Click the **Drawing Tools Format** tab. In the Shape Styles group, click the **Shape Fill** button arrow, point to **Texture**, and then click the **Woven mat** texture. Click the **Shape Outline** button arrow. Under Theme Colors, click the **White**, **Text 1** theme color. Click the **Shape Outline** button arrow again, point to **Weight**, and then click **2¼ pt**.

13. Right-click the callout shape and in the shortcut menu, click **Set as Default Shape**. Click the **Insert** tab and then click the **Shapes** button. Under Basic Shapes, select the **Heart** shape. Draw a heart shape below the Cuddles (cat) picture. The default formats are applied to the new shape. Type **Meow!**.

14. Save the changes and leave the presentation open for the next Step-by-Step.

> **TIP**
>
> Text fonts and shape effects are also saved with the default shape settings.

Inserting Animated Clip Art

You can also add animated clip art to a slide. One of the media type options in the Clip Art gallery is videos. The clip art videos are GIF (Graphics Interchange Format) files. GIF is a file format that supports animation. The animated GIF files can be inserted using the same process as inserting clip art illustrations.

TIP

You can easily insert clip art of any type (graphics or animated GIFs) that is stored on an accessible disk or server (rather than in the Clip Organizer). To insert clip art stored as a file, click the Insert tab. In the Images group, click the Insert Picture from File button, then navigate to the drive and folder where the file is stored, select the filename, and click Insert.

Once an animated clip art video has been inserted, you can resize it and position it on the slide, but you cannot edit the image as you would other clip art. To modify an animated image, you need to use a program designed especially for creating animated images. Animated clip art images play during a presentation, but unless you apply an animation effect, they do not play in Normal view.

As you apply animations to objects, the animations are numbered in sequence. You can rearrange the order of the animations in the Animation Pane. When you change the order, the animation numbers are automatically updated to reflect the new sequence. You can also add sound effects to slide transitions and animations to "make noise" as the objects and slides appear, such as an applause or the sound of a camera click.

Step-by-Step 7.4

1. If necessary, open the **Revised Happy Tails 3** file from your solution files. Save the presentation as **Revised Happy Tails 4**, followed by your initials.

2. Go to slide 5. Click the **Insert** tab. In the Images group, click the **Clip Art** button to open the Clip Art task pane.

3. In the Search for text box, type **clock**. Click the **Results should be** list arrow and enable the option **Videos**. Disable all other media file type options and click the **list arrow** to close the menu. Make sure the Include Office.com content option is enabled.

4. Click **Go**. When the search results are displayed, scroll through them and select a thumbnail similar to the one shown in **Figure 7–10**. The small icon in the lower-right corner indicates that the clip art image is animated.

FIGURE 7–10
Clip art video with animation icon

Animation icon

5. Note that the animation for the image does not preview in the task pane or in Normal view. Click the **Slide Show** button in the status bar to view the animation. Note that the animation plays automatically.

6. Press **Esc** to switch to Normal view. If you are not satisfied with your selection, delete the object and select another thumbnail from the Clip Art task pane. When you are satisfied with the animated image you have inserted on the slide, close the Clip Art task pane.

7. Resize the image so that it is approximately 2.5" high (or an appropriate height for your chosen image). Reposition the clip art object to the right of the bulleted list.

8. The clip art object should still be selected. Click the **Animations** tab. In the Animation group, click the **More** button. Under Entrance, click the **Fade** entrance effect. The animation previews, and the number *6* appears to the left of the clip art object on the slide.

9. Select the clip art object. In the Advanced Animation group, click the **Animation Pane** button. The Animation Pane opens and the new animation appears at the end of the list (#6), labeled Picture, followed by a number. If necessary, click the Expand button ⟨⟩ to show all animated objects.

10. In the Animation Pane, drag the new Picture animation and position it between animations 1 and 2, as shown in **Figure 7–11**.

FIGURE 7–11
Animated objects for slide 5 after reorganization

11. Click the **list arrow** for the new Picture animation, and then click **Start With Previous**.

12. Click the **list arrow** for the new Picture animation again, and then click **Effect Options**. Under Enhancements, click the **Sound** list arrow. Scroll down and click **Chime**. Click the **Audio** button to the right of the Sound text box to show the Volume setting. Do not make any changes. Click **OK**. A preview of the audio sound plays.

13. At the top of the Animation Pane, click **Play** to preview the animations. The preview is usually quick. Click the **Slide Show** button and preview the content on the slide, clicking through the animations. When the last bulleted item is displayed (*Cats live up to 20 years*), press **Esc** to return to Normal view.

14. Close the Animation Pane. Save the changes and leave the presentation open for the next Step-by-Step.

Understanding Graphics File Formats

Graphics files can be saved in many different formats. A *raster graphics* image, which is also referred to as a *bitmap*, consists of rows of tiny colored dots called *pixels* (short for picture elements) or *bits* that compose the image on a computer screen. Raster graphics open quickly, but when you enlarge a raster graphic, the dots are spread over the area and the image can lose definition. A *vector graphics* image consists of lines, curves, and shapes. Vector graphics take more time to open, but when you increase and decrease the image size the clarity of the image will not change. Vector graphic formats are typically used when creating documents to be sent to a printer.

▶ **VOCABULARY**
raster graphics

bitmap

pixels

bits

vector graphics

EXTRA FOR EXPERTS

Another alternative to reduce the file size is to link the picture files to the presentation so they are not saved with the presentation. The photo files must be stored on the same computer when running the presentation. To link the file, click the Insert tab and then click the Picture button. Navigate to the drive and folder where the file is stored. Click the Insert list arrow and then click Link to File.

The size of a picture file in kilobytes (or even megabytes) depends on the file format. JPEG images, for example, tend to be smaller files than TIFF images. The graphic size is also affected by the resolution. The resolution is determined by the number of pixels. The resolution size is frequently referred to as dpi (dots per inch) or ppi (pixels per inch). The higher the number of pixels, the higher the resolution.

Table 7–1 provides information about several graphics file formats that are compatible with PowerPoint.

TABLE 7–1   Graphics file formats

FILE FORMAT	FILE EXTENSION	DESCRIPTION
Bitmap (BMP)	.bmp	This raster graphic format can display millions of colors and is commonly used because it is compatible with several programs. The image quality is retained through numerous saves.
Graphics Interchange Format (GIF)	.gif	This raster graphic format supports animation and transparent background, and it is compatible with almost all Web browsers. Because it is limited to supporting 256 colors, it is good for illustrations, line drawings, and black and white images. Quality of the image is not lost when the file is decompressed, and the image quality is retained through numerous saves.
Joint Photographic Experts Group (JPEG)	.jpg	This raster graphic format can be used for high-quality photos and complex graphics containing millions of colors. It can compress photos into very compact files, so it is commonly used on Web pages and it is useful when sending images via e-mail.
Portable Network Graphics (PNG)	.png	This raster graphic format can display millions of colors, and it is commonly used on Web pages. The format does support transparent background, but unlike GIF, it does not support animation. Quality of the image is not lost when the file is decompressed, and the image quality is retained through numerous saves.
Tag Image File Format (TIFF)	.tif	This raster graphic format can display millions of colors, allows any resolution, and is compatible with many programs. Because it can produce very high-quality images, it is often used in publishing. The file sizes are typically larger than GIF or JPEG formats. This format is best for storing bitmapped images on personal computers. The image quality is retained through numerous saves.
Windows Metafile (WMF)	.wmf	This vector graphic format was designed to be portable between Office applications such as Word, PowerPoint, and Publisher. The format is compatible with both 16- and 32-bit Windows operating systems.
Enhanced Metafile (EMF)	.emf	This vector graphic format is a newer 32-bit version of the Windows Metafile format. The newer version supports more drawing features.

Modifying Pictures and Digital Images

You can use options on the Picture Tools Format tab to adjust the way the picture looks. PowerPoint provides several commands for removing the background, changing the picture colors, adding artistic effects, and formatting borders. The Soften options enable you to remove unwanted marks on a picture, and the Sharpen options enable you to enhance the picture details. The Contrast controls enable you to clarify elements by adjusting the darkest and lightest areas of a picture, and the Brightness controls enable you to adjust the relative lightness of the picture.

Step-by-Step 7.5

1. Open the **Revised Happy Tails 4** file from your solution files. Save the presentation as **Revised Happy Tails 5**, followed by your initials.

2. Go to slide 6. Click the **Insert** tab. In the Images group, click the **Insert Picture from File** button to open the Insert Picture dialog box. Navigate to the drive and folder where your Data Files are stored. Select the file **Kylie.jpg**, and then click **Insert**. The picture is inserted in the slide and most likely covers the entire slide.

3. On the Picture Tools Format tab, in the Size group, change the height to **4"**. Then reposition the picture object in the lower-right corner of the slide.

4. With the picture object still selected, in the Adjust group, click the **Remove Background** button. The picture background changes to a violet color, and the Background Removal tab appears. In the Close group, click the **Keep Changes** button.

5. In the Adjust group, click the **Corrections** button to display the picture corrections options shown in **Figure 7–12**.

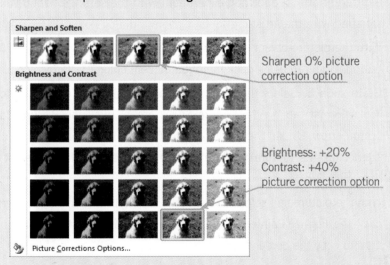

Sharpen 0% picture correction option

Brightness: +20%
Contrast: +40%
picture correction option

FIGURE 7–12
Corrections options

6. Under Sharpen and Soften, position the mouse pointer over the first option to preview the **Soften: 50%** effect. Then, position the mouse pointer over the last option in the same row, **Sharpen 50%**, to preview the effect. (The Sharpen 0% option should still be enabled.)

7. If necessary, click the Corrections button to display the picture correction options. Under Brightness and Contrast, click the **Brightness: +20% Contrast: +40%** picture correction option, the fourth option in the last row. (See Figure 7-12.)

8. With the picture object still selected, in the Adjust group, click the **Artistic Effects** button to display the options shown in **Figure 7–13**.

FIGURE 7–13
Artistic effects options

Light Screen effect

9. Position the mouse pointer over several of the options to preview the various effects. Click the **Light Screen** effect, as shown in Figure 7–13.

10. With the picture object still selected, click the **Artistic Effects** button again. At the bottom of the menu, click **Artistic Effects Options**. The Format Picture dialog box opens. If necessary, reposition the dialog box on the screen so you can see the picture. The same artistic effects options are available, but here you can tweak the settings by changing the transparency and the grid size. Experiment with the settings.

11. In the Format Picture dialog box, click the **Artistic Effect** button, choose a different effect, and then experiment with the settings. When you are satisfied with the artistic effects, close the dialog box.

12. With the picture object still selected, in the Adjust group, click the **Color** button. Under Recolor, click the **Aqua, Accent color 1 Dark** recolor option.

13. Go to slide 3. Select the picture on the left and then click the **Picture Tools Format** tab. In the Picture Styles group, click the **Picture Border** button arrow. Under Theme Colors, click the **Aqua, Accent 1** theme color. Then click the **Picture Border** button arrow again. Point to **Weight** and then click **3 pt**.

14. With the picture still selected, click the **Home** tab. In the Clipboard group, click the **Format Painter** button. Click anywhere inside the photo on the right to copy the border format.

15. Save the changes and leave the presentation open for the next Step-by-Step.

Converting Objects to a SmartArt Graphic

Once clip art images are added to a slide, you can convert the graphics to be included in a SmartArt object; and then of course, you can animate the objects in the SmartArt diagram. You can also convert shapes and WordArt objects to a SmartArt object.

Step-by-Step 7.6

1. If necessary, open the **Revised Happy Tails 5** file from your solution files. Save the presentation as **Revised Happy Tails 6**, followed by your initials.

2. Go to slide 4. Select the cat clip art object, press and hold **Ctrl**, and then select the dog clip art object. Both images should be selected, and the Picture Tools Format tab is displayed.

3. Click the **Picture Tools Format** tab. In the Picture Styles group, click the **Picture Layout** button to display the layout options, as shown in **Figure 7–14**.

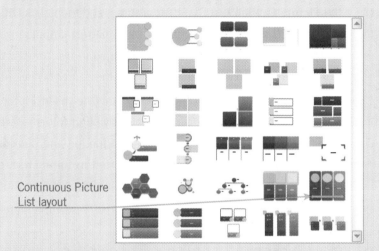

Continuous Picture List layout

FIGURE 7–14
Picture Layout options

4. Click the **Continuous Picture List** layout, as shown in Figure 7–14. The SmartArt graphic is inserted on the slide, and the clip art images are positioned in the picture placeholders within the SmartArt graphic. In the first text placeholder, type **$650**. In the second text placeholder, type **$1,000**.

5. Select the SmartArt object. The SmartArt Tools Design tab is displayed. In the Layouts group, click the **More** button. Click the **Vertical Picture Accent List** layout. Resize the SmartArt diagram so it is approximately 4" high, and center the graphic below the last line of text.

6. Go to slide 7. In the placeholder, click the **Insert SmartArt Graphic** icon to open the Choose a SmartArt Graphic dialog box. In the left

pane, click **Picture** to display the SmartArt graphic picture options, as shown in **Figure 7–15**.

FIGURE 7–15
Choose a SmartArt
Graphic dialog box

Picture Caption
List SmartArt graphic

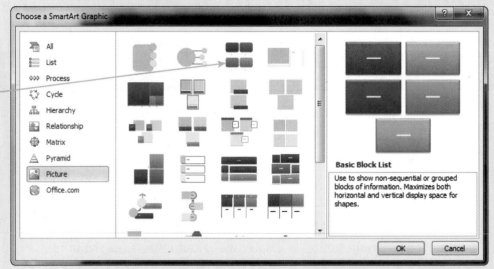

7. Click the **Picture Caption List** SmartArt graphic, and then click **OK**. Drag the center handle on the right border for the SmartArt graphic inward to reduce the width so the four objects are arranged in two rows, with two objects in each row. Reposition the graphic in the center of the slide.

8. Click the icon in the first object of the diagram. The Insert Picture dialog box opens. If necessary, navigate to the drive and folder where your Data Files are stored. Select the picture file **Blue.jpg** and click **Insert**. The picture is automatically resized and inserted in the picture placeholder. Click the **Text** placeholder below the picture, and type **Blue**.

9. Click the icon in the second object in the first row. Insert the picture file **Taffy.jpg**. Click the icon in the first object in the second row and insert the picture file **Charlie.jpg**. Insert the picture file **Cuddles.jpg** in the last object. Type the names in the caption placeholders below each picture.

10. With the SmartArt graphic selected, click the **Animations** tab. In the Animation group, click the **More** button. Under Entrance, click the **Split** entrance effect.

11. In the Animation group, click the **Effect Options** button and then, under Direction, click **Vertical Out**. A preview of the revised animation plays.

12. Click the **Effect Options** button again, and then, under Sequence, click **One by One**. A preview of the revised animation plays.

13. Go to slide 1. Click the **Slide Show** button in the status bar and review the presentation slides. When you have reviewed the animations on all slides, press **Esc** to return to Normal view.

14. Save the changes and close the presentation.

Creating a Photo Album

The Photo Album feature creates a new presentation for a group of pictures. After you identify the pictures to be included in the photo album, the pictures are arranged on individual slides. You can choose the number of pictures to show on each slide. Photo album templates with preformatted slide borders and picture placeholders are also available at Office.com, or you can create your own template using special effects including themes, transitions, colorful backgrounds, and specific layouts. You can easily rearrange the order of the slides, add captions to the pictures on the slides, format all pictures in black and white, and add frames around the pictures. To provide information about the photos, you can insert text boxes between slides.

You can enhance the appearance of the photos by adjusting the brightness and contrast. You can also recolor the photos and apply artistic effects. If necessary, you can rotate a photo to change from landscape orientation to portrait orientation.

> **TIP**
>
> PowerPoint provides several sample photo album templates that provide a variety of slide layouts for positioning photos. To access the sample templates, click the File tab, and then click New. Under Available Templates and Themes, click the Sample templates icon.

Step-by-Step 7.7

1. If necessary, open a new blank presentation. Click the **Insert** tab. In the Images group, click the **New Photo Album** button. The Photo Album dialog box opens, as shown in **Figure 7–16**.

FIGURE 7–16
Photo Album dialog box

2. Under Insert picture from, click **File/Disk**. The Insert New Pictures dialog box opens. If necessary, navigate to the drive and folder where your Data Files are stored. Select the following filenames: (*Hint*: Click the first file-name, press and hold **Ctrl**, and then click the remaining filenames.)

   A perfect catch!.jpg

   Focus.jpg

   Let's play!.jpg

   Nap time.jpg

   Run fast.jpg

3. When the five files are selected, click **Insert**.

4. Select options to format the album:

   a. Under Album Layout, click the **Picture layout** list arrow and then click **1 picture**. A preview is displayed at the right.

   b. Under Picture Options, enable the option **Captions below ALL pictures**. The picture filename will appear in the caption.

   c. Enable the option **ALL pictures black and white**. The Preview pane adapts to show the new format. Disable the option to restore the photos to the original colors.

   d. Click the **Frame shape** list arrow, and then click **Rounded Rectangle**. A preview is displayed at the right. Click the **Frame shape** list arrow again, and then click **Simple Frame, White**.

   e. Next to the Theme box, click **Browse** to open the Choose Theme dialog box. The themes saved on your computer are listed. Scroll down and select **Pushpin.thmx**, and then click **Select**.

   f. When your settings match those shown in **Figure 7–17**, click **Create**.

FIGURE 7–17
Photo Album dialog box with new settings

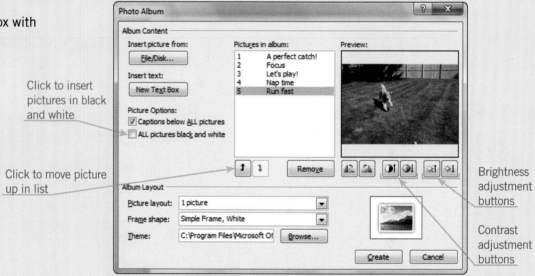

Click to insert pictures in black and white

Click to move picture up in list

Brightness adjustment buttons

Contrast adjustment buttons

5. Save the presentation as **Pet Photo Album**, followed by your initials.

6. On slide 1, select the text in the title placeholder and type **Love me....** Then press **Enter** and type **Love my dog**. If necessary, edit the name under the title to show your name.

7. Go to slide 2. Note that because of the theme graphic (the pushpin background), the captions do not fit well on all of the slides. To edit the album formats, click the **Insert** tab. In the Images group, click the **New Photo Album** button arrow and then click **Edit Photo Album**. The Edit Photo Album dialog box opens.

8. Make the following changes:

   a. Under Album Layout, click **Browse**, scroll down and select **Hardcover.thmx**, then click **Select**.

b. Under Insert picture from, click **File/Disk**. Select the picture file **Kylie.jpg**, and then click **Insert**. Under Pictures in album, the new picture is selected at the bottom of the list.

c. Under the Preview pane, click the **Rotate Right** button ![icon]. The photo rotates to a portrait layout in the Preview pane. Click the **Rotate Left** button to return the photo to the default landscape orientation.

d. Under the Preview pane, click each of the **Contrast** buttons ![icon] ![icon] as shown in Figure 7–17. The adjustments appear in the Preview pane. Also under the Preview pane, click each of the **Brightness** buttons ![icon] ![icon], as shown in Figure 7–17, and observe the adjustments in the Preview pane.

e. Under the Pictures in album list, click the **Up** arrow five times to move the *Kylie* picture to the top of the list. Use the up and down arrow buttons to rearrange the list in the following order:

Kylie

Let's play!

Focus

A perfect catch!

Run fast

Nap time

f. Under Pictures in album, select the fifth picture, **Run fast**. Under Insert text, click **New Text Box**. The list now shows seven items (six photos and a text box).

9. Click **Update**. Go to slide 7. Select the text in the placeholder and type **After a long day of retrieving the ball…**.

10. Go to slide 2. Select the picture on the slide. Click the **Picture Tools Format** tab. In the Picture Styles group, click the **More** button. In the third row, click the **Snip Diagonal Corner, White** picture style.

11. With the picture selected, in the Picture Styles group, click the **Picture Effects** button and then point to **Shadow**. Under Outer, in the second row, click **Offset Center**.

12. Select the caption text **Kylie** and change the font size to **40 point**. Note that the shadow effect is also applied to the caption text. Drag the caption text box down to position it a little lower below the picture.

TIP

You can also add new photos to the album by inserting new slides and then inserting the pictures on the new slides.

TIP

If you are unable to change the font size, right-click the text box and click Format Shape. In the left pane, click Text Box, and under Autofit, select the Do not Autofit option.

13. Select the picture. Click the **Picture Tools Format** tab. In the Adjust group, click the **Compress Pictures** button ▣. The Compress Pictures dialog box opens, as shown in **Figure 7-18**. Under Compression options, disable the option **Apply only to this picture**. Note that you can also choose to delete the cropped area of the picture. Under Target output, you can select options for Print, Screen (good for Web pages), and E-mail. Leave the target settings as is and click **OK**.

FIGURE 7–18
Compress Pictures dialog box

Disable this option

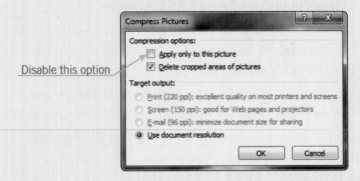

14. Save the changes and leave the presentation open for the next Step-by-Step.

Saving a Presentation as a Video

You can turn a photo album presentation into a video, or you can apply settings so that the presentation is self-running. Then you can share photos with others by publishing the photo album on the Web, saving it to a DVD, or attaching it to an e-mail. And, of course, you can also print the slides. If you add a lot of high-resolution pictures to a presentation, the file size will grow and the photos may take longer to open in the presentation. If you need to e-mail the presentation file, the file size may be too big. To reduce the file size, you can compress one or all of the pictures.

Once created, you can save the photo album (or any presentation file) as a video in a .wmv format. You can then burn the file to a DVD so you can play the video in a DVD player or play it in the default media player installed on a computer.

Step-by-Step 7.8

1. If necessary, open the **Pet Photo Album** file from your solution files.

2. Go to slide 1. Click the **Transitions** tab. In the Transition to This Slide group, click the **More** button. Under Exciting, click the **Flip** transition. A preview of the transition plays.

3. In the Timing group, note the Advance Slide setting is set for On Mouse Click. Click the **Apply To All** button. It does not appear that any changes are made to the existing slide or to any other slides, but the transition is now applied to all the slides.

4. Click the **File** tab and then click **Save & Send**. In the center pane, under File Types, click **Create a Video** to display the Save & Send options, as shown in **Figure 7–19**.

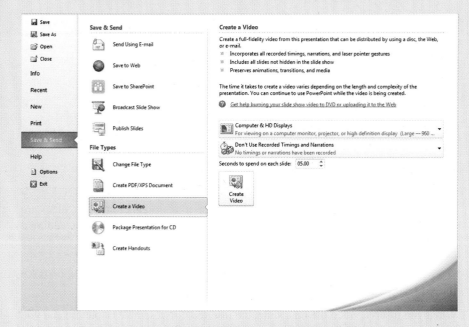

FIGURE 7–19
Save & Send options in Backstage view

5. In the right pane, click the **Computer & HD Displays** button to display additional video format options, as shown in **Figure 7–20**.

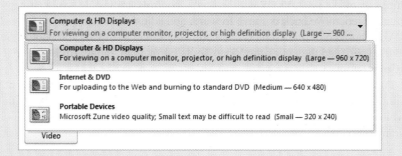

FIGURE 7–20
Video format options

6. Click **Portable Devices.**

7. Note that if timings or narrations had been recorded on the slides, you could choose to exclude them from the video.

8. Change the Seconds to spend on each slide setting to **04.00**.

9. Click the **Create Video** button. The Save As dialog box opens. Navigate to the drive and folder where your solution files are saved. The file type is already set for Windows Media Video (*.wmv), and you do not need to change the filename.

10. Click **Save** and wait for the saving process to complete. It may take a few minutes. The progress status will display in the status bar. When the file conversion is complete, the status message closes.

11. Click the **Start** button, click **Computer**, and then navigate to the drive and folder where your solution files are stored. Locate and then double-click the **Pet Photo Album.wmv** filename. The file will open in the default media player.

12. If necessary, click the **Play/Pause** button and enjoy the video! Note that the transitions occur automatically.

13. When the video stops playing, close the video and the media player window.

14. Close the presentation file without saving the changes.

Working with Video and Sound Clips

Video and sound clips can add an extra dimension to a presentation. Most slides are rather static, so you can make an audience really sit up and take notice by adding a sound object or including a video clip.

Inserting and Editing a Video Clip

When you insert a video file on a slide, the inserted clip resembles a picture and you can resize, move, recolor, and adjust contrast to the video object just as you would a picture. You can also apply a style to the video object on the slide.

You can also format the video to play automatically, and you can choose to show or hide the media controls. When the media controls are visible, you can pause or stop the video, move back or move forward, and adjust the volume.

You can recolor and correct video clips the same as clip art and photos. Select the video clip, and then click the Video Tools Format tab. In the Adjust group, click the Color button.

PowerPoint supports several video formats. *Streaming video* is media sent in a continuous flow of data that can be played from an online source without waiting to download the file. If you have a fast Internet connection, you can stream live video to your computer.

▶ **VOCABULARY**
streaming video

ETHICS IN TECHNOLOGY

You can find pictures and other multimedia objects on the Internet, and computers make it easy to copy or download those files. Often people think that information published on the Internet is in the public domain and free, but that is not always the case. Someone owns the rights to those pictures and media files, and intellectual property law ensures that the owner of the content is entitled to copyright protection. Before you download or copy something from the Internet, consider how you will use the content. For example, you can copy or download any clip art image in the Microsoft Office Clip Art and Media Library without permission and free of charge when you use the images in your own work. However, there are restrictions that prohibit you using the images in a product that you sell. If you are not sure about how you can use the content, check with the owner.

Table 7–2 provides information about the video file formats that are compatible with PowerPoint.

TABLE 7–2   Video file formats

FILE FORMAT	FILE EXTENSION	DESCRIPTION
Advanced Systems Format (ASF)	.asf	This format can be used to stream audio and video content, images, and script commands over a network.
Audio Video Interleave (AVI)	.avi	This is a common format because audio and video content is compressed.
Moving Picture Experts Group (MPEG)	.mpg or .mpeg	This format is often used for creating downloadable movies. It is a common format for videos published on the Internet.
Windows Media Video (WMV)	.wmv	This format is used for both streaming and downloading from the Internet. The format compresses audio and video and requires minimal storage space. To play the format on a non-Windows computer, an extra application must be installed.

PowerPoint offers playback features for videos. After you insert the video on a slide, you can trim the video clip to include only the content relevant to the presentation. Trimming the video clip not only saves time when showing the presentation, but it also reduces the file size. You can choose to zoom to a full-screen view of the video, loop the video so it continues to replay, rewind the video when finished, hide the object when it's not playing, and set the video volume.

When saving a presentation that includes an embedded video, you can reduce the file size and also improve playback performance by compressing the media files. PowerPoint provides three options: Presentation Quality, Internet Quality, and Low Quality. Choosing the right option is important, because the compression might affect the media quality.

EXTRA FOR EXPERTS

Video clips can be quite large and consequently take up a lot of storage space. To reduce the presentation file size, you can create links instead of embedding the videos. When a video is linked in a presentation, the video file must be stored on the same computer when you show the presentation. For best results, save the video clips in the same folder as the presentation file.

Step-by-Step 7.9

1. Open the **Revised Happy Tails 6** file from your solution files. Save the presentation as **Revised Happy Tails 7**, followed by your initials.

2. Go to slide 2. Select the clip art object, and then press **Delete**. In the placeholder, click the **Insert Media Clip** icon. The Insert Video dialog box opens. Navigate to the drive and folder where your Data Files are stored. Select the video file **Frisbee fun.wmv**, and then click **Insert**. An image of the video is inserted on the slide.

3. The media controls appear in the bar below the video object. Click the **Play/Pause** button to preview the video.

4. Click the **Video Tools Playback** tab. In the Editing group, click the **Trim Video** button to open the Trim Video dialog box, as shown in **Figure 7–21**. Your dialog box will differ.

FIGURE 7–21
Trim Video dialog box

Start time

Start and End bars

End time

5. Drag the **Start bar** to the right to advance to approximately 1½ seconds into the video clip. The time displays above the bar and in the Start Time box below the bar. (You can also trim the end time.) When your dialog box settings are similar to those shown in Figure 7–21, click **OK**.

6. The video object should still be selected. In the Editing group, under Fade Duration, change the Fade In setting to **2.00**. Change the Fade Out setting to **1.00**.

7. Go to slide 1. Click the **Slide Show** tab. In the Set Up group, make sure the Show Media Controls option is enabled. Click the **Slide Show** button in the status bar. Click once to advance to slide 2. Note that the video clip appears, but the video will not start until you position the mouse pointer over the image to show the media controls and then click the Play button. Press **Esc** to return to Normal view.

8. Select the video object. Click the **Video Tools Playback** tab. In the Video Options group, click the **Start** list arrow and then click **Automatically**. Enable the **Hide While Not Playing** option.

9. Click the **Animations** tab. In the Timing group, note that the Start box is empty because the video will start automatically. Change the Delay setting to **2.00**. There will be a 2-second delay before the video begins to play.

10. Go to slide 1. Click the **Slide Show** button in the status bar. Then click to advance to slide 2. Wait, and the video clip will start playing automatically. When the video ends, the clip will disappear. Press **Esc** to switch to Normal view.

11. To add special effects and formats, select the video object. Click the **Video Tools Format** tab and do the following:

    a. In the Video Styles group, click the **More** button. Under Intense, in the third row, click the **Metal Rounded Rectangle** video style.

    b. In the Video Styles group, click the **Video Effects** button and then point to **3-D Rotation**. Under Perspective, select **Perspective Right**.

    c. In the Adjust group, click the **Color** button and select a color option. Click the **Color** button again and then click **Video Color Options**. In the Format Video dialog box, click **Reset** to restore the video to its original color. Click **Close**.

    d. In the Size group, change the height setting to **6**. Reposition the video object in the center of the slide, on top of the title placeholder.

    e. The video object should still be selected. In the Arrange group, click the **Send Backward** button. Then select the title placeholder and position it at the top of the video object and inside the video object border.

12. Select the video object again, and then click the **Video Tools Playback** tab. In the Video Options group, click the **Volume** button, and then click **Mute**. In the Preview group, click the **Play** button to preview the video, which now plays without any sound.

13. Click the **File** tab and then click the **Compress Media** button. In the submenu, click **Internet Quality**. The Compress Media dialog box will open and show the file status. When the compression process is complete, close the Compress Media dialog box.

14. Save the changes and leave the presentation open for the next Step-by-Step.

Inserting a Sound Object

Sound objects can add interesting effects to slides, and adding a sound object is as easy as adding clip art or a picture. If you have downloaded sounds from Microsoft's Online Clip Art and Media Web site, they will appear in the Clip Art task pane. If you have an audio file that you can access on a disk or server, use the Insert Audio command on the Ribbon to locate and insert the sound.

Table 7–3 provides information about the audio file formats that are compatible with PowerPoint.

TABLE 7–3   Audio file formats

FILE FORMAT	FILE EXTENSION	DESCRIPTION
Audio Interchange File Format (AIFF)	.aiff	This high-quality format is commonly used to burn audio CDs. Files are not compressed and, therefore, can be large. The files are commonly used on Macintosh systems.
Audio File Format (AU)	.au	The format is typically used to create sound files for UNIX computers or the Web.
Musical Instrument Digital Interface (MIDI)	.mid or .midi	This is a standard format for interchanging musical information between musical instruments, synthesizers, and computers.
MPEG Audio Layer 3 (MP3)	.mp3	This compressed format is commonly used to store music files and audiobooks on computers and portable devices.
Waveform Audio File Format (WAV)	.wav	This format saves sounds as waveforms (an image that represents an audio signal or recording) and is commonly used on Windows-based computers.

A sound file is inserted on the current slide as an icon. You can test a sound without running the presentation by double-clicking the audio icon in Normal view. You can choose to play the sound automatically or when triggered by a click. If you choose to play the sound automatically, you can arrange the objects so that the audio icon is not visible.

Step-by-Step 7.10

1. Open the **Revised Happy Tails 7** file from your solution files. Save the presentation as **Revised Happy Tails 8**, followed by your initials.

2. Go to slide 4. Select the SmartArt graphic object. Click the **Animations** tab. In the Advanced Animation group, click the **Add Animation** button and then click the **Appear** entrance effect. In the Animation group, click the **Effect Options** button and then click **One by One**.

3. Click the **Insert** tab. In the Media group, click the **Insert Audio** button arrow and then click **Clip Art Audio**. In the Clip Art task pane, click the **Results should be** list arrow. If necessary, enable the **Audio** option and disable all other options. Click the **list arrow** to close the menu. If necessary, enable the option Include Office.com content.

4. In the Search for text box, type **cat** and then click **Go**. Scroll through the list of results and select a meow sound. The audio clip object, a sound icon 🔊, is inserted on the slide.

EXTRA FOR EXPERTS

If you search for clip art at the Office.com Web site (instead of using the Clip Art task pane), you can search by category. Also, if you find a particular style that you like, you can search for similar images. Hover the mouse pointer over the image and then click See Similar Images.

5. To preview the sound, click the **Play/Pause** button in the bar below the sound icon on the slide. If you are not satisfied with the audio clip, delete the object and select a different clip in the Clip Art task pane.

6. With the sound icon selected on the slide, click the **Animations** tab. In the Advanced Animation group, click the **Animation Pane** button. In addition to the audio clip, there are four items in the list because each of the two objects consists of two parts: the clip art image and the text box with the dollar amount. If necessary, click the Expand button to view the full list.

7. In the Animation Pane, click the **list arrow** for the meow audio clip object and then click **Start After Previous**.

8. In the Timing group, click the **Move Earlier** button three times to reposition the audio clip object in the task pane so it appears just above *2 Content Placeholder*. A number 1 is displayed next to the sound icon on the slide. The audio clip will play after the cat clip art appears on the slide. Drag the audio clip and position it to the left of the cat image.

9. In the Clip Art task pane, change the Search for text to **dog**. Click **Go**. Review the results and select an audio clip for a barking sound. Close the Clip Art task pane.

10. In the Animation Pane, click the **list arrow** for the barking audio clip object, and then click **Start After Previous**. Drag the audio clip object up one level, just above the Trigger line. The number 2 appears next to the sound icon on the slide, and the audio clip will play after the dog clip art appears.

11. In the Animation Pane, click the **list arrow** for the barking audio clip object, and then click **Effect Options** to open the Play Audio dialog box, as shown in **Figure 7–22**. If the audio clip is quite long, you can shorten the clip by setting a start time in the From time box. To play the audio clip over multiple slides, under Stop playing, you can enable the After option and set the number of slides. Close the dialog box, and then close the Animation Pane.

FIGURE 7–22
Effect tab in the Play Audio
dialog box

12. In the slide window, drag the sound icons to the right side of the slide border, as shown in **Figure 7–23**. The audio clips will still be saved with the slide, but they will not appear on the slide when you show the presentation.

FIGURE 7–23
Sound icons repositioned
on side of slide

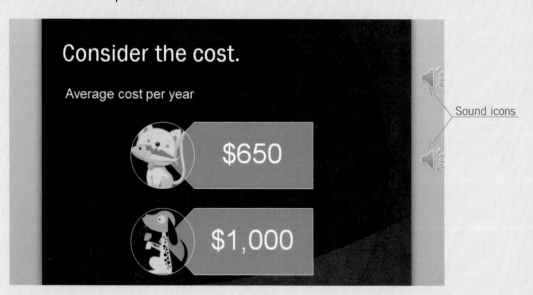

13. Click the **Slide Show** button in the status bar. Click to show the cat clip art. The meow audio clip will play immediately after the image appears. Click a second time to show the dog clip art. The barking audio clip will play immediately after the image appears.

14. Press **Esc** to switch to Normal view. Save the changes and leave the presentation open for the next Step-by-Step.

Recording a Narration

You can also record your own sound or narration. Voice narrations are effective for Web-based presentations. To record an audio clip, you must have a sound card and a microphone. The audio clip is recorded and inserted on the current slide as a sound icon. To complete the next Step-by-Step, your computer must have a sound card, a microphone, and speakers.

Step-by-Step 7.11

1. Open the **Revised Happy Tails 8** file from your solution files. Save the presentation as **Revised Happy Tails 9**, followed by your initials.

2. Go to slide 6. Delete the slide title *Also consider....*

3. Click the **Insert** tab. In the Media group, click the **Insert Audio** button arrow and then click **Record Audio** to open the Record Sound dialog box, as shown in **Figure 7–24**.

FIGURE 7–24
Record Sound dialog box

4. Select the text in the Name box, and then type **Also consider**.

5. Click the **Record** button. Say the following: **Before adopting a pet, there are some things you should also consider.** Then click the **Stop** button.

6. Click the **Play** button to listen to the recording. If you want to re-record the narration, click Cancel and then repeat Steps 3–5. When you are satisfied with the recording, click **OK**. A sound icon appears on the slide.

7. Click the **Animations** tab. In the Advanced Animation group, click the **Animation Pane** button. In the Animation Pane, reposition the **Also consider** audio clip object so that it is at the beginning of the list.

8. In the Animation Pane, click the **Also consider** list arrow. Click **Timing** to open the Timing tab in the Play Audio dialog box. Click the **Start** list arrow, and then click **After Previous** to set the audio clip to play automatically. Change the Delay setting to **1.5**, and then click **OK**. Close the Animation Pane.

9. Drag the sound icon to the right side of the slide.

10. Go to slide 8. In the last line of text, replace *Your Name* with your own name. Then click anywhere within the bulleted list to select the placeholder.

11. In the Advanced Animation group, click the **Add Animation** button and then at the bottom of the menu click **More Entrance Effects**. Scroll down to the bottom of the menu. Under Exciting, click **Credits** and then click **OK**.

12. In the Timing group, click the **Start** list arrow and then click **With Previous**.

13. Go to slide 1. Click the **Slide Show** button in the status bar and review the presentation.

14. Save the changes and close the presentation.

SUMMARY

In this lesson, you learned:

- You can easily modify graphics by resizing and repositioning them on the slide so they fit the slide design.

- You are not limited to the original colors of a graphic. You can customize a graphic by changing its colors to match the other colors in the current theme.

- One of the media type options in the Clip Art gallery is video, which consists of animated clip art images.

- Graphics files can be saved in many different formats, and the format affects both the resolution quality of the graphic and the file size.

- Graphics on a slide can be converted into a SmartArt object, and the objects in the diagram can then be animated.

- The Photo Album feature makes it quick and easy to put together a presentation of photos.

- Presentations can be saved as videos so that they can be viewed on a DVD player.

- Sound and video clips provide other multimedia interest to a slide show. You can apply animation settings to play the sound and video clips automatically or you can control when they play.

- Video clips can add an extra dimension to a presentation, and after inserting a video clip on a slide, you can trim the clip as needed.

- Sound objects can also add interesting effects to slides. In addition to using audio clips, you can add sounds or narrations that you record.

VOCABULARY REVIEW

Define the following terms:

aspect ratio	nudging	scaling
bitmap	outcrop	streaming video
bits	pixels	vector graphics
crop	raster graphics	

■ REVIEW QUESTIONS

TRUE / FALSE

Circle T if the statement is true or F if the statement is false.

T   F   **1.**   You can use the Crop tool to add white space to a graphic.

T   F   **2.**   When recoloring graphics, you are limited to the theme colors.

T   F   **3.**   You can convert a presentation file to a video file format.

T   F   **4.**   You can edit animated clip art images as you would edit any other clip art images.

T   F   **5.**   You can apply formats to a video clip on a slide just as you would apply formats to photos.

FILL IN THE BLANK

Complete the following sentences by writing the correct word or words in the blanks provided.

1. _____ is moving an object vertically or horizontally in small increments.

2. Sizing a graphic so that its proportions are precise is referred to as _____.

3. The _____ is the ratio between the image width and image height.

4. The tiny dots that compose a bitmap image are referred to as _____.

5. Raster graphics are often referred to as _____.

WRITTEN QUESTIONS

Write a brief answer to the following questions.

1. What is streaming video?

2. Why would you outcrop a graphic?

3. Compare raster and vector graphics and note the advantages and disadvantages of each file format type.

4. What file type(s) would you recommend for publishing pictures on the Internet and why?

5. When you insert photos and video clips on a slide, how do you know what file types you are working with?

■ PROJECTS

If you have a SAM 2010 user profile, your instructor may have assigned an autogradable version of the indicated project. If so, log into the SAM 2010 Web site at *www.cengage.com/sam2010* to download the instruction and start files.

PROJECT 7–1

1. Open the **Dynamic Park** file from the drive and folder where your Data Files are stored. Save the presentation as **Revised Dynamic Park**, followed by your initials.

2. Apply a design theme to all the slides in the presentation.

3. Go to slide 2. Search for and insert an appropriate illustration or picture to emphasize environmental protection, conserving energy, and promoting healthy lives.

4. Go to slide 3. Search for and insert appropriate graphics to illustrate one or more of the bulleted items on the slide.

5. If necessary, crop the images or change the aspect ratio so that they fit within the content on the slides.

6. Go to slide 4. Insert two graphics to help the audience quickly recognize those who say yes and those who say no. Then select the two images and convert them to a SmartArt graphic that shows pictures and text.

7. In the text placeholders, type **53%** for those who support the proposal and **41%** for those who do not support the proposal. If necessary, resize the SmartArt graphic.

8. Recolor the images, and remove or make the backgrounds transparent if that helps to enhance the slide content.

9. Search for and insert an animated clip and/or an audio clip that complements the content on one of the slides. Animate the objects to appear at the right time.

10. Save the changes. Review the slides in Slide Show view.

11. Save the presentation as a video in your solutions folder. Then close the presentation.

SAM PROJECT 7–2

1. Open the **Motocross.pptx** file from the drive and folder where your Data Files are stored. Save the presentation as **Final Motocross**, followed by your initials.

2. Apply a design to all the slides in the presentation.

3. Go to slide 2. Insert the picture file **MX Start.jpg**. Go to slide 3 and insert the picture file **MX Jump.jpg**.

4. Go to slide 4 and insert the video file **Motocross.wmv**. Format the video to play automatically.

5. Go to slide 5. Insert the picture file **MX Finish.jpg**. Remove the background from the picture. Then insert a clip art image of a checkered flag. Modify the flag as needed (format the background color as transparent or recolor the clip art image) so that it fits with the design and theme.

6. If necessary, crop and/or resize the images on slide 5. Apply animations to both of the images.

7. Apply a picture style to the photos on slides 2 and 3, and also apply a style to the video clip on slide 4. If necessary, adjust the picture and video sizes on slides 2, 3, and 4.

8. Add an audio clip for applause (clapping or cheering) on slide 5. Format the audio clip to play automatically, and hide the sound icon so it does not appear on the slide.

9. Record an audio clip narration for the last slide. For example, you can say "Way to go!" Hide the audio icon on the side of the slide, and format the audio clip to play with the previous, with a slight delay.

10. Add any additional effects that will enhance the presentation.

11. Preview the slides in Slide Show view, then make any necessary changes.

12. Save the changes and then close the presentation.

PROJECT 7–3

1. Create a photo album. Select the following files from your Data Files folder.

   Bright horizon.jpg

   Pink horizon.jpg

   Sunset fog.jpg

   Sunset high waves.jpg

   Sunset silhouette.jpg

   Sunset trees.jpg

   Sunset waves.jpg

   Yellow sunset.jpg

2. Save the presentation as **Hawaiian Sunsets**, followed by your initials.

3. Edit the album formatting as desired. Add an appropriate title, apply a theme, add frames to the pictures, and include picture captions.

4. Edit the captions as needed by changing the font size and repositioning as needed.

5. Format one or more pictures using artistic effects, and adjust the contrast and brightness as needed.

6. Add transitions to the slides, and if desired, advance the slides automatically by setting a time to advance after each slide.

7. If desired, rearrange the sequence of the pictures.

8. Add audio clips to some of the slides. For example, audio clips for nature and ocean waves are available in the Clip Art task pane. Hide the audio icons on the side of the slide, and format the audio clips to play automatically for one or more slides.

9. Save the changes to the presentation. Review the slides in Slide Show view, and make any necessary changes.

10. Save the changes and then close the presentation.

PROJECT 7–4

1. Open the **Service.pptx** file from the drive and folder where your Data Files are stored. Save the presentation as **Revised Service**, followed by your initials.

2. Edit the WordArt on slide 1 to change the title to **Service Quality Feedback**.

3. Convert the WordArt object to a SmartArt object. (*Hint:* Right-click on the WordArt object, then click **Convert to SmartArt** on the shortcut menu.) Apply the **Target List** SmartArt style.

4. Go to slide 2. Select the bulleted list and convert the text to a SmartArt object. Apply the **Target List** SmartArt style.

5. Go to slide 3. Insert a **Smiley Face** shape (under Basic Shapes) on the right side of the slide, approximately 2½ inches high. Drag the diamond handle on the mouth upward to change the shape to a frowning face.

6. Change the shape fill color to **Yellow**. Change the shape outline color to **Indigo**, **Text 2**, and change the outline weight to **2¼ pt**. Even though this shape does not contain text, you can apply a font color for text by right-clicking or using the buttons on the Home tab. Change the font color to **Indigo**, **Text 2**.

7. Set the shape as the default shape.

8. Go to slide 4. Insert a **Smiley Face** shape, approximately 2½ inches high, on the right side of the slide.

9. Go to slide 5. Insert a **Smiley Face** shape, approximately 2½ inches high, on the right side of the slide.

10. Go to slide 6. Insert a **5-Point Star** shape (under Stars and Banners), approximately 3 inches high, on the right side of the slide. With the shape still selected, type **92%**. Select the new text and change the font size to **28**.

11. Save the changes and then close the presentation

◼ CRITICAL THINKING

ACTIVITY 7–1

When you completed the projects for this lesson, you had the liberty to add special effects to enhance the presentation. With a partner, review your solution files for Projects 7-1, 7-2, and 7-3. Explain to your partner why you chose the design themes, graphics, slide transitions, and sound effects for each presentation. Ask your partner to provide constructive feedback regarding whether or not he or she thinks your choices were effective. Summarize your partner's comments.

ACTIVITY 7–2

You are working with a colleague to prepare a presentation that will be used at a trade show and also published online. Your colleague e-mails you a picture that she says is perfect for the presentation, but she doesn't provide the source of the picture. What questions should you ask your colleague, and what steps should you take, before you use the file? Write a brief report that answers these questions.

Estimated Time: 1.5 hours

LESSON 8

Customizing Slides

OBJECTIVES

Upon completion of this lesson, you should be able to:

- Customize a color scheme and the slide background.
- Customize text and text box shapes.
- Customize slide masters.
- Create a new layout master.
- Insert a new slide master.
- Create a new design template.
- Create a custom show with an agenda slide.
- Use sections to organize slides.

VOCABULARY

agenda slide

color scheme

gradient fill

Using design templates makes formatting slides quick and easy, but as you create presentations, you might find that none of the design templates is exactly right for the slides you want to create. Perhaps you don't like one color in the template—or you like all the colors, but the font is not appropriate. PowerPoint offers many ways to customize slide designs and layouts.

Modifying an Existing Design Template

If you like the look of a particular PowerPoint design template, you can start with that template, add to it, and modify the formats until you are happy with the results. You can apply a new color scheme, create a new slide background, remove graphic elements from a design, change text box shapes, and modify the fonts and the alignment of the text within a text box.

Customizing the Color Scheme

▶ VOCABULARY

color scheme

Each built-in PowerPoint theme has associated color schemes that are accessible in the Theme Colors gallery. A *color scheme* is a set of 12 coordinated colors. Two light colors and two dark colors are used for text and background. Six of the colors are used to apply accents to charts, tables, and other objects. One color is used for hyperlinks, and one color is used for followed hyperlinks. You can modify the color scheme, and if desired, you can save the modified color scheme in the Theme Colors gallery for future use.

Step-by-Step 8.1

You will create a custom color scheme and save it in the Theme Colors gallery. Because you may share your computer with others, you will remove the custom theme from the gallery after you create it.

1. Open the **National Parks** file from the drive and folder where your Data Files are stored. Save the presentation as **National Parks Draft 1**, followed by your initials.

2. Scroll through the slides to preview the content. You do not need to review every slide; the presentation has 63 slides. Slides 4 through 62 provide information about the individual U.S. national parks. The intent is to provide a photo for each national park, but for now only the slide for the first park, Acadia, includes a photo.

3. Go to slide 3. To view the color schemes that are available, click the **Design** tab. In the Themes group, click the **Colors** button. The available theme color schemes are displayed, as shown in **Figure 8–1**. Custom color schemes may be listed at the top of your gallery.

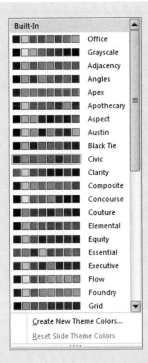

FIGURE 8–1
Theme Colors gallery

4. Position the mouse pointer over several of the color schemes. As you point to each color scheme, a live preview of the color combinations will appear in the Slide pane. Live previews show the changes in text colors, objects, and background colors.

5. Click the **Couture** theme color scheme. The new color scheme is applied to all the slides.

6. In the Themes group, click the **Colors** button. At the bottom of the gallery, click **Create New Theme Colors**. The Create New Theme Colors dialog box opens, as shown in **Figure 8–2**. Note that the dialog box provides two samples of text, objects, and charts in the Sample pane.

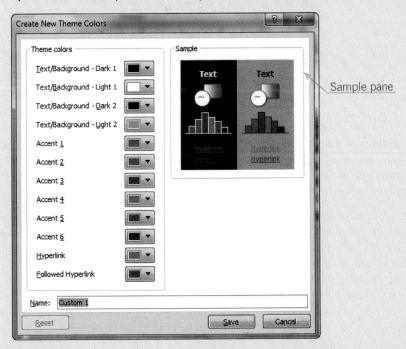

FIGURE 8–2
Create New Theme Colors
dialog box

7. To explore the color scheme options:

    a. In the left pane, under Theme colors, click the **Text/Background – Dark 1** list arrow.

    b. Normally you would select a theme color, but to help distinguish the color scheme options, under Standard colors, click the **Dark Red** standard color. The text in the Sample pane reflects the change.

    c. In the left pane, under Theme colors, click the **Accent 1** list arrow. Under Standard Colors, click the **Yellow** standard color. The changes appear in the objects and the charts in both samples.

    d. In the left pane, under Theme colors, click the **Hyperlink** list arrow, and then under Standard Colors, click the **Light Blue** standard color. The hyperlink text changes in both samples.

    e. In the left pane, under Theme colors, click the **Followed Hyperlink** list arrow. At the bottom of the color palette, click **More Colors**. In the Colors dialog box, click the **Standard** tab, and then select a green color. Click **OK**. The followed hyperlink text changes in both samples.

8. At the bottom of the Create New Theme Colors dialog box, in the Name text box, change the color scheme name to **MyTheme**, followed by your initials. (You cannot enter blank spaces.) Then click **Save**.

9. In the Themes group, click the **Colors** button. The new color scheme appears under the heading Custom at the top of the gallery. Right-click the **MyTheme** color scheme, and then click **Delete**. When prompted to delete the theme colors, click **Yes**.

10. Even though you deleted the custom theme, the custom color formats remain. Click the **Colors** button, and then click the **Office** theme color scheme.

11. Save the changes and leave the presentation open for the next Step-by-Step.

Customizing the Slide Background

Depending upon the design template, the background might be a plain color, a shaded color, a texture, or a pattern. The background in a design template might also include graphic elements such as horizontal lines, curves, and objects. If you do not want the graphics to appear on your slides, you can hide the graphics from the background.

You can change the slide background to a new fill color from your current color scheme, to any other color on the standard palette, or to a custom color. To add interest to a relatively simple background, you can change the background to a *gradient fill*, which is composed of two or more colors that gradually blend from one color to another. You can also use a picture (clip art or photo) to fill the background. Although solid and gradient fill colors are commonly used for backgrounds, sometimes the color is not enough. To add a different emphasis to the slide background, you can

▶ **VOCABULARY**
gradient fill

apply a texture or pattern background. To tailor the background to your content, you can apply different backgrounds to each slide in a presentation.

Making changes to a background may create the need to modify other objects on the slide. For example, a texture background might make it difficult to read the text, or the text color may not be visible on a color background. So, you may need to change a font color and change the font size or apply the bold format so that the text is easy to read.

Step-by-Step 8.2

1. If necessary, open the **National Parks Draft 1** file from your solution files. Save the presentation as **National Parks Draft 2**, followed by your initials.

2. Go to slide 1. If necessary, click the **Design** tab. In the Background group, enable the **Hide Background Graphics** option. The graphics are removed from the current slide.

3. In the Background group, click the **Background Styles** button. The Background Styles gallery opens, as shown in **Figure 8–3**. The styles are based on the color scheme.

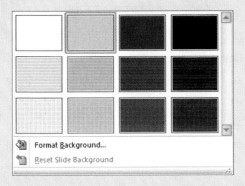

FIGURE 8–3
Background Styles gallery

4. Click **Format Background** to open the Format Background dialog box, as shown in **Figure 8–4**. Currently, the design shows a solid fill. If necessary, drag the dialog box to the right so you can see a portion of the Slides tab and some of the Slide pane.

FIGURE 8–4
Format Background dialog box

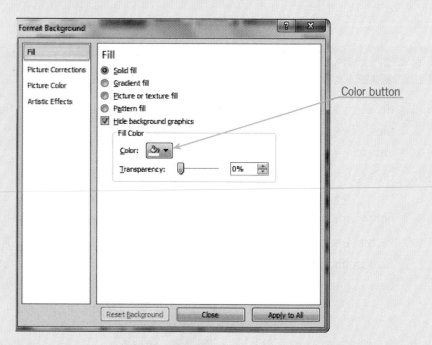

5. Under Fill Color, click the **Color** button to display the color palette. Under Theme Colors, in the top row, click the **Olive Green, Accent 3** theme color.

6. Enable the **Pattern fill** option. Thumbnails for numerous patterns are displayed in the dialog box. Explore the pattern options:

   a. Click a few of the patterns. Each pattern changes the background in the Slide pane.

   b. Click the **Foreground Color** button, and then select a new theme color. The slide background changes.

   c. Click the **Background Color** button, and then select a new theme color.

   d. At the bottom of the dialog box, click **Reset Background**.

7. Enable the **Gradient fill** option. The dialog box options change, as shown in **Figure 8–5**. Your dialog box will differ because of previously applied gradient formats.

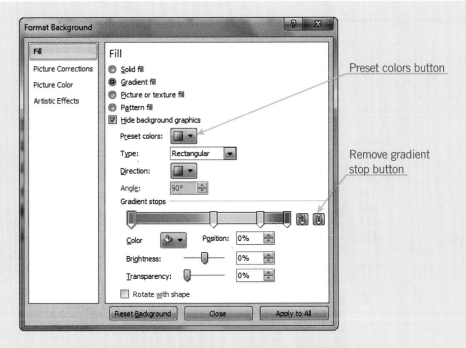

FIGURE 8–5
Gradient fill options

8. Explore the gradient fill options:

   a. Click the **Preset colors** button. A gallery of 24 options opens. In the second row, click the **Fog** preset option.

   b. Click the **Type** list arrow, and then click **Rectangular**.

   c. Click the **Direction** button, and then click the second option **From Bottom Left Corner**.

   d. Click the **Color** button. Under Theme Colors, in the first row, click the **Olive Green, Accent 3** theme color.

   e. The bar shows four Gradient stop options. Drag the second stop from the left back and forth on the bar to see the effect it has on the gradient fill. With the second gradient stop selected, click the **Remove gradient stop** button.

9. Note that the Hide background graphics option is enabled. Click **Apply to All**.

10. Enable the **Picture or texture fill** option. The slide background changes to a Papyrus background. Click the **Texture** button [image] to open the Texture Styles gallery, as shown in **Figure 8–6**. Click the **Texture** button again to close the gallery.

FIGURE 8–6
Texture Styles gallery

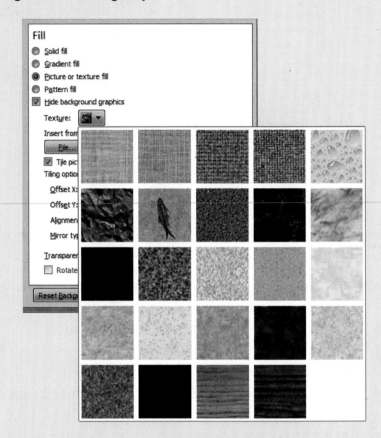

11. Under Insert from, click **File**. Navigate to the drive and folder where your Data Files are stored. Select the filename **Grand Canyon.jpg**, and then click **Insert**. The picture is inserted as the slide background.

12. At the bottom of the dialog box, change the Transparency setting to **15%**. Close the dialog box.

13. Scroll through the first five or six slides to preview the backgrounds and font colors. Adjustments are needed and will be made in the next Step-by-Step.

14. Save the changes and leave the presentation open for the next Step-by-Step.

Customizing Text

There are several ways to add text to a slide. You can add text to placeholders, create a WordArt object, and enter text in shapes. Callout shapes include an embedded text box, but you can, of course, use the Text Box button to create a custom size text box and then format the text box as desired, and even change its shape. Text boxes are especially useful when you want to position several blocks of text on a slide, or when you want to show some text on the slide in a different orientation from the other text. Like all other objects and shapes, you can change the fill color, background, and outline for the text box. And, you can enhance the text within the text box.

In the next Step-by-Step, you will explore options for formatting the text box and the text within the shape. You will explore options to apply text effects, set the text alignment, create columns, set internal margins, and adjust the flow of text within a text box using manual settings or the Autofit setting. To save your formatting changes, you can set the current text box formatting as the default for new text boxes.

All of the formats you apply to a text box shape and the text within the text box are also available for text placeholders, Word Art objects, and other shapes.

Step-by-Step 8.3

1. If necessary, open the **National Parks Draft 2** file from your solution files. Save the presentation as **National Parks Draft 3**, followed by your initials.

2. Go to slide 1, and select all the text in the Title placeholder. Right-click the selected text, and then at the bottom of the shortcut menu, click **Format Text Effects** to open the dialog box shown in **Figure 8–7**.

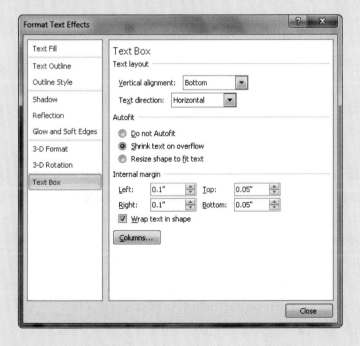

FIGURE 8–7
Format Text Effects dialog box

3. Format the selected text:
   a. In the left pane, click **Text Fill**. New options appear in the right pane. In the right pane, under Fill Color, click the **Color** button. Under Theme Colors, click the **White, Background 1** theme color.

    b. In the left pane, click **Shadow**. New options appear in the right pane. In the right pane, click the **Color** button. Under Theme Colors, click the **Black, Text 1** theme color.

    c. Click **Close** to close the dialog box.

    d. Deselect the text on slide 1. The title is now much easier to read.

4. If necessary, click the **Home** tab. In the Slides group, click the **New Slide** button arrow, and then click the **Blank** layout. If necessary, show the Ruler. Click the **Insert** tab. In the Text group, click the **Text Box** button. The mouse pointer changes to a Text Box Pointer ↓. Click in the Slide pane approximately 1 inch from the upper-left corner, then drag the mouse down and to the right to create a text box approximately 6 inches wide. Note that regardless of how tall you draw the text box, when you release the mouse button, the vertical height of the text box size is automatically adjusted.

5. Type the text below. Note that the text wraps in the text box and the height of the text box automatically adjusts to show the text.

If you enjoy the outdoors, national parks are great destinations for vacations. While enjoying the scenery, you can also learn about American history.

6. Right-click the text and then click **Format Text Effects**. In the left pane, Text Box is selected, and the Text Box options appear in the right pane. Under Internal margin, note that the option to wrap text in the shape is also enabled. Under Autofit, enable the option **Shrink text on overflow**. Click **Close**.

7. Position the insertion point after the period in the last sentence in the text box, press **spacebar**, and then type **If you're looking for adventure,**. Note that as you enter the new text, the font size shrinks so that the text fits within the current text box size.

8. Drag the lower-right **corner** handle toward the center of the text box size to make the text box smaller. The font size shrinks even more. Drag the lower-right **corner** handle down and to the right to increase the text box size to approximately 6 inches wide by 3 inches high. The font size increases, but even though there is space in the text box, the font does not exceed 18 point, which is the original font size.

9. Right-click the text and then click **Format Text Effects**. Under Autofit, enable the option **Do not Autofit**. Click **Close**.

10. Drag the lower-right **corner** handle inward so the text box is about half of the original size. Note that the font size does not change, and when the text box becomes too small to contain all the text, the text overflows the text box. Even though all of the text does not fit within the text box, all of the text will still appear on the slide.

11. The text box should be selected. Click the **Drawing Tools Format** tab. In the Size group, change the shape height setting to **2.5"**. Change the shape width setting to **7"**.

12. Right-click the text and then click **Format Text Effects**. If necessary, move the dialog box to the right so you can see some of the text box in the Slide pane. Change the text box settings:

    a. Under Text layout, click the **Vertical alignment** list arrow and then click **Middle Centered**. You will see the text move down in the text box.

    b. Under Autofit, enable the option **Resize shape to fit text**. The text box size changes, and there is no longer space at the bottom of the text box.

    c. Under Internal margin, change all four settings to **0.2"**. As you change the settings, you will see the adjustments in the text box.

    d. Under Internal margin, click **Columns**. In the Columns dialog box, change the Number setting to **2** and change the Spacing setting to **0.5"**. Click **OK**.

    e. Close the Format Text Effects dialog box.

13. Position the insertion point after the last character in the text box, press **spacebar**, and then type **you'll find endless opportunities for hiking, biking, whitewater rafting, kayaking, camping, wildlife watching, fishing, rock climbing, and horseback riding.** As you enter the new text, the size of the text box will adapt.

14. Save the changes and leave the presentation open for the next Step-by-Step.

Customizing Text Box Shapes

Just as you can customize backgrounds for slides, you can customize the backgrounds for text boxes. Formatting text boxes is the same as formatting shapes. In the next Step-by-Step, you will explore options for formatting the text box shape.

Step-by-Step 8.4

1. If necessary, open the **National Parks Draft 3** file from your solution files. Save the presentation as **National Parks Draft 4**, followed by your initials.

2. If necessary, go to slide 2. Right-click the text box and then click **Format Shape** to open the dialog box shown in **Figure 8–8**.

FIGURE 8–8
Format Shape dialog box

3. Format the text box background and border:

   a. In the left pane, Fill is already selected. In the right pane, under Fill, click the **Solid fill** option. Under Fill Color, click the **Color** button. Under Theme Colors, click the **Orange, Accent 6** theme color.

   b. In the left pane, click **Line Color**. In the right pane, click the **Solid line** option. Click the **Color** button. Under Theme Colors, click the **Dark Blue, Text 2** theme color.

   c. In the left pane, click **3-D Format**. In the right pane, under Bevel, click the **Top** button. Under Bevel, click the first option in the second row, **Angle**.

   d. In the left pane, click **Glow and Soft Edges**. In the right pane, click the **Presets** button. Under Glow Variations, click the last option, **Orange, 18 pt glow, Accent color 6**.

   e. Click **Close**.

4. Set the text box formatting as the default for new text boxes:

   a. The text box should be selected. If necessary, click the text box border to select the text box. (If a broken line appears around the text box, the text box is not selected.)

   b. Right-click the selected text box and then click **Set as Default Text Box**.

   c. Deselect the text box. Click the **Insert** tab. In the Text group, click the **Text Box** button. Draw a text box at the bottom of the slide and type your first and last names.

   d. Click outside the text box to see the formatting on the new text box.

   e. On the Quick Access Toolbar, click the **Undo** button arrow and then click **Insert Text Box** to remove the new text box.

5. Go to slide 3. Click anywhere in the Title placeholder to select it. Format the shape with a picture fill:

   a. Right-click the placeholder and then click **Format Shape**.

   b. Under Fill, enable the **Picture or texture fill** option.

   c. Under Insert from, click **File**. Navigate to the drive and folder where your Data Files are stored. Click the filename **Grand Canyon** and then click **Insert**.

   d. Click **Close**.

6. Format the text effects:

   a. Right-click the title **FACTS** and then click **Format Text Effects**.

   b. In the left pane, click **Text Fill**. In the right pane, under Fill color, click the **Color** button. Under Theme Colors, click the **White, Background 1** theme color.

   c. In the left pane, click **Shadow**. In the right pane, click the **Color** button. Under Theme Colors, click the **Black, Text 1** theme color.

   d. Click **Close**.

7. Change the shape and the shape size:

   a. The placeholder should still be selected. Click the **Drawing Tools Format** tab.

   b. In the Insert Shapes group, click the **Edit Shape** button, and then point to **Change Shape**. Under Rectangles, click the fifth option, **Snip Diagonal Corner Rectangle**.

   c. On the Drawing Tools Format tab, in the Size group, change the shape height to **3.5"** and the shape width to **1.8"**. Do not be concerned that the shape overlaps other objects on the slide.

8. Format the alignment of the text in the text box:

   a. Right-click the placeholder and then click **Format Text Effects**.

   b. In the right pane, under Text layout, click the **Text direction** list arrow and then click **Stacked**.

   c. Under Internal margin, change the Left and Right settings to **0.4"**.

   d. Disable the option to **Wrap text in shape**.

   e. Click **Close**.

9. On the Drawing Tools Format tab, in the Arrange group, click the **Align** button. Click **Align Right**. Click the **Align** button again, and then click **Align Top**.

10. Save the changes and leave the presentation open for the next Step-by-Step.

Working with Multiple Slide Objects

When positioning multiple objects on a slide, you can layer the objects. The Selection Pane is useful when working with layered objects on a slide. In the Selection Pane, you can select, rename, reorder, and group objects.

Sometimes when objects are layered, an object may not be visible because it is positioned behind other objects. The Selection Pane will help you identify all the objects on the slide. You can also choose to hide one or more objects on the slide so you can focus on other objects. When an object is hidden on the slide, the object does not appear on the slide in Slide Show view.

Step-by-Step 8.5

1. If necessary, open the **National Parks Draft 4** file from your solution files. Save the presentation as **National Parks Draft 5**, followed by your initials.

2. If necessary, go to Slide 3. In the Slide pane, select the **Facts** text box. Click the **Drawing Tools Format** tab. In the Arrange group, click the **Selection Pane** button. The Selection Pane shown in **Figure 8–9** displays to the right of the Slide pane. Your Selection Pane may differ.

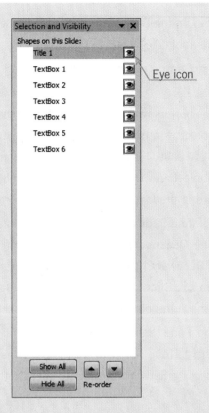

FIGURE 8–9
Selection Pane

3. Note that the Title 1 item (the Facts text box) is selected in the Selection Pane. In the Selection Pane, click the **Eye** icon ⊡ to the right of Title 1. The icon is now blank, indicating that the object is hidden. Click the blank icon again to make the Title placeholder visible again.

4. In the Selection Pane, click the **TextBox 1** item in the list. The text box object *84,000,000 acres of land* is selected in the Slide pane. In the Selection Pane, click the selected **TextBox 1** object a second time. The insertion point is now positioned in the text box for the list item. Delete the existing text and then type **Acres**.

5. Rename the other *TextBox* items in the Selection Pane list.

   a. Click the **TextBox 2** item in the list. Click a second time and then replace the text with **Oceans**.

   b. Rename the **TextBox 3** item in the list **Landmarks.**

   c. Rename the **TextBox 4** item in the list **Structures**.

   d. Rename the **TextBox 5** item in the list **Heritage**.

   e. Rename the **TextBox 6** item in the list **Parks**.

6. Click the **Eye** icons to hide the objects **Acres**, **Landmarks**, and **Heritage**. Then at the bottom of the Selection Pane, click **Show All**.

7. In the Selection Pane, click the **Title 1** item. Press and hold **Ctrl**, and click each of the other items in the list. All the objects are selected in the Slide pane. Press and hold **Ctrl** and then click the **Title 1** item to deselect it. All but one of the objects are selected.

8. On the Home tab, in the Drawing group, click the **Arrange** button. Under Position Objects, point to **Align**. In the submenu, click **Align Left**.

9. Click the **Arrange** button again. Point to **Align**, and then click **Distribute Vertically**.

10. Click the **Arrange** button again. Point to **Align**, and then click **Align Middle**. The selected objects are now all layered, and only two of the objects are visible in the Slide pane. However, the Selection Pane confirms that there are still seven objects on the slide. None of the objects are hidden, but because they are layered, you cannot see all of them.

11. Click anywhere in the Slide pane to deselect the objects. In the Selection Pane, select the **Oceans** item. At the bottom of the Selection Pane, click the **Send Backward** ⬇ button. The order changes in the Selection Pane list and in the Slide pane. Click the **Send Backward** button three more times to move the object to the end of the list.

12. In the Selection Pane, select the **Parks** item and then click the **Bring Forward** button ⬆ four times to move it up the list. Use the Send Backward and Bring Forward buttons to reorder the text box items as follows:

Parks

Landmarks

Heritage

Structures

Acres

Oceans

13. Switch to Slide Show view. Click only once to trigger the animations for the layered objects on the slide. Entrance and exit animations have already been applied. Changing the layered order does not affect the animation order, so the objects will still appear on the slide in the same sequence.

14. When the animations stop and the Oceans object appears, switch to Normal view. Close the Selection Pane.

15. Save the changes and leave the presentation open for the next Step-by-Step.

Customizing the Slide Master and Layout Masters

The slide master is useful when you work with a presentation with a large number of slides because it controls the formatting for all the slides in the presentation. The formats stored in the slide master include themes (color schemes, fonts, and effects) and backgrounds. The slide master also controls placeholders, and it can contain graphics that are part of the design template.

Each slide master has several associated layout masters that define formats for the slide layouts available for the presentation. Each of the layout masters contains the same theme as the associated slide master. When you edit a layout master, the changes apply only to slides formatted with that specific layout. For example, if you change the font for bulleted text on the Title and Content layout master, it will affect only the bulleted items on slides using the Title and Content layout. However, when you edit the slide master, the changes affect all the layout masters. If you change the font for bulleted text on the slide master, all the bulleted items throughout the entire presentation will show the new font.

The slide master and the layout masters contain placeholders for the slide layouts, such as title, subtitle, and content placeholders. You can remove the placeholders or add new placeholders. You can also insert custom graphics or text boxes on slide masters so that the information appears throughout the presentation. This is a good way to add a company logo or name to every slide in a presentation.

The masters include placeholders specifically designed for headers and footers, slide numbers, and dates. You can resize and reposition placeholders, and you can change the text formats. To customize the text for headers and footers on slide masters and layout masters, you must use the Header & Footer button to open the Header and Footer dialog box. You can have the header or footer appear on just one of the slide layouts, on just the title slide, or on all slides in the presentation.

You can also format transitions on slide masters and layout masters, and while working in Slide Master view, you can modify the transition effects and apply sounds.

Step-by-Step 8.6

1. If necessary, open the **National Parks Draft 5** file from your solution files. Save the presentation as **National Parks Draft 6**, followed by your initials.

2. Click the **View** tab. In the Master Views group, click the **Slide Master View** button. Thumbnails for the slide master and each of the layout masters associated with the presentation are displayed in the slide thumbnail pane, as shown in **Figure 8–10**.

FIGURE 8–10
Slide thumbnails pane

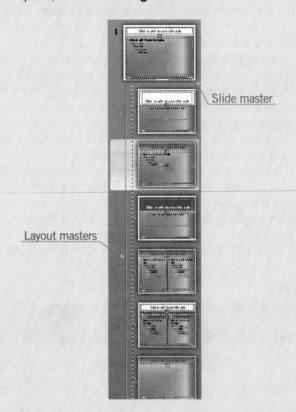

Slide master

Layout masters

3. The first thumbnail is the slide master. Position the mouse pointer over the thumbnail to show the ScreenTip *1_Civic Slide Master: used by slides(s) 1-64*, which references the design theme (Civic) and the slides to which the formats are applied (slides 1–64).

4. Point to the second thumbnail. This is the layout master for the Title Slide layout, and as the ScreenTip indicates, the layout is currently used for only one slide. Move the mouse pointer over some of the remaining thumbnails. You'll see that some of the layout masters are not used in this presentation.

5. In the slide thumbnail pane, click the **Slide Master** thumbnail at the top. In the Edit pane on the right, click anywhere within the first bulleted item (*Click to edit Master text styles*). Click the **Home** tab. In the Paragraph group, click the **Bullets** button arrow, and then at the bottom of the menu, click **Bullets and Numbering** to open the Bullets and Numbering dialog box. In the lower-left corner of the dialog box, click the **Color** button, and then select the **Dark Blue, Text 2** theme color. Click **OK**. All first-level bullets throughout the presentation will appear in the darker blue color.

6. Click the **Insert** tab. In the Text group, click the **Header & Footer** button to open the Header and Footer dialog box, as shown in **Figure 8-11**. Enable the **Date and time** option. The Update automatically option should be enabled. Enable the **Footer** option, and in the text box type your first and last names. Enable the option **Don't show on title slide**. Click **Apply**. Note that the dates will differ.

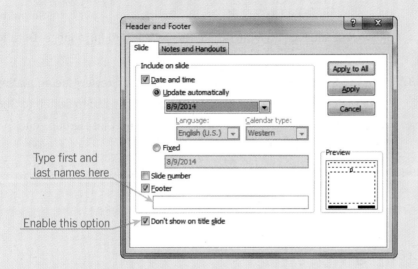

Type first and last names here

Enable this option

FIGURE 8–11
Header and Footer dialog box

7. In the Edit pane, select the text in the footer text box (in the lower-left corner). Use the Mini toolbar to change the font color to **Dark Blue, Text 2**. Select the date and time field in the date and time footer box and change the font color to **Dark Blue, Text 2**.

8. In the slide thumbnail pane, click the third layout master: the **Section Header layout** thumbnail. Click anywhere within the **Click to edit Master title style** text to select the Title placeholder. Click the **Home** tab, and in the Font group, click the **Increase Font Size** button twice to change the font size to 48 point. Click the **Font Color** button arrow, and then select the **Dark Blue, Text 2** theme color. The changes will only appear on slides formatted with the Section Header layout.

9. At the top of the slide thumbnail pane, click the **Slide Master** thumbnail. Select all five levels of the bulleted list. Click the **Animations** tab. In the Advanced Animation group, click the **Add Animation** button. Under Entrance, click the **Fade** entrance effect.

10. In the Timing group, click the **Start** list arrow and then click **On Click**. In the Animation group, click the **Effect Options** button and make sure the By Paragraph option is selected. Click anywhere to close the menu. All bulleted lists throughout the presentation will be animated, so you won't need to apply the animation format each time you create a bulleted list. A symbol is added to the left of the slide master to indicate animations.

11. In the slide thumbnail pane, click the **Title and Content layout** thumbnail (the second layout master). Click the **Transitions** tab. In the Transition to This Slide group, click the **More** button. Under Subtle, click the **Reveal** transition. The transition will be applied to all slides formatted using the Title and Content layout format.

12. In the Transition to This Slide group, click the **Effect Options** button and then click **Smoothly From Left**. In the Timing group, click the **Sound** list arrow and then click **Camera**. In the Timing group, change Duration setting to **3.00**.

13. Click the **Slide Show** button in the status bar and review the animations and slide transitions for the first four slides. Press **Esc** to switch to Slide Master view. Click the **Slide Master** tab. In the Close group, click the **Close Master View** button.

14. Save the changes and leave the presentation open for the next Step-by-Step.

Creating a New Layout Master

If you have content that is not well-suited to the current slide layouts, you can add a new layout master and create a custom slide layout. To create the new slide layout, you simply insert a new layout master and then insert placeholders on it. The placeholders that you insert are automatically formatted based on the slide master formats. If desired, however, you can customize the placeholder formats for the new layout master, and then the customized formats will apply to all slides using that layout.

After creating the new layout master, you can apply the new layout to new slides as well as to existing slides.

Step-by-Step 8.7

1. If necessary, open the **National Parks Draft 6** file from your solution files. Save the presentation as **National Parks Draft 7**, followed by your initials.

2. Click the **View** tab. In the Master Views group, click the **Slide Master View** button to open the slide thumbnail pane.

3. In the slide thumbnail pane, select the **Two Content layout** thumbnail (the fourth layout master).

4. On the Slide Master tab, in the Edit Master group, click the **Insert Layout** button. A new layout master thumbnail is inserted in the slide thumbnail pane, following the selected thumbnail.

5. Position the mouse pointer over the new layout master thumbnail. The name *Custom Layout Layout* has already been applied. In the Edit Master group, click the **Rename** button. In the Layout name text box, select the existing text, type **Custom Text and Picture**, and then click **Rename**.

6. In the Master Layout group, click the **Insert Placeholder** button arrow and then click **Text**. The mouse pointer changes to a cross-hair $+$.

7. Drag the mouse pointer to create a placeholder on the left side of the slide. Use the rulers to create a placeholder approximately 5 inches wide and 3 inches high. (*Hint*: You can also click the Drawing Tools Format tab, and set the dimensions in the Size group.) Position the text box below the title placeholder and near the left border of the slide.

8. In the Master Layout group, click the **Insert Placeholder** button arrow and then click **Picture**. Create a placeholder approximately 6 inches wide and 4 inches high. Position the new placeholder so that it aligns with the lower-right corner of the slide. The picture placeholder will overlap the text and date placeholders.

9. In the Close group, click the **Close Master View** button.

10. Go to slide 1. On the Home tab, in the Slides group, click the **New Slide** button arrow. Note that the new layout option appears in the menu. Click the **Custom Text and Picture** thumbnail. A new slide with the new layout formats is added to the presentation. Click **Undo** to remove the new slide from the presentation.

11. On the Slides tab, select the **slide 5** thumbnail. Press and hold down **Ctrl** and **Shift**, and then press **End**. The range of slides 5:64 is selected.

12. With the range of slides selected, in the Slides group, click the **Layout** button and then click the **Custom Text and Picture** thumbnail. The layouts for all the selected slides are now converted to the new slide layout.

13. Go to slide 64. In the Slides group, click the **Layout** button and then click the **Section Header** layout.

14. Save the changes and leave the presentation open for the next Step-by-Step.

> **EXTRA FOR EXPERTS**
>
> To save time, you can base the new layout master on an existing layout master. Right-click the existing layout master thumbnail, and then click Duplicate Layout. The layout master is copied, and a new thumbnail appears in the slide thumbnail pane. Modify the new layout master and rename it.

Inserting a New Slide Master

Each theme has its own set of unique slide layouts. For more complexity and flexibility, you can add additional slide masters. This enables you to access more design templates with more backgrounds, colors, and effects.

Step-by-Step 8.8

1. If necessary, open the **National Parks Draft 7** file from your solution files. Save the presentation as **National Parks Draft 8**, followed by your initials.

2. Click the **View** tab. In the Master Views group, click the **Slide Master View** button to open the slide thumbnail pane.

3. In the Edit Master group, click the **Insert Slide Master** button. A new slide master thumbnail with the number 2 is inserted in the slide thumbnail pane, along with 11 layout masters. Scroll up in the pane. Note that the #1 slide master and the associated 11 layout masters still appear at the top of the list.

4. Position the mouse pointer over the #2 slide master and layout masters thumbnails to see that the formats are not applied to any slides.

5. The #2 slide master should still be selected. In the Background group, click the **Background Styles** button. In the second row of the Background Styles gallery, click the **Style 7** background style.

6. In the Edit Theme group, click the **Themes** button. Scroll down through the Built-In themes and click the **Trek** theme. Note that a new slide master thumbnail with the number 3 appears below the #2 slide master and layout masters.

7. With the #3 slide master thumbnail selected, in the Edit Master group, click the **Rename** button. In the Layout name box, select the existing text, type **My Custom Design** followed by your initials, and then click **Rename**.

8. Position the mouse pointer over the #3 slide master and layout masters thumbnails. Note that the new formats and designs have not been applied to slides in the presentation.

9. In the Edit window, select the text in the Title placeholder. Right-click the selected text, and then use the Mini toolbar to change the font style to **Comic Sans MS** and the font size to **32** point.

10. In the Edit Master group, click the **Preserve** button. A pushpin icon ⊞ appears to the left of the #3 slide master thumbnail. Even though the master is not being used at this time, the master will be stored with the presentation.

11. Scroll up in the slide thumbnail pane and right-click the **#2 Custom Design Slide Master** thumbnail. Click **Delete Master**. The slide master is removed from the slide thumbnail pane, and the #3 Slide Master is now assigned the number 2.

12. In the Close group, click the **Close Master View** button.

13. If necessary, click the **Home** tab. In the Slides group, click the **New Slide** button arrow. Note that there are two sets of layouts for slides. Click outside the menu to close the menu without selecting a layout.

14. Save the changes and leave the presentation open for the next Step-by-Step.

Customizing the Handout and Note Masters

The handout master controls how the slide thumbnails are arranged for handouts. PowerPoint provides seven different layout options for handouts, so there are seven different handout masters. On each handout master, you can add custom information to the header and footer placeholders.

To control items you want to appear on the notes pages, you use the notes master. You can change the page setup and define the paper size; you can also change the orientation for the slides and notes page. You can also resize the placeholders for the slides and the notes, and you can add custom information to the header and footer placeholders.

Instead of printing handouts directly from PowerPoint, you can create handouts and send them to a Word document. Then you can use Word to format the content and add new content. The slide content is pasted into the Word document. You can choose to paste the content using a link so that when the slides in the presentation change, the handout is automatically updated.

Step-by-Step 8.9

1. If necessary, open the **National Parks Draft 8** file from your solution files. Save the presentation as **National Parks Draft 9**, followed by your initials.

2. Click the **View** tab. In the Master Views group, click the **Handout Master View** button. A layout with six slides appears. In the Page Setup group, click the **Slides Per Page** button. Note that there are seven layout options. Click **6 Slides**.

3. Click the **Insert** tab, and in the Text group, click the **Header & Footer** button. On the Notes and Handouts tab, enable the **Header** option, and in the text box, type **National Parks**. Enable the **Footer** option, and in the text box, type your first and last names. Click **Apply to All**.

4. Click the **Handout Master** tab. Click the **header** placeholder on the left side of the handout window to select the placeholder. Click the **Home** tab. Change the font size to **14 point** and the font color to the **Dark Blue, Text 2** theme color. Select the **footer** placeholder on the left side and apply the same font formats.

5. Click the **Handout Master** tab. In the Close group, click the **Close Master View** button.

6. Click the **File** tab, and then click **Print**. Under Settings, click the **Full Page Slides** button to show the options, as shown in **Figure 8–12**.

FIGURE 8–12
Print options

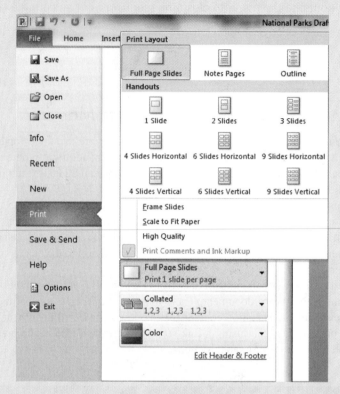

7. Under Handouts, select the **4 Slides Horizontal** layout. Note in the preview pane that the information is displayed in the header and footer panes. In the left pane, click **Save & Send**. In the center pane, click **Create Handouts**, and then in the right pane, click the **Create Handouts** button to open the dialog box shown in **Figure 8–13**.

FIGURE 8–13
Send to Microsoft Word dialog box

8. Enable the option **Blank lines next to slides**. Also enable the **Paste link** option, and then click **OK**. Switch to the Word document. Wait patiently for the process to complete, and then save the Word document as **National Parks Handout**, followed by your initials. Exit Word.

9. Click the **View** tab. In the Master Views group, click the **View Notes Master** button.

10. Click the **Insert** tab. In the Text group, click the **Header & Footer** button to open the Header and Footer dialog box. Note that because you already formatted the header and footer for the handout master, the information is already available. Click **Apply to All**.

11. Select the **header** placeholder on the left side. Click the **Home** tab. Change the font size to **14** point and the font color to the **Dark Blue, Text 2** theme color. Select the text in the footer placeholder on the left side and apply the same font formats.

12. Click the **Notes Master** tab. In the Close group, click the **Close Master View** button.

13. Click the **File** tab, and then click **Print**. Under Settings, click the **4 Slides Horizontal** button. Under Print Layout, click **Notes Pages**. Note that the page number appears in the lower-right corner. Click the **Home** tab.

14. Save the changes and leave the presentation open for the next Step-by-Step.

Creating a New Design Template

Using a custom design template is a good way to lend a uniform appearance to presentations generated for specific purposes or by particular presenters. A business, for example, might want to standardize all the presentations created for its use. You've done a lot of work to customize the design for the National Parks presentation. Changes you made to the masters apply only to the current presentation. To save the revisions for future use, you can save the revised design template using a new template name.

You can save your template with your own files or you can let PowerPoint place it in the Templates folder where you can easily choose it for other presentations. If you save the template somewhere other than the Templates folder, you can still apply its formats to a new slide show.

In the next Step-by-Step, you will select and delete multiple slides simultaneously. You can select multiple slides in the Slide pane in Normal view or in Slide Sorter view.

Step-by-Step 8.10

1. If necessary, open the **National Parks Draft 9** file from your solution files.

2. On the Slides tab, click the **slide 1** thumbnail. Press and hold **Ctrl**, and then select the **slide 3** and **slide 4** thumbnails.

3. Click the **slide 1** thumbnail. Press and hold **Shift** and then click the **slide 6** thumbnail. Then press **Ctrl+A** to select all the slides. Press **Delete**.

4. Click the **File** tab, and then click **Save As** to open the Save As dialog box. In the File name box, type **Custom Template**, followed by your initials. In the Save as type box, click the **list arrow** and then click **PowerPoint Template (*.potx)**. The Templates folder should appear in the path at the top of the dialog box. Click **Save**.

5. Click the **File** tab, and then click **Save As**. Navigate to the drive and folder where your solution files are stored. Then click **Save**. The template is now also saved to your solutions folder. Close the template file.

6. Click the **File** tab, and then click **New**. Under Available Templates and Themes, click the **My templates** icon. The New Presentation dialog box opens, showing the personal templates available, as shown in **Figure 8–14**.

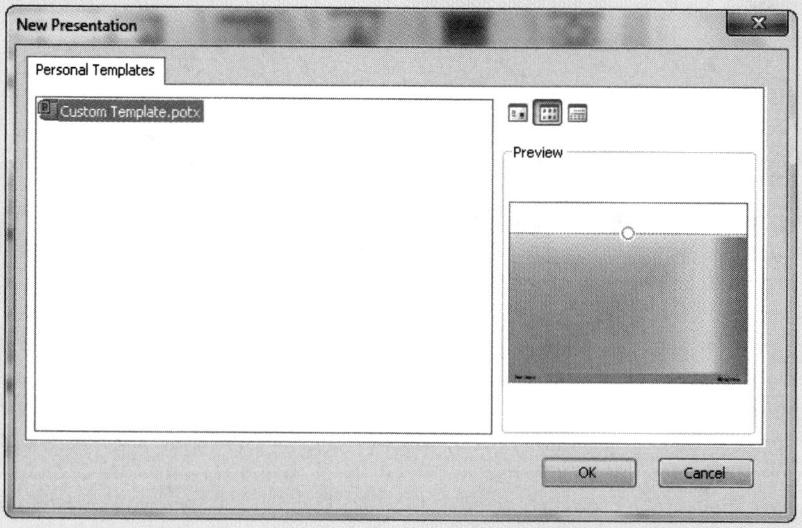

FIGURE 8–14
New Presentation dialog box with
Personal Templates tab

7. If necessary, select **Custom Template** and then click **OK**. A new presentation is opened.

8. In the Slides group, click the **New Slide** button arrow. Note that all the layout options are available, including the Custom Text and Picture layout. Click outside the menu to close the menu without inserting a new slide.

9. Click the **View** tab. In the Master Views group, click the **Slide Master View** button. Note that the #1 slide master includes the animation formats. Scroll down through the slide thumbnail pane, and you'll see the #2 slide master and layout masters. In the Close group, click the **Close Master View** button.

10. Click the **File** tab, and then click **New**. Under Available Templates and Themes, click the **My templates** icon. In the New Presentation dialog box, on the Personal Templates tab, right-click **Custom Template**, and then click **Delete**. When prompted to move the file to the Recycle Bin, click **Yes**.

11. Click **Cancel** to close the dialog box. Click the **Home** tab to close Backstage view.

12. Close the new presentation without saving any changes.

Creating a Custom Show with an Agenda Slide

A custom show is actually a presentation within a presentation. To create a custom show, you identify a group of related slides within a presentation. Creating custom shows gives you flexibility when a presentation contains a large number of slides because you can group related topics in the presentation and focus on the slides that are appropriate for a particular audience. For example, the National Parks presentation contains 59 slides providing information about national parks across the United States. If you're presenting to an audience in Utah, you can create a custom show and include only the slides for the parks in Utah. Once you have identified the slides for the custom show, you can reorder them within the custom show.

You are not limited to one show; you can create multiple custom shows from the same presentation. At any time, you can edit, remove, and even make a copy of a custom show.

Once you have created custom shows, you can create an *agenda slide* that provides an outline of topics for the presentation. Agenda slides are especially useful for presentations with custom shows. You can identify the topics on the agenda slide and create a hyperlink for each topic so you can easily navigate to different sections of the presentation. You can also apply a format so that you will automatically return to the agenda slide after the last slide in the custom show appears.

▶ **VOCABULARY**
agenda slide

Step-by-Step 8.11

1. Open the **National Parks Draft 9** file from your solution files. Save the presentation as **National Parks Draft 10**, followed by your initials.

2. Click the **Slide Show** tab. In the Start Slide Show group, click the **Custom Slide Show** button, and then click **Custom Shows**. The Custom Shows dialog box opens. Click **New** to open the Define Custom Show dialog box, as shown in **Figure 8–15**.

FIGURE 8–15
Define Custom
Show dialog box

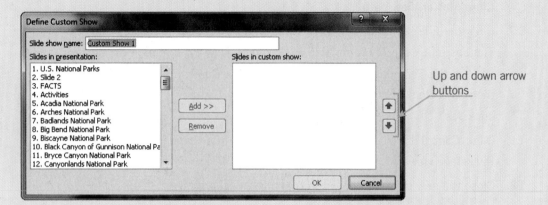

Up and down arrow buttons

3. In the Slide show name text box, type **Utah National Parks**. Under Slides in presentation, click **6. Arches National Park**. Press and hold **Ctrl** and click the following slides:

   11. **Bryce Canyon National Park**

   12. **Canyonlands National Park**

   13. **Capitol Reef National Park**

   63. **Zion National Park**

4. Click **Add>>**. The selected slides are copied to the pane on the right.

5. Under Slides in custom show, select **2. Bryce Canyon National Park**, and then click the **up arrow** button. Then select **3. Canyonlands National Park** and then click the **down arrow** button to move the slide down in the list. Return the list to alphabetical order, and then click **OK**.

6. In the Custom Shows dialog box, click the **New** button and create a new custom show named **California National Parks**. Add the following slides to the new custom show, and then click **OK**.

   15. **Channel Islands National Park**

   19. **Death Valley National Park**

   36. **Joshua Tree National Park**

   39. **Kings Canyon National Park**

   42. **Lassen Volcanic National Park**

   50. **Redwood National Park**

   53. **Sequoia National Park**

   62. **Yosemite National Park**

7. Click **New** and create a third custom show named **Alaska National Parks**. Add the following slides to the new custom show and click **OK**, then close the Custom Shows dialog box.

   20. **Denali National Park**

   23. **Gates of the Arctic National Park**

   24. **Glacier Bay National Preserve**

   37. **Katmai National Park**

   38. **Kenai Fjords National Park**

   40. **Kobuk Valley National Park**

   41. **Lake Clark National Park**

   60. **Wrangell-Saint Elias National Park**

8. Go to slide 4. To create an agenda slide, click the **Home** tab. In the Slides group, click the **New Slide** button arrow and then click the **Blank** layout from the #1 layout masters. Click the **Insert** tab. In the Illustrations group, click the **Insert SmartArt Graphic** button. Under List, in the second row, click the **Vertical Box List** SmartArt graphic, and then click **OK**.

9. In the first placeholder, type **Alaska**. In the second placeholder, type **California**. And in the third placeholder, type **Utah**.

10. Select and then right-click the text in the **Alaska** SmartArt object, and then click **Hyperlink**. In the Insert Hyperlink dialog box, under Link to, click **Place in This Document**. Under Select a place in this document, scroll down to Custom Shows and click **Alaska National Parks**. Enable the **Show and return** option. When your dialog box matches the one shown in **Figure 8–16**, click **OK**.

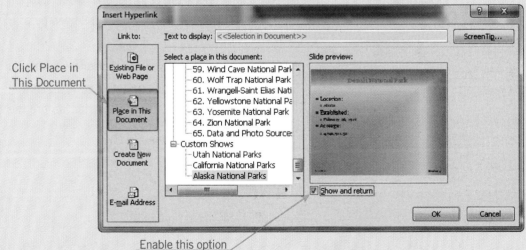

Click Place in This Document

Enable this option

FIGURE 8–16
Insert Hyperlink dialog box

11. Create similar hyperlinks to the remaining two custom shows. Be sure to enable the **Show and return** option.

12. Click the **Design** tab. In the Themes group, click the **Colors** button. At the bottom of the menu, click **Create New Theme Colors**. Under Theme colors, click the **Hyperlink** list arrow and change the color setting to the **White, Text 1** theme color. Click **Save**. The hyperlinked text is now visible on the SmartArt objects.

13. Save the changes. Click the **Slide Show** button on the status bar. Click the last hyperlink, **Utah,** and preview the slides in the custom show. When you advance through all the slides in the Utah National Parks custom show, PowerPoint will return to slide 5. If time permits, preview the slides in the other two custom shows. When you click at the end of each custom show, you will return to the agenda slide.

14. Switch to Normal view. Save the changes and leave the presentation open for the next Step-By-Step.

TIP

To start a custom show, click the Slide Show tab. In the Start Slide Show group, click Custom Slide Show and then click Custom Shows. In the Custom shows list, select a show and then click Show.

Using Sections to Organize Slides

When a presentation has numerous slides, like the National Parks presentation, navigating through the slides can be tedious. To organize the slides, you can separate slides in a presentation into different sections. After creating the sections, you can view them in both Slide Sorter view and Normal view. You can collapse one or more sections, which will enable you to focus on a specific section of slides in the presentation. The sections are also useful if you share presentations with others because you can direct them to a specific section.

Step-by-Step 8.12

1. If necessary, open the **National Parks Draft 10** file from your solution files. Save the presentation as **National Parks Draft 11**, followed by your initials.

2. Go to slide 6 and, in the status bar, click the **Slide Sorter view** button. If necessary, click the **Home** tab. In the Slides group, click the **Section** button and then click **Add Section**. A section bar is inserted before the selected slide, as shown in **Figure 8–17**.

Section bar

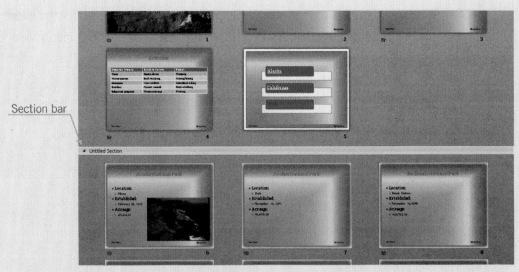

FIGURE 8–17
New section added in
Slide Sorter view

3. In the Slides group, click the **Section** button and then click **Rename Section**. The Rename Section dialog box opens. In the Section name text box, type **Parks A-C** and then click **Rename**.

4. Scroll down and click the **slide 20** thumbnail. In the Slides group, click the **Section** button and then click **Add Section**. Right-click the new section bar and click **Rename Section**. In the Section name text box, type **Parks D-G** and then click **Rename**.

5. Switch to Normal view. On the Slides tab, scroll down and click the **slide 33** thumbnail. If necessary, click the **Home** tab. In the Slides group, click the **Section** button and then click **Add Section**. A new section bar appears in the Slides tab, as shown in **Figure 8–18**.

FIGURE 8–18
New section added in
Normal view

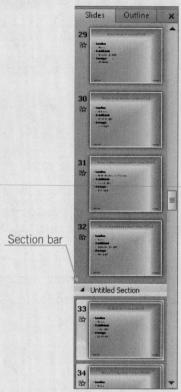

Section bar

6. In the Slides tab, right-click the section bar and then click **Rename Section**. In the Section name text box, type **Parks H-N** and then click **Rename**.

7. In the Slides tab, click the **slide 49** thumbnail, create a new section, and name the section **Parks O-Z**. Double-click the **Parks O-Z** section bar. The section is collapsed and the slides are hidden. The section bar shows that there are 17 slides in the section.

8. Scroll up and double-click the **Parks A-C** section bar. Then double-click the **Parks D-G** section bar.

9. Scroll to the top of the Slides tab. Right-click the **Default Section** section bar and rename the section **Introduction**. Then, collapse the slides in the section.

10. In the Slides tab, drag the Parks D-G section bar to move the section above the Parks A-C section.

11. Switch to Slide Sorter view. Click the **Parks H-N** section bar to select all the slides in that section. Then double-click the **Parks H-N** section bar to collapse the slides. All the sections should now be collapsed.

12. Right-click the **Parks D-G** section bar, and then click **Move Section Down** to reposition the section so that it follows the Parks A-C section.

13. Right-click any one of the section bars, and then click **Expand All**. All the sections are expanded. Right-click any one of the section bars, and then click **Collapse All**. Then, expand the **Introduction** section.

14. Save the changes and close the presentation.

SUMMARY

In this lesson, you learned:

- Changing the color scheme is a quick way to give slides a fresh new look. To fine-tune the look of a presentation, you can change individual colors in the color scheme and you can save the custom scheme in the Theme Colors gallery.

- You have many options for changing the background of a slide. You can change the color, create a gradient of one or more colors, add a texture, or use a pattern. You can also use graphics to create backgrounds.

- There are several features available for modifying the appearance and flow of text within a text box. You can also add backgrounds, outlines, and special effects to text boxes.

- Slide masters and layout masters control the placement of text and other items on a slide, as well as color, font, style, and size of text. When you modify a slide master, the new formats are applied to all slides based on the master.

- Masters also provide placeholders specifically designed for headers and footers, slide numbers, and dates. To customize your presentation, resize and reposition these placeholders and/or change the text formats.

- You can add additional layout masters to a presentation, and you can customize the layout and placeholder formats on the layout master.

- More than one slide master can be added to a presentation, giving you access to a wider range of design templates.

- After modifying the slide designs and layouts, you can save the customized settings as a new design template and make the template available for future use.

- Custom shows are like presentations within presentations. Gathering slides into a custom show allows you to control groups of slides during a presentation.

- Slides can be organized in sections, making it easier to navigate the slides—especially when a presentation consists of a large number of slides.

■ VOCABULARY REVIEW

Define the following terms:

| agenda slide | color scheme | gradient fill |

REVIEW QUESTIONS

TRUE / FALSE

Circle T if the statement is true or F if the statement is false.

T   F   **1.**   A presentation is limited to 11 layout masters.

T   F   **2.**   You can use pictures and clip art to create a slide background.

T   F   **3.**   If you change the alignment of a title on a layout master, you will see the same change in all titles on all slides in the presentation.

T   F   **4.**   When you edit the slide master, the changes affect all the layout masters.

T   F   **5.**   If you choose to hide design graphics on a slide, the graphics are automatically removed from all slides in the presentation.

FILL IN THE BLANK

Complete the following sentences by writing the correct word or words in the blanks provided.

1. A(n) _____ is a set of coordinated colors.

2. A(n) _____ provides an outline of topics for the presentation.

3. A(n) _____ is composed of two or more colors that gradually blend from one color to another.

4. The _____ controls the formatting for all the slides in the presentation.

5. When saving a design template, you use the _____ file extension.

WRITTEN QUESTIONS

Write a brief answer to the following questions.

1. What types of formats are stored in a slide master?

2. After customizing slide designs and layouts, how can you save the changes so you can apply the same design and formats in future projects?

3. What are the advantages of creating multiple slide masters for a presentation?

4. What are the benefits of creating custom shows?

5. Why does a color scheme provide two different color settings for hyperlinks?

■ PROJECTS

PROJECT 8–1

1. Open the **Time Management** file from the drive and folder where your Data Files are stored. Save the presentation as **Final Time Management**, followed by your initials.

2. On slide 1, replace *Your Name* with your first and last names.

3. Create three custom shows:

   a. Name the first custom show **Step 1** and include slides 7–10.

   b. Name the second custom show **Step 2** and include slides 11–13.

   c. Name the third custom show **Step 3** and include slides 14–16.

4. Go to slide 6. Format the text in each SmartArt object to link to the related custom shows. Choose the setting to return to slide 6 once you have advanced through the custom show slides.

5. Apply a new color scheme and/or modify the color scheme as needed. For example, make sure the color scheme is appropriate for the presentation content, and make sure the hyperlink colors work in the SmartArt object on slide 6.

6. Go to slide 18. Hide the background graphics. Then format the slide background using clip art.

7. If necessary, adjust the font formats so you can easily read the text on the slide.

8. If time permits, add clip art to the slides to enhance the presentation.

9. Preview the presentation in Slide Show view.

10. Save the changes and close the presentation.

PROJECT 8–2

1. Open the **Building Renovation** file from the drive and folder where your Data Files are stored. Save the presentation as **Final Building Renovation**, followed by your initials.

2. Format the slide background using clip art of a blueprint (or another appropriate image). Apply the background to all slides in the presentation. If necessary, adjust the image transparency.

3. Depending on the background image, you may want to modify the theme colors.

4. Modify the slide master:

   a. Change the master title style font to **Arial Rounded MT Bold**.

   b. Change the font size to **40 point**.

   c. If necessary, change the font color to complement the background image.

   d. Insert the footer text **Twilight Enterprises** on all pages. Change the footer font size to **16 point**, and change the font color to fit with the color scheme you selected.

5. Modify the Title and Content layout master:

   a. If necessary, change the font color and size for the bulleted text so that you can easily read it with the slide background image.

   b. Apply a different bullet style for the first-level bullet.

   c. Animate the bulleted lists with an entrance effect, starting On Click.

   d. Apply a slide transition.

6. Insert and format a new layout master.

   a. Name the new layout master **Custom Credits**.

   b. Remove the title and footer placeholders.

   c. Insert a text placeholder that fills most of the slide.

   d. Remove the bullets formats in the placeholder.

   e. Select the text placeholder and apply the entrance effect **Credits**. Format the animation to start **With Previous**.

7. Format a header and footer for the handout and notes masters. The header should show *Building Renovation* and the footer should show *Twilight Enterprises*.

8. In Normal view, create a new slide at the end of the presentation based on the new Custom Credits layout. In the placeholder, type the following, and then add your name at the bottom of the list.

   Thanks to:

   Angela Forest

   Joshua Winton

   Kong Zo Chang

9. Preview the slides in Slide Show view. Make any necessary corrections or apply additional formats to enhance the slides.

10. Preview the handouts and notes pages in Backstage view to make sure the headers and footers appear. Save the changes to the presentation.

11. Delete all the slides in the presentation, and then save the presentation as a template with your solution files. Name the new template file **Building Renovation Design**, followed by your initials.

12. Close the presentation template.

PROJECT 8–3

1. Click the File tab, and then click New. Under Available Templates and Themes, click the Sample templates icon. Select the Five Rules thumbnail, and then click the Create button.

2. Save the new document as **Organized Five Rules**, followed by your initials.

3. Scroll through the slides to become familiar with the content. Note that there are 56 slides in the presentation. You may not have time now to review the entire presentation thoroughly, but when you do, preview all the slides in Slide Show view. There's a lot to learn from the content, and you'll view some very effective uses of animations, transitions, and audio clips.

4. Switch to Slide Sorter view. Create sections to organize the slides. Name each section so you can easily identify the slide content. Note that you may need to fully review the slide content to determine the section breaks.

5. Collapse all of the sections except the first section.

6. Save the changes and close the presentation.

■ CRITICAL THINKING

ACTIVITY 8–1

In a Word document, write a brief paragraph to compare working with sections in a PowerPoint presentation to working in Outline view in a Word document.

ACTIVITY 8–2

In this lesson, you worked with the handout master and the notes master. You may have noticed that in these views the Ribbon provided commands for themes, colors, and backgrounds. Do you think you would ever use these features to format handouts and notes pages? Write a brief paragraph, and explain the reason for your response.

LESSON 9

Importing and Exporting Information

■ OBJECTIVES

Upon completion of this lesson, you should be able to:

- Reuse slides from another presentation.
- Copy and paste slides to Word documents.
- Create slides from a Word outline.
- Import a table from a Word document.
- Export slide information to a Word outline.
- Embed worksheet data and link an Excel chart in a slide.
- Copy data from an Access table.
- Save a slide as a graphic file.

■ VOCABULARY

export

import

integration

slide library

This lesson introduces you to techniques for exchanging information between PowerPoint presentations and between PowerPoint and other Office applications, including Word, Excel, and Access.

Reusing Slides from Another Presentation

Suppose you are creating a presentation and realize that you already prepared some slides for the topic in another presentation. Do you have to re-create the slides? No way! You can easily copy and paste selected content onto a new slide, or you can copy and reuse entire slides.

To copy and paste slides from one presentation to another, both presentations must be open. If the presentation containing the slides you want to copy is large and you want to pick and choose among the slides, the Reuse Slides command is probably a better choice. You can scroll through the entire presentation and select individual slides you want to reuse, or you can insert all of the slides at once. Reusing slides has the additional advantage that you do not have to open the presentation file containing the slides you want to import.

When you use either method to copy slides from one presentation to another, the design template for the current (or destination) presentation is applied to the copied slides by default. However, you can choose to keep the formatting from the original (or source) presentation of the copied slides.

You can also reuse files from a *slide library*, which is a special type of library used to store presentation slides. Those who have access to a slide library can publish slides to the library as well as use slides that are stored in the library. When you reuse slides from a slide library, you can choose to receive notification when changes are made to the slide stored in the slide library. To access slides in a slide library, you must have a connection to a server running Microsoft Office SharePoint Server 2007 or Microsoft SharePoint Server 2010, which is beyond the scope of this lesson.

▶ **VOCABULARY**
slide library

Step-by-Step 9.1

1. Open the **Community Service** file from the drive and folder where your Data Files are stored. Save the presentation as **Revised Community Service 1**, followed by your initials. Scroll through the slides to get familiar with the content.

2. Open the **Blood Drive** file from the drive and folder where your Data Files are stored. Go to slide 1. In the Slide pane, select all the text (including the Register symbol) in the placeholder in the lower-right corner of the slide. In the Clipboard group, click the **Copy** button.

3. Switch to the Revised Community Service 1 presentation. On slide 1, click anywhere within the Subtitle placeholder. In the Clipboard group, click the **Paste** button.

4. Switch to the Blood Drive presentation. On the Slides tab, select the **slide 2** thumbnail and then click the **Copy** button. Close the Blood Drive presentation file without saving any changes.

5. In the Revised Community Service 1 presentation, on the Slides tab, select the **slide 4** thumbnail. In the Clipboard group, click the **Paste** button. The slide from the Blood Drive presentation is inserted after slide 4, with the formatting of the Revised Community Service 1 presentation.

6. In the Slides group, click the **New Slide** button arrow, and then at the bottom of the menu, click **Reuse Slides**. The Reuse Slides pane, similar to the one shown in **Figure 9–1**, opens on the right side of the document window. Your pane will differ.

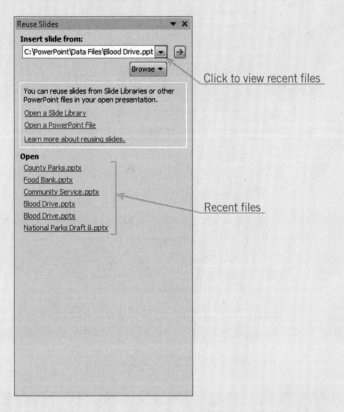

FIGURE 9–1
Reuse Slides pane

7. In the Reuse Slides pane, under Insert slide from, click the **list arrow**. Recently accessed files appear in the list. Click the **list arrow** again to hide the list.

8. In the Reuse Slides pane, click **Browse** and then click **Browse Slide Library**. The Select a Slide Library dialog box opens. If your computer is connected to a server running SharePoint, you can browse to access the slide library here. Click **Cancel** to close the dialog box.

9. In the Reuse Slides pane, click **Browse** and then click **Browse File**. Navigate to the drive and folder where your Data Files are stored. Select the filename **Blood Drive** and then click **Open**. On the Slides tab, click the **slide 5** thumbnail. Thumbnails for the slides in the Blood Drive presentation appear in the Reuse Slides pane, as shown in **Figure 9–2**. If you are accessing slides from a slide library in SharePoint, the Reuse Slides pane will look very similar.

FIGURE 9–2
Thumbnails for the
Blood Drive slides

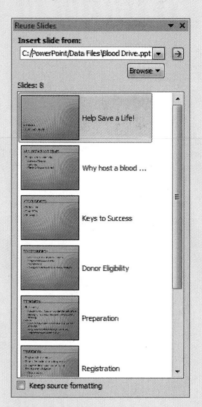

10. In the Reuse Slides pane on the right, position the mouse pointer over the **Keys to Success** (slide 3) thumbnail to view a large image of the thumbnail, as shown in **Figure 9–3**. The slide title appears at the bottom of the slide.

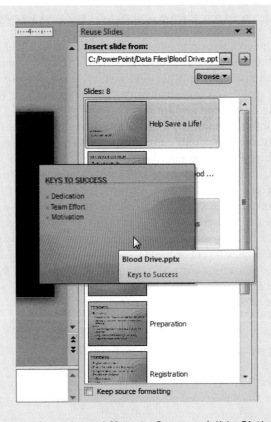

FIGURE 9–3
Enlarged preview of the Keys to Success (slide 3) thumbnail

11. Click to select the enlarged **Keys to Success** (slide 3) thumbnail. In the Slide Thumbnail pane on the left, you will see that the slide has been inserted into the Revised Community Service presentation after slide 5. Also note that the new slide is formatted with the same design as the other slides in the presentation, and the slide title appears at the top of the slide.

12. Switch to Slide Sorter view. Position the insertion point between slide 7 and slide 8, scrolling down if necessary. In the Reuse Slides pane, click **Browse** and then click **Browse File**. Select the filename **Food Bank**, and then click **Open**. Thumbnails of the presentation file appear in the Reuse Slides pane.

13. In the Reuse Slides pane, click the **Organize a Food Drive** (slide 2) thumbnail. Then click the **Volunteer at the Food Bank** (slide 3) thumbnail. Then click the **Donate Professional Services** (slide 5) thumbnail.

14. In the upper-right corner of the Reuse Slides pane, click the **Close** button. Save the changes and leave the presentation open for the next Step-by-Step.

TIP

To maintain the original design of the reused slides, at the bottom of the Reuse Slides pane, enable the Keep source formatting option.

TIP

To reuse all slides in a presentation, right-click any one of the thumbnails and then click Insert All Slides.

Sharing Information among Applications

If information already exists in another Office application, such as Word, Excel, or Access, you do not need to type and format the information again in PowerPoint. Instead, you can import or export the information. When you *import* content, you bring it into one application from another compatible application. When you *export* content, you send it from one application to another.

Sharing the information among the applications is often referred to as *integration*. Integrating applications not only saves time, but it also ensures consistency in data because when you retype information, you risk making errors. To share the information, you can copy and paste content, link data from one application to another, embed content as an object, or convert the content to a different file format.

When you link data to a slide, you can edit the data only in its source application. For example, if a slide contains a link to data in an Excel worksheet, you must return to the worksheet in Excel to edit the data. Changes you make in the Excel worksheet then appear in the linked object on a slide. A linked object is stored in the source file (in this example, the Excel worksheet), but it is not stored in the destination file (in this example, the PowerPoint presentation). A linked object on a PowerPoint slide is actually a picture of the object in the source application. Linking is not permanent—you can easily break a link if you no longer want the linked object to update in the destination document. When a link is broken, the object remains in the destination document as a picture and you can still resize and move it on the slide, but you cannot edit the data.

When you embed an object on a slide, you can edit the data in PowerPoint using commands from the source application. For example, if a slide contains an embedded Excel worksheet, you double-click the embedded worksheet to edit the data. Excel's commands will be displayed, and you can make the edits without leaving PowerPoint. An embedded object is stored in the destination file (in this example, the presentation).

You might wonder when you should use each of these four integration options. **Table 9–1** describes when you would use each method.

VOCABULARY
import

export

integration

TABLE 9–1   Integration options

OPTION	WHEN TO USE
Copy and Paste (default setting)	Useful when the imported information does not need to be updated. Most information can be copied and pasted, and there are usually format options available when pasting copied information.
Link	Useful when you want to keep the data current. The object is not stored in the destination file, so linking is an advantage if file space for the destination file is limited.
Embed	Useful when you want the imported information to be stored in the destination file and you want to be able to edit the source data in the destination application. Because the embedded object is stored in the destination file, the destination file size might be quite large.
Convert	Useful when the shared information must be stored in a specific format to be recognized in the destination application.

Copying and Pasting Content between Slides and Word Documents

PowerPoint offers features that enable you to easily create slides from existing content in Word documents. Text, tables, and charts created in Word can be imported into a PowerPoint presentation, and information contained on PowerPoint slides can be exported to a Word document.

Not only do slides provide information, but they are also usually quite decorative. You can add both information and pizzazz to documents created in other Office applications by copying PowerPoint slides and pasting them into Word documents. When you paste a copied slide into Word, the slide is inserted as a picture. Like any other graphic object, you can move, resize, and control how text wraps around the picture. You can also use the picture tools to format the picture. You can choose to paste the picture as a linked object so that when changes are made in the presentation file, the linked picture in the Word document is also updated.

Step-by-Step 9.2

1. If necessary, open the **Revised Community Service 1.pptx** file. Save the presentation as **Revised Community Service 2**, followed by your initials.

2. Launch Word. Open the **Long-Term Care.docx** file from the drive and folder where your Data Files are stored. Save the document as **Revised Long-Term Care**, followed by your initials.

3. Switch to the PowerPoint window. If necessary, switch to Normal view. On the Slides tab, scroll up and select the **slide 1** thumbnail. In the Clipboard group, click the **Copy** button.

4. Switch to the Word window. At the top of the document, position the insertion point after the last character in the title.

5. In the Clipboard group, click the **Paste** button arrow and then click **Paste Special**. The Paste Special dialog box opens, as shown in **Figure 9–4**. Note that the default setting will paste the copied slide as a picture in PNG format.

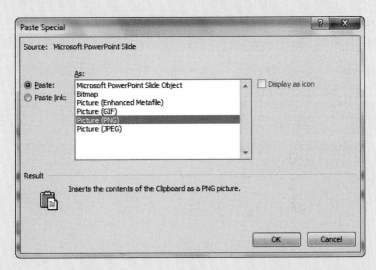

FIGURE 9–4
Paste Special dialog box

6. In the dialog box, enable the **Paste link** option. The list of options changes, and the Microsoft PowerPoint Slide Object is automatically selected. Note that Result information at the bottom of the dialog box indicates that the contents will be inserted as a picture with a shortcut link to the source file. Click **OK**. The picture is inserted in the document.

7. Right-click the **picture**, and then in the shortcut menu, click **Format Object**. In the Format Object dialog box, click the **Size** tab. Under Height, change the Absolute setting to **1"**. Under Width, click the **Absolute** text box. The width is automatically adjusted to 1.34".

8. In the Format Object dialog box, click the **Layout** tab. Under Wrapping style, click the **Square** option and then click **OK**. The picture is resized and repositioned on the page.

9. Use the mouse to drag and reposition the slide object to the right of the title and just above the blue line below the title. Right-click the **picture**, and then click **Format Object**. Click the **Layout** tab and, under Wrapping style, click the **Behind text** option and then click **OK**. The blue underline below the title is now visible across the entire width of the page.

10. Switch to the PowerPoint window. On slide 1, position the insertion point in front of the text *Strategic Solutions, Inc.*®. Press **Enter**, and then position the insertion point in the new blank line. Type **Community Service Projects**.

11. Switch to the Word document. Right-click the **slide** object, and then click **Update Link**. The picture now shows the new text.

12. Right-click the **slide** object, and then in the shortcut menu, point to **Linked Slide Object**. In the submenu, click **Links** to open the Links dialog box, as shown in **Figure 9–5**. Click **Break Link**. When prompted to break the selected link, click **Yes**. The picture of the object remains unchanged, but any changes made in the source file will no longer affect the object on the slide.

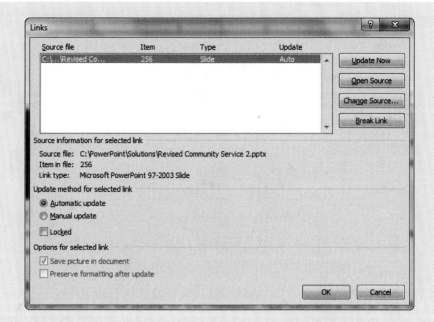

FIGURE 9–5
Links dialog box

13. Save the changes to the Word document and close the file. Leave the Word application open.

14. Switch to the PowerPoint window. Save the changes to the presentation and leave the presentation open for the next Step-by-Step.

Creating Slides from a Word Outline

One of the easiest ways to import information into PowerPoint is to create slides from an outline created in a Word document. You don't need to retype the information from the outline onto the slides or even open the Word document. PowerPoint imports all the content formatted with heading styles to create titles and bulleted lists at various levels. If heading styles are not applied in the Word document, an individual slide is created for each paragraph in the document.

PowerPoint creates only Title and Text layout slides, so if you are importing the information into a new blank presentation file, you might need to create a Title slide at the beginning of the presentation.

Step-by-Step 9.3

1. If necessary, open the **Revised Community Service 2.pptx** file. Save the presentation as **Revised Community Service 3**, followed by your initials.

2. Switch to Slide Sorter view. Scroll down to the end of the slides and position the insertion point to the right of slide 12.

3. In the Slides group, click the **New Slide** button arrow and then click **Slides from Outline**. The Insert Outline dialog box opens, as shown in **Figure 9–6**. Your dialog box will differ.

FIGURE 9–6
Insert Outline dialog box

4. Navigate to the drive and folder where your Data Files are stored. Select the filename **Long-Term Care.docx**, and then click **Insert**. Five new slides are created and inserted at the end of the presentation, with the same design applied. Note that each new slide is formatted with the Title and Text layout.

5. Double-click the **slide 13** thumbnail to show the slide in Normal view. Select the slide title and use the Mini toolbar to change the font color to white.

6. On the Slides tab, click the **slide 16** thumbnail. If necessary, select and reposition the placeholder on the slide so that all of the content appears on the slide.

7. Save the changes and leave the presentation open for the next Step-by-Step.

Importing a Table from Word

Although PowerPoint offers features for creating and formatting a table on a slide, if the table already exists in a Word document, importing the table from Word will save you time. To import table data, you select the data and copy it to the Clipboard. In PowerPoint, you can choose from several Paste Special options to paste the copied data. **Table 9–2** describes the benefits of each Paste Special option.

When you copy a table onto a PowerPoint slide, the table content is embedded in the slide and you can then use the PowerPoint table commands to format the table and rearrange the table contents.

TABLE 9–2   Paste Special options

OPTION	BENEFITS
Use Destination Styles	The table formats in the presentation theme are applied to the imported table.
Keep Source Formatting	The table formats applied in the Word document are applied to the imported table.
Embed	The table is embedded with the source formatting. You can use the PowerPoint table commands to edit the table data and modify the table styles.
Picture	The table is inserted as a picture. You can resize and reposition the picture, but you cannot edit the table data or modify the table styles.
Keep Text Only	All formatting is removed, and only the table text is imported on the slide. You can edit and format the text as desired.

Step-by-Step 9.4

1. If necessary, open the **Revised Community Service 3.pptx** file. Save the presentation as **Revised Community Service 4**, followed by your initials.

2. If necessary, launch Word. Open the **Items.docx** file from the drive and folder where your Data Files are stored. Save the document as **Updated Items**, followed by your initials.

3. Select the entire table, and then copy the table to the Clipboard.

4. Switch to the PowerPoint window. If necessary, switch to Normal view. Go to slide 8. Select and then delete the content placeholder with the bulleted items.

5. Right-click the Slide pane. Note that in the shortcut menu, under Paste Options, there are five buttons. See **Figure 9–7**. Position the mouse pointer over each button to show a ScreenTip and a live preview of the pasted contents on the slide.

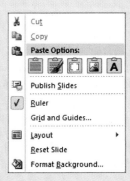

FIGURE 9–7
Paste Options in shortcut menu

TIP

When you use the Paste button to paste the copied table, a Paste Options button appears in the lower-right corner of the pasted table. If the Paste Options button does not appear, click the File tab, click Options, and then click Advanced. Under Cut, copy, and paste, enable the option Show Paste Options button when content is pasted.

6. In the shortcut menu, under Paste Options, click the **Use Destination Styles** button 🖿. The table is imported on the slide, and the presentation design theme is applied to the table. The copied data is inserted in a PowerPoint table, and the Table Tools tabs are available.

7. Drag a table corner handle to enlarge the table. Note that as the table gets bigger, the font size stays the same. If you adjust the font size, you will likely also need to adjust the column widths. Click **Undo** on the Quick Access Toolbar two times to remove the table from the slide.

8. In the Clipboard group, click the **Paste** button arrow and then click **Paste Special** to open the Paste Special dialog box. Enable the **Paste link** option. Under As, the option Microsoft Word Document Object is already selected. Click **OK**.

9. Drag a table corner handle to enlarge the table. Because the data is pasted as a picture, when you resize the object, the text also appears larger. Adjust the size of the picture to fit on the slide, and then reposition the picture as needed.

10. Switch to the Word window. Select the first column and then drag and drop the column so it is the second column. The first column is now *Cleaning Items*, the second column is *Food Items*, and the third column is *Hygiene Items*.

11. Select all the rows in the first column, except for the heading, and remove the bold format.

12. Switch to the PowerPoint window. The table is updated with the new data arrangement.

13. Save the changes to the presentation file, and leave the file open for the next Step-by-Step.

14. Switch to the Word window. Save the changes to the document and then close the document. Leave the Word application open.

Exporting Slide Information to a Word Outline

You have already seen how easily you can import information from a Word document into a PowerPoint presentation. You can just as easily export slide information to a Word document by converting the presentation information to an outline in Rich Text Format.

When you export PowerPoint data as an outline, the information appears in a new Word document with outline heading styles. Exported outlines contain no graphics, tables, or charts; the exported information includes only the slide text. In the Word document, you can modify the styles to reduce the font size and remove unnecessary font styles.

Step-by-Step 9.5

1. If necessary, open the **Revised Community Service 4.pptx** file. Save the presentation as **Revised Community Service 5**, followed by your initials.

2. Click the **File** tab, and then click **Save As** to open the Save as dialog box. If necessary, navigate to the drive and folder where you save your solution files.

3. In the File name text box, replace the existing text with **Community Service Outline**, followed by your initials.

4. Click the **Save as type** list arrow and select **Outline/RTF (*.rtf)**. Then click **Save**.

5. If necessary, launch Word. Open the **Community Service Outline.rtf** file from the drive and folder where you save your solution files. The outline document shows all the text content from the presentation slides. Note that many of the font colors are white, so the text doesn't show in the document.

6. Press **Ctrl+A** to select the entire document, and then change the font color to **Automatic** (black).

7. Note that the font sizes are quite large, because text on PowerPoint slides is formatted to appear much larger for easy reading. Press and hold **Ctrl**, and then press the left bracket key (**[**) about 20 times to shrink all the text by 20 points.

8. Scroll down through the document. Note that there are two levels of bulleted items.

9. Switch to Outline view. Note that there is no body text. All the content is formatted with a heading style.

10. Switch to Print Layout view.

11. Save the changes to the document and then exit Word.

12. Save the changes to the presentation and leave the presentation open for the next Step-by-Step.

Embedding Excel Worksheet Data in a Slide

If the data you need for a slide already exists in an Excel worksheet, you can import the information to the slide using the copy and paste, link, and embed options.

Copying and pasting information from Excel to a slide is very similar to copying and pasting information from a Word document, but there are some differences. When you copy worksheet data and use the default Paste command, the copied information is inserted on the slide as a table. To embed or link the data, you must use the Paste Special command. When the data is embedded, you can use Excel commands to edit the data. When the data is linked, changes to the data in the Excel application are automatically updated on the slide.

Step-by-Step 9.6

1. If necessary, open the **Revised Community Service 5.pptx** file, and when prompted, update the links. Save the presentation as **Revised Community Service 6**, followed by your initials.

2. Launch Excel. Open the **Donations.xlsx** file from the drive and folder where your Data Files are stored. Save the workbook as **Updated Donations**, followed by your initials.

3. Select the cell range **A1:E3** and copy the data to the Clipboard.

4. Switch to the PowerPoint window. Go to slide 4.

5. In the Clipboard group, click the **Paste** button. The worksheet data is imported in the slide in a table format. The table is quite small, and if you drag the table corner handles to enlarge the table, you'll need to adjust the font sizes and column widths. Click the **Undo** button on the Quick Access Toolbar to remove the table.

6. Right-click the Slide pane. In the shortcut menu, under Paste Options, click the **Embed** button 🖼. Because the slide background is black, the Excel data is not visible.

7. Double-click the table picture. The Ribbon changes to show Excel commands, and the worksheet data is now visible. The cell range A1:E3 is still selected.

8. On the Home tab, in the Font group, click the **Fill Color** 🖊▾ button arrow and then select a dark orange color.

9. Click anywhere outside the Excel data to hide the Excel commands.

10. Drag the picture corner handles to enlarge the picture, and reposition the picture on the slide.

11. Switch to the Excel worksheet. Click cell **E3**, type **331**, and then press **Enter**. Save the changes and close the workbook. Leave Excel open.

12. Switch to the PowerPoint window. You cannot update the Excel data because no link was created. Double-click the picture to access the Excel commands.

13. Click cell **E3**, and then type **331**. Do not press Enter because that will create a new blank row. Instead, click outside the worksheet data to hide the Excel commands. The picture now reflects the new data for 2014.

14. Save the changes and leave the presentation open for the next Step-by-Step.

Linking an Excel Chart to a Slide

Linking chart data is similar to linking worksheet data. A linked chart appears on the slide surrounded by a border and selection handles. You can resize or move the chart on the slide the same way you would any other object. You also have access to most of the Chart Tools commands to modify the chart effects and elements, such as the chart title. The object on the slide maintains a link to the source document, but only changes to the chart data in the source document appear in the chart on the slide.

Step-by-Step 9.7

1. If necessary, open the **Revised Community Service 6.pptx** file, and when prompted, update the links. Save the presentation as **Revised Community Service 7**, followed by your initials.

2. If necessary, launch Excel. Open the **Participation.xlsx** file from the drive and folder where your Data Files are stored. Save the workbook as **Updated Participation**, followed by your initials.

3. Select the chart and copy it to the Clipboard.

4. Switch to the PowerPoint window. Go to slide 6, and then right-click the Slide pane. In the shortcut menu, under Paste Special, position the mouse pointer over each button to show a ScreenTip and a live preview of the pasted contents on the slide.

5. Click the **Use Destination Theme & Link Data** button 🖿. The chart is inserted on the slide and formatted for the current presentation design theme.

6. Enlarge and reposition the chart next to the bulleted list on the slide.

7. Select the legend *# employees* on the right and change the font size to **14** point.

8. Switch to the Excel window. Click cell **F3** and change the number to **42**.

9. Right-click the chart and, in the shortcut menu, click **Change Chart Type**. The Change Chart Type dialog box opens, as shown in **Figure 9–8**. In the right pane, under Line, click the fourth option **Line with Markers** and then click **OK**.

FIGURE 9–8
Change Chart Type dialog box

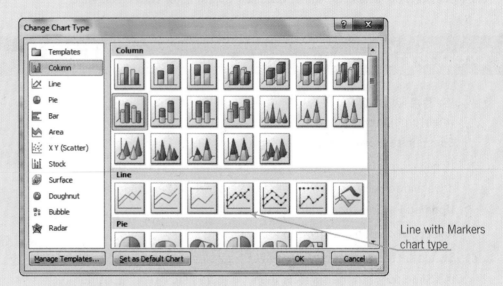

Line with Markers chart type

10. Save the changes to the worksheet and then exit Excel.

11. In the PowerPoint window, the data in the chart is already updated. The chart type did not change because only the underlying chart data is linked.

12. Save the changes to the presentation and leave the presentation open for the next Step-by-Step.

Copying Data from an Access Table

You cannot link or embed data from an Access table or form. However, you can copy the data and paste it into other Office applications. When copied data from an Access table is pasted onto a slide using the default Paste command, the data is formatted in a table. You can use the PowerPoint table commands to modify the table formats, reorder columns and rows, and arrange the table on the slide. When using the Paste Special command to paste copied data, you can choose to use the destination theme or keep the source formatting. You can also paste the copied data as text only.

Step-by-Step 9.8

1. If necessary, open the **Revised Community Service 7.pptx** file, and when prompted, update the links. Save the presentation as **Revised Community Service 8**, followed by your initials.

2. Insert a new slide at the end of the presentation using the Title Only layout. In the Title placeholder, type **PARTICIPATION IS GROWING!**.

3. Launch Access. Open the **Volunteer Participation.accdb** file from the drive and folder where your Data Files are stored.

4. In the left pane, if necessary, click any expand buttons ⟨⟩ to show all Access Objects, as shown in **Figure 9–9**. If necessary, click Enable Content in the yellow message bar.

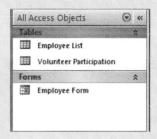

FIGURE 9–9
Access Objects pane

5. Under Tables, double-click **Volunteer Participation** to open the Volunteer Participation table.

6. The first cell in the Service column is selected. Press and hold **Shift**, and then click the last cell with data in the 2014 column (*65*). All the table data is selected. In the Clipboard group, click the **Copy** button.

7. Switch to the PowerPoint window. Go to slide 18. Right-click the slide and in the shortcut menu, under Paste Options, click **Use Destination Theme** 🖼. The copied data is inserted in a table, but because of the background colors, you cannot see the text.

8. Click the **Table Tools Design** tab. In the Table Styles group, click the **More** button and in the second row under Best Match for Document, select the **Themed Style 2 – Accent 2** style.

9. Select all the data in the table including the table title, and then use the Mini toolbar to change the font size to **24 point**.

10. Position the mouse pointer on the border between the *Service* and *2010* column headings. When the pointer changes to a double-headed ⟷ arrow, double-click to AutoFit the column width for the contents. Then AutoFit each of the remaining five columns.

11. Position the insertion point anywhere within the row *County Park Cleanup*. Click the **Table Tools Layout** tab. In the Rows & Column group, click the **Insert Above** button. A new blank row is inserted in the table.

12. Select the last row in the table. Drag and drop the selected content to the new blank row. Then right-click the blank row at the bottom of the table, and in the shortcut menu, click **Delete Rows**.

13. On the Table Tools Layout tab, in the Arrange group, click the **Align** button and then click **Align Center**. Click the **Align** button again and then click **Align Middle**.

14. Save the changes and leave the presentation and the Access database open for the next Step-by-Step.

Saving a Slide as a Graphic File

Slides usually include graphics and design elements to draw attention and hold interest. You can save slides as individual graphic files, and then you can use the files to insert pictures in other applications.

Step-by-Step 9.9

1. If necessary, open the **Revised Community Service 8.pptx** file, and when prompted, update the links.

2. If necessary, launch Access and open the **Volunteer Participation.accdb** file from the drive and folder where your Data Files are stored. Save the database as **Revised Volunteer Participation**, followed by your initials.

3. In the PowerPoint window, select the first slide. Click the **File** tab, and then click **Save As**. Navigate to the drive and folder where you save your solution files.

4. In the File name text box, type **Title Slide**.

5. Click the **Save as type** list arrow, and then select **JPEG File Interchange Format (*.jpg)**. Click **Save**, and when prompted to export every slide or only the current slide, click **Current Slide Only**. (When you select the Every Slide option, each slide in the presentation is saved as an individual graphic slide.)

6. Switch to the Access window. If necessary, in the Objects pane, click the arrows to expand the list to show all objects.

7. Under Forms, double-click **Employee Form**. A form for entering employee data opens in the right pane, as shown in **Figure 9–10**.

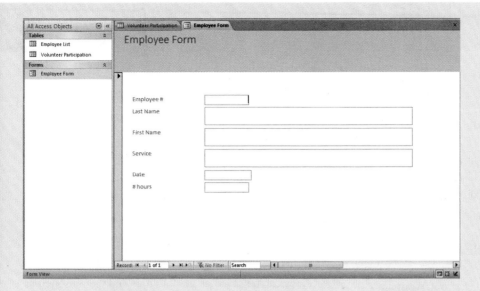

FIGURE 9–10
Employee Form

8. In the Views group, click the **View** button arrow and then click **Design View**.

9. If necessary, click the **Form Design Tools Design** tab. In the Controls group, click the **Insert Image** button. Click **Browse** and navigate to the drive and folder where you save your solution files.

10. Select the filename **Title Slide.jpg**, and then click **OK**. The mouse pointer changes to a crosshair with a picture icon . To the right of the form text boxes, drag the mouse pointer to create a shape to specify the image size, as shown in **Figure 9–11**.

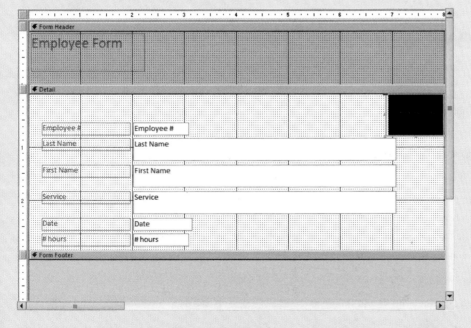

FIGURE 9–11
Inserted image in Design view

11. In the Views group, click the **View** button arrow and then click **Form View**. The slide picture now appears with the form.

12. Click the **Save** button on the Quick Access Toolbar to save the changes to the form. Then exit Access.

13. Close the presentation file without saving any changes.

SUMMARY

In this lesson, you learned:

- You can quickly access and reuse slides that have been created in another presentation.

- To share information among applications, you can copy and paste the information, link the data, embed the content, or convert the information to a different file format.

- When you paste a copied slide into Word or Excel, the copied slide is inserted as a picture.

- You can easily create slides from outlines already created in a Word document.

- When copying and pasting table data from Word into PowerPoint, there are several Paste Special options that enable you to control how the data on the slide can be edited.

- Content on slides can be exported to a Word document by converting the presentation content to a different file format.

- Excel worksheet data and charts can be copied and pasted onto slides with the options to link or embed the data. To embed or link the data, you must use the Paste Special command.

- Access table data can be copied and pasted onto slides, but the data cannot be linked or embedded.

- Slides can be saved as graphic files and then inserted as pictures in other applications.

 ## VOCABULARY REVIEW

Define the following terms:

export   integration
import   slide library

 ## REVIEW QUESTIONS

TRUE / FALSE

Circle T if the statement is true or F if the statement is false.

T   F   **1.**   When a copied slide is pasted into a Word or Excel document, the slide is inserted as a picture.

T   F   **2.**   When copying and pasting slides from one presentation to another, both presentations must be open.

T   F   **3.**   When using the Reuse Slides command to import slides, you can only import one slide at a time.

T   F   **4.**   An embedded document can be edited in the destination document.

T   F   **5.**   A linked object on a PowerPoint slide is actually a picture of the object in the source application.

MULTIPLE CHOICE

Select the best response for the following statements.

1. To keep data current, when pasting copied table data you should choose to _____ the data.

   A.   copy and paste (default setting)

   B.   link

   C.   embed

   D.   convert

2. An embedded object is stored in the _____ document.

    A.   source

    B.   destination

    C.   integrated

    D.   exported

3. When importing slides from one presentation to another, _____.

    A.   the design template for the current presentation is applied to the imported slides by default

    B.   you can choose to keep the source formatting of the imported slides

    C.   you must reapply a design theme

    D.   A and B

4. When Access table data is copied and pasted onto a slide, _____.

    A.   the copied data appears in a table on the slide

    B.   the copied data is linked to the source file

    C.   the copied data is embedded on the slide

    D.   none of the above

5. When slide information is exported to a Word outline, _____ are not included in the Word document.

    A.   graphics

    B.   tables

    C.   charts

    D.   all of the above

WRITTEN QUESTIONS

Write a brief answer to the following questions.

1. You use the Slides from Outline command to import information from a Word document to a presentation. What happens if none of the information in the Word document is formatted with heading styles?

2. When you change the chart type in the source document, why doesn't the change appear in the linked chart object?

3. What are the advantages to pasting copied data as a picture?

4. When presentation information is exported to an outline in a Word document, why are the font sizes so large?

5. What are the benefits of sharing information among applications?

■ PROJECTS

If you have a SAM 2010 user profile, your instructor may have assigned an autogradable version of the indicated project. If so, log into the SAM 2010 Web site at *www.cengage.com/sam2010* to download the instruction and start files.

PROJECT 9–1

1. Create a new blank presentation. Save the presentation as **Final Preserving Wetlands**, followed by your initials.

2. On the Title slide, in the title placeholder, type **Preserving Our Wetlands**. In the subtitle placeholder, type your first and last names.

3. Import slides from an outline created in Word. The **Wetlands Outline.docx** file is stored in the Data Files folder.

4. Apply a design theme. If desired, modify the slide master and layout masters and/or change the color scheme.

5. Reuse slides that were created in another presentation, the **Preserving Wetlands.pptx** file, which is stored in the Data Files folder. Reuse slides 7, 8, and 9, which all display charts and show the titles *Local Wetland Losses* and *Rate of Wetland Loss*. Position all three slides in the same sequence before the last slide in the presentation. Apply the destination formatting to the reused slides.

6. If necessary, modify the chart formats on the reused slides so that the data is clearly displayed.

7. Create a graphic file of slide 11. Save the file in JPEG format and name the file **Wetland Losses**, followed by your initials.

8. Save the changes and close the presentation.

SAM PROJECT 9–2

1. Open the **County Parks.pptx** file from the drive and folder where your Data Files are stored. Save the presentation as **Revised County Parks 1**, followed by your initials.

2. Launch Word and open the **Visitor Centers.docx** file from the drive and folder where your Data Files are stored. Copy the table and, in PowerPoint, paste it as a picture onto slide 6. Resize and reposition the table and modify the picture colors so the information fits well in the design theme and can be read easily. In Word, close the document without saving changes.

3. Launch Excel and open the **Park Visitors.xlsx** file from the drive and folder where your Data Files are stored. Save the worksheet as **Revised Park Visitors**, followed by your initials. Select and copy the worksheet data (*range A1:E9*) and then, in PowerPoint, link the data to slide 4. Resize and reposition the picture of the table to fill the blank area on the slide. If necessary, modify the picture colors. Leave the worksheet open.

4. Switch to Excel and, in the worksheet, click cell **E9** and type **1590**. Save the changes, and then confirm that the edit is updated in the presentation file. Leave the worksheet open.

5. In Excel, select and copy the chart in the worksheet. In PowerPoint, embed the chart on slide 5, using the destination theme. Resize and reposition the chart to fill the blank area on the slide. If necessary, modify the chart fonts so the legend and axis titles are easy to read. Exit Excel, saving any changes to the worksheet.

6. Save the changes to the presentation. Then save the slide information as an outline in Rich Text Format. Name the new file **County Parks Outline**, followed by your initials.

7. In Word, open the outline file **County Parks Outline**. If necessary, change the font color for all the text. Change the font size and paragraph alignments. Save the changes to the document and exit Word.

8. Leave the presentation open for the next Project.

PROJECT 9–3

1. If necessary, open the **Revised County Parks 1** file from the folder where you save your solution files and save the presentation as **Revised County Parks 2**, followed by your initials.

2. Launch Access and open the **Popular County Parks.accdb** file from the drive and folder where your Data Files are stored. Open the Park Information table.

3. Select all the table data except the ID values, and do not include the bottom blank row in the selection. Then copy the selected data to the Clipboard.

4. Switch to PowerPoint and paste the copied data as a table on slide 3, using the destination theme. Increase the font sizes and resize and reposition the table in the blank area on the slide. AutoFit each of the column widths in the table, and make any other adjustments so the table data is easy to read.

5. Exit Access without saving any changes to the database.

6. Save the changes to the presentation and then exit PowerPoint.

■ CRITICAL THINKING

ACTIVITY 9–1

When copying and pasting a table from a Word document to a slide, one of the Paste Special options is to Keep Text Only. Practice using this paste option to view the results. Write a brief paragraph explaining why you would or would not use this option to paste table data on a slide.

ACTIVITY 9–2

In this lesson, you learned several ways to integrate content between applications. Refer to **Table 9–1** and describe a scenario for using each of the four integration options. For example, you would use the copy and paste option to copy a URL in a Works Cited Page at the end of a report and then paste the information on a slide so that you can create a hyperlink on the slide.

LESSON 10

Sharing and Delivering Presentations

■ OBJECTIVES

Upon completion of this lesson, you should be able to:

- Add, edit, and delete comments.
- Compare and combine presentations.
- Rehearse timings and record narrations.
- Save and send presentations.
- Protect presentations and attach a digital signature.
- Annotate slides during the presentation.
- Set up a self-running slide show.
- Broadcast presentations.

■ VOCABULARY

broadcasting

case sensitive

comment

digital signature

document workspace site

encryption

kiosk

markup

Portable Document Format (PDF)

PowerPoint Viewer

XML Paper Specification (XPS)

ADVANCED   **Microsoft PowerPoint Unit**

The content and format of the slides for your presentation are almost completed. You are now ready to make some final edits and then explore options for sharing and delivering the presentation. In this lesson, you will learn about the final preparations before distributing a presentation and features you can use when delivering the presentation.

Collaborating on a Presentation

Team members commonly collaborate on creating a presentation. Often a presentation is reviewed by several individuals before the final version is completed. As team members review the presentation, they edit the content, add new content, change formats, and share their thoughts. PowerPoint offers several features for providing feedback and comparing changes.

Editing Slide Content

When you think about editing slide content, you probably first think about editing the words in the text boxes. You can, of course, also edit the text box formats. In the next Step-by-Step, you will apply colors to both text and text box borders and shape effects to enhance the appearance of the slides. You will also apply column and indentation formats to customize the text layout. You can personalize the edits you make by setting your own user name and initials in the PowerPoint Options dialog box. This helps reviewers to identify who made the changes in the presentation.

Step-by-Step 10.1

1. Open the **Festival** file from the drive and folder where your Data Files are stored.

2. Click the **File** tab, and then click **Options** to open the PowerPoint Options dialog box, as shown in **Figure 10–1**. Your settings will differ. Under Personalize your copy of Microsoft Office, make note of the User name and Initials text boxes. Then, if necessary, input your first and last name and your initials. Click **OK**.

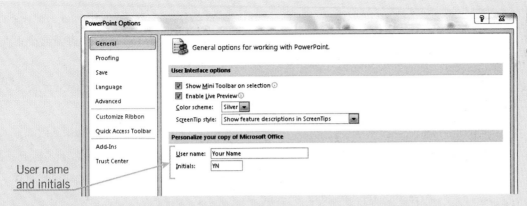

FIGURE 10–1
PowerPoint Options
dialog box

3. Save the presentation as **Revised Festival 1**, followed by your initials.

4. Go to slide 7. Click anywhere in the paragraph to select the text box. On the Home tab in the Paragraph group, click the **Columns** button ▤ ▾ and then click **More Columns**. In the Number box, change the setting to **2**. In the Spacing box, if necessary, set the spacing at **0.5"**. Click **OK**. In the Paragraph group, click the **Justify** button ▤.

5. The text box should still be selected. Format the text box shape fill and outline:

   a. Click the **Drawing Tools Format** tab. In the Shape Styles group, click the **Shape Fill** button arrow. In the submenu, click the **Red, Text 2, Darker 50%** theme color.

   b. In the Shape Styles group, click the **Shape Outline** button arrow. Point to **Weight**. In the submenu, click **More Lines**. The Format Shape dialog box opens.

   c. Under Line Style, in the Width box, enter the setting **6 pt**.

   d. Click the **Compound type** button arrow, and then select the third option, **Thick Thin**.

   e. In the left column, click **Line Color**. Then in the right column, click the **Color** list arrow. In the submenu, click the **Gray-50%, Accent 1** theme color.

   f. Close the Format Shape dialog box.

6. Triple-click the paragraph to select the entire paragraph. Click the **Home** tab. In the Font group, click the **Font Color** button arrow and then click the **White, Background 1** theme color.

7. Click the **Drawing Tools Format** tab, and in the Shape Styles group, click the **Shape Effects** button. Point to **Bevel**, and in the submenu under Bevel, click the first option, **Circle**.

8. Go to slide 2. Select all the paragraphs in the bulleted list. In the Paragraph group, click the **Dialog Box Launcher** to open the Paragraph dialog box.

9. Under Indentation, change the Before text setting to **.8** and then click **OK**. The bulleted items shift to the right.

10. Click the **Undo** button to restore the bulleted list to the default setting.

11. Go to slide 4. Insert a clip art image of a king or a crown. After inserting the clip art image, close the Clip Art pane. Resize, reposition, and recolor the image as needed.

12. Save the changes and leave the presentation open for the next Step-by-Step. (If you are ending your PowerPoint session, click the File tab and then click Options. Restore the user name and initials to the settings you noted in Step 2 above.)

Adding, Editing, and Deleting Comments

A *comment* is an annotation that is added within a document by the author or reviewer. Comments provide an easy way to share ideas and suggestions without changing the content of the presentation. PowerPoint automatically assigns numbers to comments as they are inserted in the presentation, and initials for the commenter's user name are included. The numbers are sequential, regardless of the user name. By default, comments appear in the upper-left corner of the slide, but you can drag and drop the comment icons to reposition them. You can easily navigate the comments by using the Previous Comment and Next Comment buttons, and you can delete one or all of the comments.

Comments inserted on slides are often referred to as *markup*. Markup appears in Normal view, but it doesn't appear in Slide Show view. You can specify whether or not to include markup when you print slides or handouts. If you don't want the markup to appear as you work with slides in Normal view, you can toggle the feature off.

Step-by-Step 10.2

1. If necessary, open the **Revised Festival 1** file from your solution files. Save the presentation as **Revised Festival 2**, followed by your initials.

2. Go to slide 2. Click the **Review** tab. In the Comments group, click the **New Comment** button. A text box showing your user name and the current date appears in the upper-left corner of the slide. To the left of the text box is an icon showing your initials and the number 1. See **Figure 10–2**.

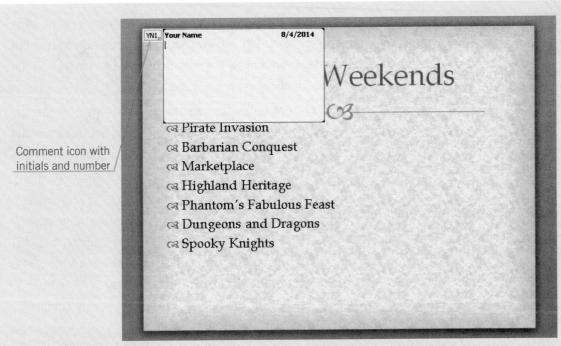

FIGURE 10–2
New comment
text box

Comment icon with
initials and number

3. With the insertion point positioned in the comment text box, type **Add the dates for each of these themes.**. Click anywhere in the Slide pane outside the comment box, to collapse the text box. The comment icon still appears in the upper-left corner.

4. Double-click the **comment icon** to reopen the comment text box. (When you click the icon only once, the comment text appears, but you cannot edit the content.) Position the insertion point in front of the word *dates*, type **scheduled**, and then press the **spacebar**. The revised sentence should now read *Add the scheduled dates for each of these themes.*.

5. Click outside the comment text box to collapse it so that only the icon appears. In the Comments group, click the **Show Markup** button to toggle the Show Markup feature off. The comment icon no longer appears on the slide.

6. Go to slide 4. Click the **New Comment** button. The Show Markup feature is automatically toggled back on. Note that the comment box is labeled with your initials and the number 2. In the comment text box, type **Insert a photo of the Queen's Kitchen.**. Then click outside the text box to collapse it.

7. In the Comments group, click the **Previous Comment** button. The Comment 1 text box on slide 2 opens. Click the **New Comment** button. A new icon with the number 3 and a new text box overlays Comment 1. Although a new comment is inserted between Comments 1 and 2, the comment numbers are not adjusted. Type **Need to confirm that these theme titles are accurate.**. Collapse the comment text box.

TIP

You can also edit a comment by right-clicking the comment icon and then clicking Edit Comment in the shortcut menu.

8. Select the **Comment 1** icon, and then drag it to the bottom of the slide and position it in the lower-left corner. Leave the number 3 comment at the top of the slide. Even though the sequence of the comments on the slide changes, the numbers are not adjusted.

9. Click the **Next Comment** button to navigate to Comment 3 at the top of the slide. Even though the comment numbers are not in sequential order on the slides, the next comment is the number 3 comment on this same slide. Click the **Next Comment** button again to move to Comment 2 on slide 4.

10. Click the **Previous Comment** button twice to navigate to Comment 1 on slide 2. In the Comments group, click the **Delete Comment** button arrow and then click **Delete**. The comment is removed from the slide. However, the comment at the top of the slide still shows the number 3. When you delete a comment, the numbers of the remaining comments are not updated.

11. Click the **File** tab and then click **Print**. If you print the slides in a presentation, the comment icons will appear on the slides, as shown in **Figure 10–3**.

> **TIP**
>
> To delete a comment, you can also right-click the comment icon and then click Delete Comment in the shortcut menu.

FIGURE 10–3
Print preview of a
slide with
a comment

12. In the preview pane, click the **Next Page** button. The comment text will print on a separate page, as shown in **Figure 10–4**. Advance to page 6 to view the comment for slide 4. Under Settings, click **Full Page Slides** to view the Print Layout settings. Disable the **Print Comments and Ink Markup** option. The comments no longer show in the preview pane.

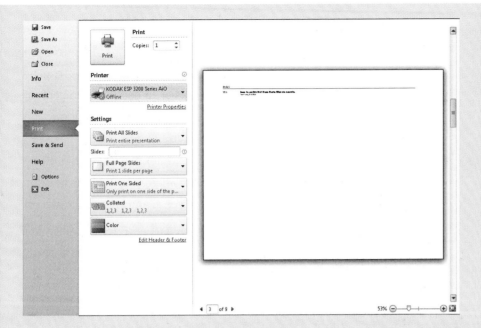

FIGURE 10–4
Print preview of comment text with a reference to slide number

13. Click the **Review** tab. In the Comments group, click the **Delete** button arrow and then click **Delete All Markup in this Presentation**. When prompted to delete all comments and ink annotations, click **Yes**.

14. Save the changes and leave the presentation open for the next Step-by-Step. (If you are ending your PowerPoint session, click the File tab and then click Options. Restore the user name and initials to the settings you noted earlier in Step-by-Step 10.1, Step 2, and then click OK.)

Comparing and Combining Presentations

To compare different versions of presentations, you can arrange slides on the screen to view more than one presentation at a time. Another option is to merge two presentations to compare the content. Once combined, differences between the two presentations are listed in the Reviewing pane. Differences can include inserted or deleted slides and new text, graphics, and formats. The user name associated with the saved presentation is shown, and you can choose which version of content you want to keep in the merged document.

Step-by-Step 10.3

1. If necessary, open the **Revised Festival 2** file from your solution files. Save the presentation as **Revised Festival 3**, followed by your initials. Then open the **Festival Reviewer A** file from the drive and folder where your Data Files are stored.

2. Click the **View** tab. In the Window group, click the **Cascade Windows** button 🖺. The windows are stacked.

3. In the Window group, click the **Arrange All** button 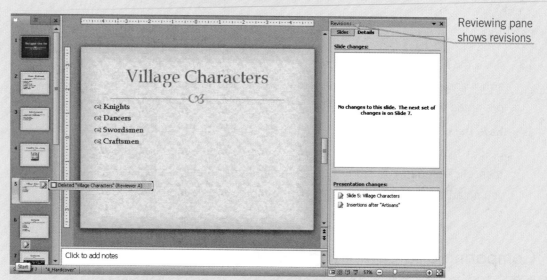 to view the presentations side by side. As you scroll through the slides in each window and compare the two presentations, you'll find that it can be difficult to identify the differences. It is easier to compare the content using the Compare feature. Close the Festival Reviewer A window, and then maximize the Revised Festival 3 window.

4. Click the **Review** tab. In the Compare group, click the **Compare** button. If necessary, navigate to the drive and folder where your solution files are stored. Select the filename **Festival Reviewer A** and then click **Merge**. The Reviewing pane opens, as shown in **Figure 10–5**. Note that the Reviewing pane displays two sections on the Details tab: Slide changes and Presentation changes.

FIGURE 10–5
Reviewing pane for
a merged presentation

Reviewing pane
shows revisions

5. On the Slides tab on the left, click the **slide 2** thumbnail. In the Reviewing pane on the right, under Slide changes, click **Content Placeholder 2: Pirate Invasion Ba....** A markup summary ScreenTip appears to the right of the content placeholder in the slide window indicating that the Reviewer A presentation includes *Oktoberfest*. See **Figure 10–6**.

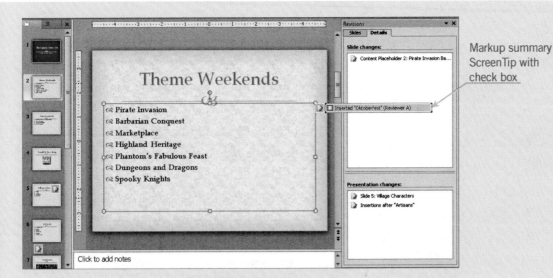

FIGURE 10–6
Markup indicating text inserted in the Reviewer A presentation

Markup summary ScreenTip with check box

6. In the Reviewing pane, click the **Slides** tab to view the Theme Weekends slide as it appears in the Reviewer A presentation. See **Figure 10–7**. Click the blue check box above the slide thumbnail to accept all changes by Reviewer A. The bulleted item *Oktoberfest* is added to the list in the placeholder in the slide window.

FIGURE 10–7
A thumbnail of the slide in the Reviewer A presentation

Thumbnail image of slide

7. On the Slides tab on the left, click the **slide 4** thumbnail. In the Reviewing pane on the right, click the **Details** tab. Under Slide changes, click **Picture 2**. A markup summary ScreenTip to the right of the content placeholder in the Slide pane indicates that the Reviewer A presentation shows the canvas contents (in other words, the content holder is blank). Click anywhere in the slide window to collapse the markup without making any changes. The clip art you inserted on the slide will remain.

8. In the Slide pane position the mouse pointer over the icon to the right of the title placeholder to show a markup summary ScreenTip. Click to show the ScreenTip with a check box. To accept this change, you would enable the check box. Instead, click anywhere in the Slide pane to collapse the markup without making any changes.

9. In the Reviewing pane, under Presentation changes, click **Slide 5: Village Characters**. A markup summary ScreenTip appears next to the slide 5 thumbnail on the Slides tab, as shown in **Figure 10–8**. The markup indicates that the slide was deleted in the Reviewer A presentation. Click the blue check box on the markup summary ScreenTip to accept the change. Slide 5 is removed from the merged presentation.

> **TIP**
>
> You can also accept and reject changes by clicking the Accept Change and Reject Change buttons in the Compare group on the Review tab.

FIGURE 10–8
Markup indicating a deleted slide in the Reviewer A presentation

Click to accept deletion

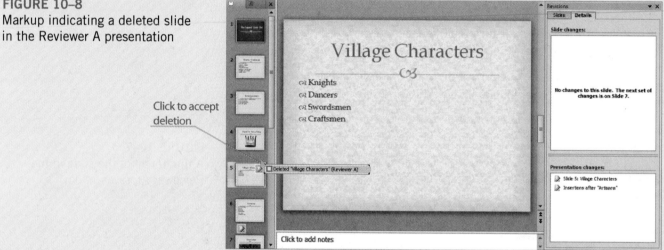

10. On the Slides tab, click the icon between the slide 5 and slide 6 thumbnails. The markup indicates that a slide with the title *Competitions* was inserted in the Reviewer A presentation. Click the blue check box to accept the change and add the new slide to the merged presentation. Note that a new thumbnail for slide 6 now shows an icon with a check mark. The ScreenTip for the icon indicates that the new slide from Reviewer A was added to the presentation.

11. Go to slide 7. Click the icon to the right of the content placeholder in the Slide pane. A list of several differences is displayed, as shown in **Figure 10–9**. Click the check box at the top of the list to accept all the differences as they appear in the Reviewer A document. Note that all the text box formats you applied are now removed. Uncheck the top check box to restore the text box settings.

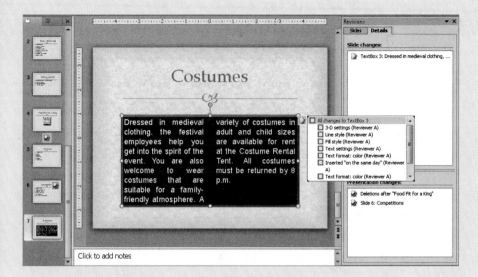

FIGURE 10–9
List of differences on slide 7

12. In the list, enable the change **Inserted "on the same day" (Reviewer A)**. Then click anywhere in the Slide pane to collapse the markup summary. Select the text in the text box and format the font color **White, Background 1**.

13. Close the Reviewing pane. Click the **Review** tab. In the Compare group, click the **End Review** button. When prompted to end the review for the current document, click **Yes**. All markup is removed from the presentation.

14. Click the **File** tab, and then click **Options**. Restore the user name and initials to the settings you noted earlier in Step-by-Step 10.1, Step 2. Click **OK**. Save the changes and leave the presentation open for the next Step-by-Step.

Coauthoring Presentations

Word features enable multiple users to work on the same presentation at the same time. You can upload presentations to a ***document workspace site***, which is a Web site that provides a central location for storing and sharing files. Files are stored in a library and can be password protected so that users must know the password to gain access or to open folders or files.

Microsoft SharePoint provides a document workspace site that enables a business to customize file storage and handling to suit its needs. Files can be stored and updated, file status information is provided, and employees can access the files remotely, enabling team members to collaborate and work together in real time. You need authorization to publish or access files at a SharePoint site, so introducing and showing SharePoint features is beyond the scope of this lesson.

Microsoft also offers SkyDrive, a free Windows Live service that provides password-protected online storage. You can assign passwords to control who has access to your files. To access SkyDrive, you must have a Windows Live account. If you use Hotmail, Live Messenger, or Xbox LIVE, you already have a Windows Live ID. If not, it only takes a minute to sign up. The following Step-by-Step will guide you in setting up a personal SkyDrive account.

▶ **VOCABULARY**
document workspace site

Step-by-Step 10.3

1. If necessary, open the **Revised Festival 3** file from your solution files. Save the presentation as **Revised Festival 4**, followed by your initials.

2. Click the **File** tab, and then click **Save & Send**. In the center pane, click **Save to Web**.

3. If you have a Windows Live ID, click the **Sign In** button, enter your ID (e-mail address) and password, and then click **OK**. (If you do not have an account, click the link to sign up for Windows Live and follow the directions to create a new account.)

4. If necessary, under Personal Folders, click the **My Documents** folder to select it. Then click the **Save As** button. The Save As dialog box opens. There may be a slight delay before the dialog box opens. Note that the path where the file will be stored shows a Windows Live network address.

5. You do not need to change the filename, so leave everything as is and click **Save**.

6. Close the Revised Festival 4 document. The document has been uploaded to the server.

7. Using your browser, go to **www.windowslive.com**. If necessary, sign in. Click **Office**, and if necessary, open the Your documents folder and the My Documents folder, and then click the **Revised Festival 4** file. The presentation will open in the PowerPoint Web App. You will see options to open the file in PowerPoint, edit the file in your browser, share the file, and start the slide show.

8. If you want full access to the PowerPoint features to edit the presentation, you can open the presentation in PowerPoint. Above the slide window, click the option **Open in PowerPoint**. If a prompt appears asking if you trust the source, click **OK**. The presentation will open in PowerPoint on your computer. When prompted to enter your Windows Live ID credentials, type your password and click **OK**. Close the presentation.

9. Return to your browser, and if necessary, sign back into your Windows Live account. View your online files and open the **My Documents** folder. Point to the **Revised Festival 4.pptx** file, and then click the **Delete** button ☒. When prompted, click **OK** to confirm the deletion.

10. In your browser, click **sign out** in the upper-right corner to sign out of Windows Live. Close your browser.

📠 EXTRA FOR EXPERTS

When you click Edit in Browser, some of the Ribbon commands appear in the Web App and you can make common edits such as adding and deleting slides and changing font and paragraph formats. The file is saved automatically in the default folder on your computer.

Rehearsing Timings and Recording Narrations

If you have set automatic slide timings, you can use the Rehearse Timings button to find out if you have allowed enough time for each slide. This feature is also beneficial if you want to know how long it might take a person to go through the show slide by slide. When you choose Rehearse Timings on the Slide Show menu, the presentation immediately starts running. A toolbar containing a stopwatch box appears on the screen to show how much time you have spent viewing each slide and the presentation as a whole. After you have finished the presentation, PowerPoint reports how long it took you to progress through all the slides and prompts you to choose to use your rehearsal timings the next time you view the slides.

If your computer has a microphone, you can record narrations for your presentation. This is a useful option for a slide show that runs automatically on the Web. After selecting settings for recording narrations, PowerPoint starts the slide show. A narration is saved for each slide, and you can also save the slide timings to fit the narrations. If you have already rehearsed timings and saved them for the slides in the presentation, you can choose to save the new timings that are required for the recorded narrations. You do not need to record a narration for every slide. You can start recording narrations from the beginning of a slide show, or you can start recording from the current slide. Each slide that contains a narration displays a sound object in the lower-right corner. Voice narration takes precedence over any other kind of sound on your slides. If you have recorded narration, you will not hear other sounds you have inserted.

Step-by-Step 10.4

To complete Steps 9–13, you must have a microphone and a sound card installed in your computer.

1. Open the **Revised Festival 4** file from your solution files.

2. Click the **Slide Show** tab. In the Set Up group, click the **Rehearse Timings** button. The presentation opens in Slide Show view. The Recording toolbar, shown in **Figure 10–10**, appears in the upper-left corner of the screen.

FIGURE 10–10
Recording toolbar

3. Click the **Pause** button ⏸ on the Recording toolbar to stop the clock. The dialog box shown in **Figure 10–11** appears.

FIGURE 10–11
Dialog box indicating recording is paused

4. Click **Resume Recording**, and then click the slide (or press Page Down or the down arrow key) to advance to the next slide. Wait at least four or five seconds for each slide, and then advance to the next slide. When you click the last slide, a prompt will appear asking if you want to keep the slide timings. Click **Yes**.

5. If necessary, switch to Slide Sorter view. The timings for each slide are displayed below the lower-left corner of each slide thumbnail.

6. Click the **slide 7** thumbnail. Click the **Transitions** tab. In the Timing group, under Advance Slide, change the setting in the After box to **00:15.00**. This will add more time to view slide 7.

7. Click the **Slide Show** tab. In the Start Slide Show group, click the **From Beginning** button. The slides will automatically advance based on the timings you rehearsed as well as the one timing you edited. When the slide show ends, click to exit Slide Show view.

8. Save the changes.

9. Go to slide 2. On the Slide Show tab, in the Set Up group, click the **Record Slide Show** button arrow and then click **Start Recording from Current Slide**. The Record Slide Show dialog box opens.

10. Make sure both options are enabled, as shown in **Figure 10–12**. By enabling the Slide and animation timings option, the rehearsed timings in the earlier steps will be replaced with the new timings needed for the recorded narrations.

FIGURE 10–12
Record Slide Show dialog box

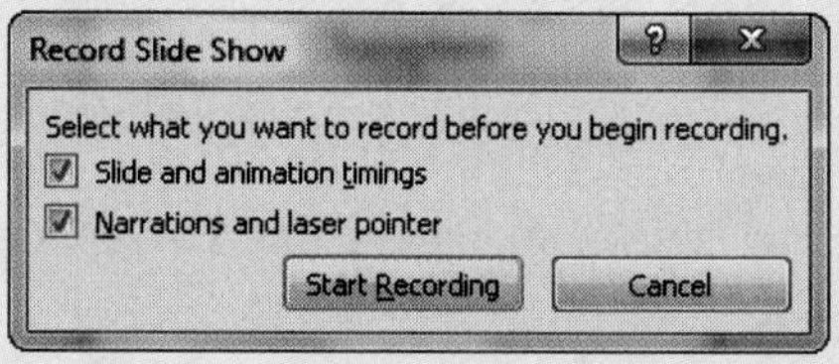

11. Click **Start Recording**. The Recording toolbar will appear in the upper-left corner. Start talking about the content on the slide. Say the following: "As you can see, there are several upcoming adventures. Special events are planned for each theme."

12. Wait a second or two, and then press the **down arrow** to advance to the next slide. Say the following: "Each weekend there are a variety of shows and activities that provide opportunities for people of all ages to learn and have fun." Press **Esc** to stop recording, and then switch to Slide Sorter view.

13. Note that the timing for slides 1, 4, 5, 6, and 7 did not change. Also note that there is an audio icon in the lower-right corner of slides 2 and 3. Start the slide show from the beginning. Allow the slides to advance automatically, and listen to the recordings for slides 2 and 3. (If you are not satisfied with the recording, you can delete the audio icon on the slide and re-record the narration.)

14. Save the changes and leave the presentation open for the next Step-by-Step.

Preparing Presentations for Distribution

After finalizing the presentation content, the next step is to prepare the presentation for distribution. PowerPoint provides several options for saving presentation files to share with others. Before distributing the files, you should consider protecting them so others cannot edit the content. Also, before distributing presentation files, you may want to verify your identity and confirm that the information in the file is valid.

Saving and Sending Presentations

To distribute presentation files, you can send the file via e-mail or in a fax message. Obviously, to send the file via e-mail, you must have a network or Internet connection, and you must have sufficient bandwidth (the speed of data transfer) for transferring the file. Publishing to a slide library or to a SharePoint site is another alternative so that others can access the slides.

Not all users have access to the PowerPoint application. If your audience only needs access to the presentation content, you can save the files in other formats. The *Portable Document Format (PDF)* was created by Adobe Systems in 1993. Microsoft first offered the *XML Paper Specification (XPS)* format in Office 2007. Both the PDF and XPS document formats are designed to preserve the visual appearance and layout of each page and enable fast viewing and printing.

▶ **VOCABULARY**
Portable Document Format (PDF)
XML Paper Specification (XPS)

Table 10–1 lists some of the presentation file types and describes the benefits of using each file type.

TABLE 10–1   Presentation file types

PRESENTATION FILE TYPE	BENEFITS OF USE
Presentation (*.pptx)	This is the default PowerPoint 2010 presentation format; the file can be opened in PowerPoint 2007 and 2010.
PDF Document Format (*.pdf)	Preserves the document formatting and enables file sharing when users have the Adobe software that enables editing.
XPS Document Format (*.xps)	Preserves the document formatting in a final form.
OpenDocument Presentation (*.odp)	Files can be opened in presentation applications that use the OpenDocument format, which makes it possible to share and collaborate on documents across multiple systems and multiple platforms; formatting might be lost.
PowerPoint Show (*.ppsx)	Saves time because the file automatically opens in Slide Show view. To quickly access the file when giving a presentation, save the file to the Desktop.
PowerPoint 97-2003 Presentation (*.ppt)	The file can be opened using previous software versions from PowerPoint 97 to Office PowerPoint 2003.
Template (*.potx)	Use to format future presentations.
PowerPoint Picture Presentation (*.pptx)	Each slide is converted to a picture; the file size is reduced, and some information may be lost, such as narrations and audio. When you open the file, you will not be able to edit the content.
PNG Portable Network Graphics (*.png)	Prints quality image files of each slide.
JPEG File Interchange Format (*.jpg)	Produces Web-quality image files of each slide.

By default, presentations are created for on-screen viewing. This means that the slides you see on your screen have been sized to fit the proportions of a monitor screen. However, PowerPoint gives you a number of other standard slide sizes from which to choose, or you can set a custom size. You can also adjust the slide layout and change the page setup and orientation to fit other formats, such as the 16:9 aspect ratio of the widescreen format.

Step-by-Step 10.5

1. If necessary, open the **Revised Festival 4** file from your solution files.
2. Click the **File** tab, and then click **Save & Send**. The options for sending a presentation via e-mail appear in the right pane, as shown in **Figure 10–13**.

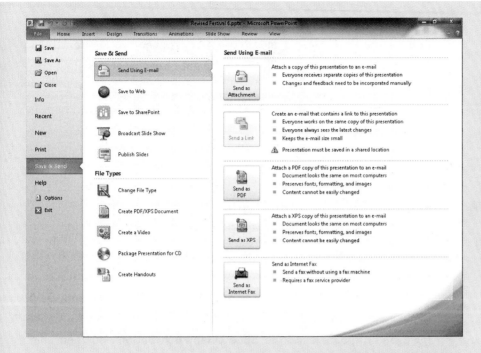

FIGURE 10–13
Send Using E-mail options

3. In the center pane, under File Types, click **Create PDF/XPS Document**. Then in the right pane, click the **Create PDF/XPS** button. The Publish as PDF or XPS dialog box opens. Click the Save as type list arrow and then click **PDF (*.pdf)**. If you have Adobe Reader installed on your computer, when you save the document using the PDF format, the document will open in the Adobe Reader application.

4. Navigate to the file and folder where you save your solution files. Click the **Save as type** list arrow, and then click **XPS Document (*.xps)**. You do not need to change the filename. Click **Publish**. The new presentation opens in XPS Viewer.

5. The XPS Viewer does not include automatic slide timings. Scroll down to view the slides. The audio icons still appear on the slides, but you cannot play the narrations. Close the XPS viewer.

6. Click the **File** tab, and then click **Save As**. Click the **Save as type** list arrow, and then click **PowerPoint Show (*.ppsx)**. Click **Save**.

7. Close the presentation and exit PowerPoint. Then navigate to the drive and folder where your solution files are stored. Double-click the filename **Revised Festival 4.ppsx**. Note that the file automatically opens in Slide Show view, and the slides start playing.

8. Press **Esc** to stop the slide show. Note that when you stop the slide show, the file closes and PowerPoint is not open.

9. Open the **Revised Festival 4.pptx** file from your solutions folder.

TIP

If you do not see the file extension (*.ppsx), open the Control Panel and then open Appearance and Personalization. Click Folder Options, and then click the View tab. Under Advanced settings, make sure the option Hide extensions for known file types is disabled.

10. Click the **Design** tab. In the Page Setup group, click the **Page Setup** button. The Page Setup dialog box opens, as shown in **Figure 10–14**. Note that you can use the Width and Height boxes to set a custom size.

FIGURE 10–14
Page Setup dialog box

11. Change the height to **6.1** inches. Then click the **Slides sized for** list arrow, and then click the standard size **On-screen Show (16:10)**. In the Orientation section, under Slides, enable the **Portrait** option. Click **OK**. The slide layout changes are obvious in Slide Sorter view. In the Page Setup group, click the **Slide Orientation** button and then click **Landscape**.

12. Click **File**, and then click **Save As**. Click the **Save as type** list arrow, click **OpenDocument Presentation (*.odp)**, and then click **Save**. When prompted to continue to save in this format, click **Yes**. Close the presentation.

13. Open the **Revised Festival 4.pptx** file from your solution files. Click **File**, and then click **Save As**. In the File name box, change the filename to **Revised Festival Picture**, followed by your initials. Click the **Save as type** list arrow, and near the end of the list of formats, click **PowerPoint Picture Presentation (*.pptx)** and then click **Save**. When prompted that a copy has been saved, click **OK**. Close the presentation.

14. Open the **Revised Festival Picture** presentation. Note that you cannot make any edits. Switch to Slide Show view and review the presentation. Note that the audio icons on slides 2 and 3 do not play. Close the presentation.

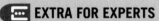

EXTRA FOR EXPERTS

The default setting in PowerPoint is Unrestricted Access. You can use the Restrict Permission by People feature to grant designated people access to your presentations, yet they still cannot edit, copy, or print the files. To use the Restrict Permission by People feature, you must be able to authenticate the credentials of people by using an Information Rights Management (IRM) service.

Protecting Presentations

When sharing a presentation file, you may want to consider protecting the presentation so that others do not make changes to the file. When you use the Mark as Final command, you are indicating that the status of the document is final. PowerPoint saves the file as a read-only document, but this does not provide secure protection. If users want to make edits, they can easily toggle off the Mark as Final feature.

To restrict access to presentations, you can encrypt the files so they are not readable without a password. *Encryption* is a standard method for encoding data. When assigning passwords in PowerPoint, the characters can be any combination of letters, numerals, spaces, and symbols. A strong password includes a combination of text, numbers, and symbols and consists of at least eight characters. The password is *case sensitive*, which means that when entering a password to open a file, the upper and lower casing of the letters must be identical to the casing of the letters in the assigned password. If the casing of the letters differs, the file will not open. Passwords can be changed or deleted using the Encrypt Document dialog box.

VOCABULARY
encryption
case sensitive

Step-by-Step 10.6

1. Open the **Revised Festival 4.pptx** file from your solution files. Save the presentation as **Revised Festival 5**, followed by your initials.

2. Click the **File** tab. In the center pane, click the **Protect Presentation** button and then click **Mark as Final**. When prompted to mark the presentation as final, click **OK**. Read the dialog box that explains the purpose of marking the document final, and then click **OK** to close it. The information in the center pane changes to show Permissions, as shown in **Figure 10–15**.

FIGURE 10–15
Backstage view with Permissions setting

3. Click the **Home** tab. Note the yellow message bar at the top of the document indicating that the presentation has been marked as final. Also note that the Marked as Final button  appears in the status bar.

4. Click **Edit Anyway** in the yellow message bar at the top of the slide window. The presentation can now be edited.

5. Click the **File** tab and, in the center pane, click the **Protect Presentation** button. Click **Encrypt with Password**. The Encrypt Document dialog box opens, as shown in **Figure 10–16**.

FIGURE 10–16
Encrypt Document dialog box

6. In the Password text box, type **RF2014!**. Click **OK**. The Confirm Password dialog box opens. In the Reenter password text box, type **RF2014!** and then click **OK**.

7. Save the changes to the presentation, and then close the file.

8. Reopen the **Revised Festival 5** presentation from your solution files. When prompted to enter the password, type **RF2014!** and then click **OK**.

9. Click the **File** tab, and then click the **Protect Presentation** button. Click **Encrypt with Password** to open the Encrypt Document dialog box. Delete the current password, and then type the new password **RF2014#1**. Then click **OK**. Then reenter the new password and click **OK**.

10. Save the changes and leave the presentation open for the next Step-by-Step.

WARNING

If you forget a password, you cannot access a presentation. Write down passwords and keep them in a secure location, or use a password management application.

Attaching a Digital Signature

VOCABULARY
digital signature

A *digital signature* is an attachment to a file or e-mail message certifying that the information in the file is authentic and safe. The digital signature is embedded in the presentation, and although it is not visible, recipients of the presentation can see that the file has been digitally signed. Signed files are marked as final and remain signed until the file is changed. If the presentation is edited, the signature is removed. You can embed multiple digital signatures in the same presentation.

Digital signatures are easy to create using the Digital Certificate for VBA Projects tool. However, when you use this feature, you create a self-signed digital certificate, which does not verify your identity and, therefore, is only appropriate for personal use. Furthermore, the digital certificate can only be used on the computer where it is created.

The Digital Certificate for VBA Projects tool is used in this lesson to demonstrate how to attach a digital signature to a document. If you need an authenticated certificate, you must secure a service from a third-party vendor; several commercial certification authority services are compatible with Office applications.

Step-by-Step 10.7

1. If necessary, open the **Revised Festival 5** file from your solution files. (To open the file, you will need to enter the password **RF2014#1**.) Save the presentation as **Revised Festival 6**, followed by your initials.

2. Click the **File** tab, and then click the **Protect Presentation** button. Click **Encrypt with Password**. Delete the current password, leave the text box blank, and then click **OK**. The file is no longer password protected.

3. View the digital signatures on your computer:

   a. Launch Internet Explorer.

   b. Click the **Tools** button, and then click **Internet Options**.

   c. In the Internet Options dialog box, click the **Content** tab. Under Certificates, click **Certificates**. A list of digital signatures available on your computer appears. Check to see if your digital signature appears in the list.

   d. Close both dialog boxes, and then close Internet Explorer.

   e. If your personal signature was not in the list, go to Step 4. If your personal signature was in the list, go to Step 5.

4. Create a new digital certificate:

   a. On the taskbar, click the **Start** button, click **All Programs**, click **Microsoft Office**, click **Microsoft Office 2010 Tools**, and then click **Digital Certificate for VBA Projects**.

   b. In the Create Digital Certificate dialog box, in the Your certificate's name box, type your first and last names. Click **OK**.

   c. A message box appears indicating that a new certificate has been successfully created. Click **OK** to close the dialog boxes.

5. If necessary, click the File tab. In the center pane, click the **Protect Presentation** button and then click **Add a Digital Signature**. A message box appears explaining that Microsoft does not warrant a digital signature's legal enforceability. Click **OK**.

6. In the Sign dialog box, under Purpose for signing this document, type **To confirm the validity of the information in this presentation.**. If your name does not appear in the Signing as: box, click Change, select your certificate, and then click OK.

7. In the Sign dialog box, click **Sign**. If a prompt appears saying that the signature cannot be verified, it is because your certificate is a self-signed certificate and the certificate was not issued by a trusted certificate authority (CA). If so, click Yes to use the certificate.

8. A message box opens confirming that the signature has been successfully saved with the document. If any changes are made to the document, the signature will be invalid. Click **OK**.

9. In the center pane, you may see a warning about an invalid signature. In the center pane, click the **View Signatures** button to open the Signatures pane.

10. Point to your signature in the pane, and then click the **down arrow** to the right of your signature. A menu of options for the selected signature opens, as shown in **Figure 10–17**. Your settings may look different.

FIGURE 10–17
Signatures pane showing options for signatures

11. Click **Signature Details**. If your certificate is not trusted, click the link Click here to trust this user's identity.

12. Click **View** to review the certificate information. Click **OK**, and then click **Close** to close the dialog box.

13. A yellow message bar at the top of the slide window shows that the document has been marked as final to discourage editing. The Signatures icon 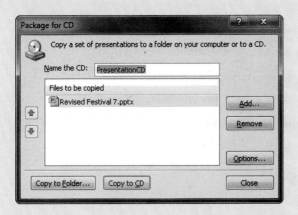 appears in the status bar, indicating that the document contains a signature.

14. The signature was automatically saved with the document. Close the Signatures pane. Leave the presentation open for the next Step-by-Step.

Package a Presentation

If you plan to show a presentation on a different computer, you can compress and save the file to a folder (such as a flash drive) or to a CD. You can choose to include linked files and/or to embed TrueType fonts. You can also restrict access by assigning passwords, and you can inspect the file.

If the destination computer does not have PowerPoint installed, you can use *PowerPoint Viewer*, a Microsoft application that enables you to open PowerPoint presentations when the PowerPoint application is not installed on the computer. You will need to download and install the PowerPoint Viewer on the destination computer. When using the PowerPoint Viewer, you can view and print presentations, but you cannot edit the presentations.

▶ **VOCABULARY**
PowerPoint Viewer

Step-by-Step 10.8

1. If necessary, open the **Revised Festival 6** presentation from your solution files. Save the presentation as **Revised Festival 7**, followed by your initials. When prompted about invalidating all the signatures, click **Yes**.

2. In the yellow message bar at the top of the slide window, click **Edit Anyway**. When prompted to continue, click **Yes**, and then when prompted to remove the signature and save the document, click **OK**.

3. Click the **File** tab, and then click **Save & Send**. In the center pane, under File Types, click **Package Presentation for CD**. Then in the right pane, click the **Package for CD** button. The Package for CD dialog box opens. Under Files to be copied, the current filename appears, as shown in **Figure 10–18**.

FIGURE 10–18
Package for CD dialog box

4. Replace the text in the Name the CD text box with **Festival CD**, followed by your initials.

5. Click **Options** to open the Options dialog box, as shown in **Figure 10–19**.

FIGURE 10–19
Options dialog box

6. Under Include these files, make sure the options Linked files and Embedded TrueType fonts are enabled. In the first password box, type the password **RF2014#1**. In the second password box, type **RF20114!** and then enable the option **Inspect presentations for inappropriate or private information**. Click **OK**.

7. When prompted to confirm the password to open each presentation, type **RF2014#1** and click **OK**. When prompted to confirm the password to modify each presentation, type **RF20114!** and then click **OK**.

8. If you were to click Copy to CD, the files would be burned to a CD using the CD/DVD drive on your computer. Instead of burning a CD, click **Copy to Folder**. The Copy to Folder dialog box opens.

9. Click **Browse**, navigate to the drive and folder where your solution files are saved, and then click **Select**. The path to your solutions folder appears in the Location box.

10. In the Copy to Folder dialog box, click **OK**. When prompted to include linked files in your package, click **Yes**.

11. The Document Inspector window opens. Click **Inspect**. When the inspection results appear, click **Remove All** to remove the document properties and personal information. Then close the Document Inspector dialog box.

12. A window showing the contents of the Final Festival folder opens. Double-click the **PresentationPackage** folder. Note that the folder contains seven files and all are related to the Revised Festival 7 file.

13. Close the window. Then close the Package for CD dialog box.

14. Leave the Revised Festival 7 presentation open for the next Step-by-Step.

Delivering Presentations

The most traditional way to deliver a presentation is for a presenter to stand up in front of the audience and control the slides. When delivering a presentation this way, you can use tools to underline or highlight text and objects on the slide. However, PowerPoint offers several other features that enable you to deliver the presentation to an audience in a remote location or to create a self-running presentation.

Annotating Slides during a Presentation

You might occasionally want to draw or write on your slides as you present them. PowerPoint has several options for writing new content and highlighting existing content. After adding annotations, you can erase them. If you don't erase the annotations, you have the option of keeping or discarding them when you exit the slide show.

You can also use the mouse pointer as a laser pointer and customize the color.

Step-by-Step 10.9

1. If necessary, open the **Revised Festival 7** presentation from your solution files.

2. Click the **Slide Show** tab. In the Set Up group, click the **Set Up Slide Show** button to open the Set Up Show dialog box, as shown in **Figure 10–20**.

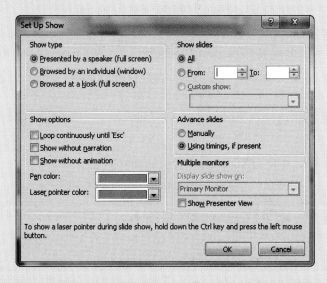

FIGURE 10–20
Set Up Show dialog box

3. Under Show type, the default option Presented by a speaker (full screen) should already be enabled. Under Show options, change the Pen color setting to blue and change the Laser pointer color setting to green.

4. Under Advance slides, enable the option **Manually**. Then click **OK**.

5. Select the **slide 5** thumbnail. Then switch to Slide Show view.

6. Hover the mouse pointer over the lower-left corner of the screen. Four transparent buttons will be displayed. Click the **Pen** button 🖊, and then in the shortcut menu, click **Pen**. The mouse pointer changes to a small blue dot.

7. Click and drag the mouse pointer to create a circle around the word *Pottery*. Then click and drag the mouse pointer to underline the word *Blacksmithing*.

8. Press **Esc** to toggle off the pen.

9. Press and hold the **Ctrl** key as you click and hold down the left mouse button and drag the mouse around to move the laser pointer on the screen.

10. Click the **Pen** button in the lower-left corner, and then click **Eraser**. The mouse pointer changes to an Eraser ✎. Click the blue circle around the word *Pottery* to remove the annotation.

11. Right-click anywhere on the slide. In the shortcut menu, point to **Pointer Options** and then click **Highlighter**. The mouse pointer changes to a vertical yellow bar . Drag the mouse pointer over the word *Leatherwork* to highlight the text. Press **Esc** to toggle off the highlighter.

12. Because you are using the mouse for annotations, you cannot click to advance slides during a presentation. Press **PageDown** (or press the down arrow key) to advance to the next slide.

13. Advance to the end of the slide show and click to exit. A prompt will appear asking if you want to keep the ink annotations. Click **Keep**.

14. Save the changes and leave the presentation open for the next Step-by-Step.

Setting Up the Show

Before you present your slides, you should use the Set Up Show command to verify your current settings and to specify additional settings. For example, you can hide specific slides or select a range of slides to display.

You can also specify the show type. For example, you can prepare the slide show to be self-running for a *kiosk,* an interactive computer terminal available for public use. Or, you can set up the presentation so that an individual can view the slides and control when to advance them. You can also control whether the slides appear with or without narrations and animations.

The Show Set Up group also includes a feature to record the presentation. When you use this feature, PowerPoint records both the timings and narrations as you deliver the presentation. A recording of the presentation enables you to go back and listen to your narrations afterwards, and those who missed your presentation can review the slides and listen to your narration at a later point.

▶ **VOCABULARY**
kiosk

📼 **EXTRA FOR EXPERTS**

If you want to show only one of your custom shows, click the Custom show option and select the show. Additional options allow you to adjust the resolution of your presentation and to display it on multiple monitors.

Step-by-Step 10.10

1. If necessary, open the **Revised Festival 7** presentation from your solution files. Save the presentation as **Revised Festival 8**, followed by your initials.

2. If necessary, switch to Normal view. Go to slide 5. Point to the highlight annotation, click to select the object, and then press **Delete**. Then delete the blue underline.

3. On the Slides tab, click the **slide 4** thumbnail. Then, if necessary, click the **Slide Show** tab. In the Set Up group, click the **Hide Slide** button. Note that on the Slides tab, the number for the selected slide shows a diagonal line, indicating that it will not appear in the slide show.

4. In the Set Up group, click the **Set Up Slide Show** button to open the Set Up Show dialog box.

5. Under Show type, enable the **Browsed at a kiosk (full screen)** option. Under Show options, the Loop continuously until 'Esc' option is automatically enabled. The option is grayed out, so you cannot disable it. Under Advance slides, enable the **Using timings, if present** option. Click **OK**.

6. In the Start Slide Show group, click the **From Beginning** button and watch the presentation. The slides will advance using the timing settings, and the narrations will also play. The slide with the title *Food Fit for a King* will not appear in the slide show. When the last slide appears, the presentation will play again.

7. Press **Esc** to switch to Normal view. Save the changes to the presentation.

8. Save the presentation as **Revised Festival 9**, followed by your initials.

9. Create Action buttons:
   a. Go to slide 1. Click the **Insert** tab. In the Illustrations group, click the **Shapes** button. At the bottom of the menu, under Action Buttons, click **Action Button: Forward or Next**. The mouse pointer changes to a cross.
   b. Drag the mouse pointer in the lower-right corner of the slide to create a button approximately 1" wide by ½" high. When you release the mouse button, the Action Settings dialog box will open. Click **OK**. Select the action button and copy it to the Clipboard.
   c. Go to slide 2. Paste the forward action button copied from slide 1 to slide 2. Do not be concerned about the button overlaying the audio icon. Audio icons do not appear during a slide show.

d. Click the **Shapes** button. Under Action Buttons, click **Action Button: Back or Previous**. Draw a similar sized shape in the lower-left corner of slide 2, then click **OK**. Reposition and resize the two buttons as needed.

e. Select both action buttons and copy them to the Clipboard. Then copy the buttons to slides 3–7. You need to copy only a Back or Previous button on slide 7.

10. Go to slide 4. Click the **Slide Show** tab, and in the Set Up group, click the **Hide Slide** button to toggle the feature off. The diagonal line no longer appears on the slide number on the Slides tab.

11. In the Set Up group, click the **Set Up Slide Show** button. Under Show type, enable the **Browsed by an individual** option. Under Show options, make sure the Loop continuously until 'Esc' option is disabled.

12. Under Show slides, in the From box, enter **2**. In the To box, if necessary, enter **7**. Under Advance slides, enable the option **Manually**. Then click **OK**.

13. In the Start Slide Show group, click the **From Beginning** button and review the presentation. You will need to click the Forward or Next action button to advance to the next slide. When the last slide appears, you can click the Back or Previous action button.

14. Press **Esc** to switch to Normal view. Save the changes and leave the presentation open for the next Step-by-Step.

EXTRA FOR EXPERTS

You can also insert the Action Button: Beginning shape to create a hyperlink to the first slide in the presentation or the Action Button: End shape to create a hyperlink to the last slide in the presentation.

▶ **VOCABULARY**
broadcasting

Broadcasting Presentations

Broadcasting is a way to present slides to an audience that cannot convene in one location for the presentation. If, for example, you work in a very large company or for a company that has branch offices located over a wide geographic area, broadcasting is a sensible way to reach all your potential viewers. A broadcast presentation is saved in HTML format, which means your viewers do not need PowerPoint to view the slides. Instead, they view the slides using their standard Web browser.

Using the Broadcast Slide Show command, you connect to the Microsoft PowerPoint Broadcast Service. You must first sign in with your Windows Live ID. Then you provide the URL link to those you want to invite to watch a synchronized view of your slide show. Up to 50 remote attendees may participate in the broadcast. When they access the Web page, they can view the presentation and see animations and transitions just as they would view the slide show on your computer. You can manually control the slide display, or you can set automatic timings.

Step-by-Step 10.11

You must have a Windows Live ID to complete these steps.

1. If necessary, open the **Revised Festival 9** presentation from your solution files.

2. If necessary, click the **Slide Show** tab. In the Start Slide Show group, click the **Broadcast Slide Show** button to open the Broadcast Slide Show dialog box.

3. Click **Start Broadcast**. When prompted, sign into your Windows Live account. The Broadcast Slide Show dialog box opens. Click **Send in Email**. A new e-mail message opens in Outlook. All you would need to enter is the recipient's e-mail address. The subject line and body of the message are already complete.

4. Close Outlook.

5. In the Broadcast Slide Show dialog box, click **Start Slide Show**. Remote viewers can now view the slide show online.

6. Press **Esc** to switch to Normal view. In the yellow message bar, click **End Broadcast**. When the prompt to disconnect all remote viewers appears, click **End Broadcast**.

7. Close the presentation.

TIP

If you do not have Outlook installed on your computer, you can click Copy Link and then create an e-mail message in your e-mail application and paste the link into the body of the message.

SUMMARY

In this lesson, you learned:

- When collaborating on a presentation, team members can use comments to provide feedback on slides. You can easily add, edit, and delete comments.

- You can view presentations side by side, but the Compare feature makes it easier to identify the differences between two presentations.

- To enable team members to collaborate and work together in real time, presentations can be stored and updated so that employees can access the file remotely.

- The Rehearse Timings button is beneficial in helping you estimate how much time you need to show the slides in the presentation.

- If you have access to a microphone, you can record narrations that will play during the slide show.

- PowerPoint provides several options for saving and sending presentations, including the Web, e-mail, and fax. There are also several options for file formats suitable for a variety of uses.

- You can protect presentations to ensure that others do not make changes to the file, and you can restrict access by assigning a password. You can also certify that the information in the file is authentic.

- As you present a slide show, you can use tools to annotate the slides, and then you can choose to keep or discard the annotations.

- Your audience does not need to be in the same room with you to view your presentation. PowerPoint provides several options for delivering presentations remotely.

VOCABULARY REVIEW

Define the following terms:

broadcasting   document workspace site   Portable Document Format (PDF)
case sensitive   encryption   PowerPoint Viewer
comment   kiosk   XML Paper Specification (XPS)
digital signature   markup

 # REVIEW QUESTIONS

TRUE / FALSE

Circle T if the statement is true or F if the statement is false.

T   F   **1.**   When comments are deleted from slides, the remaining comment numbers are automatically updated.

T   F   **2.**   Marking a document as final is one of the more secure ways to protect a document.

T   F   **3.**   Multiple users can work on the same presentation at the same time.

T   F   **4.**   When annotating slides during a slide show, the annotations are automatically saved with the slides.

T   F   **5.**   Voice narrations take precedence over any other kind of sound on your slides.

FILL IN THE BLANK

Complete the following sentences by writing the correct word or words in the blanks provided.

1. A(n) _____ is a central location for storing and sharing documents.

2. A(n) _____ is an attachment to a file or e-mail message certifying that the information in the file is authentic and safe.

3. _____ is a way to present slides to an audience that cannot convene in one location for the presentation.

4. _____ is a standard method for encoding data.

5. A(n) _____ is an interactive computer terminal available for public use.

WRITTEN QUESTIONS

Write a brief answer to the following questions.

1. What are the benefits of saving a document in a PDF or XPS format?

2. Explain how you can print copies of the comments added to slides.

3. Explain how rehearsing timings helps you estimate how long it will take you to go through a presentation.

4. What are the advantages of packaging a presentation to a CD (or copying the presentation to a file folder)?

5. What are the advantages to using the Compare feature to review changes made in multiple versions of a presentation?

■ PROJECTS

If you have a SAM 2010 user profile, your instructor may have assigned an autogradable version of the indicated project. If so, log into the SAM 2010 Web site at *www.cengage.com/sam2010* to download the instruction and start files.

PROJECT 10–1

1. Open the file **Karate 1** from the drive and folder where your Data Files are stored. Save the presentation as **Revised Karate 1**, followed by your initials.

2. Note the current settings for the user name and initials. Change the user name to your name, and change the initials.

3. Go to slide 6. Add the comment **Do you think we should apply related font colors to the words in this list?**. Collapse the comment text box.

4. Edit the comment text by adding the following sentence at the beginning of the comment: **Are the colors in the correct sequence?**. Collapse the comment text box.

5. Save the changes to the presentation. Restore the user name settings.

6. Save the file as **Revised Karate 2**, followed by your initials.

7. Use the Compare feature to compare the **Revised Karate 2** presentation to the **Karate Reviewer A** file in the Data Files folder.

8. Accept the following changes from Reviewer A:

   a. Reordering of the bulleted items on slide 2. (*Hint*: Look at the Karate Reviewer A slide on the Slides tab of the Reviewing pane.)

   b. All font color changes on slide 6.

   c. The new slide at the end of the presentation.

9. Do not accept the changes on slide 5.

10. Delete all the comments in the presentation, and end the review.

11. Save the changes to the presentation.

12. Package the presentation to a CD (copy the file to a folder in your Solutions folder). Name the folder **Final Karate**, followed by your initials. Create a password to modify each presentation: **#1ETARAK**. Include linked files and inspect the files for private information. Remove all personal information.

13. Restore the user name settings noted in Step 2. Close all open files, folders, and dialog boxes.

⟨SAM⟩ PROJECT 10–2

1. Open the file **Scarecrow 1** from the drive and folder where your Data Files are stored. Save the presentation as **Revised Scarecrow 1**, followed by your initials.

2. Rehearse the timings for all the slides. Animations have been applied throughout the slides, so be sure to click and advance to each item on a slide before moving on to the next slide.

3. Save the timings. Then set the time for slide 5 to **15**.

4. Save the changes to the presentation.

5. Save the presentation in the PDF format, using the same filename.

6. Protect the Revised Scarecrow 1.pptx file by encrypting it with a password. Use the password **014@FRCC#**.

7. Save the changes and close the file.

PROJECT 10–3

1. Open the file **Scarecrow 2** from the drive and folder where your Data Files are stored. Save the presentation as **Revised Scarecrow 2**, followed by your initials.

2. Go to slide 2. Apply an emphasis effect to the text box. (*Hint*: Use the More Emphasis Effects command to make sure you see all available effects.) Trigger the effect to start after the previous, and adjust the timing if necessary.

3. Beginning with the first slide, record the entire slide show. Record the slide and animation timings as well as narrations and laser pointer. Take your time advancing through the slides, and record narrations on at least two of the slides. (*Hint*: You can read the slide content, or you can add your own comments regarding the content.) Review the narrations, and re-record them if necessary.

4. Set the slide show up to run all slides at a kiosk. The show should include the narrations and animations.

5. Save the changes to the presentation.

6. Attach your digital signature to the presentation. The purpose of the signature is to confirm that the file is authentic and safe.

7. Close the file.

PROJECT 10–4

1. Open the **Karate 2** file from the drive and folder where your Data Files are stored. Save the presentation as **Revised Karate 3**, followed by your initials.

2. Add action buttons to slides 1–7 so the individual can navigate forward and backward through the slides.

3. Show the presentation from the beginning. When you get to slide 5, use the Pen tool to underline each of the bulleted terms. Discard all annotations.

4. In the Set Up Show options, change the show type to be browsed by an individual who can manually advance through the slides. Show all the slides.

5. Save the changes to the presentation.

6. Close the file.

■ CRITICAL THINKING

ACTIVITY 10–1

Ask a classmate or friend to partner with you so you can experience broadcasting a presentation. Then reflecting on the experience, answer the following questions: What did it feel like presenting without seeing your audience? Did your partner feel that it was a positive experience? Do you think you are likely to use the broadcasting feature anytime in the near future?

ACTIVITY 10–2

Describe a scenario for which you would create a self-running presentation to be browsed at a kiosk. Would you include narrations on some or all of the slides? Why or why not?

UNIT REVIEW

Advanced Microsoft PowerPoint

▪ REVIEW QUESTIONS

MATCHING

Match the correct term in Column 2 to its description in Column 1.

Column 1

_____ 1. An interactive computer terminal available for public use.

_____ 2. Provides an outline of topics and is useful for presentations with custom shows.

_____ 3. A list of coordinates related to a specific image.

_____ 4. Tiny colored dots that compose the image on a computer screen.

_____ 5. A standard method for encoding data.

_____ 6. An object that becomes part of the destination file and can be edited in the destination file.

_____ 7. A line bordering the chart plot area used as a frame of reference for measurement.

_____ 8. Reviews the topics in a presentation and can be used as an introduction to or a review of a presentation.

_____ 9. An object inserted as a static object that accesses data stored in the source file.

_____ 10. Related data points that are plotted in a chart.

Column 2

A. agenda slide

B. axis

C. bitmap

D. data series

E. embedded object

F. encryption

G. hot spot

H. image map

I. kiosk

J. legend

K. linked object

L. pixels

M. summary slide

MULTIPLE CHOICE

Select the best response for the following statements.

1. A _____ image takes more time to open, but when you increase and decrease the image size, the clarity of the image will not change.

    A. dpi

    B. vector

    C. raster

    D. ppi

2. The PowerPoint proofing tools check _____

    A. spelling and grammar

    B. capitalization

    C. formats

    D. all of the above

3. The option to _____ data is most useful when you want to keep the data current.

    A. convert

    B. embed

    C. link

    D. copy and paste

4. A _____ chart is effective for showing how parts relate to a whole.

    A. column

    B. line

    C. pie

    D. radar

5. The _____ controls the formatting for all the slides in the presentation.

    A. layout master

    B. custom design template

    C. main layout master

    D. slide master

6. To restrict access to a presentation file, you can _____.

    A. encrypt the file

    B. attach a digital signature

    C. mark the presentation as final

    D. all of the above

7. PowerPoint's _____ feature will automatically correct commonly misspelled words, without prompting you.

    A. AutoCorrect

    B. AutoComplete

    C. AutoType

    D. Custom Dictionary

8. To change column width in a table, you can use the _____ command.

    A. AutoFit

    B. Distribute Columns

    C. Adjust Columns

    D. A or B

9. To add blank space around a graphic, you can _____.

    A.   drag the side handles of the graphic

    B.   drag the corner handles of the graphic

    C.   outcrop the graphic

    D.   any of the above

10. Sizing a graphic to exact proportions is referred to as _____.

    A.   scaling

    B.   nudging

    C.   cropping

    D.   aspect ratio

WRITTEN QUESTIONS

Write a brief answer to the following questions.

1. What two factors affect the size of a picture file?

2. Why is it important to select the right chart type?

3. What are the benefits of organizing slides into sections?

4. Why would you use Paste Special options when copying slides from one presentation to another?

5. How can you reduce the file size of a presentation that includes pictures, video clips, and audio clips?

6. What is progressive disclosure?

7. When would you use PowerPoint Viewer?

8. What formats does a table style provide?

9. How are slide masters useful?

10. When you export PowerPoint data to a Word document, what information appears in the Word outline?

■ PROJECTS

PROJECT 1

1. Open the **Fire Instructions** file from the drive and folder where your Data Files are stored. Save the presentation as **Revised Fire Instructions**, followed by your initials.

2. Go to slide 4. Remove the second-level bullet formats. Replace the first-level bullets with a custom bullet, using a symbol of your choice.

3. Insert a new Title and Content slide between slides 1 and 2. Create a bar chart using the data below. Add the slide title **Previous Year Fires**.

	ZONE 1	ZONE 2	ZONE 3
Cooking	33	21	28
Heating equipment	14	7	17
Arson	5	4	2
Other equipment	7	5	6
Electrical distribution	11	8	9

4. Go to slide 6. Select the list of terms in the content placeholder and convert the text to a vertical list SmartArt object. Apply a SmartArt style. Animate the objects with an entrance effect so that each level of the chart appears one by one.

5. Go to slide 8. Change the bulleted list to a numbered list. Change the number style to the 1) format, and change the number size to 125% of the text.

6. On slide 3, add a clip art image (illustrations or photographs) of a smoke alarm. On slide 8, add a clip art image of a fire extinguisher. Crop, resize, and reposition the graphics as needed. Also, recolor the graphics to fit the color scheme, or remove the picture background.

7. Apply entrance effect animations to the bulleted lists on slides 3 and 5 so that each bulleted item appears on click. Apply exit effect animations to the bulleted list on slide 8 so that each bulleted item disappears on click. (*Hint*: Be sure to use the More Entrance Effects and More Exit Effects commands so you can choose from all options available.) Also on slide 8, apply a custom motion path to move the image from left to right on the slide, and then from left to right again. Adjust the timing of the motion effect as needed, and format the motion animation to appear after the previous animation.

8. Go to slide 9. Select the list of terms in the content placeholder and convert the text to a Process SmartArt Object. Apply a SmartArt style. Animate the objects with an entrance effect so that each level of the chart appears one by one.

9. Go to slide 10. Format the two lists:

   a. Increase the font size in both lists to 44 pt.

   b. Click to the left of the first list to select the blank text box. In the text box, type **RACE**. Format the text direction with the **Stacked** option and center align the text. Change the font size to 44 pt and apply the bold format.

   c. Click to the left of the second list to select another blank text box. Type **PASS**, and then apply the same text formats as described in Step 9b.

10. Select all four text boxes. Using theme colors, apply a shape fill and a shape outline.

11. Change the slide background by using a solid, gradient, picture or texture, or pattern fill. Apply the new background format to all slides.

12. Save slide 10 as a picture in the JPEG format and using the filename **Guide**, followed by your initials.

13. Rehearse the timing for each of the slides, starting at the beginning of the presentation.

14. Save the changes with the timings and close the presentation.

PROJECT 2

1. Open the **Codes** file from the drive and folder where your Data Files are stored. Save the presentation as **Revised Codes**, followed by your initials.

2. Change the slide background to a gradient fill using the preset styles or by creating your own gradient style. Be sure to format a background that is compatible with the font colors on slides 3–7. It may be necessary to reapply the black font color on slide 4.

3. Insert a new Title and Content slide at the end of the presentation. Delete the blank title placeholder. Create a table using the data below.

CODE	ALERT
Blue	Emergency in the area designated; real emergencies such as cardiac arrest
Red	Fire discovered in designated area; "red code" used to avoid panic among patients
Black	A disaster has struck in the city, county, or area; the facility will accept the injured
Yellow	A bomb threat has been received; maintain the safety of patients, visitors, and personnel
A	Suspected abduction of an infant or child; follow protocol for unit shutdown
Gray	Security response is needed or anticipated; follow protocol for your unit

4. Remove the background graphic for slide 8. AutoFit the column widths and resize the table to fill the slide area. If desired, change the table style.

5. Apply an entrance effect animation for the table.

6. Go to slide 6 and add the following comment to the slide: **Be sure to mention that Code A used to be referred to as Code Purple.**

7. Use the slide master to format animations for the first-level bulleted lists. Choose an entrance effect triggered on click, and set the effect options to appear by first-level paragraphs.

8. On the slide master, format a transition for each of the slides. Then preview each slide to make sure the slide master formats are correct. Make any necessary corrections and save the file.

9. Inspect the presentation and remove document properties and personal information from the file, but do not remove comments and annotations.

10. Protect the presentation by encrypting the file using the password ***BLP/911**.

11. Save the changes and close the file.

PROJECT 3

1. Open the **Cabins** file from the drive and folder where your Data Files are stored. Save the file as **Revised Cabins,** followed by your initials.

2. Create a new custom dictionary named **WWCR** and save the dictionary in your solutions folder. Add the words *Whyspering* and *Michigamme* to the dictionary.

3. Create a slide background using a clip art image of a cabin, woods, or an outdoor scene to apply to all slides in the presentation. Adjust the transparency of the background image so you can easily read text on the slides. Apply the background to all slides.

4. If necessary, change the font color(s) on the slide master to complement the background image and also to make the text easier to read.

5. On the slide master, format a slide transition. Set up a duration of 3 seconds for the transition. Apply a sound to play with the transition, such as wind.

6. On the slide master, format entrance effects for the first- and second-level bulleted lists. Format the bulleted items to appear after previous, with a 2 second delay.

7. Go to slide 6. Set the transition to advance after 10 seconds.

8. Set up the show for self-running at a kiosk. Show all slides, using the timings.

9. Remove the custom dictionary from the dictionary list.

10. Save the changes and close the presentation.

PROJECT 4

1. Create a new photo album using the following picture files, which are stored in the drive and folder where your Data Files are stored.

   Buffalo.jpg

   Elephant.jpg

   Leopard.jpg

   Lion.jpg

   Rhinoceros.jpg

2. Choose the **1 picture** layout option, and apply the **Compound Frame, Black** frame shape. Add captions below all pictures, and format all the pictures black and white.

3. Arrange the pictures in the following sequence:

   Leopard

   Lion

   Buffalo

   Rhinoceros

   Elephant

4. Title the photo album **The Big 5!,** and if necessary, replace *Your Name* in the Subtitle placeholder with your first and last names.

5. Save the presentation as **Big 5a,** followed by your initials.

6. Reset all the pictures in the photo album.

7. Go to slide 2. To make it easier to locate the leopard in the photo, apply the **Glow Diffused** artistic effect.

8. Apply a different artistic effect to each of the remaining photos in the album, and if desired, change the picture colors.

9. Save the presentation as **Big 5b**, followed by your initials.

10. Reset all the pictures in the photo album. Edit the photo album as follows:

    a.   Disable the caption option.

    b.   Disable the black and white option.

    c.   Apply a theme.

    d.   Change the frame shape so that it complements the designated theme.

11. After applying the new photo album settings, make adjustments as necessary. Apply a transition to all slides, and change the setting to advance the slide after 5 seconds for all slides.

12. Use the Compress Pictures command on the Picture Tools Format tab, using the document resolution as the target output to compress all the pictures in the presentation. Then save the presentation as **Big5c**, followed by your initials.

13. Save the presentation as a video, using the portable device setting. Use the recorded timings. Assign the filename **Big5d**, followed by your initials, and use the .wmv format.

14. Close the Big5c presentation.

PROJECT 5

1. Open the **Diving** file from the drive and folder where your Data Files are stored. Save the presentation as **Diving Videos**, followed by your initials.

2. Go to slide 2. In the content placeholder, insert the **1 meter.avi** file from the drive and folder where your Data Files are stored.

3. Trim the video to not play the first 3 seconds, and stop playing the video before the cheer at the end of the clip.

4. Go to slide 3. In the content placeholder, insert the **3 meter.avi** file from the drive and folder where your Data Files are stored. Set the playback volume to **Low**.

5. Go to slide 4. In the content placeholder, insert the **10 meter.avi** file from the drive and folder where your Data Files are stored. Set the playback volume to **Low**.

6. Format the playback for each of the video objects on slides 2–4 as follows:

    a.   Resize and reposition the video to fill the area below the slide title.

    b.   Start the video automatically.

    c.   Hide the video when it is not playing.

7. Apply video style formats, or borders and styles, to the video objects on slides 2–4.

8. If you have access to a microphone, record the narrations described below for slides 2–4. Hide the audio objects during the show, and format the audio clips to play automatically. In the Animations pane, rearrange the order of the animated objects so that the audio clips play before the videos.

    a.   For slide 2, say **Dive 405c, inward 2 ½ somersaults in the tuck position.**

    b.   For slide 3, say **Dive 107b, forward 3 ½ somersaults in the pike position.**

    c.   For slide 4, say **Dive 614b, armstand forward 2 somersaults in the pike position.**

9. Apply a transition to all of the slides with a 3 second duration. Set the transition to automatically advance to the next slide after a 1 second delay. The animations should be arranged so that the audio clip plays before the video starts to play.

10. Set up the show so that the media controls do not appear when you position the mouse over a media object.

11. Compress the media files using the Presentation Quality setting, and save the presentation.

SIMULATION

You work for Santos-Pearce, an insurance company. Your supervisor will be speaking at an upcoming conference sponsored by the local Chamber of Commerce. Businesspeople and community residents will attend the session. Your supervisor has asked you to prepare a presentation to provide an overview of the types of insurance offered by the company.

JOB 1

The company offers several types of insurance. Fortunately, you have a file used for new employee orientation that outlines the various insurance types. A coworker recently prepared a similar presentation, so you can access information from that file, too. Then you can apply a design and customize the formats.

1. Open a new presentation and create new slides by inserting an outline from the document **Insurance Overview.docx** located in the drive and folder where your Data Files are stored. Save the new presentation as **Revised Insurance 1**, followed by your initials.

2. Delete slide 2. On slide 1, in the Title placeholder, Type **Santos-Pearce**. In the Subtitle placeholder, type **Protect Yourself and Your Loved Ones**.

3. Open the slide master and apply the following formats:

   a. Apply the **Newsprint** theme.

   b. Change the color theme to **Hardcover**.

   c. Customize the Hardcover theme colors by changing the Hyperlink color to **White, Text 1** and changing the Followed Hyperlink color to **Gold, Hyperlink**.

   d. Create a custom bullet.

   e. Change the font size for level 1 bullets to **32 pt.** Change the font size for level 2 bullets to **28 pt.**

   f. Create a footer using the company name Santos-Pearce. Do not show the footer on the title slide.

4. At the end of the presentation, reuse some slides from the presentation **New Insurance**, located in the drive and folder where your Data Files are stored. Select the slides with the titles *Farm Insurance* (second slide) and *Specialty Insurance* (last slide).

5. Divide the slides into sections and name the sections as indicated below.

   Slides 1 and 2: **Introduction**

   Slides 3–6: **Life and Health**

   Slides 7–9: **Vehicle**

   Slides 10–14: **Property**

   Slides 15–16: **Farm and Specialty**

6. Collapse the slides and rearrange the order so that the *Property* section appears after *Life and Health* and before *Vehicle*.

7. Save the changes and leave the presentation open for the next Job.

JOB 2

At the company Web site, clients can provide feedback about their satisfaction with the company products and services. The data is updated each week. The feedback has been very positive, and you decide that a chart showing the current results will add credibility to the presentation.

1. If necessary, open the **Revised Insurance 1** file from the drive and folder where your solution files are stored. Save the presentation as **Revised Insurance 2**, followed by your initials.

2. In Excel, open the **Client Survey.xlsx** file from the drive and folder where your Data Files are stored. Save the worksheet as **Current Client Survey**, followed by your initials.

3. Copy the chart to the Clipboard. Switch to the presentation window. Insert a new Title and Text layout slide at the end of the presentation. Paste the chart onto the slide, using the destination theme and linking the data.

4. In the Title placeholder, type **Customer Satisfaction**. Increase the chart area to fill the area on the slide, and enlarge the pie chart as much as possible.

5. Change the legend font size to **18 pt**. Format the layout for the data labels by enabling the option **Percentage** and disabling the option **Value**. Position the data labels in the center of the categories in the chart. Select the data labels and format the font size to **18 pt** and change the font color to white.

6. Animate the chart with an entrance effect, and format the animation so that the parts of the chart appear by category. Add a subtle sound (such as a click) to the animations.

7. Save the changes and leave the presentation open for the next Job.

JOB 3

You decide it will be easier for the audience to comprehend the differences between insurance types by including a table in the presentation. To introduce the table content in increments, you decide to format the table for progressive disclosure.

1. If necessary, open the **Revised Insurance 2** file from the drive and folder where your solution files are stored. Save the presentation as **Revised Insurance 3**, followed by your initials.

2. Go to slide 4. Insert a new Title and Content slide. In the Title placeholder, type **Comparison**. Insert a table with 5 columns and 6 rows. Enter the following data in the table. Use a symbol to create the check marks and, if necessary, increase the font size of the symbol.

	TERM	WHOLE	UNIVERSAL	VARIABLE
Death benefit	√	√	√	√
Flexible payments			√	√
Invested in market				√
Guaranteed cash value		√	√	
Tax advantages	√	√	√	√

3. Resize the table and make it as big as possible to fit on the slide. AutoFit the column widths to fit the content. Distribute the rows equally and center the text vertically in the cells. Modify the table style if desired.

4. Copy slide 5, and then paste the copied slide four times between slides 5 and 6. Remove table rows from the copied slides to create progressive disclosure of the table.

5. Save the changes and leave the presentation open for the next Job.

JOB 4

To enhance the presentation, you decide to add graphics to some of the slides. Providing a visual image for each type of insurance will help the audience relate to and remember the presentation content.

1. If necessary, open the **Revised Insurance 3** file from the drive and folder where your solution files are stored. Save the presentation as **Revised Insurance 4**, followed by your initials.

2. Insert a new Content with Caption layout slide at the beginning of the Life and Health section (before slide 3). In the Title placeholder, type **Life Insurance**. In the text box on the left, type **Relieve anxiety over life's uncertainties!**. Then insert a clip art image (an illustration or a photograph) of a family.

3. Insert a new Content with Caption layout slide between slides 10 and 11. In the Title placeholder, type **Health Insurance**. In the text box on the left, type **Live well!**. Then insert a clip art image (an illustration or a photograph) related to health, fitness, or the medical field.

4. Insert a new Content with Caption layout slide at the beginning of the Property section (before slide 14). In the Title placeholder, type **Property Insurance**. In the text box on the left, type **Protect your assets!**. Then insert a clip art image (an illustration or a photograph) of the interior or exterior of a home.

5. Insert a new Content with Caption layout slide at the beginning of the Vehicle section (before slide 20). In the Title placeholder, type **Vehicle Insurance!**. In the text box on the left, type **Ride safely!**. Then insert a clip art image (an illustration or a photograph) of a vehicle, such as an auto or a motorcycle.

6. Insert a new Content with Caption layout slide at the beginning of the Farm and Specialty section (before slide 24). In the Title placeholder, type **Farm Insurance**. In the text box on the left, type **Protection against perils!**. Then insert a clip art image (an illustration or a photograph) of a farm.

7. Insert a new Content with Caption layout slide between slides 25 and 26. In the Title placeholder, type **Specialty Insurance**. In the text box on the left, type **Avoid the risks!**. Then insert a clip art image (an illustration or a photograph) related to travel, pets, and so on.

8. Modify the clip art images you added to fit in with the color scheme and design. For example, recolor or remove the picture backgrounds, apply a picture style, modify the borders, make corrections, or change the color and add artistic effects.

9. Go to slide 2. Convert the text in the bulleted list to a SmartArt object, such as the Target List option.

10. Save the changes and leave the presentation open for the next Job.

JOB 5

The slide content is complete, so you can now create an agenda slide and add some transitions to the slides.

1. If necessary, open the **Revised Insurance 4** file from the drive and folder where your solution files are stored. Save the presentation as **Revised Insurance 5**, followed by your initials.

2. Create the following custom shows:

   Slides 3–10: **Life Insurance**

   Slides 11–13: **Health Insurance**

   Slides 14–19: **Property Insurance**

   Slides 20–23: **Vehicle Insurance**

   Slides 24–25: **Farm Insurance**

   Slides 26–27: **Specialty Insurance**

3. At the end of the Introduction section (after slide 2), insert a new Title and Content slide. Create an agenda slide:

   a. Insert a **Vertical Box List** SmartArt object, and add three additional shapes.

   b. Enter the custom show names in the shapes.

   c. Create hyperlinks to the custom shows, and enable the option to return to the agenda slide at the end of each custom show.

   d. Resize and reposition the SmartArt object so it fits on the slide.

4. Choose a transition format and apply the transition to all the slides. Set the transition to trigger on mouse click.

5. Preview all the slides and animations, and make any necessary corrections. Review the progressive disclosure on slides 7–11 and make any necessary adjustments.

6. Save the changes and leave the presentation open for the next Job.

JOB 6

Your supervisor is very pleased with your work and asks you to save the presentation in other formats to make it easy to share the information and design with others.

1. If necessary, open the **Revised Insurance 5** file from the drive and folder where your solution files are stored. Save the presentation as **Revised Insurance 6**, followed by your initials.

2. Inspect the document, and then remove all document properties and personal information.

3. Save the presentation as a video, using the same filename and the Portable Devices setting. Use the default setting to spend 5 seconds on each slide.

4. Save the presentation as an XPS document, using the same filename. Close the XPS viewer.

5. Add your digital signature to the presentation. The purpose for signing the document is to verify the integrity of the content.

6. Save the presentation as a template. Be sure to save the file in your solutions folder. Name the file **S-P Template**, followed by your initials, and change the file type to **PowerPoint Template (*.potx)**. When prompted about removing the digital signature and proceeding, click **Yes**.

7. Delete all slides except the first slide. Remove all sections.

8. Save the changes and close the presentation.

A COMPREHENSIVE GUIDE TO MICROSOFT OFFICE SPECIALIST OBJECTIVES, POWERPOINT® 2010

STANDARDIZED CODING NUMBER	OBJECTIVES & ABBREVIATED SKILL SETS	INTRO UNIT PAGE #	ADVANCED UNIT PAGE #
OBJECTIVE 1	Managing the PowerPoint environment		
1.1	Adjust views		
1.1.1	Adjust views by using Ribbon	PPT 11, 37, 51	PPT Adv 111
1.1.2	Adjust views by status bar commands	PPT 8, 11, 16, 17, 19	
1.2	Manipulate the PowerPoint window		
1.2.1	Work with multiple presentation windows simultaneously		PPT Adv 151-152
1.3	Configure the Quick Access Toolbar		
1.3.1	Show the Quick Access Toolbar (QAT) below the Ribbon		PPT Adv 8
1.4	Configure PowerPoint file options		
1.4.1	Use PowerPoint Proofing	PPT 57–59	
1.4.2	Use PowerPoint Save options	PPT 10–11, 160	
OBJECTIVE 2	Creating a slide presentation		
2.1	Construct and edit photo albums		
2.1.1	Add captions to picture		PPT Adv 71–74

1

POWERPOINT® 2010 OBJECTIVES *(continued)*

STANDARDIZED CODING NUMBER	OBJECTIVES & ABBREVIATED SKILL SETS	INTRO UNIT PAGE #	ADVANCED UNIT PAGE #
2.1.2	Insert text		PPT Adv 71–74
2.1.3	Insert images in black and white		PPT Adv 71–74
2.1.4	Reorder pictures in an album		PPT Adv 71–74
2.1.5	Adjust image		PPT Adv 71–74
2.1.5.1	Rotation		PPT Adv 71–74
2.1.5.2	Brightness		PPT Adv 71–74
2.1.5.3	Contrast		PPT Adv 71–74
2.2	**Apply slide size and orientation settings**		
2.2.1	Set up a custom size		PPT Adv 160–162
2.2.2	Change the orientation	PPT 37	PPT Adv 160, 162
2.3	**Add and remove slides**		
2.3.1	Insert an outline	PPT 126–127	PPT Adv 129–130
2.3.2	Reuse slides from a saved presentation	PPT 42, 136–138	PPT Adv 122–125
2.3.3	Reuse slides from a slide library	PPT 136	PPT Adv 122–125
2.3.4	Duplicate selected slides	PPT 42	PPT Adv 35
2.3.5	Delete multiple slides simultaneously		PPT Adv 109–111

POWERPOINT® 2010 OBJECTIVES *(continued)*

STANDARDIZED CODING NUMBER	OBJECTIVES & ABBREVIATED SKILL SETS	INTRO UNIT PAGE #	ADVANCED UNIT PAGE #
2.3.6	Include non-contiguous slides in a presentation		PPT Adv 122–123
2.4	**Format slides**		
2.4.1	Format sections	PPT 148	PPT Adv 114–117
2.4.2	Modify themes	PPT 33–36	PPT Adv 86–88
2.4.3	Switch to a different slide layout	PPT 59–60	PPT Adv 100–101, 104–105
2.4.4	Apply a formatting to a slide	PPT 37	PPT Adv 86–92
2.4.4.1	Fill color	PPT 37	PPT Adv 88–92
2.4.4.2	Gradient		PPT Adv 88–92
2.4.4.3	Picture	PPT 37–38	PPT Adv 88, 97
2.4.4.4	Texture		PPT Adv 88–92
2.4.4.5	Pattern		PPT Adv 88–92
2.4.5	Set up slide footers	PPT 32–33	PPT Adv 101, 103
2.5	**Enter and format text**		
2.5.1	Use text effects	PPT 14–15, 82–84	PPT Adv 93–95
2.5.2	Change text format	PPT 14–15, 52–53	PPT Adv 93–95

POWERPOINT® 2010 OBJECTIVES *(continued)*

STANDARDIZED CODING NUMBER	OBJECTIVES & ABBREVIATED SKILL SETS	INTRO UNIT PAGE #	ADVANCED UNIT PAGE #
2.5.2.1	Indentation	PPT 52	PPT Adv 93, 95, 146–148
2.5.2.2	Alignment	PPT 52–53	
2.5.2.3	Line spacing	PPT 52–53	
2.5.2.4	Direction		PPT Adv 93, 97
2.5.3	Change the formatting of bulleted and numbered lists	PPT 54–55	PPT Adv 101–102
2.5.4	Enter text in a placeholder text box	PPT 45–46	
2.5.5	Convert text to SmartArt	PPT 76–77	
2.5.6	Copy and pasting text		PPT Adv 126–127
2.5.7	Use Paste Special	PPT 130–132	PPT Adv 127, 130–133, 135–137
2.5.8	Use Format Painter	PPT 143–144	
2.6	**Format text boxes**		
2.6.1	Apply formatting to a text box		PPT Adv 93–98, 146–148
2.6.1.1	Fill color		PPT Adv 95–98, 147
2.6.1.2	Gradient		PPT Adv 95

POWERPOINT® 2010 OBJECTIVES *(continued)*

STANDARDIZED CODING NUMBER	OBJECTIVES & ABBREVIATED SKILL SETS	INTRO UNIT PAGE #	ADVANCED UNIT PAGE #
2.6.1.3	Picture		PPT Adv 95–98
2.6.1.4	Texture		PPT Adv 95
2.6.1.5	Pattern		PPT Adv 95
2.6.2	Change the outline of a text box		PPT Adv 95–96, 146–147
2.6.2.1	Color		PPT Adv 95–96, 147
2.6.2.2	Weight		PPT Adv 95, 146
2.6.2.3	Style		PPT Adv 95–96, 147
2.6.3	Change the shape of the text box	PPT 49–50	PPT Adv 93–95, 97
2.6.4	Apply effects		PPT Adv 93–97, 148
2.6.5	Set the alignment	PPT 52–53	PPT Adv 93–95, 97, 147
2.6.6	Create columns in a text box		PPT Adv 93–95, 97, 147
2.6.7	Set internal margins		PPT Adv 93–95, 97, 147
2.6.8	Set the current text box formatting as the default for new text boxes		PPT Adv 93, 96

POWERPOINT® 2010 OBJECTIVES *(continued)*

STANDARDIZED CODING NUMBER	OBJECTIVES & ABBREVIATED SKILL SETS	INTRO UNIT PAGE #	ADVANCED UNIT PAGE #
2.6.9	Adjust text in a text box		PPT Adv 93–95, 97, 146–148
2.6.9.1	Wrap	PPT 109	PPT Adv 95, 97
2.6.9.2	Size	PPT 55–56	PPT Adv 94
2.6.9.3	Position		PPT Adv 93–95, 97
2.6.10	Use AutoFit		PPT Adv 93–95
OBJECTIVE 3	**Working with graphical and multimedia elements**		
3.1	**Manipulate graphical elements**		
3.1.1	Arrange graphical elements	PPT 41, 106–108, 114	
3.1.2	Position graphical elements		PPT Adv 59–61
3.1.3	Resize graphical elements	PPT 38, 41, 98	PPT Adv 59–61
3.1.4	Apply effects to graphical elements	PPT 41, 103, 105	PPT Adv 67–68
3.1.5	Apply styles to graphical elements	PPT 41	PPT Adv 69, 73
3.1.6	Apply borders to graphical elements	PPT 41	PPT Adv 67–68
3.1.7	Add hyperlinks to graphical elements	PPT 150–151	PPT Adv 17–20

POWERPOINT® 2010 OBJECTIVES *(continued)*

STANDARDIZED CODING NUMBER	OBJECTIVES & ABBREVIATED SKILL SETS	INTRO UNIT PAGE #	ADVANCED UNIT PAGE #
3.2	**Manipulate images**		
3.2.1	Apply color adjustments	PPT 41–42	PPT Adv 61–63
3.2.2	Apply image corrections		PPT Adv 67–68
3.2.2.1	Sharpen		PPT Adv 67–68
3.2.2.2	Soften		PPT Adv 67–68
3.2.2.3	Brightness		PPT Adv 67–68
3.2.2.4	Contrast		PPT Adv 67–68
3.2.3	Add artistic effects to an image	PPT 41, 105–106	PPT Adv 67–68
3.2.4	Remove a background	PPT 114–115	PPT Adv 67
3.2.5	Crop a picture		PPT Adv 56–58
3.2.6	Compress selected pictures or all pictures	PPT 41–42	PPT Adv 73–74
3.2.7	Change a picture		PPT Adv 59–61
3.2.8	Reset a picture	PPT 41	PPT Adv 56–58, 60, 62
3.3	**Modify WordArt and shapes**		
3.3.1	Set the formatting of the current shape as the default for future shapes		PPT Adv 61–63

POWERPOINT® 2010 OBJECTIVES *(continued)*

STANDARDIZED CODING NUMBER	OBJECTIVES & ABBREVIATED SKILL SETS	INTRO UNIT PAGE #	ADVANCED UNIT PAGE #
3.3.2	Change the fill color or texture	PPT 82–84, 102–104	PPT Adv 61–63
3.3.3	Change the WordArt	PPT 82–84	PPT Adv 69, 87
3.3.4	Convert Word Art to SmartArt		PPT Adv 69, 87
3.4	**Manipulate SmartArt**		
3.4.1	Add and remove shapes		PPT Adv 48–49
3.4.2	Change SmartArt styles	PPT 77–78	
3.4.3	Change the SmartArt layout	PPT 79	PPT Adv 69–70
3.4.4	Reorder shapes	PPT 80, 142	PPT Adv 17–18
3.4.5	Convert a SmartArt graphic to text		PPT Adv 49–50
3.4.6	Convert SmartArt to shapes		PPT Adv 17–18
3.4.7	Make shapes larger or smaller		PPT Adv 17–18
3.4.8	Promote bullet levels	PPT 80	PPT Adv 48–49
3.4.9	Demote bullet levels	PPT 78–80	PPT Adv 48–49
3.5	**Edit video and audio content**		
3.5.1	Apply a style to video or audio content	PPT 118	PPT Adv 76–79

POWERPOINT® 2010 OBJECTIVES *(continued)*

STANDARDIZED CODING NUMBER	OBJECTIVES & ABBREVIATED SKILL SETS	INTRO UNIT PAGE #	ADVANCED UNIT PAGE #
3.5.2	Adjust video or audio content		PPT Adv 76–82
3.5.3	Arrange video or audio content		PPT Adv 72–80
3.5.4	Size video or audio content		PPT Adv 76–82
3.5.5	Adjust playback options	PPT 62, 119	PPT Adv 76–82
OBJECTIVE 4	**Creating charts and tables**		
4.1	**Construct and modify tables**		
4.1.1	Draw a table		PPT Adv 31–33
4.1.2	Insert a Microsoft Excel spreadsheet	PPT 130	PPT Adv 126, 133–136
4.1.3	Set table style options	PPT 92–93	PPT Adv 33–35, 137
4.1.4	Add shading	PPT 92	PPT Adv 33–35
4.1.5	Add borders	PPT 92	PPT Adv 33–35
4.1.6	Add effects	PPT 92	PPT Adv 33–35
4.1.7	Columns and Rows	PPT 91, 94	PPT Adv 28–30, 137–138
4.1.7.1	Change the alignment	PPT 94	PPT Adv 30, 32–34, 138

POWERPOINT® 2010 OBJECTIVES *(continued)*

STANDARDIZED CODING NUMBER	OBJECTIVES & ABBREVIATED SKILL SETS	INTRO UNIT PAGE #	ADVANCED UNIT PAGE #
4.1.7.2	Resize	PPT 94	PPT Adv 131–132
4.1.7.3	Merge	PPT 94	PPT Adv 28–30
4.1.7.4	Split	PPT 94	PPT Adv 28–30
4.1.7.5	Distribute		PPT Adv 28–30
4.1.7.6	Arrange		PPT Adv 28–32
4.2	**Insert and modify charts**		
4.2.1	Select a chart type	PPT 85–87	PPT Adv 38–41
4.2.2	Enter chart data	PPT 85–87	PPT Adv 46
4.2.3	Change the chart type	PPT 88–89	PPT Adv 38–41
4.2.4	Change the chart layout	PPT 88	PPT Adv 38, 41
4.2.5	Switch row and column		PPT Adv 41–42
4.2.6	Select data		PPT Adv 41–42
4.2.7	Edit data		PPT Adv 41–42, 135–136
4.3	**Apply chart elements**		
4.3.1	Use chart labels	PPT 88, 89	PPT Adv 37, 43–45

POWERPOINT® 2010 OBJECTIVES *(continued)*

STANDARDIZED CODING NUMBER	OBJECTIVES & ABBREVIATED SKILL SETS	INTRO UNIT PAGE #	ADVANCED UNIT PAGE #
4.3.2	Use axes	PPT 87	PPT Adv 37, 43
4.3.3	Use gridlines		PPT Adv 43–46
4.3.4	Use backgrounds		PPT Adv 38–40
4.4	**Manipulate chart layouts**		
4.4.1	Select chart elements		PPT Adv 43–45
4.4.2	Format selections		PPT Adv 43–45
4.5	**Manipulate chart elements**		
4.5.1	Arrange chart elements		PPT Adv 43–45
4.5.2	Specify a precise position		PPT Adv 43–45
4.5.3	Apply effects		PPT Adv 43–45, 47–48
4.5.4	Resize chart elements		PPT Adv 43–44
4.5.5	Apply Quick Styles	PPT 88	PPT Adv 38, 40
4.5.6	Apply a border		PPT Adv 38, 43
4.5.7	Add hyperlinks		PPT Adv 47–48, 143

POWERPOINT® 2010 OBJECTIVES *(continued)*

STANDARDIZED CODING NUMBER	OBJECTIVES & ABBREVIATED SKILL SETS	INTRO UNIT PAGE #	ADVANCED UNIT PAGE #
OBJECTIVE 5	**Applying transitions and animations**		
5.1	**Apply built-in and custom animations**		
5.1.1	Use More Entrance Effects	PPT 66, 68, 112	PPT Adv 11, 12, 48, 84
5.1.2	Use More Emphasis Effects	PPT 66	PPT Adv 11, 176
5.1.3	Use More Exit Effects	PPT 66	PPT Adv 11, 36
5.1.4	Use More Motion Paths	PPT 66	PPT Adv 11, 36
5.2	**Apply effect and path options**		
5.2.1	Set timing	PPT 67, 113, 116	PPT Adv 11–14, 74, 78, 81, 84
5.2.2	Set start options	PPT 66–67, 112–113	
5.3	**Manipulate animations**		
5.3.1	Change the direction of an animation		PPT Adv 11–13
5.3.2	Attach a sound to an animation		PPT Adv 64–65
5.3.3	Use Animation Painter	PPT 110–112	PPT Adv 13
5.3.4	Reorder animation		PPT Adv 64–65

POWERPOINT® 2010 OBJECTIVES *(continued)*

STANDARDIZED CODING NUMBER	OBJECTIVES & ABBREVIATED SKILL SETS	INTRO UNIT PAGE #	ADVANCED UNIT PAGE #
5.3.5	Selecting text options		PPT Adv 11–13
5.4	**Apply and modify transitions between slides**		
5.4.1	Modifying a transition effect	PPT 69	PPT Adv 101–104
5.4.2	Adding a sound to a transition		PPT Adv 64, 101, 104
5.4.3	Modify transition duration	PPT 157	PPT Adv 104
5.4.4	Set up manual or automatically timed advance options	PPT 69, 156–157	PPT Adv 169, 172
OBJECTIVE 6	**Collaborating on presentations**		
6.1	**Manage comments in presentations**		
6.1.1	Insert and edit comments	PPT 146–147	PPT Adv 148–151
6.1.2	Show or hide markup	PPT 146	PPT Adv 148–150
6.1.3	Move to the previous or next comment	PPT 147	PPT Adv 148–150
6.1.4	Delete comments		PPT Adv 148, 150–151
6.2	**Apply proofing tools**		
6.2.1	Use Spelling and Thesaurus features	PPT 57–59	PPT Adv 4–8
6.2.2	Compare and combine presentations	PPT 147	PPT Adv 151–155

POWERPOINT® 2010 OBJECTIVES *(continued)*

STANDARDIZED CODING NUMBER	OBJECTIVES & ABBREVIATED SKILL SETS	INTRO UNIT PAGE #	ADVANCED UNIT PAGE #
OBJECTIVE 7	**Preparing presentations for delivery**		
7.1	**Save presentations**		
7.1.1	Save the presentation as a picture presentation		PPT Adv 160, 162
7.1.2	Save the presentation as a PDF		PPT Adv 159–161
7.1.3	Save the presentation as a XPS		PPT Adv 159–161
7.1.4	Save the presentation as an outline		PPT Adv 132–133
7.1.5	Save the presentation as an OpenDocument		PPT Adv 160, 162
7.1.6	Save the presentation as a show(.ppsx)		PPT Adv 160–161
7.1.7	Save a slide or object as a picture file		PPT Adv 138–139
7.2	**Share presentations**		
7.2.1	Package a presentation for CD delivery	PPT 161–162	PPT Adv 167–168
7.2.2	Create video		PPT Adv 74–76
7.2.3	Create handouts (send to Microsoft Word)	PPT 138–139	PPT Adv 107–109
7.2.4	Compress media	PPT 41–42	PPT Adv 76–79

POWERPOINT® 2010 OBJECTIVES *(continued)*

STANDARDIZED CODING NUMBER	OBJECTIVES & ABBREVIATED SKILL SETS	INTRO UNIT PAGE #	ADVANCED UNIT PAGE #
7.3	**Print presentations**		
7.3.1	Adjust print settings	PPT 20–22	
7.4	**Protect presentations**		
7.4.1	Set a password		PPT Adv 163–164
7.4.2	Change a password		PPT Adv 163–165
7.4.3	Mark a presentation as final	PPT 164	PPT Adv 162–163
OBJECTIVE 8	**Delivering presentations**		
8.1	**Apply presentation tools**		
8.1.1	Add pen and highlighter annotations	PPT 18, 153	PPT Adv 169–170
8.1.2	Change the ink color	PPT 153	PPT Adv 169
8.1.3	Erase an annotation	PPT 153	PPT Adv 169–170
8.1.4	Discard annotations upon closing	PPT 154	PPT Adv 169, 176
8.1.5	Retain annotations upon closing		PPT Adv 169–170
8.2	**Set up slide shows**		
8.2.1	Set up a Slide Show	PPT 154–155	PPT Adv 170–172

POWERPOINT® 2010 OBJECTIVES *(continued)*

STANDARDIZED CODING NUMBER	OBJECTIVES & ABBREVIATED SKILL SETS	INTRO UNIT PAGE #	ADVANCED UNIT PAGE #
8.2.2	Play narrations		PPT Adv 83–84
8.2.3	Set up Presenter view	PPT 155	
8.2.4	Use timings	PPT 155–157	PPT Adv 157
8.2.5	Show media controls		PPT Adv 77–79
8.2.6	Broadcast presentations	PPT 157	PPT Adv 172–173
8.2.7	Create a Custom Slide Show	PPT 149	PPT Adv 111–114
8.3	**Set presentation timing**		
8.3.1	Rehearse timings	PPT 156–157	PPT Adv 157–159
8.3.2	Keep timings	PPT 156–157	PPT Adv 157–159
8.3.3	Adjust a slide's timing	PPT Adv 157	PPT Adv 157–159
8.4	**Record presentations**		
8.4.1	Starting recording from the beginning of a slide show		PPT Adv 157
8.4.2	Starting recording from the current slide of the slide show		PPT Adv 157–158

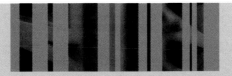

APPENDIX A

Computer Concepts

The Computer: An Overview

A computer is a machine that is used to store, retrieve, and manipulate data. A computer takes *input*, uses instructions to *process* and *store* that data, and then produces *output*. You enter the data into the computer through a variety of input devices, such as a keyboard or mouse. The processor processes the data to produce information. Information is output presented in many ways such as an image on a monitor, printed pages from a printer, or sound through speakers. Computer *software* is stored instructions or programming that runs the computer. *Memory* inside the computer stores the programs or instructions that run the computer as well as the data and information. Various *storage devices* are used to transfer or safely store the data and information on *storage media*.

A *computer system* is made up of components that include the computer, input, and output devices. Computer systems come in many shapes, sizes, and configurations. The computer you use at home or in school is often called a *personal computer*. *Desktop computers* often have a 'computer case' or a *system unit*, which contains

APPENDIX A

processing devices, memory, and some storage devices. **Figure A–1** shows a typical desktop computer. Input devices such as the mouse or pointing device, and keyboard are attached to the system unit by cables or wires. Output devices, such as the monitor (display device), speakers, and printer are also attached to the system unit by cables or wires. *Wireless technology* makes it possible to eliminate wires and use the airwaves to connect devices. *Laptop* or *notebook* computers have all the essential parts: the keyboard, pointing device, and display device all in one unit. See **Figure A–2** for a typical notebook computer.

FIGURE A–1   A desktop computer system

FIGURE A–2   A laptop computer

When learning about computers, it is helpful to organize the topics into a discussion about the hardware and the software, and then how the computer processes the data.

Computer Hardware

The physical components, devices, or parts of the computer are called *hardware*. Computer hardware includes the essential components found on all computers such as the central processing unit (CPU), the monitor, the keyboard, and the mouse. Hardware can be divided into categories: Input devices, processors, storage devices, and output devices. ***Peripheral devices*** are additional components, such as printers, speakers, and scanners that enhance the computing experience. Peripherals are not essential to the computer, but provide additional functions for the computer.

Input Devices

There are many different types of input devices. You enter information into a computer by typing on a keyboard or by pointing, clicking, or dragging a mouse. A ***mouse*** is a handheld device used to move a pointer on the computer screen. Similar to a mouse, a ***trackball*** has a roller ball that turns to control a pointer on the screen. Tracking devices, such as a ***touchpad***, are an alternative to the trackball or mouse. Situated on the keyboard of a laptop computer, they allow you to simply move and tap your finger on a small electronic pad to control the pointer on the screen.

    Tablet PCs allow you to input data by writing directly on the computer screen. Handwriting recognition technology converts handwritten writing to text. Many computers have a microphone or other ***sound input device*** which accepts speech or sounds as input and converts the speech to text or data. For example, when you telephone a company or bank for customer service, you often have the option to say your requests or account number. That is ***speech recognition technology*** at work!

    Other input devices include scanners and bar code readers. You can use a ***scanner*** to convert text or graphics from a printed page into code that a computer can process. You have probably seen ***bar code readers*** being used in stores. These are used to read bar codes, such as the UPC (Universal Product Code), to track merchandise or other inventory in a store. See **Figure A–3**.

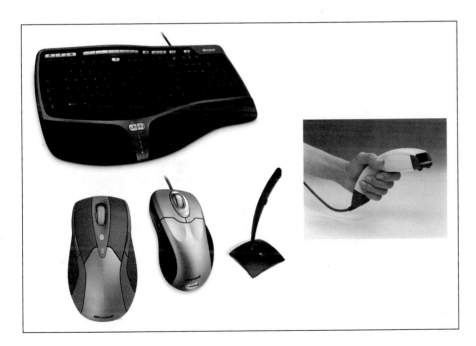

FIGURE A–3 Examples of input devices

Processing Devices

Processing devices are mounted inside the system unit of the computer. The **motherboard** is where the computer memory and other vital electronic parts are stored. See **Figure A–4**. The **central processing unit** (**CPU**) is a silicon chip that processes data and carries out instructions given to the computer. The CPU is stored on the motherboard of the computer. The **data bus** includes the wiring and pathways by which the CPU communicates with the peripherals and components of the computer.

FIGURE A–4   A motherboard

Storage Devices

Computers have to store and retrieve data for them to be of any use at all. Storage devices are both input and output devices. A **storage medium** holds data. Storage media include hard drives, tape, memory cards, solid state flash drives, CDs, and DVDs. A **storage device** is the hardware that stores and retrieves data from a storage medium. Storage devices include hard drives, card readers, tape drives, and CD and DVD drives.

Storage devices use magnetic, optical, or solid state technologies. Magnetic storage uses magnetic fields to store data and can be erased and used over and over again. Optical technology uses light to store data. Optical storage media use one of three technologies: read-only (ROM), recordable (R), or rewritable (RW). Solid state storage uses no moving parts and can be used over and over again. There are advantages and disadvantages to each technology.

Most computers have more than one type of storage device. The main storage device for a computer is the **hard drive** that is usually inside the system unit. Hard drives use magnetic storage. The hard drive reads and writes data to and from a round magnetic platter, or disk. **Figure A–5** shows a fixed storage unit. It is not removable from the computer.

FIGURE A–5   An internal hard drive

External and removable hard drives that can plug into the USB port on the system unit are also available. External drives offer flexibility; allowing you to transfer data between computers easily. See **Figure A–6**. At the time this book was written, typical hard drives for a computer system that you might buy for your personal home use range from 500 gigabytes (GB) to 2 terabytes.

FIGURE A–6   An external hard drive

The *floppy disk drive* is older technology that is no longer available on new computers. Some older computers still have a floppy disk drive which is mounted in the system unit with access to the outside. A floppy disk is the medium that stores the data. You put the floppy disk into the floppy disk drive so the computer can read and write the data. The floppy disk's main advantage was portability. You can store data on a floppy disk and transport it for use on another computer. A floppy disk can hold up to 1.4MB (megabytes) of information. A Zip disk is similar to a floppy disk. A *Zip disk* is also an older portable disk technology that was contained in a plastic sleeve. Each disk held 100MB or 250MB of information. A special disk drive called a *Zip drive* is required to read and write data to a Zip disk.

Optical storage devices include the *CD drive* or *DVD drive* or *Blu-ray drive*. CDs, DVDs, and *Blu-ray drive (BD)* use optical storage technology. See **Figure A–7**.

FIGURE A–7   A CD/DVD/Blu-ray drive

These drives are typically mounted inside the system unit, although external versions of these devices are also available. Most new computers are equipped with CD/DVD burners. That means they have read and write capabilities. You use a CD/DVD drive to read and write CDs and DVDs. A *CD* is a compact disc, which is a form of optical storage. Compact discs can store 700 MB of data. These discs have a great advantage over other forms of removable storage as they can hold vast quantities of information—the entire contents of a small library, for instance. They are also fairly durable. Another advantage of CDs is their ability to hold graphic information, including moving pictures, with the highest quality stereo sound. A *DVD* is also an optical disc that looks like a CD. It is a high-capacity storage device that can contain up to 4.7GB of data, which is a seven-fold increase over a CD. There are two variations of DVDs that offer even more storage—a 2-layer version with 9.4GB capacity and double-sided discs with 17GB capacity. A DVD holds 133 minutes of data on each side, which means that two two-hour full-length feature movies can be stored on one disc. Information is encoded on the disk by a laser and read by a CD/DVD drive in the computer. ***Blu-ray discs (BD)*** offer even more storage capacity. These highest-capacity discs are designed to record full-length high-definition feature films. As of this writing, a BD can store upwards of 35GB of data. Special Blu-ray hardware, including disc players available in gaming systems and Blu-ray burners, are needed to read Blu-ray discs.

A CD drive only reads CDs, a DVD drive can read CDs and DVDs, a Blu-ray drive reads BDs, CDs, and DVDs. CD/DVD/BD drives look quite similar, as do the discs. See **Figure A–8**.

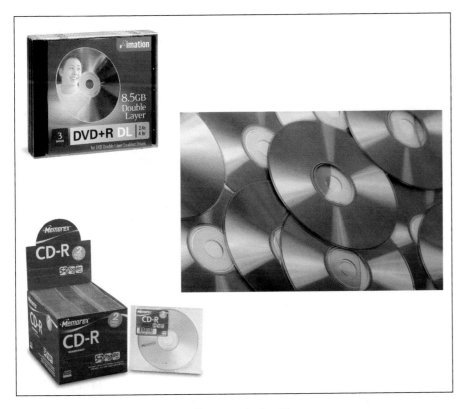

FIGURE A–8   CDs, DVDs, and Blu-rays look alike

APPENDIX A

Solid state storage is another popular storage technology. A *USB flash drive* is a very portable small store device that works both as a drive and medium. It plugs directly into a USB port on the computer system unit. You read and write data to the flash drive. See **Figure A–9**.

FIGURE A–9   A flash drive

Solid state card readers are devices that can read solid state cards. Solid state storage is often used in cameras. See **Figure A–10**.

FIGURE A–10   Solid state card and card reader

Magnetic tape is a medium most commonly used for backing up a computer system, which means making a copy of files from a hard drive. Although it is relatively rare for data on a hard drive to be completely lost in a crash (that is, for the data or pointers to the data to be partially or totally destroyed), it can and does happen. Therefore, most businesses and some individuals routinely back up files on tape. If you have a small hard drive, you can use DVDs or CD-ROMs or solid state storage such as a flash drive or memory card to back up your system. **Figure A–11** shows a tape storage system.

FIGURE A–11   Tape storage system

Output Devices

The *monitor* on which you view your computer work is an output device. It provides a visual representation of the information stored in or produced by your computer. The typical monitor for today's system is a flat-screen monitor similar to a television. Computer monitors typically use *LCD technology*. LCD stands for Liquid Crystal Display. See **Figure A–12**. LCD monitors provide a very sharp picture because of the large number of tiny dots, called *pixels*, which make up the display as well as its ability to present the full spectrum of colors. *Resolution* is the term that tells you how clear an image will be on the screen. Resolution is measured in pixels. A typical resolution is 1024 × 768. A high-quality monitor may have a resolution of 1920 × 1080, or 2560 × 1440 or higher. Monitors come in different sizes. The size of a monitor is determined by measuring the diagonal of the screen. Laptops have smaller monitors than desktop computers. A laptop monitor may be 13", 15", or 17". Desktop monitors can be as large as 19"–27" or even larger.

FIGURE A–12   An LCD monitor

Printers are a type of output device. They let you produce a paper printout of information contained in the computer. Today, most printers use either inkjet or laser technology to produce high-quality print. Like a copy machine, a *laser printer* uses heat to fuse a powdery substance called *toner* to the page. *Ink-jet printers* use a spray of ink to print. Laser printers give the sharpest image and often print more pages per minute (ppm) than ink-jet printers. Ink-jet printers provide nearly as sharp an image, but the wet printouts can smear when they first are printed. Most color printers, or photo printers for printing photographs, are ink-jet printers. Color laser printers are more costly. These printers allow you to print information in a full array of colors, just as you see it on your monitor. See **Figure A–13**.

FIGURE A–13   Printers

Laptop or Notebook Computer

A *laptop computer*, also called a *notebook computer*, is a small folding computer that can literally fit in a person's lap or in a backpack. Within the fold-up case of a laptop is the CPU, data bus, monitor (built into the lid), hard drive (sometimes removable), USB ports, CD/DVD drive, and trackball or digital tracking device. The advantage of the laptop is its portability—you can work anywhere because you can use power either from an outlet or from the computer's internal, rechargeable batteries. Almost all laptops have wireless Internet access built into the system. The drawbacks are the smaller keyboard, smaller monitor, smaller capacity, and higher price, though some laptops offer full-sized keyboards and higher quality monitors. As technology allows, storage capacity on smaller devices is making it possible to offer laptops with as much power and storage as a full-sized computer. See **Figure A–14**.

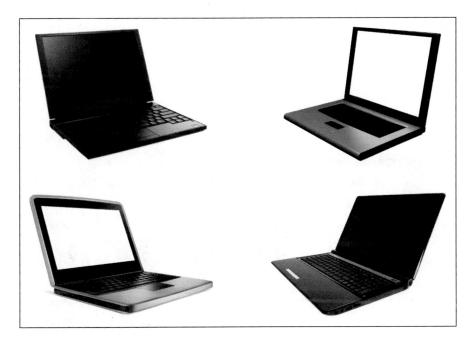

FIGURE A–14   Laptop computers

Personal Digital Assistants (PDA) and Smartphones

A *Personal Digital Assistant (PDA)* is a pocket-sized electronic organizer that helps you to manage addresses, appointments, expenses, tasks, and memos. If you own a cell phone, chances are it is a *Smartphone* and it can do more than just make and receive phone calls. Today, many handheld devices, such as cell phones and Personal Digital Assistants include features such as a full keypad for text messaging and writing notes, e-mail, a browser for Web access, a calendar and address book to manage contacts and appointments, a digital camera, radio, and digital music player. Most handheld devices also include software for games, financial management, personal organizer, GPS, and maps. See **Figure A–15**.

FIGURE A–15   Smartphones

The common input devices for PDAs and some Smartphones include touch-sensitive screens that accept input through a stylus pen or small keyboards that are either built in to the device or available as software on the screen. Data and information can be shared with a Windows-based or Macintosh computer through a process called synchronization. By placing your handheld in a cradle or through a USB port attached to your computer, you can transfer data from your PDA's calendar, address book, or memo program into your computer's information manager program and vice versa. The information is updated on both sides, making your handheld device a portable extension of your computer.

How Computers Work

All input, processing, storage, and output devices function together to make the manipulation, storage, and distribution of data and information possible. Data is information entered into and manipulated or processed within a computer. Processing includes computation, such as adding, subtracting, multiplying, and dividing; analysis planning, such as sorting data; and reporting, such as presenting data for others in a chart or graph. This next section explains how computers work.

Memory

Computers have two types of memory—RAM and ROM. *RAM*, or *random access memory*, is the silicon chips in the system unit that temporarily store information when the computer is turned on. RAM is what keeps the software programs up and running and provides visuals that appear on your screen. You work with data in RAM up until you save it to a storage media such as a hard disk, CD, DVD, or solid state storage such as flash drive.

Computers have sophisticated application programs that include a lot of graphics, video, and data. In order to run these programs, computers require a lot of memory. Therefore, computers have a minimum of 512MB of RAM. Typical computers include between 2GB and 4GB of RAM to be able to run most programs. Most computer systems are expandable and you can add on RAM after you buy the computer. The more RAM available for the programs, the faster and more efficiently the machine will be able to operate. RAM chips are shown in **Figure A–16**.

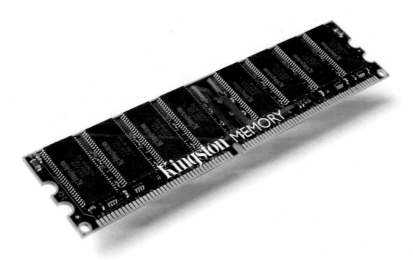

FIGURE A–16   RAM chips

ROM, or *read-only memory*, is the memory that stays in the computer when it is turned off. It is ROM that stores the programs that run the computer as it starts or "boots up." ROM holds the instructions that tell the computer how to begin to load its operating system software programs.

Speed

The speed of a computer is measured by how fast the computer processes each instruction. There are several factors that affect the performance of a computer: the speed of the processor, or the *clock speed*, the *front side bus speed*—the speed of the bus that connects the processor to main memory—the speed in which data is written and retrieved from the hard drive or other storage media, and the speed of the graphics card if you are working on programs that use a lot of graphic images. These all factor into a computer's performance.

The speed of a computer is measured in *megahertz (MHz)* and *gigahertz (GHz)*. Processor speed is part of the specifications when you buy a computer. For example, to run Windows 7 on a computer, you need a processor that has 1 gigahertz (GHz) or faster 32-bit (x86) or 64-bit (x64) processor. Processors are sold by name and each brand or series has its own specifications. Processor manufacturers include AMD, Intel, and Motorola.

Networks

Computers have expanded the world of communications. A *network* is defined as two or more computers connected to share data. *LANs (local area networks)* connect computers within a small area such as a home, office, school, or building. Networks can be wired or wireless. The *Internet* is the largest network in the world connecting millions of computers across the globe. Using the Internet, people can communicate across the world instantly.

Networks require various communication devices and software. *Modems* allow computers to communicate with each other by telephone lines. Modem is an acronym that stands for "MOdulator/DEModulator." Modems convert data in bytes to sound media in order to send data over the phone lines and then convert it back to bytes after receiving data. Modems operate at various rates or speeds. *Network cards* in the system unit allow computers to access networks. A *router* is an electronic device that joins two or more networks. For example, a home network can use a router and a modem to connect the home's LAN to the Internet. A *server* is the computer hardware and software that "serves" the computers on a network. Network technology is sometimes called "client-server." A personal computer that requests data from a server is referred to as a *client*. The computer that stores the data is the *server*. On the Internet, the computer that stores Web pages is the *Web server*. **Figure A–17** shows a network diagram.

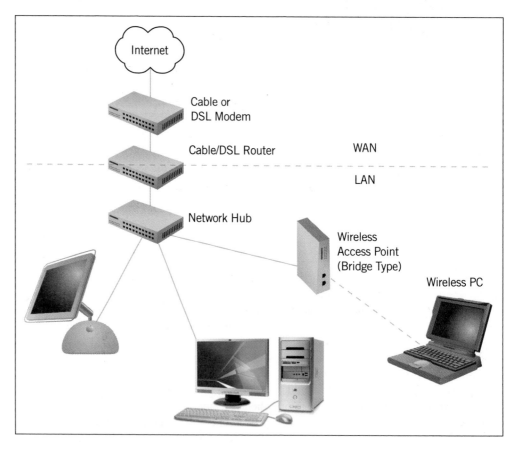

FIGURE A–17   Diagram of a network

Networks have certain advantages over stand-alone computers: they allow communication among the computers; they allow smaller capacity computers to access the larger capacity of the server computers on the network; they allow several computers to share peripherals, such as one printer; and they can make it possible for all computers on the network to have access to the Internet.

Connect to the Internet

To connect to the Internet you need to subscribe to an ***Internet Service Provider (ISP)***. There are several technologies available. Connection speeds are measured in bits per second. Upload speeds are slower than download speeds. ***Dial-up*** is the oldest, and the slowest Internet access technology that is offered by local telephone companies. To get access to the Internet, your computer has to dial out through a phone line. Many people have moved to ***always-on connection technologies***. The computer is always connected to the Internet if you turn the computer on, so you don't have to dial out. These always-on faster technologies, known as a ***Digital Subscriber Line (DSL)***, include cable connections, satellites, and fiber optic. They are offered by telephone and cable television companies, as well as satellite service providers. It can be noted that satellite Internet access is the most expensive and dialup is the cheapest. DSL is through phone lines. **Table A–1** shows a brief comparison of these technologies based on the time this book was written and average speed assessments.

TABLE A–1 Comparing average Internet access options

FEATURE	SATELLITE	DSL	CABLE	FIBER OPTIC
Max. High Speed	Download speeds ranging anywhere from 768 Kbps up to 5.0 Mbps	Download speed 10 Mbps/ upload speed 5 Mbps	Download speed 30 Mbps/ upload speed 10 Mbps	Download speed 50 Mbps/ upload speed 20 Mbps
Access is through	Satellite dish	Existing phone line	Existing TV cable	Fiber-optic phone lines
Availability	Available in all areas; note that satellite service is sensitive to weather conditions	Generally available in populated areas	Might not be available in rural areas	Might not be available in all areas as fiber-optic lines are still being installed in many areas

Software

A ***program*** is a set of instructions that the computer uses to operate. ***Software*** is the collection of programs and other data input that tells the computer how to run its devices, how to manipulate, store, and output information, and how to accept the input you give it. Software fits into two basic categories: systems software and applications software. A third category, network software, is really a type of application.

Systems Software

The ***operating system*** is the main software or ***system software*** that runs a computer and often defines the type of computer. There are two main types or platforms for personal computers. The Macintosh computer, or Mac, is produced by Apple Computer, Inc. and runs the Mac operating system. The PC is a Windows-based

APPENDIX A

computer produced by many different companies, but which runs the Microsoft Windows operating system.

Systems software refers to the operating system of the computer. The operating system is a group of programs that is automatically copied in from the time the computer is turned on until the computer is turned off. Operating systems serve two functions: they control data flow among computer parts, and they provide the platform on which application and network software work—in effect, they allow the "space" for software and translate its commands to the computer. The most popular operating systems in use today are the Macintosh operating system, MAC OS X and several different versions of Microsoft Windows, such as Windows XP, Windows Vista, or Windows 7. See **Figure A–18** and **Figure A–19**.

FIGURE A–18   Windows 7 operating system

FIGURE A–19 Mac OS

Since its introduction in the mid-1970s, Macintosh has used its own operating system, a graphical user interface (GUI) system that has evolved over the years. The OS is designed so users "click" with a mouse on pictures, called icons, or on text to give commands to the system. Data is available to you in the WYSIWYG (what-you-see-is-what-you-get) format; that is, you can see on-screen what a document will look like when it is printed. Graphics and other kinds of data, such as spreadsheets, can be placed into text documents. However, GUIs take a great deal of RAM to keep all of the graphics and programs operating.

The original OS for IBM and IBM-compatible computers (machines made by other companies that operate similarly) was DOS (disk operating system). It did not have a graphical interface. The GUI system, Windows™, was developed to make using the IBM/IBM-compatible computer more "friendly." Today's Windows applications are the logical evolution of GUI for IBM and IBM-compatible machines. Windows is a point-and-click system that automatically configures hardware to work together. You should note, however, that with all of its abilities comes the need for more RAM, or a system running Windows will operate slowly.

Applications Software

When you use a computer program to perform a data manipulation or processing task, you are using applications software. Word processors, databases, spreadsheets, graphics programs, desktop publishers, fax systems, and Internet browsers are all applications software.

Network Software

A traditional network is a group of computers that are hardwired (connected together with cables) to communicate and operate together. Today, some computer networks use RF (radio frequency) wireless technology to communicate with each other. This is called a *wireless network*, because you do not need to physically hook the network together with cables. In a typical network, one computer acts as the server, controlling the flow of data among the other computers, called nodes, or clients on the network. Network software manages this flow of information.

APPENDIX A

History of the Computer

Though various types of calculating machines were developed in the nineteenth century, the history of the modern computer begins about the middle of the last century. The strides made in developing today's personal computer have been truly astounding.

Early Development

The ENIAC, or Electronic Numerical Integrator and Computer, (see **Figure A–20**) was designed for military use in calculating ballistic trajectories and was the first electronic, digital computer to be developed in the United States. For its day, 1946, it was quite a marvel because it was able to accomplish a task in 20 seconds that normally would take a human three days to complete. However, it was an enormous machine that weighed more than 20 tons and contained thousands of vacuum tubes, which often failed. The tasks that it could accomplish were limited, as well.

FIGURE A–20 The ENIAC

From this awkward beginning, however, the seeds of an information revolution grew. The invention of the silicon chip in 1971, and the release of the first personal computer in 1974, launched the fast-paced information revolution in which we now all live and participate.

Significant dates in the history of computer development are listed in **Table A–2**.

TABLE A–2   Milestones in the development of computers

YEAR	DEVELOPMENT
1948	First electronically stored program
1951	First junction transistor
1953	Replacement of tubes with magnetic cores
1957	First high-level computer language
1961	First integrated circuit
1965	First minicomputer
1971	Invention of the microprocessor (the silicon chip) and floppy disk
1974	First personal computer (made possible by the microprocessor)

The Personal Computer

The PC, or personal computer, was mass marketed by Apple beginning in 1977, and by IBM in 1981. It is this desktop device with which people are so familiar and which, today, contains much more power and ability than did the original computer that took up an entire room. The PC is a small computer (desktop size or less) that uses a microprocessor to manipulate data. PCs may stand alone, be linked together in a network, or be attached to a large mainframe computer. See **Figure A–21**.

FIGURE A–21   An early IBM PC

Computer Utilities and System Maintenance

Computer operating systems let you run certain utilities and perform system maintenance to keep your computer running well. When you add hardware or software, you make changes in the way the system operates. With Plug and Play, most configuration changes are done automatically. The *drivers*, software that runs the peripherals, are installed automatically when your computer identifies the new hardware. When you install new software, many changes are made to the system automatically that determine how the software starts and runs.

In addition, you might want to customize the way the new software or hardware works with your system. You use *utility software* to make changes to the way hardware and software works. For example, you can change the speed at which your mouse clicks, how quickly or slowly keys repeat on the keyboard, and the resolution of the screen display. Utilities are included with your operating system. If you are running Windows XP, Windows Vista, or Windows 7, the Windows Control Panel provides access to the many Windows operating system utilities. **Figure A–22** shows the System and Security utilities in the Control Panel for Windows 7.

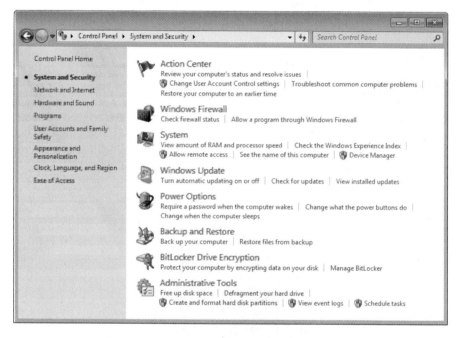

FIGURE A–22   Control Panel for Windows 7

Virus and Spyware Protection

Certain maintenance should be performed regularly on computers. *Viruses* are malicious software programs that can damage the programs on your computer causing the computer to either stop working or run slowly. These programs are created by people, called *hackers*, who send the programs out solely to do harm to computers. Viruses are loaded onto your computer without your knowledge and run against your wishes. *Spyware* is also a form of a program that can harm your computer. There are utilities and programs called *antispyware* and *antivirus* programs that protect your computer from spyware and viruses.

You should install and update your antivirus and spyware protection software regularly, and scan all new disks and any incoming information from online sources for viruses. Some systems do this automatically; others require you to install software to do it.

Disk Maintenance

From time to time, you should run a program that scans or checks the hard drive to see that there are not bad sectors (areas) and look for corrupted files. Optimizing or defragmenting the hard disk is another way to keep your computer running at its best. Scanning and checking programs often offers the option of "fixing" the bad areas or problems, although you should be aware that this could result in data loss.

Society and Computers

The electronic information era has had global effects and influenced global change in all areas of people's lives including education, government, society, and commerce. With the changes of this era have come many new questions and responsibilities. There are issues of ethics, security, and privacy.

Ethics

When you access information—whether online, in the workplace, or via purchased software—you have a responsibility to respect the rights of the person or people who created that information. Digital information, text, images, and sound are very easy to copy and share, however, that does not make it right to do so. You have to treat electronic information with respect. Often images, text, and sound are copyrighted. *Copyright* is the legal method for protecting the intellectual property of the author— the same way as you would a book, article, or painting. For instance, you must give credit when you copy information from the Web or another person's document.

If you come across another person's personal information, you must treat it with respect. Do not share personal information unless you have that person's permission. For example, if you happen to pass a computer where a person left personal banking information software open on the computer or a personal calendar available, you should not share that information. If e-mail comes to you erroneously, you should delete it before reading it.

When you use equipment that belongs to your school, a company for which you work, or others, here are some rules you should follow:

1. Do not damage computer hardware.

2. Do not add or remove equipment without permission.

3. Do not use an access code or equipment without permission.

4. Do not read others' e-mail.

5. Do not alter data belonging to someone else without permission.

6. Do not use the computer for play during work hours or use it for personal profit.

7. Do not access the Internet for nonbusiness related activities during work hours.

8. Do not install or uninstall software without permission.

9. Do not make unauthorized copies of data or software or copy company files or procedures for personal use.

10. Do not copy software programs to use at home or at another site in the company without permission.

APPENDIX A

Security and Privacy

The Internet provides access to business and life-enhancing resources, such as distance learning, remote medical diagnostics, and the ability to work from home more effectively. Businesses, colleges and universities, and governments throughout the world depend on the Internet every day to get work done. Disruptions in the Internet can create havoc and dramatically decrease productivity.

With more and more financial transactions taking place online, *identity theft* is a growing problem, proving a person's online identity relies heavily upon their usernames and passwords. If you do online banking, there are several levels of security that you must pass through, verifying that you are who you claim to be, before gaining access to your accounts. If you divulge your usernames and passwords, someone can easily access your accounts online with devastating effects to your credit rating and to your accounts.

Phishing is a criminal activity that is used by people to fraudulently obtain your personal information, such as usernames, passwords, credit card details, and your Social Security information. Your Social Security number should never be given out online. Phishers send e-mails that look legitimate, but in fact are not. Phishing e-mails will often include fake information saying that your account needs your immediate attention because of unusual or suspected fraudulent activity. You are asked to click a link in the e-mail to access a Web site where you are then instructed to enter personal information. See **Figure A–23** and **Figure A–24**. Phishing e-mail might also come with a promise of winning some money or gifts. When you get mail from people you don't know, the rules to remember are "you never get something for nothing," and "if it looks too good to be true, it's most likely not true."

PayPal would not use a yahoo.com Domain for e-mail

No recipient

Fake URL as you can see from ScreenTip

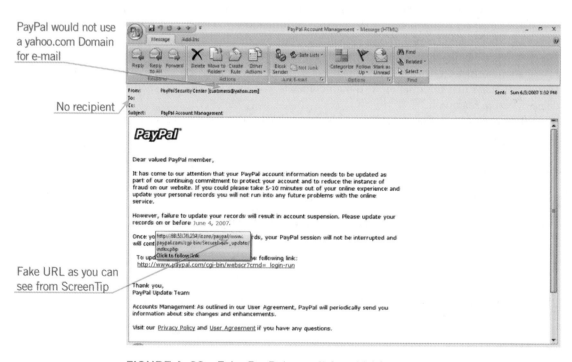

FIGURE A–23 Fake PayPal e-mail for phishing

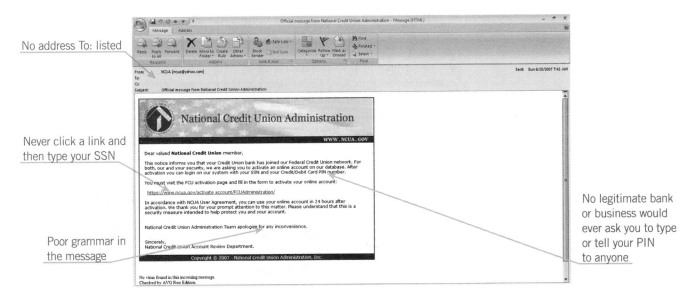

No address To: listed

Never click a link and then type your SSN

Poor grammar in the message

No legitimate bank or business would ever ask you to type or tell your PIN to anyone

FIGURE A–24 Fake Credit Union e-mail for phishing

Whatever the ruse, when you click the link provided in the phishing e-mail, your browser will open a Web site that looks real, perhaps like your bank's site, eBay, or PayPal. But, in fact, this is a fake site set up to get you to give up your personal information. Phishing sites are growing. You should never click a link provided in an e-mail to get to sites such as your bank, eBay, or PayPal. Your bank or any other legitimate Web site will never ask you to type personal information on a page linked from an e-mail message. Always type the Web page address directly in the browser. Banks and Web sites have been trying to stop phishing sites through technology. Other attempts to reduce the growing number of reported phishing incidents include legislation and simply educating users about the practice.

Just as you would not open someone else's mail, you must respect the privacy of e-mail sent to others. When interacting with others online, you must keep confidential information confidential. Do not endanger your privacy, safety, or financial security by giving out personal information to someone you do not know.

> **EXTRA FOR EXPERTS**
>
> Ebay is an online auction Web site that provides people a way to buy and sell merchandise through the Internet. PayPal is a financial services Web site that provides a way to transfer funds between people who perform financial transactions on the Internet.

Career Opportunities

In one way or another, all careers involve the computer. Whether you are a grocery store clerk using a scanner to read the prices, a busy executive writing a report that includes charts, graphics, and detailed analysis on a laptop on an airplane, or a programmer writing new software—almost everyone uses computers in their jobs. Farmers use computers to optimize crops and order seeds and feed. Most scientific research is done using computers.

There are specific careers available if you want to work with computers in the computer industry. Schools offer degrees in computer programming, computer repair, computer engineering, and software design. The most popular jobs are systems analysts, computer operators, database managers, database specialists, and programmers. Analysts figure out ways to make computers work (or work better) for a particular business or type of business. Computer operators use the programs and devices to conduct business with computers. Programmers write the software for applications or new systems. There are degrees and jobs for people who want to create and maintain Web sites. Working for a company maintaining their Web site can be a very exciting career.

There are courses of study in using CAD (computer-aided design) and CAM (computer-aided manufacturing). There are positions available to instruct others in computer software use within companies and schools. Technical writers and editors must be available to write manuals about using computers and software. Computer-assisted instruction (CAI) is a system of teaching any given subject using the computer. Designing video games is another exciting and ever-growing field of computer work. And these are just a few of the possible career opportunities in an ever-changing work environment. See **Figure A–25**.

FIGURE A–25   Working in the computer field

What Does the Future Hold?

The possibilities for computer development and application are endless. Things that were dreams or science fiction only 10 or 20 years ago are now reality. New technologies are emerging constantly. Some new technologies are replacing old ways of doing things; others are merging with those older methods and devices. Some new technologies are creating new markets. The Internet (more specifically, the Web), cell phones, and DVD videos are just a few inventions of the past decades that did not have counterparts prior to their inventions. We are learning new ways to work and play because of the computer. It is definitely a device that has become part of our offices, our homes, and our lives.

Social networking has moved from the streets and onto the Web. People meet and greet through the Internet using sites such as MySpace, Facebook, and Twitter.

Emerging Technologies

Today the various technologies and systems are coming together to operate more efficiently. Convergence is the merging of these technologies. Telephone communication is being combined with computer e-mail and Web browsing so users can set a time to meet online and, with the addition of voice technology, actually speak to each other using one small portable device.

The Web, now an important part of commerce and education, began as a one-way vehicle where users visited to view Web pages and get information. It has evolved into sites where shopping and commerce takes place and is now evolving into a technology where users create the content. Web 2.0 and sites such as Facebook.com, flickr.com, LinkedIn.com, twitter.com, wikipedia.com, and youtube.com have content generated by the people that visit the Web sites. See **Figure A–26**.

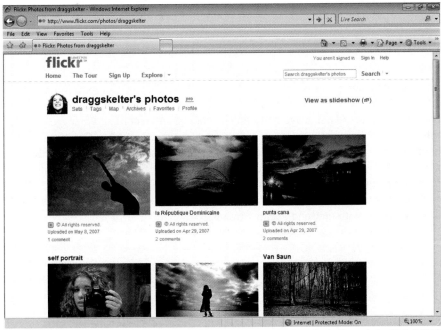

FIGURE A–26   User generated content

Computers have radically changed the way the medical profession delivers health care. Through the medical community, computers have enhanced medicine and healthcare throughout the world.

Trends

There are many trends that drive the computer industry. One trend is for larger and faster storage. From megabytes, to gigabytes, to terabytes, storage is becoming less an issue as the cost of storage is also dropping. RAM today is increasing exponentially. The trend is to sell larger blocks of RAM with every new personal computer. Newer processors also operate at speeds that are faster than the previous generation processors.

The actual size of computers is decreasing. Technology is allowing more powerful components to fit into smaller devices—laptops are lighter, monitors take up less space on the desktop, and flash drives can fit in your pocket and store gigabytes of data.

Home Offices

More and more frequently, people are working out of their homes—whether they are employees who are linked to their office in another location or individuals running their own businesses. *Telecommuting* meets the needs of many industries. Many companies allow workers to have a computer at home that is linked to their office and employees can use laptop computers to work both from home and on the road as they travel. A laptop computer, in combination with a wireless network, allows an employee to work from virtually anywhere and still keep in constant contact with her or his employer and customers.

Business communication is primarily by e-mail and telephone. It is very common for serious business transactions and communications to occur via e-mail rather than through the regular mail. Such an arrangement saves companies time and workspace and, thus, money.

Home Use

More and more households have personal computers. The statistics are constantly proving that a computer is an essential household appliance. Computers are used to access the Internet for shopping, education, and leisure. Computers are used to maintain financial records, manage household accounts, and record and manage personal information. More and more people are using electronic banking. Games and other computer applications offer another way to spend leisure dollars, and the convergence of television, the Internet, and the computer will find more households using their computers for media such as movies and music.

The future is computing. It's clear that this technology will continue to expand and provide us with new and exciting trends.

APPENDIX B

Keyboarding Touch System Improvement

Introduction

- *Your Goal—Improve your keyboarding skills using the touch system so you are able to type without looking at the keyboard.*

Why Improve Your Keyboarding Skills?

- To type faster and more accurately every time you use the computer
- To increase your enjoyment while using the computer

Instead of looking back and forth from the page to see the text you have to type and then turning back to the keyboard and pressing keys with one or two fingers, using the touch system you will type faster and more accurately.

> **WARNING**
>
> Using two fingers to type while looking at the keyboard is called the "hunt and peck" system and is not efficient when typing large documents.

Getting Ready to Build Skills

In order to get ready you should:

1. **Prepare your desk and computer area.**
   a. Clear your desk of all clutter, except your book, a pencil or pen, the keyboard, the mouse, and the monitor.
   b. Position your keyboard and book so that you are comfortable and able to move your hands and fingers freely on the keyboard and read the book at the same time.
   c. Keep your feet flat on the floor, sit with your back straight, and rest your arms slightly bent with your finger tips on the keyboard.
   d. Start a word-processing program, such as Microsoft Word, or any other text editor. You can also use any simple program such as the Microsoft Works word processor or WordPad that is part of the Windows operating system. Ask your teacher for assistance.

📟 EXTRA FOR EXPERTS

There are two forms that you will complete as you work through this appendix to improve your typing skills: the **Timed Typing Progress Chart** and the **Keyboarding Technique Checklist**. Both forms are printed as the last two pages at the end of this Appendix.

2. Take a two-minute timed typing test according to your teacher's directions.

3. Calculate your words a minute (WAM) and errors a minute (EAM) using the instructions on the timed typing progress chart. This will be the base score you will compare to future timed typing.

4. Record today's Date, WAM, and EAM on the Base Score line of the writing progress chart.

5. Repeat the timed typing test many times to see improvements in your score.

6. Record each attempt on the Introduction line of the chart.

Getting Started

Keyboarding is an essential skill in today's workplace. No matter what your job, most likely you have to learn to be an effective typist. Follow the hints below to help you achieve this goal:

- Ignore errors.
- To complete the following exercises, you will type text that is bold and is not italicized and looks **like this**.
- If you have difficulty reaching for any key, for example the y key, practice by looking at the reach your fingertips make from the j key to the y key until the reach is visualized in your mind. The reach will become natural with very little practice.
- To start on a new line, press Enter.

Skill Builder 1

Your Goal—Use the touch system to type the letters j u y h n m and to learn to press the spacebar.

Keys

What to Do

1. Place your fingertips on the home row keys as shown in **Figure B–1**.

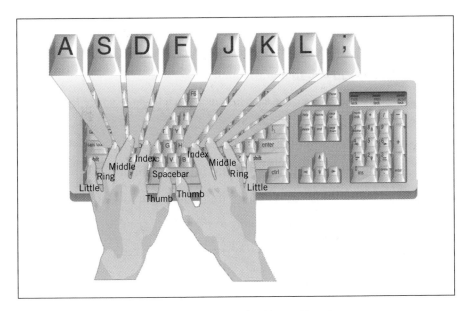

FIGURE B–1 Place your fingertips on the Home Row keys

2. Look at **Figure B–2**. In step 3, you will press the letter keys j u y h n m. To press these keys, you use your right index finger. You will press the spacebar after typing each letter three times. The spacebar is the long bar beneath the bottom row of letter keys. You will press the spacebar with your right thumb.

> ### TIP
>
> The home row keys are where you rest your fingertips when they are not typing. The index finger of your right hand rests on the J key. The index finger of your left hand rests on the F key. Feel the slight bump on these keys to help find the home row keys without looking at the keyboard.

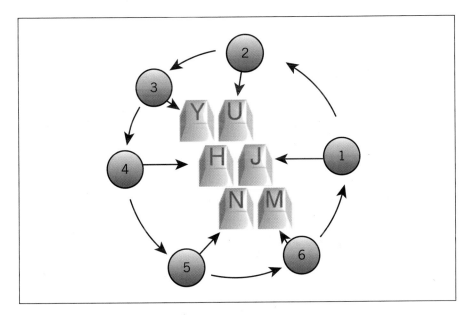

FIGURE B–2 Pressing the J U Y H N M keys

3. Look at your keyboard. Repeat the letters silently to yourself as you move your right index finger from the j key to press each key three times, and then press the spacebar. Start typing:

jjj uuu jjj yyy jjj hhh jjj nnn jjj mmm

jjj uuu jjj yyy jjj hhh jjj nnn jjj mmm jjj

4. Repeat the same drill as many times as it takes for you to reach your comfort level.

jjj uuu jjj yyy jjj hhh jjj nnn jjj mmm

jjj uuu jjj yyy jjj hhh jjj nnn jjj mmm jjj

5. Close your eyes and visualize each key under each finger as you repeat the drill in step 4.

6. Look at the following two lines and type:

jjj jjj jjj juj juj juj jyj jyj jyj jhj jhj jhj jnj jnj jnj jmj jmj jmj

jjj jjj jjj juj juj juj jyj jyj jyj jhj jhj jhj jnj jnj jnj jmj jmj jmj

7. Repeat step 6, this time concentrating on the rhythmic pattern of the keys.

8. Close your eyes and visualize the keys under your fingertips as you type the drill in step 4 from memory.

9. Look at the following two lines and type these groups of letters:

j ju juj j jy jyj j jh jhj j jn jnj j jm jmj j ju juj j jy jyj j jh jhj j jn jnj j jm jmj

jjj ju jhj jn jm ju jm jh jnj jm ju jmj jy ju jh j u ju juj jy jh jnj ju jm jmj jy

10. You may want to repeat Skill Builder 1, striving to improve typing letters that are most difficult for you.

Skill Builder 2

The left index finger is used to type the letters f r t g b v. Always return your left index finger to the f key on the home row after pressing the other keys.

Your Goal—Use the touch system to type f r t g b v .

Keys

What to Do

1. Place your fingertips on the home row keys as you did in Skill Builder 1, Figure B–1.

2. Look at **Figure B–3**. Notice how you will type the letters f r t g b v and then press the spacebar with your right thumb.

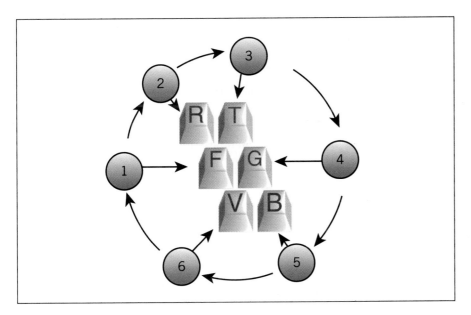

FIGURE B–3   Pressing the F R T G B V keys

3. Look at your keyboard. To press these keys, you use your left index finger. You will press the spacebar after typing each letter three times. The spacebar is the long bar beneath the bottom row of letter keys. You will press the spacebar with your right thumb.

   After pressing each letter in the circle, press the home key f three times as shown. Don't worry about errors. Ignore them.

   fff rrr fff ttt fff ggg fff bbb fff vvv

   fff rrr fff ttt fff ggg fff bbb fff vvv fff

4. Repeat the same drill two more times using a quicker, sharper stroke.

   fff rrr fff ttt fff ggg fff bbb fff vvv

   fff rrr fff ttt fff ggg fff bbb fff vvv fff

5. Close your eyes and visualize each key under each finger as you repeat the drill in step 4.

6. Look at the following two lines and key these groups of letters:

   fff fff fff frf frf frf ftf ftf ftf fgf fgf fgf fbf fbf fbf fvf fvf fvf

   fff fff fff frf frf frf ftf ftf ftf fgf fgf fgf fbf fbf fbf fvf fvf fvf

7. Repeat step 6, this time concentrating on a rhythmic pattern of the keys.

8. Close your eyes and visualize the keys under your fingertips as you type the drill in step 4 from memory.

9. Look at the following two lines and type these groups of letters:

   fr frf ft ftf fg fgf fb fbf fv fvf

   ft fgf fv frf ft fbf fv frf ft fgf

10. You are about ready to type your first words. Look at the following lines and type these groups of letters (remember to press the spacebar after each group):

jjj juj jug jug jug rrr rur rug rug rug

ttt tut tug tug tug rrr rur rub rub rub

ggg gug gum gum gum mmm mum

mug mug mug hhh huh hum hum hum

11. Complete the Keyboarding Technique Checklist.

Skill Builder 3

Your Goal—Use the touch system to type k i , d e c.

Keys  (comma)

What to Do

1. Place your fingertips on the home row keys. The home row key for the left middle finger is d. The home row key for the right middle finger is k. You use your left middle finger to type d, e, c. You use your right middle finger to type k, i, , as shown in **Figure B–4**.

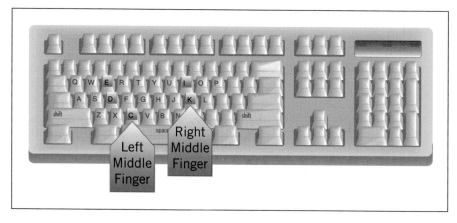

FIGURE B–4   Pressing the K I , D E C keys

2. Look at your keyboard and locate these keys: k i , (the letter k key, the letter i key, and the comma key).

3. Look at your keyboard. Repeat the letters silently to yourself as you press each key three times and put a space between each set of letters and the comma to type:

kkk iii kkk ,,, kkk iii kkk ,,, kkk iii kkk ,,, kkk iii kkk ,,, kkk iii kkk ,,, kkk

4. Look at the characters in step 3 and repeat the drill two more times using a quicker, sharper stroke.

5. Close your eyes and repeat the drill in step 3 as you visualize each key under each finger.

6. Repeat step 3, do not look at the keyboard, and concentrate on the rhythmic pattern of the keys.

Keys D E C

What to Do

1. Place your fingertips on the home row keys.

2. Look at your keyboard and locate these keys: d e c (the letter d key, the letter e key, and the letter c key).

3. Look at your keyboard. Repeat the letters silently to yourself as you press each key three times and put a space between each set of letters to type:

   ddd eee ddd ccc ddd eee ddd ccc ddd eee ddd ccc ddd eee ddd ccc ddd

4. Look at the letters in step 3 and repeat the drill two more times using a quicker, sharper stroke.

5. Close your eyes and repeat the drill in step 3 as you visualize each key under each finger.

6. Repeat step 3, do not look at the keyboard, and concentrate on the rhythmic pattern of the keys.

7. Look at the following lines of letters and type these groups of letters and words:

   fff fuf fun fun fun ddd ded den den den

   ccc cuc cub cub cub vvv vev vet

   fff fuf fun fun fun ddd ded den den den

   ccc cuc cub cub cub vvv vev vet

8. Complete the Keyboarding Technique Checklist.

Skill Builder 4

Your Goal—Use the touch system to type l o . s w x and to press the left Shift key.

Keys L O . (period)

What to Do

1. Place your fingertips on the home row keys. The home row key for the left ring finger is s. The home row key for the right ring finger is l. You use your left ring finger to type s w x. You use your right ring finger to type l o . as shown in **Figure B–5**.

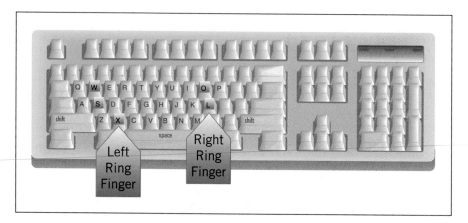

FIGURE B–5   Pressing the L O . S W X keys

2. Look at your keyboard and locate the following keys: l o . (the letter l key, the letter o key, and the period key).

3. Look at your keyboard. Repeat the letters silently to yourself as you press each key three times and put a space between each set of letters and the periods to type:

    lll ooo lll ... lll ooo lll ... lll ooo lll ... lll ooo lll ... lll ooo lll ... lll ooo lll ... lll

4. Look at the line in step 3 and repeat the drill two more times using a quicker, sharper stroke.

5. Close your eyes and repeat the drill in step 3 as you visualize each key under each finger.

6. Repeat step 3, do not look at the keyboard, and concentrate on the rhythmic pattern of the keys.

Keys ⓢ ⓦ ⓧ

1. Place your fingertips on the home row keys.

2. Look at your keyboard and locate the following letter keys: s w x

3. Look at your keyboard. Repeat the letters silently to yourself as you press each key three times and put a space between each set of letters to type:

    sss www sss xxx sss www sss xxx sss www sss xxx sss www sss xxx sss

4. Look at the line in step 3 and repeat the same drill two more times using a quicker, sharper stroke.

5. Close your eyes and repeat the drill in step 3 as you visualize each key under each finger.

6. Repeat step 3, do not look at the keyboard, and concentrate on the rhythmic pattern of the keys.

Key Shift ⟨SHIFT⟩ (Left Shift Key)

You press and hold the Shift key as you press a letter key to type a capital letter. You press and hold the Shift key to type the character that appears above the numbers in the top row of the keyboard and on a few other keys that show two characters.

Press and hold down the left Shift key with the little finger on your left hand while you press each letter to type capital letters for keys that are typed with the fingertips on your right hand. See **Figure B–6**.

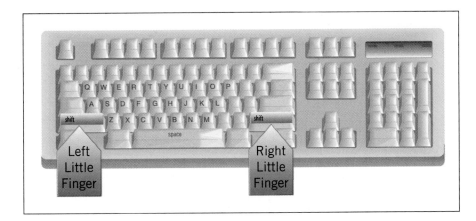

FIGURE B–6   Using the Shift keys

1. Type the following groups of letters and the sentence that follows.

    jjj JJJ jjj JJJ yyy YYY yyy YYY nnn NNN nnn NNN mmm MMM

    Just look in the book. You can see well.

2. Complete a column in the Keyboarding Technique Checklist.

Skill Builder 5

Your Goal—Use the touch system to type a q z ; p / and to press the right Shift key.

Keys ⟨;⟩ (Semi-Colon) ⟨P⟩ ⟨/⟩

APPENDIX B

What to Do

1. Place your fingertips on the home row keys. The home row key for the left little finger is a. The home row key for the right little finger is ;. You use your left little finger to type a q z. You use your right little finger to type ; p / as shown in **Figure B–7**.

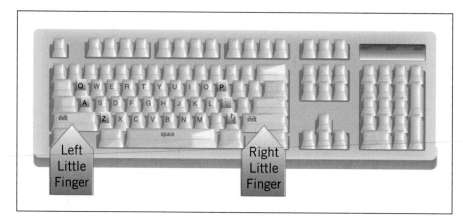

FIGURE B–7   Pressing the A Q Z ; P / and the right Shift key

2. Look at your keyboard and locate the following keys: ; p / (the semi-colon, the letter p, and the forward slash).

3. Repeat the letters silently to yourself as you press each key three times and put a space between each set of characters to type:

    ;;; ppp ;;; /// ;;; ppp ;;; /// ;;; ppp ;;; ///

    ;;; ppp ;;; /// ;;; ppp ;;; /// ;;; ppp ;;; /// ;;;

4. Look at the lines in step 3 and repeat the drill two more times using a quicker, sharper stroke.

5. Close your eyes and repeat the drill in step 3 as you visualize each key under each finger.

6. Repeat step 3, do not look at the keyboard, and concentrate on a rhythmic pattern of the keys.

Keys Ⓐ Ⓠ Ⓩ

1. Place your fingertips on the home row keys.

2. Look at your keyboard and locate the following keys: a q z (the letter a, the letter q, and the letter z).

3. Look at your keyboard. Repeat the letters silently to yourself as you press each key three times and put a space between each set of letters and type:

    aaa qqq aaa zzz aaa qqq aaa zzz aaa qqq aaa zzz aaa qqq aaa zzz aaa

4. Look at the line in step 3 and repeat the same drill two more times using a quicker, sharper stroke.

5. Close your eyes and repeat the drill in step 3 as you visualize each key under each finger.

6. Repeat step 3, do not look at the keyboard, and concentrate on the rhythmic pattern of the keys.

Key Shift (SHIFT) (Right Shift Key)

Press and hold down the right Shift key with the little finger on your right hand while you press each letter to type capital letters for keys that are typed with the fingertips on your left hand.

1. Type the following lines. Press and hold down the right Shift key with the little finger of your right hand to make capitals of letters you type with the fingertips on your left hand.

   sss SSS rrr RRR

   Press each key quickly. Relax when you type.

2. Complete another column in the Keyboarding Technique Checklist.

Skill Builder 6

You will probably have to type slowly at first, but with practice you will learn to type faster and accurately.

Your Goal—Use the touch system to type all letters of the alphabet.

What to Do

1. Close your eyes. Do not look at the keyboard and type all letters of the alphabet in groups of three with a space between each set as shown:

   aaa bbb ccc ddd eee fff ggg hhh iii jjj

   kkk lll mmm nnn ooo ppp qqq rrr sss

   ttt uuu vvv www xxx yyy zzz

2. Repeat step 1, concentrating on a rhythmic pattern of the keys.

3. Repeat step 1, but faster than you did for step 2.

4. Type the following sets of letters, all letters of the alphabet in groups of two with a space between each set as shown:

   aa bb cc dd ee ff gg hh ii jj kk ll mm nn oo pp qq rr ss tt uu vv ww xx yy zz

5. Type the following letters, all letters of the alphabet with a space between each letter as shown:

   a b c d e f g h i j k l m n o p q r s t u v w x y z

6. Continue to look at this book. Do not look at the keyboard, and type all letters of the alphabet backwards in groups of three with a space between each set as shown:

   zzz yyy xxx www vvv uuu ttt sss rrr

   qqq ppp ooo nnn mmm lll kkk jjj iii

   hhh ggg fff eee ddd ccc bbb aaa

7. Repeat step 6, but faster than the last time.

8. Type each letter of the alphabet once backwards:

   z y x w v u t s r q p o n m l k j i h g f e d c b a

9. Think about the letters that took you the most amount of time to find the key on the keyboard. Go back to the Skill Builder for those letters, and repeat the drills until you are confident about their locations.

Timed Typing

Prepare to take the timed typing test, according to your teacher's directions.

1. **Prepare your desk and computer area.**
   a. Clear your desk of all clutter except your book, a pencil or pen, the keyboard, the mouse, the monitor, and the computer if it is located on the desk.
   b. Position your keyboard and book so that you are comfortable and able to move your hands and fingertips freely.
   c. Keep your feet flat on the floor, sitting with your back straight, resting your arms slightly bent with your fingertips on the keyboard.

2. Take a two-minute timed typing test according to your teacher's directions.

3. Calculate your words a minute (WAM) and errors a minute (EAM) scores using the instructions on the Timed Typing Progress Chart in this book.

4. Record the date, WAM, and EAM on the Skill Builder 6 line in the Timed Typing Progress Chart printed at the end of this appendix.

5. Repeat the timed typing test as many times as you can and record each attempt in the Timed Typing Progress Chart.

Skill Builder 7

Your Goal—Improve your typing techniques—which is the secret for improving your speed and accuracy.

What to Do

1. Rate yourself for each item on the Keyboarding Technique Checklist printed at the end of this appendix.

2. Do not time yourself as you concentrate on a single technique you marked with a "0." Type only the first paragraph of the timed typing.

3. Repeat step 2 as many times as possible for each of the items marked with an "0" that need improvement.

4. Take a two-minute timed typing test. Record your WAM and EAM on the Timed Typing Progress Chart as 1st Attempt on the Skill Builder 7 line. Compare this score with your base score.

5. Looking only at the book and using your best techniques, type the following technique sentence for one minute:

   .   **2**   .   **4**   .   **6** .   **8**   .   **10**   .   **12**   .   **14**   .   **16**

Now is the time for all good men and women to come to the aid of their country.

6. Record your WAM and EAM in the Timed Typing Progress Chart on the 7 Technique Sentence line.

7. Repeat steps 5 and 6 as many times as you can and record your scores in the Timed Typing Progress Chart.

Skill Builder 8

Your Goal—Increase your words a minute (WAM) score.

What to Do

You can now type letters in the speed line very well and with confidence. Practicing all of the other letters of the alphabet will further increase your skill and confidence in keyboarding.

1. Take a two-minute timed typing test.

2. Record your WAM and EAM scores as the 1st Attempt in the Timed Typing Progress Chart.

3. Type only the first paragraph only one time as fast as you can. Ignore errors.

4. Type only the first and second paragraphs only one time as fast as you can. Ignore errors.

5. Take a two-minute timed typing test again. Ignore errors.

6. Record only your WAM score as the 2nd Attempt in the Timed Typing Progress Chart. Compare only this WAM with your 1st Attempt WAM and your base score WAM.

Get Your Best WAM

1. To get your best WAM on easy text for 15 seconds, type the following speed line as fast as you can, as many times as you can. Ignore errors.

   .   **2**   .   **4**   .   **6**   .   **8**   .   **10**

Now is the time, now is the time, now is the time,

2. Multiply the number of words typed by four to get your WAM (15 seconds × 4 = 1 minute). For example, if you type 12 words for 15 seconds, 12 × 4 = 48 WAM.

3. Record only your WAM in the 8 Speed Line box in the Timed Typing Progress Chart.

4. Repeat steps 1–3 as many times as you can to get your very best WAM. Ignore errors.

5. Record only your WAM for each attempt in the Timed Typing Progress Chart.

Skill Builder 9

Your Goal—Decrease errors a minute (EAM) score.

What to Do

TIP

How much you improve depends upon how much you want to improve.

1. Take a two-minute timed typing test.

2. Record your WAM and EAM as the 1st Attempt in the Timed Typing Progress Chart.

3. Type only the first paragraph only one time at a controlled rate of speed so you reduce errors. Ignore speed.

4. Type only the first and second paragraphs only one time at a controlled rate of speed so you reduce errors. Ignore speed.

5. Take a two-minute timed typing test again. Ignore speed.

6. Record only your EAM score as the 2nd Attempt in the Timed Typing Progress Chart. Compare only the EAM with your 1st Attempt EAM and your base score EAM.

Get Your Best EAM

1. To get your best EAM, type the following accuracy sentence (same as the technique sentence) for one minute. Ignore speed.

   Now is the time for all good men and women to come to the aid of their country.

2. Record only your EAM score on the Accuracy Sentence 9 line in the Timed Typing Progress Chart.

3. Repeat step 1 as many times as you can to get your best EAM. Ignore speed.

4. Record only your EAM score for each attempt in the Timed Typing Progress Chart.

Skill Builder 10

Your Goal—Use the touch system and your best techniques to type faster and more accurately than you have ever typed before.

What to Do

1. Take a one-minute timed typing test.

2. Record your WAM and EAM as the 1st Attempt on the Skill Builder 10 line in the Timed Typing Progress Chart.

3. Repeat the timed typing test for two minutes as many times as necessary to get your best ever WAM with no more than one EAM. Record your scores as 2nd, 3rd, and 4th Attempts.

> **TIP**
>
> You may want to get advice regarding which techniques you need to improve from a classmate or your instructor.

Assessing Your Improvement

1. Circle your best timed typing test for Skill Builders 6-10 in the Timed Typing Progress Chart.

2. Record your best score and your base score. Compare the two scores. Did you improve?

	WAM	EAM
Best Score	_____	_____
Base Score	_____	_____

3. Use the Keyboarding Technique Checklist to identify techniques you still need to improve. You may want to practice these techniques now to increase your WAM or decrease your EAM.

Timed Typing

Every five strokes in a timed typing test is a word, including punctuation marks and spaces. Use the scale above each line to tell you how many words you typed.

```
        .       2       .       4       .       6       .
If you learn how to key well now, it
    8       .       10      .       12      .       14      .       16
is a skill that will help you for the rest
        .       18      .       20      .       22      .       24
of your life. How you sit will help you key
    .       26      .       28      .       30      .       32      .       34
with more speed and less errors.  Sit with your
        .       36      .       38      .       40      .       42      .
feet flat on the floor and your back erect.
        44      .       46      .       48      .       50
To key fast by touch, try to keep your
    .       52      .       54      .       56      .       58      .
eyes on the copy and not on your hands or
    60      .       62      .       64      .       66      .       68
the screen.  Curve your fingers and make sharp,
    .       70      .
quick strokes.
    72      .       74      .       76      .       78      .
Work for speed first.  If you make more
    80      .       82      .       84      .       86      .       88
than two errors a minute, you are keying too
    .       90      .       92      .       94      .       96      .
fast. Slow down to get fewer errors. If you
        98      .       100     .       102     .       104     .
get fewer than two errors a minute, go for
    106     .
speed.
```

Timed Typing Progress Chart

Timed Writing Progress Chart

Last Name: _____   *First Name:* _____

Instructions

Calculate your scores as shown in the following sample. Repeat timed writings as many times as you can and record your scores for each attempt.

Base Score	Date	WAM	EAM	Time

To calculate WAM: Divide words keyed by number of minutes to get WAM. For example: 44 words keyed in 2 minutes = 22 WAM [44/2=22]

To calculate EAM: Divide errors made by minutes of typing to get EAM

For example: 7 errors made in 2 minutes of typing = 3.5 EAM [7/2=3.5]

		1st Attempt		2nd Attempt		3rd Attempt		4th Attempt	
Skill Builder	**Date**	**(a) WAM**	**(b) EAM**	**WAM**	**EAM**	**WAM**	**EAM**	**WAM**	**EAM**
Sample	9/2	22	3.5	23	2.0	25	1.0	29	2.0
Introduction									
6									
7									
8					-----				
9				-----					
10									
7 Technique Sentence									
8 Speed Line			-----		-----		-----		-----
9 Accuracy Sentence		-----		-----		-----		-----	

APPENDIX B

Keyboarding Technique Checklist

Last Name: _____   *First Name:* _____

Instructions

1. Write the Skill Builder number, the date, and the initials of the evaluator in the proper spaces.

2. Place a check mark (✓) after a technique that is performed satisfactorily.

3. Place a large zero (0) after a technique that needs improvement.

Skill Builder Number:	Sample										
Date:	9/1										
Evaluator:	SL										
Technique											
Attitude											
1. Enthusiastic about learning	✓										
2. Optimistic about improving	✓										
3. Alert but relaxed	✓										
4. Sticks to the task; not distracted	✓										
Getting Ready											
1. Desk uncluttered	✓										
2. Properly positions keyboard and book	✓										
3. Feet flat on the floor	✓										
4. Body erect, but relaxed	0										
Keyboarding											
1. Curves fingers	0										
2. Keeps eyes on the book	✓										
3. Taps the keys lightly; does not "pound" them	0										
4. Makes quick, "bouncy," strokes	0										
5. Smooth rhythm	0										
6. Minimum pauses between strokes	✓										

APPENDIX C

Differences between Windows 7, Windows Vista, and Windows XP

The Windows Experience

- Microsoft offers many new features in Windows 7 that are not available in Windows XP and Windows Vista.

- The overall Windows experience has been vastly improved from Windows XP to Windows 7. If you make the jump from XP to Windows 7, you will discover a great number of changes that are for the better. In addition, many of the new features introduced in Windows Vista were retained in this latest version of the popular operating system. Upgrading to Windows 7 is also an easier, more streamlined transition.

- With Windows 7, Microsoft has simplified everyday tasks and works more efficiently. This is all in response to issues users had with the Windows XP and Windows Vista experience. The major differences between Windows XP, Windows Vista, and Windows 7 are in the Start menu, dynamic navigation, desktop gadgets, improved security, search options, parental controls, and firewall, as well as improvements to the Windows Aero feature, see **Figure C–1**.

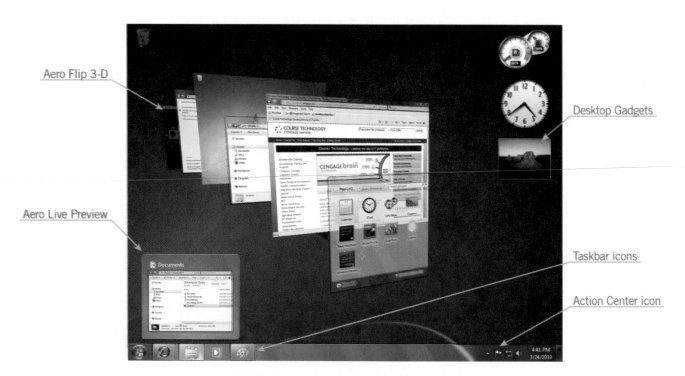

FIGURE C–1 Windows 7 Features

Windows Aero

- Windows Aero is a new graphic interface feature which gives a "transparent" quality to windows, dialog boxes, and other items in the Windows Vista and Windows 7 environment.

- Flip 3-D, or simply Flip, shows mini versions of windows and thumbnails in the Windows 7 environment when turned on.

Windows XP users had to download Windows Desktop Enhancements and PowerTools from the Microsoft Web site to change their Windows experience. Windows Vista and Windows 7 now have many different themes and options built into the operating system, making it easy to modify the Windows experience. One theme, introduced in Windows Vista is Aero.

Windows Aero is a feature which was first introduced in Windows Vista and is not available in the Windows XP operating system. Windows Aero, enabled by default in Windows 7, is a more aesthetically pleasing user interface to Windows Vista and Windows 7 systems. For example, Windows XP utilizes ScreenTips only when pointing to items on the Taskbar, Desktop, and Menus. The basic ScreenTips found in Windows XP have been enhanced to show live "sneak-previews" of windows with a simple point to the icon on the taskbar , as shown in **Figure C–2**.

Windows 7 made major improvements to the function of Aero. These new features include Aero Peek, Aero Shake, Aero Snap, Touch UI, and many other visual effects covered in this section. Compare the evolution of the Taskbar ScreenTip in Windows XP to Windows Vista and finally in Windows 7 in the figures below.

FIGURE C–2   Comparing Windows XP taskbar with Windows Vista and Windows 7

Understanding the Desktop

- Gadgets, introduced in Windows Vista, and Jump Lists, introduced in Windows 7, are two new desktop features.
- Windows 7 also includes multiple Aero themes to customize your desktop including the Desktop Background Slideshow.

APPENDIX C

At first glance, the Windows XP desktop only appears to differ slightly from that of Windows Vista, but the new features available with Windows 7 are substantial. The icons, shortcuts, folders, and files are generally the same; however, there are major aesthetic visual differences in this version. The most obvious addition from XP to Vista is the desktop gadget. Gadgets were not available in Windows XP. In **Figure C–4**, notice the appearance of three gadgets on the sidebar. Desktop gadgets are also available in Windows 7; however the sidebar function has been abandoned. Users simply add the gadget to the desktop.

The Taskbar in Windows XP includes the notification area, quick launch (when enabled), Start button, and icon(s) representing open programs. Beginning with Windows 7, you can now easily pin items to the Taskbar instead of using a quick launch feature. Jump lists, Aero themes and the Desktop Background Slideshow, explained in this chapter, are also new features to Windows 7.

FIGURE C–3 Windows XP Start menu and Desktop

The Start menu has been slightly enhanced from Windows XP to Windows 7. All Programs no longer appears on an additional menu, it has been merged with the Start menu. Windows Vista introduced a search function built into the Start menu, which allows users to search the computer easily for documents, applications, and help. Compare the evolution in desktops from Windows XP to Windows 7 in **Figures C–3, C–4,** and **C–5.**

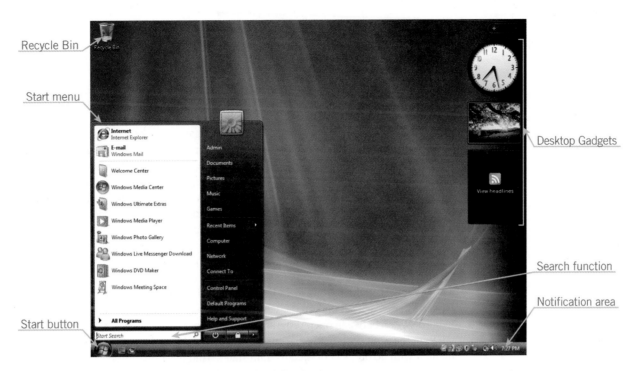

FIGURE C–4 Windows Vista Start menu and Desktop

FIGURE C–5 Windows 7 Start menu and Desktop

APPENDIX C

Navigating in Windows

- The Address bar in Windows 7 now functions differently, with more direct navigation functions.
- Windows 7 now includes a comprehensive Navigation pane in Windows Explorer.

Windows Explorer provides the tools to navigate and locate items on your computer. The Address bar has been upgraded from Windows XP to allow for easier movement between folders. In Windows XP, the only available methods were the Back button and drop-down arrow. See **Figure C–6**. A big difference is in the function of the path. You may now click the folder in your path to move back. You may also begin a search directly from the Address bar, which is a new Windows 7 feature. Windows XP users' only option to search was to utilize the Search Companion.

The Navigation pane, which provides links to common or recently used folders, is dramatically different in Windows 7, compared to Windows XP, which only featured Favorites. "My Documents", the default user folder in Windows XP, is now a collection of folders grouped in Libraries in Windows 7. These folders, as well as Favorites, are easily found on the new Navigation pane and are easily customizable.

To switch between open programs easily, Windows XP's only option aside from clicking the icon on the Taskbar, was to tab through available programs, in a basic method with no preview of the program state. Windows Flip, introduced in Windows Vista, allows you to move to an open file, window or program by pressing the Alt+Tab keys, while showing a preview of the program's current state in Aero. The Windows Vista version of Flip was enhanced for Windows 7 users, although the function remains the same. See **Figures C–8** and **C-9** on the following pages.

FIGURE C–6   Windows Explorer as seen in Windows XP

Dynamic Address bar

Back button

Favorite Links pane

Search text box

View headlines

Explorer window in Tiles view

FIGURE C–7   Windows Explorer as seen in Windows Vista

Aero Flip tabs through open programs

Taskbar buttons for open programs

FIGURE C–8   Flip in Windows Vista

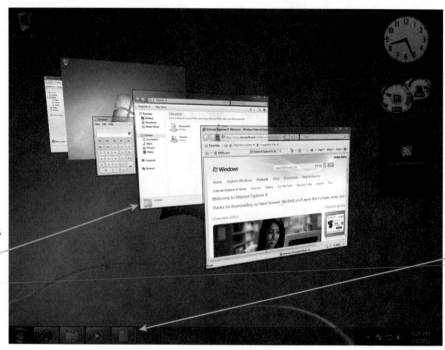

Aero Flip 3-D tabs through open programs

Taskbar buttons for open programs

FIGURE C–9   Flip 3-D in Windows 7

Using Windows

- The new Aero Shake and Aero Snap allow you to easily move, resize, minimize and maximize open windows.
- The Control Panel now includes additional descriptive links, making it easy to find the item you are looking to modify.

Moving and resizing windows in Windows 7 provides the same essential functions as it did in previous Windows versions, with a few additions. In Windows XP and Vista, you had to manipulate each window individually, by clicking and dragging. You can still click and drag to resize and move windows; however this function has been upgraded and revamped in Windows 7. Aero Shake allows you to "shake" all open windows except that particular window to a minimized state. Aero Snap is a new way to easily resize open windows to expand vertically, or side-by-side.

The Control Panel, revamped in Windows Vista, has a new look in Windows 7, compared to that in Windows XP. The Search text box allows you to search for the Control Panel task you wish to perform. There are also descriptive linked items now replacing the "classic" icon format. **Figures C–10**, **C–11**, and **C–12**, which are shown on the following pages, illustrate the differences in the Control Panel from Windows XP to Windows 7.

Switch to Classic View for basic icon arrangement

Control Panel

Grouped categories

FIGURE C–10   Windows XP Control Panel

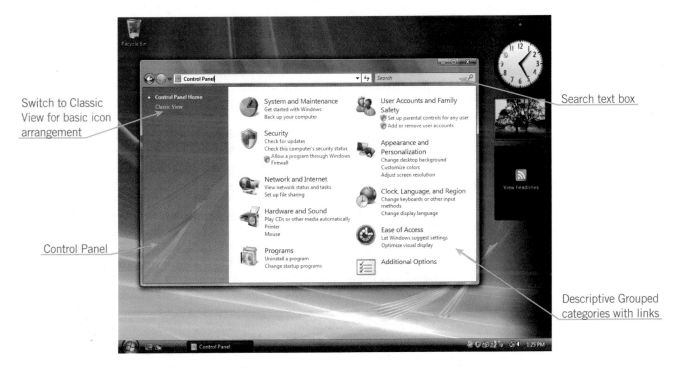

Switch to Classic View for basic icon arrangement

Control Panel

Search text box

Descriptive Grouped categories with links

FIGURE C–11   Windows Vista Control Panel

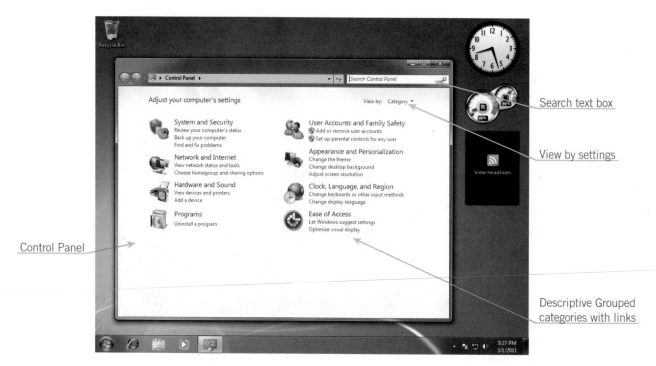

FIGURE C–12 Windows 7 Control Panel

Managing Your Computer

- The Action Center is a new feature in Windows 7 which consolidates message traffic from Windows maintenance and security features.
- Basic system utilities, such as Disk Cleanup and Disk Defragmenter, remain essentially the same from Windows XP to Windows 7.

Windows XP and Windows Vista's only method of receiving information on security and maintenance was the Security Center, available from the Control Panel. Windows 7 has improved this function, by creating a new Action Center, which communicates with the firewall, spyware protection, and antivirus software. Windows 7 users can now navigate to the Action Center by visiting the System and Security section of the Control Panel to view computer status and resolve issues. The Action Center is also pre-configured in Windows 7 to send important alerts to the Notification area of the taskbar.

One of the major upgrades in Windows 7 is in performance. Windows 7 was designed to run on less memory, shutting down services when not in use. In the Control Panel of Windows 7, there is a new Performance and Information Tools section. If you are a previous Windows XP user, you should familiarize yourself with this new feature. You will be able to assess your computer's performance, adjust settings, run disk cleanup, and launch advanced tools to manage your computer.

Windows Defender, introduced in Windows Vista is Microsoft's answer to spyware protection. This was not available for Windows XP users, pre Windows XP Service Pack 2. Windows XP Service Pack 2 users could download it from the Microsoft Web site and install it manually. Windows 7 also includes Windows Defender by default.

Windows Update, introduced in Windows XP has remained the same throughout the transitions through Windows Vista and Windows 7. Windows Update, which automatically downloads and installs important updates, was one of the only ways

Microsoft offered to maintain a secure PC with Windows XP. Now, in Windows 7, the Action Center, Performance Information and Tools, Windows Defender, and Windows Update work together to keep your computer secure. **Figures C–13**, **C–14**, and **C–15**, which are shown on the next few pages, compare Windows XP and Vista's Security Centers with Windows 7 Security Center and Action Center.

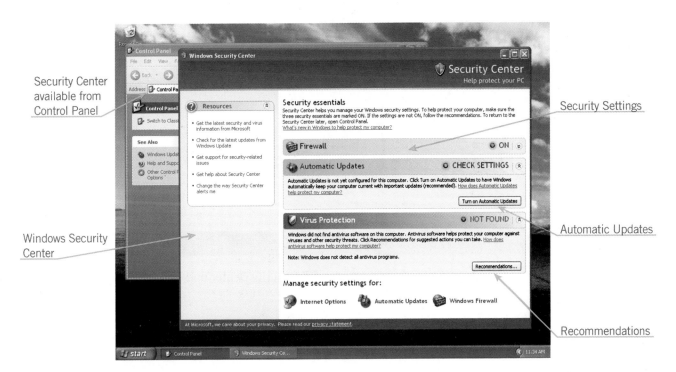

FIGURE C–13 Windows XP Security Center

FIGURE C–14 Windows Vista Security Center

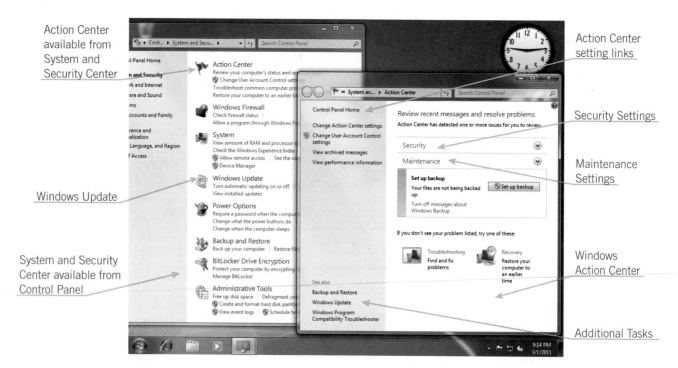

FIGURE C–15 Windows 7 Security Center and Action Center

APPENDIX D

Using SkyDrive and Office Web Apps

■ OBJECTIVES

Upon completion of this lesson, you should be able to:

- Explore cloud computing and Windows Live.
- Obtain a Windows Live ID and sign in to Windows Live.
- Upload files to SkyDrive.
- Use Office Web Apps View and Edit modes.
- Create folders on SkyDrive.
- Organize files on SkyDrive.
- Give permission for access to a folder on your SkyDrive.
- Co-author using the Excel Web App.

■ VOCABULARY

cloud computing

co-author

Office Web Apps

OneNote

SkyDrive

Windows Live

If the computer you are using has an active Internet connection, you can go to the Microsoft Windows Live Web site and use SkyDrive to store and share files. From SkyDrive, you can also use Office Web Apps to create and edit Word, PowerPoint, Excel, and OneNote files, even when you are using a computer that does not have Office 2010 installed. In this Appendix, you will learn how to obtain a Windows Live ID, how to share files with others on SkyDrive, and how to use the Word, Excel, and PowerPoint Web Apps, including co-authoring in the Excel Web App.

Understanding Cloud Computing and Windows Live

Cloud computing refers to data, applications, and even resources that are stored on servers that you access over the Internet rather than on your own computer. With cloud computing, you access only what you need when you need it. Many individuals and companies are moving towards "the cloud" for at least some of their needs. For example, some companies provide space and computing power to developers for a fee. Individuals might subscribe to an online backup service so that data is automatically backed up on a computer at the physical location of the companies that provide that service.

Windows Live is a collection of services and Web applications that you can use to help you be more productive both personally and professionally. For example, you can use Windows Live to send and receive email, chat with friends via instant messaging, share photos, create a blog, and store and edit files. Windows Live is a free service that you sign up for. When you sign up, you receive a Windows Live ID, which you use to sign into your Windows Live account. **Table D–1** describes the services available on Windows Live.

► VOCABULARY

cloud computing

Windows Live

TABLE D–1   Services available via Windows Live

SERVICE	DESCRIPTION
Email	Send and receive e-mail using a Hotmail account
Instant Messaging	Use Messenger to chat with friends, share photos, and play games
SkyDrive	Store files, work on files using Web Apps, and share files with people in your network
Photos	Upload and share photos with friends
People	Develop a network of friends and coworkers and use it to distribute information and stay in touch
Downloads	Access a variety of free programs available for download to a PC
Mobile Device	Access applications for a mobile device: text messaging, using Hotmail, networking, and sharing photos

SkyDrive is an online storage and file sharing service. With a Windows Live account, you receive access to your own SkyDrive, which is your personal storage area on the Internet. You upload files to your SkyDrive so you can share the files with other people, access the files from another computer, or use SkyDrive's additional storage. On your SkyDrive, you are given space to store up to 25 GB of data online. Each file can be a maximum size of 50 MB. You can also use your SkyDrive to share files with friends and coworkers. After you upload a file to your SkyDrive, you can choose to make the file visible to the public, to anyone you invite to share your files, or only to yourself. You can also use SkyDrive to access Office Web Apps. When you save files to SkyDrive on Windows Live, you are saving your files to an online location. SkyDrive is like having a personal hard drive "in the cloud."

Office Web Apps are versions of Microsoft Word, Excel, PowerPoint, and *OneNote*, an electronic notebook program included with Microsoft Office, that you can access online from your SkyDrive. Office Web Apps offer basic functionality, allowing you to create and edit files created in Word, PowerPoint, and Excel online in your Web browser. An Office Web App does not include all of the features and functions included with the full Office version of its associated application. However, you can use the Office Web Apps from any computer that is connected to the Internet, even if Microsoft Office 2010 is not installed on that computer.

Obtaining a Windows Live ID

To save files to SkyDrive or to use Office Web Apps, you need a Windows Live ID. You obtain a Windows Live ID by going to the Windows Live Web site and creating a new account.

Note: If you already have a Windows Live ID, you can skip Step-by-Step D.1.

Step-by-Step D.1

1. Start Internet Explorer. Click in the Address bar, type **www.windowslive.com**, and then press **Enter**. The page where you can sign into Windows Live opens.

2. Click the **Sign up** button. The Create your Windows Live ID page opens.

3. Follow the instructions on the screen to create an ID with a new, live.com email address or create an ID using an existing email address.

4. After completing the process, if you signed up with an existing email address, open your email program or go to your Web-based email home page, and open the email message automatically sent to you from the Windows Live site. Click the link to open the Sign In page again, sign in with your user name and password if necessary, and then click the **OK** button in the page that appears telling you that your email address is verified.

5. Exit Internet Explorer.

VOCABULARY
SkyDrive
Office Web Apps
OneNote

WARNING

If the URL doesn't bring you to the page where you can sign into Windows Live, use a search engine to search for *Windows Live*.

Uploading Files to SkyDrive

You can access your SkyDrive from the Windows Live page in your browser after you signed in with your Windows Live ID, or from Word, Excel, PowerPoint, or OneNote. Then you can upload a file to a private or public folder on your SkyDrive.

Uploading a File to SkyDrive from Backstage View

If you are working in a file in Word, Excel, or PowerPoint, you can save the file to your SkyDrive from Backstage view. To do this, you click the File tab, click Save & Send in the navigation bar, and then click Save to Web. After you do this, the right pane changes to display a Sign In button that you can use to sign in to your Windows Live account. See **Figure D–1**.

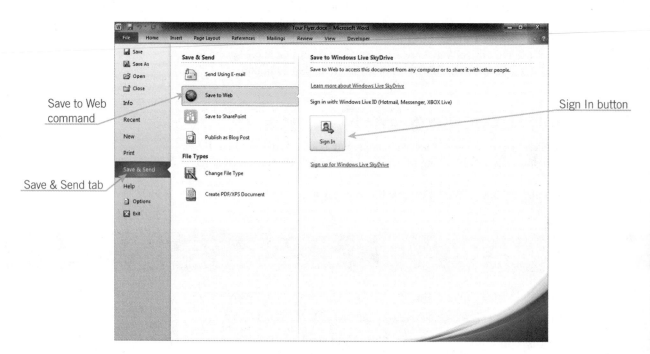

FIGURE D–1 Save & Send tab in Backstage view in Word after clicking Save to Web

Click the Sign In button to sign into Windows Live. After you enter your user name and password, the right pane in Backstage view changes to list the folders on your SkyDrive and a Save As button now appears in the right pane. See **Figure D–2**.

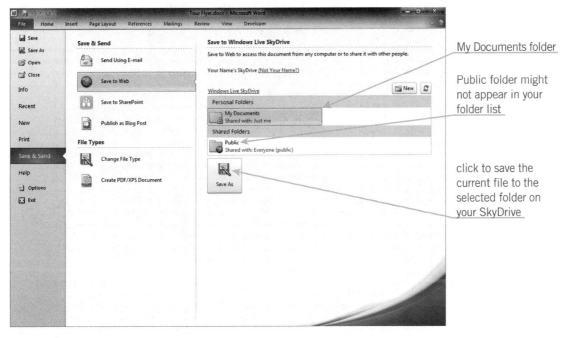

FIGURE D–2   Save & Send tab after connecting to Windows Live

To save the file, click the correct folder, and then click the Save As button.

Step-by-Step D.2

1. Start Word. Open the file named **Tour Flyer.docx** document from the drive and folder where your Data Files are stored.

2. Click the **File** tab, and then click **Save & Send** on the navigation bar. The Save & Send options appear in Backstage view as shown in Figure D–1.

3. Under Save & Send, click **Save to Web**.

4. Click the **Sign In** button. The Connecting to docs.live.net dialog box opens. See **Figure D–3**. If you are already signed into Windows Live, you will see the folders in your SkyDrive account listed instead of the Sign In button. Skip this step (Step 4) and Step 5.

FIGURE D–3
Connecting to docs.live.net dialog box

5. In the E-mail address box, type the email address associated with your Windows Live ID account. Press **Tab**, and then type the password associated with your Windows Live account in the Password box. Click the **OK** button. The dialog box closes, and another dialog box appears briefly while you connect to the Windows Live server. After you are connected, the folders on your SkyDrive appear in the right pane in Backstage view, as shown in Figure D–2.

6. In the right pane, click the **My Documents** folder, and then click the **Save As** button. Backstage view closes, and then after a few moments, the Save As dialog box opens. The path in the Address bar identifies the Public folder location on your SkyDrive.

7. Click the **Save** button. The dialog box closes and the Tour Flyer file is saved to the My Documents folder on your SkyDrive.

8. Exit Word.

Uploading a File to SkyDrive in a Browser

You can also add files to SkyDrive by starting from an Internet Explorer window. To do this, go to www.windowslive.com, and then log in to your Windows Live account. See **Figure D–4**.

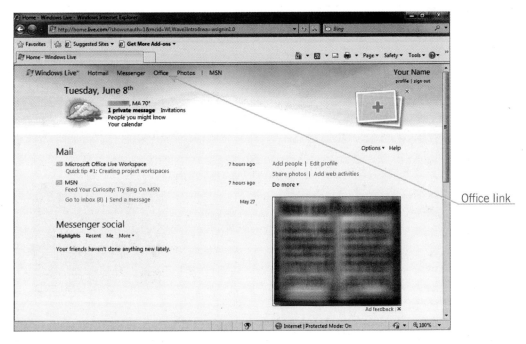

FIGURE D–4 Windows Live home page

To get to your SkyDrive, you click the Office link in the list of navigation links at the top of the window. To see all the folders on your SkyDrive, click View all in the Folders list on the left. See **Figure D–5**.

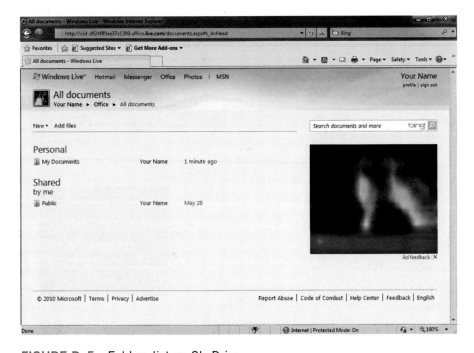

FIGURE D–5 Folders list on SkyDrive

Click the folder to which you want to add the file to open it. See **Figure D–6**.

click to add files
to this folder

contents of folder
are listed here

FIGURE D–6   My Documents folder page on SkyDrive

Click the Add files link to open the Add documents to *Folder Name* page; for example, if you click the Add files link in the My Documents folder, the Add documents to My Documents page appears. See **Figure D–7**.

page name

click this link to
display the Open
dialog box

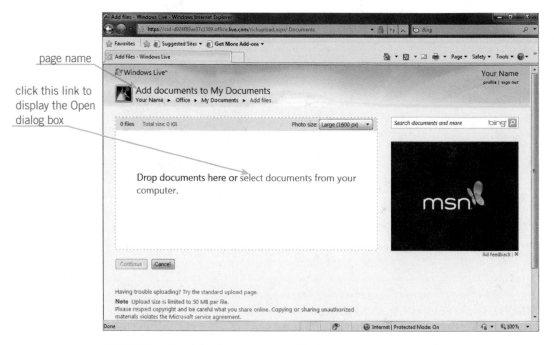

FIGURE D–7   Add documents to My Documents page on SkyDrive

Click the "select documents from your computer" link to display the Open dialog box. Locate the drive and folder where the file is stored, click it, and then click Open. The file uploads and is listed in the box. Click Continue to display the folder containing the files you uploaded to your SkyDrive.

Step-by-Step D.3

1. Start Internet Explorer. Click in the Address bar, type **www.windowslive. com**, and then press **Enter**.

2. If the Sign In page appears, type your Windows Live ID user name and password in the appropriate boxes, and then click **Sign in**. Your Windows Live home page appears similar to the one shown in Figure D–4.

3. In the list of command links at the top of the window, click **Office**. Your SkyDrive page appears.

4. In the list under Folders on the left, click **View all**. All the folders on your SkyDrive appear, similar to Figure D–5.

5. Click the **My Documents** folder. The My Documents page appears, similar to Figure D–6.

6. In the list of command links, click the **Add files** link. The Add documents to My Documents page appears, as shown in Figure D–7.

7. Click the **select documents from your computer** link, navigate to the drive and folder where your Data Files are stored, click **Tour Sales.pptx**, and then click the **Open** button. The file uploads and appears in the box on the Add documents to My Documents page.

8. At the bottom of the box, click the **select more documents from your computer** link. In the Open dialog box, click **Tour Data.xlsx**, and then click **Open**. The Excel file is listed in the box along with the PowerPoint file.

9. Below the box, click **Continue**. The My Documents folder page appears listing the files in that folder.

10. Keep the My Documents folder page displayed in Internet Explorer for the next Step-by-Step.

Using Office Web Apps

There are two ways to work with files using the Office Web Apps. You can view a file or you can edit it using its corresponding Office Web App. From your SkyDrive, you can also open the document directly in the full Office 2010 application if the application is installed on the computer you are using. You do not need to have Microsoft Office 2010 programs installed on the computer you use to access Office Web Apps.

Using a Web App in View Mode

To use a Web App in View mode, simply click its filename in the folder. This opens the file in View mode in the Web App. **Figure D–8** shows the Tour Flyer Word file open in the Word Web App in View mode.

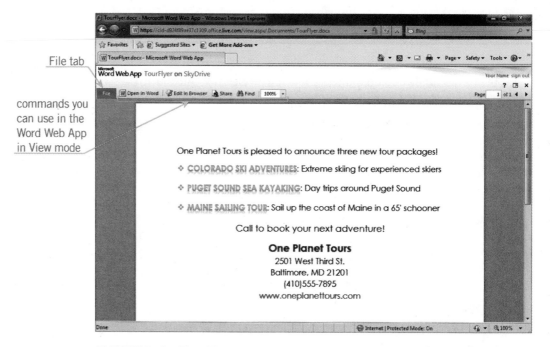

FIGURE D–8   Tour Flyer document open in View mode in Word Web App

Step-by-Step D.4

1. Click **Tour Flyer**. The Tour Flyer document opens in the Word Web App in View mode, as shown in Figure D–8.

2. Click anywhere in the document window, and then type any character. Nothing happens because you are allowed only to view the document in View mode.

3. Click the **File** tab. A list of commands opens. Note that you can print the document using the Print command on this menu.

4. Click **Close**. The document closes and the My Documents folder page appears again.

5. Leave the My Documents folder page open for the next Step-by-Step.

TIP

Position the mouse over a file icon to see the full filename and other details about the file.

Using a Web App in Edit Mode

You can also edit documents in the Office Web Apps. Although the interface for each Office Web App is similar to the interface of the full-featured program on your computer, a limited number of commands are available for editing documents using the Office Web App for each program. To edit a file in a Web App, point to the file in the folder page, and then click the Edit in browser link. You will see a Ribbon with a limited number of tabs and commands on the tabs. **Figure D–9** shows the file Tour Sales open in the PowerPoint Web App in Edit mode.

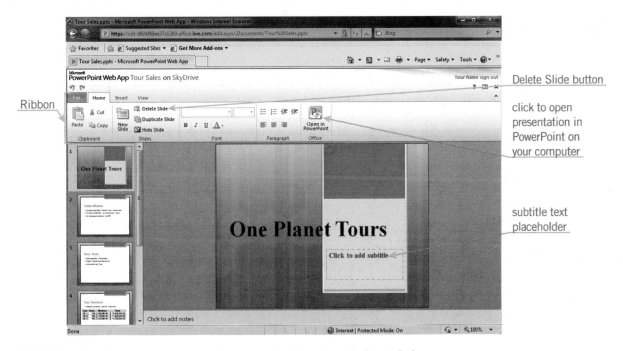

FIGURE D–9 Tour Sales presentation open in Edit mode in PowerPoint Web App

Step-by-Step D.5

1. In the list of files in the My Documents folder, point to **Tour Sales**. A list of commands for working with the file appears.

2. In the list of commands, click the **Edit in browser** link. The Tour Sales presentation appears in the PowerPoint Web App in Edit mode, as shown in Figure D–9. In Edit mode, you see a version of the familiar Ribbon.

3. In the Slide pane, click in the subtitle text placeholder, and then type your name.

4. In the Slides tab, click **Slide 3** to display it in the Slide pane. The slide title is *New Tours*.

5. On the Home tab, in the Slides group, click the **Delete Slide** button. The *New Tours* slide is deleted from the presentation and the new Slide 3 (*Tour Revenue*) appears in the Slide pane. Now you will examine the other two tabs available to you in the PowerPoint Web App.

6. Click the **Insert** tab on the Ribbon. The only objects you can insert in a slide using the PowerPoint Web App in Edit mode are pictures and SmartArt. You can also create a hyperlink.

7. Click the View tab. Note that you cannot switch to Slide Master view in the PowerPoint Web App.

8. Leave the Tour Sales file open in the PowerPoint Web App for the next Step-by-Step.

Editing a File Stored on SkyDrive in the Program on Your Computer

If you are working with a file stored on your SkyDrive and you want to use a command that is available in the full-featured program on your computer but is not available in the Web App, you need to open the file in the full-featured program on your computer. You can do this from the corresponding Office Web App by clicking the Open in *Program Name* button on the Home tab on the Web App Ribbon.

Step-by-Step D.6

1. Click the **Home** tab. In the Office group, click the **Open in PowerPoint** button. The Open Document dialog box appears warning you that some files can harm your computer. This dialog box opens when you try to open a document stored on a Web site.

2. Click the **OK** button. PowerPoint starts on your computer and the revised version of the Tour Sales presentation opens on your computer. The presentation is in Protected view because it is not stored on the local computer you are using.

3. In the yellow Protected View bar, click the **Enable Editing** button. Now you can insert a footer on the slides.

4. Click the **Insert** tab, and then click the **Header & Footer** button in the Text group.

5. Click the **Footer** check box, type **2013 Sales Projections** in the Footer box, and then click the **Apply to All** button. When you use the full-featured version of a program, you do need to save the changes you made, even when it is stored in a folder on your SkyDrive.

6. On the Quick Access Toolbar, click the **Save** button 🖫. The modified file is saved to your SkyDrive.

7. In the PowerPoint window title bar, click the **Close** button . The PowerPoint program closes and you see your browser window listing the contents of the My Documents folder.

8. Click the **Tour Sales** file. Slide 1 of the Tour Sales file appears in the PowerPoint Web app in View mode.

9. At the bottom of the window, click the **Next Slide** button ▶️ twice. Slide 3 (*Tour Revenue*) appears in the window. Remember that you deleted the original Slide 3, *New Tours*. Also note that the footer you added is on the slide.

10. Click the **File** tab, and then click **Close**. The PowerPoint Web App closes and the My Documents page appears.

11. Leave the My Documents page open for the next Step-by-Step.

◆— WARNING

You can also open a document stored on your SkyDrive in the program stored on your computer from View mode in the corresponding Office Web App.

◆— WARNING

If the Connecting to dialog box opens asking for your Windows Live ID credentials, type the email address associated with your Windows Live ID in the E-mail address box, type your password in the Password box, and then click the OK button.

APPENDIX D

Creating Folders on Your SkyDrive

You can keep your SkyDrive organized by using file management techniques, similar to the way you organize files on your computer's hard drive. You can create a folder in your SkyDrive in the Internet Explorer window or from Backstage view in the program on your computer.

To create a folder on your SkyDrive in Internet Explorer, click the New link in the list of commands, and then click Folder to open the Create a new folder page on your SkyDrive. See **Figure D–10**.

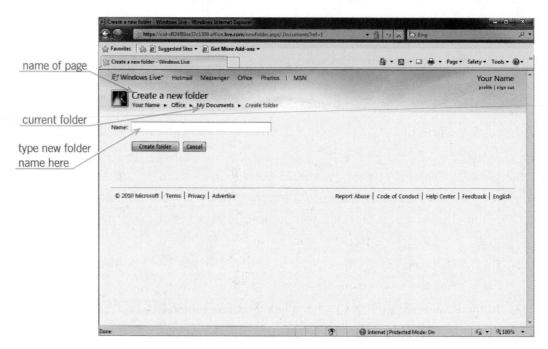

FIGURE D–10   Create a new folder page on SkyDrive

To create a new folder on your SkyDrive from the Save & Send tab in Backstage view in an application, click the New button in the upper-right. This opens the same Create a new folder page shown in Figure D–10.

Type the name for the new folder in the Name box, and then click Next. The Add files to *Folder Name* page that you saw earlier appears. If you want to upload a file to the new folder, you can do so at this point. If you don't, you can click the link for the new folder or click the SkyDrive link to return to your SkyDrive home page.

Step-by-Step D.7

1. In the list of command links, click the **New** link, and then click **Folder**. The Create a new folder page appears with the insertion point in the Name box.

2. In the Name box, type **Sales**, and then click **Create folder**. The new empty folder is displayed in the browser window. You can see that you are looking at the contents of the new folder by looking at the navigation links. See **Figure D–11**.

navigation links

command links

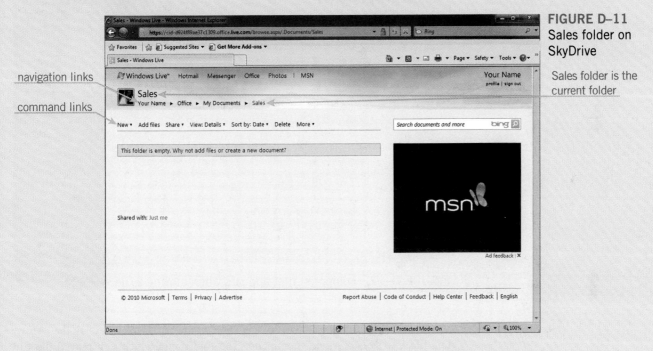

FIGURE D–11
Sales folder on SkyDrive

Sales folder is the current folder

3. Leave the Sales folder page open for the next Step-by-Step.

Organizing Files on Your SkyDrive

As on your hard drive, you can move and delete files on your SkyDrive. To move or delete a file, first display the commands for working with the file by pointing to its name in the file list in the folder. To move a file, click the More link, and then click Move to open the "Where would you like to move *File Name*?" page. See **Figure D–12**.

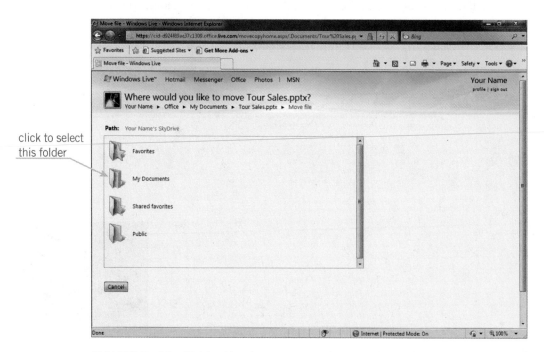

FIGURE D–12   Folder list that appears when moving a file

In the list of folders, click a folder. Then, at the top of the list, click the "Move this file into *Folder Name*" command. The folder into which you moved the file appears, along with a message telling you that the file was moved.

To delete a file, point to it to display the commands for working with the file, and then click the Delete button in the list of command links.

Step-by-Step D.8

1. In the list of navigation links, click the **My Documents** link. Point to **Tour Sales**. The commands for working with this file appear.

2. In the list of command links, click the **More** link, and then click **Move**. The "Where would you like to move Tour Sales.pptx?" page appears, and a list of folders on your SkyDrive appears.

⎯⎯⎯ **WARNING**

Depending on the resolution of your computer, you might not need to click the More link to access the Move command.

3. In the list of folders, click the **My Documents** folder to display the list of folders located inside that folder. Click the **Sales** folder. The contents of the Sales folder appear in the list of folders. Because this folder does not contain any additional folders, you see only a command to create a New folder and the command to move the file.

4. In the list of folders, click **Move this file into Sales**. After a moment, the contents of the Sales folder appear, along with a message telling you that you have moved the Tour Sales file from the My Documents folder.

5. In the list of navigation links, click the **My Documents** link. The contents of the My Documents folder appear.

6. Point to **Tour Flyer**. In the list of command links, click the **Delete** button . A dialog box opens warning you that you are about to permanently delete the file.

7. Click **OK**. The dialog box closes, the file is deleted from the My Documents folder on your SkyDrive.

8. Leave the My Documents folder page open for the next Step-by-Step.

Giving Permission for Access to a Folder on Your SkyDrive

If you upload a file to a private folder, you can grant permission to access the file to anyone else with a Windows Live ID. You can grant permission to folders located at the same level as the My Documents folder. You cannot grant permission to individual files or to folders located inside a locked folder. If you grant permission to someone to access a folder, that person will have access to all the files in that folder.

To grant permission to someone, click the folder to display its contents, click the Share link in the list of navigation links, and then click Edit permissions. The Edit permissions for *Folder Name* page appears. You can use the slider bar to make the contents of the new folder public by sharing it with everyone, your friends as listed on your Windows Live ID account and their friends, just your friends, or only some friends. You can also share it only with specific people that you list in the box in the Add Specific People section. When you type someone's name or email address associated with the person's Windows Live ID account in the box in the Add specific people section, and then press Enter, the person's name appears in a box below with a check box next to the name or email address. The box to the right of the person's name or email address indicates that the person can view files in the shared folder. You can then click the arrow to change this so that the person can view, edit, or delete files. See **Figure D–13**. Click Save at the bottom of the window to save the permissions you set.

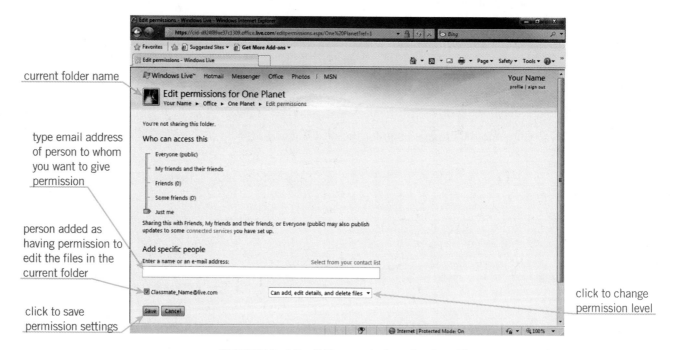

FIGURE D–13   Edit permissions for One Planet page on SkyDrive

To complete the next Step-by-Step, you need to work with a partner who also has a Windows Live ID account.

Step-by-Step D.9

1. In the list of navigation links, click the **Office** link, and then in the list of links on the left, click **View all**. The All documents page appears.

2. In the list of command links, click the **New** link, and the click **Folder**. The Create a folder page appears with a temporary folder name in the Name box. The temporary name is selected, so you can just type the new name.

3. In the Name box, type **One Planet**. Click **Next**. The One Planet folder page appears.

4. In the list of navigation links, click the **Office** link. In the list of folders on the left, click the **My Documents** link. The My Documents folder page appears.

5. In the file list, point to **Tour Data**, click the **More** link, and then click **Move**. The Where would you like to move Tour Data.xlsx? page appears.

6. In the list of folders, click **One Planet**. In the new list that appears, click the **Move this file into One Planet**. The One Planet page appears with the Tour Data file listed.

7. In the list of command links, click the **Share** link. Click **Edit permissions**. The Edit permissions for One Planet page appears.

8. Under Add specific people, click in the **Enter a name or an e-mail address** box, type the email address of your partner, and then press **Enter**. The email address you typed appears below the box. A check box next to the email address is selected, and a list box to the right identifies the level of access for this person. The default is Can add, edit details, and delete files, similar to Figure D–13. You want your partner to be able to edit the file, so you don't need to change this.

9. At the bottom of the window, click **Save**. The Send a notification for One Planet page appears. You can send a notification to each individual when you grant permission to access your files. This is a good idea so that each person will have the URL of your folder. Your partner's email address appears in the To box.

TIP

Because you are creating a folder at the same level as the My Documents folder, there is a Share with box below the Name box. You can set the permissions when you create the folder if you want.

TIP

To make the contents of the folder available to anyone, drag the slider up to the top so it is next to the Everyone (public).

> **WARNING**
>
> If you do not receive a message from Windows Live, make sure you are checking the email account associated with your Windows Live ID. If you created a new live.com or hotmail.com email address when you signed up with Windows Live, you need to use Hotmail to see the email message sent to you.

10. Click in the Include your own message box, type **You can now access the contents of the One Planet folder on my SkyDrive.**, and then click **Send**. Your partner will receive an email message from you advising him or her that you have shared your One Planet folder. If your partner is completing the steps at the same time, you will receive an email message from your partner.

11. Check your email for a message from your partner advising you that your partner has shared his or her Sales folder with you. The subject of the email message will be "*Your Partner's Name* has shared documents with you."

12. If you have received the email, click the **View folder** button in the email message, and then sign in to Windows Live if you are requested to do so. You are now able to access your partner's One Planet folder on his or her SkyDrive. See **Figure D–14**.

FIGURE D–14
One Planet folder on someone else's SkyDrive

name of person who gave you permission to access the One Planet folder on his or her SkyDrive

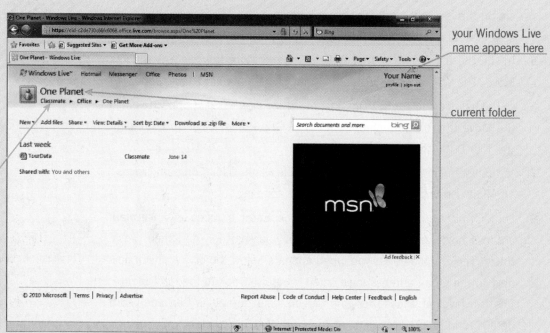

your Windows Live name appears here

current folder

13. Leave Internet Explorer open for the next Step-by-Step.

Co-Authoring with the Excel Web App

When you work with the Excel Web App, you can use its *co-authoring* feature to simultaneously edit an Excel workbook at the same time as a colleague. When you co-author a workbook, a list of the people currently co-authoring the workbook appears at the bottom of the window. Co-authoring is not available in the Word or PowerPoint Web Apps. When you open a file in the Excel Web App, a notification appears at the right end of the status bar notifying you that two people are editing the document. See **Figure D–15**. You can click this to see the email addresses of the people currently editing the workbook.

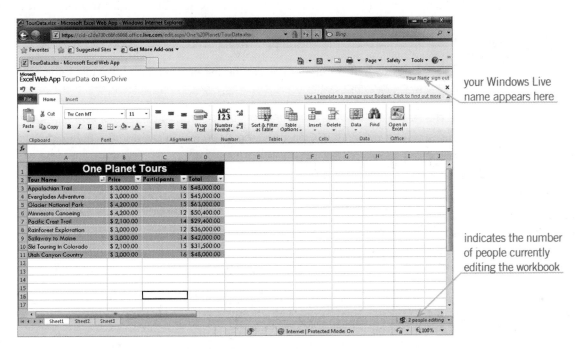

your Windows Live name appears here

indicates the number of people currently editing the workbook

FIGURE D–15   Tour Data file open in Edit mode in Excel Web App with two people editing

To complete this next Step-by-Step, you need to continue working with the partner who has permission to access the One Planet folder on your SkyDrive and who gave you permission to access his or her One Planet folder.

Step-by-Step D.10

1. Decide with your partner whether you will modify the Tour Data file stored on your SkyDrive or on his or her SkyDrive. After you decide the SkyDrive account with which you are going to work, both of you display the contents of that One Planet folder.

2. Point to **Tour Data**, and then in the list of command links, click the **Edit in browser** link.

3. In the status bar, click the **2 people editing** button. A list pops up identifying you and your partner as the two people editing the document.

   Decide with your partner which one of you will execute Step 4. The other person will then execute Step 5.

4. Either you or your partner click cell **A12**, type **Gulf Islands Sailing**, press **Tab**, type **3000**, press **Tab**, type **10**, and then press **Tab**. The formula in the other cells in column D is copied automatically to cell D12 because the data in the original Excel file was created and formatted as an Excel table. Both you and your partner see the data entered in row 12.

   If you entered the data in row 12, you partner should execute Step 5; if your partner entered the data in row 12, you should execute Step 5.

5. Either you or your partner—the person who did not execute Step 4—click cell **B12**, type **3700**, and then press **Tab**. The data entered is reformatted in the Accounting number format, and the total in cell D12 is recalculated. Again, both you and your partner see the change executed.

   Both you and your partner should execute the rest of the steps in this section.

6. Click the **File** tab, and then click **Close**. The changes you made to the Excel workbook are saved automatically on the current SkyDrive account. You are finished working with the Office Web Apps, so you can sign out of Windows Live.

7. In the upper-right of the SkyDrive window, click the **sign out** link. You are signed out of Windows Live.

8. In the title bar of your Web browser window, click the **Close** button to exit your Web browser.

OneNote Web App

The other Office Web App is OneNote. As with Word, Excel, and PowerPoint files, you can share OneNote files on SkyDrive directly from OneNote. Note that you need to click the Share tab in the navigation bar in Backstage view, and then click Web and specify Windows Live as the Web location. After you upload a OneNote file to SkyDrive, you can work with it in its corresponding Web App.

GLOSSARY

A

action button   An interactive button that performs instructions such as going to a specific slide or other object that you can create by drawing from the Shapes gallery.

adjustment handle   A yellow diamond-shaped handle that appears on a selected object. Drag the handle to change the appearance of the object.

agenda slide   A slide that provides an outline of topics for a presentation.

Align   Used to arrange objects to line up with the other objects on the slide or place an object relative to other objects on the slide. Align commands include: Left, Center, Right, Top, Middle, and Bottom.

animation   Adds motion to an object.

aspect ratio   The ratio between the width and height of an graphic.

axis   A line bordering the chart plot area used as a frame of reference for measurement.

axis title   A chart label that clarifies what is being measured, such as dollars, number of units, or time spans.

B

background   The area behind the text and graphics on a slide.

bitmap   A file format that consists of rows of tiny colored dots called pixels that compose an image on a computer screen.

bits   Tiny colored dots that compose an image on a computer screen. (See also *pixels*)

blank presentation   A new presentation that does not have theme elements, text, or objects.

broadcast   Placing a link to a presentation on the Web to allow others to watch your presentation as you give it from a remote location through a Web browser.

bullet   A small graphic symbol used to identify items in a list. Text in the content placeholder on a slide is usually preceded by a round or square bullet.

C

case sensitive   When entering a password to open a file, the upper and lower-casing of the letters must be identical to the casing of the letters in the assigned password.

category axis   The identifying labels listed on the horizontal axis in a chart.

cell   The intersection of a column and a row in a table or worksheet.

chart   A visual representation of numerical data; can be in the form of lines, bars, wedges in pies, or other graphics. *Also called* a graph.

clip art   Graphics stored in the Clip Organizer or available online that you can insert in any presentation.

color scheme   A set of 12 coordinated colors associated with a built-in theme.

column   A vertical stack of cells in a table or worksheet.

comment   An annotation that is added within a presentation by the author or reviewer.

crop   Removing a portion of a graphic or adding white space around a graphic.

Custom show   A feature that allows you to create presentations for different audiences by selecting specific slides from a presentation.

D

data label   Text or numbers that provide additional information about a value in the data series.

data series   Related data points that are plotted in a chart.

datasheet   A worksheet that appears with a chart on the slide and contains the numbers for the chart.

destination file   The file that an object is embedded in or linked to, such as a presentation file. *See also* source file.

digital signature   An attachment to a file or e-mail message that certifies that the information in the file is authentic and safe.

Document Inspector   A feature that enables you to check for hidden metadata or personal information in a presentation.

Document properties   Information about the presentation file including title, author, and keywords.

document workspace site   A central location for storing and sharing files.

E

Effects options   The Entrance, Exit, Emphasis, and Motion Path animation features such as pinwheel, diamond, and fly effects that you can use to animate objects.

embed   To place an object that was created in another application such as Microsoft Word or Excel in a slide. When you select the object, the original program will open for editing.

embedded object   An object that becomes part of the destination file; an embedded object can be edited in the destination file.

encryption   A standard method for encoding data.

export   To send information from one application to another application.

F

Format Painter   A feature that copies format attributes such as colors, borders, and fill effects from an object or text in order to apply the same formatting to another object or text.

G

grid   Vertical and horizontal lines that appear on the Slide pane and help you place text and objects.

gradient fill   A background fill composed of two or more colors that gradually blend from one color to another.

grouping   A feature that allows you to move, format, or resize several objects as if they were one object.

guidelines   Vertical and horizontal lines that you can display on the Slide pane to help place objects on the slide.

H

handles   Appear when an object is selected and are used to drag to resize the object.

Handout master   The master view for the audience handouts; includes placeholders for the slides, a header, footer, and the date and slide number.

handouts   Printouts that include a small image of the slides and an area to take notes. Handouts can be formatted in several different ways using the Handout master formatting and Backstage view print options.

hot spot   A hyperlink created for part of an image map.

hyperlink   Text or an object that when clicked "jumps to" another slide in the current slide show or another PowerPoint presentation, opens a Word, Excel, or Access file, or a browser window. *Also called* a link.

I

image map   A graphic that contains multiple hyperlinks on various parts of the image without dividing the graphic into separate objects.

import   To bring any object, data, graphics, or another file into a presentation.

integration   To share information among applications.

K

kiosk   An interactive computer terminal available for public use.

L

layout   The way content and text placeholders are placed on the slide.

Layout master   In the slide master, the individual layouts that determine the location of content and text placeholders for the slides.

legend   A list in a chart that identifies the data series indicated by the colors, patterns, or symbols used in the chart.

link   *See* hyperlink.

linked object   A file, chart, table, or other object that is created in another application such as Excel, stored in a source file, and inserted into a destination file, such as a PowerPoint slide, while maintaining a connection between the two files.

Live Preview   The Office 2010 feature that lets you point to the various choices in a gallery or palette and see the results in the slide before applying.

M

markup   Revision marks and annotations that appear in a presentation.

motion path   A way to animate an object by drawing the path on the slide. Allows you to make an object move along a specified path on the slide.

N

Normal view   The view in PowerPoint that includes the Slides/Outline tabs on the left, the Slide pane showing the selected slide in the center, and the Notes pane beneath the Slide pane. Commonly used to place objects on the slide.

Notes master   The master view for the notes pages. Includes placeholders for the slide, notes, header, footer, date, and slide number.

Notes Page view   A view in PowerPoint for working on the speaker notes page; includes placeholders for the slide notes.

Notes pane   The area below the Slide pane in which you can type speaker notes.

nudge   To move an object vertically or horizontally in small increments.

O

object   Any graphic, text element, or media clip on a slide that can be moved, edited, grouped, formatted, or animated.

organization chart   A SmartArt graphic used to show hierarchy and relationships of people or objects.

outcrop   Add blank space around a graphic.

Outline tab   A tab used to enter text in Normal view, located on the left side of the window in the same pane as the Slides tab.

P

Package for CD   A feature that allows you to save a presentation to a CD to be viewed on a computer that does not have PowerPoint installed.

pixels   Short for picture elements; tiny colored dots that compose an image on a computer screen. (See also *bits*)

placeholder   A boxed outline on a slide that can be used to insert text or an object when clicked.

plot area   A rectangular border that encloses the two axes and the data series; depending on the chart formats, the plot area may also include category names, data labels, and axes titles.

Portable Document Format (PDF)   A format developed by Adobe Systems designed to preserve the visual appearance and layout of each page and enable fast viewing and printing.

PowerPoint presentation   A computer slide show created in PowerPoint.

PowerPoint Viewer   A Microsoft application that enables you to open PowerPoint presentations when the PowerPoint application is not installed on the computer.

Presenter view   Offers a way for you to view your presentation with the speaker notes showing on one computer screen, while an audience views the presentation without viewing the speaker notes on another computer screen.

progressive disclosure   A technique that reveals slide content in increments.

publishing   Placing a presentation in a format for others to use; published presentations include handouts, Package for CD, and presentations on a document management server, in a document workspace, and on the Web.

Q

Quick Access Toolbar   A small customizable toolbar at the top of the screen with buttons for common commands such as Save and Print.

R

raster graphics   Graphics created in a file format that consists of rows of tiny colored dots called pixels that compose an image on a computer screen.

Reading view   A PowerPoint view you can use to display your presentation; very much like Slide Show view, the slide does not quite fill the screen and you can use navigation buttons on the status bar beneath the slide.

Ribbon   The graphical interface in Office 2010 with command buttons that are grouped and placed on tabs.

Rotate handle   The green handle on a selected object that you can drag to turn the object clockwise or counterclockwise.

row   The horizontal placement of cells in a table or worksheet.

S

scaling   Sizing a graphic so that its proportions are precise.

slide layout   The placement of placeholders or objects on a slide that determines how all of the objects on a slide are arranged.

slide library   A special type of library used in SharePoint to store presentation slides.

slide master   Determines the graphics and layout for the slides in a presentation. Each theme has a slide master, and slide masters include layout masters.

Slide pane   The main work area for the selected slide in Normal view.

Slide Show view   A view in PowerPoint that shows the slides on the full screen with animations and transitions.

Slide Sorter view   A view in PowerPoint that displays a thumbnail of each slide in the order in which they appear in the presentation; used to rearrange slides, check timings, and view slide transitions.

slide transition   The animated way in which a slide appears and leaves the screen during a slide show.

Slides tab   In Normal view, the tab on the left slide of the PowerPoint window that displays thumbnails of each slide.

SmartArt graphic   A graphic diagram that visually illustrates text and includes formatted graphics.

snap to   When an object is drawn to the guide or grid as though it were magnetic; used for exact placement of objects.

source file   The file in which a linked or embedded object is stored in a presentation.

Spell checker   A feature used to locate and correct spelling errors.

status bar   The area at the bottom of the PowerPoint window that tells you information about the presentation and contains the View Shortcuts buttons and the Zoom Slider.

streaming video   Media sent in a continuous stream of data that can be played from an online source without waiting to download the file.

summary slide   A slide that reviews the topics in a presentation.

T

Tab   A section of the Ribbon.

table   Text or graphics organized in columns and rows.

Taskbar   The area at the bottom of the Windows screen that contains the Start button as well as program or window buttons for open programs.

template   A predesigned presentation that has graphics and some content, such as theme elements, text, and graphics used to create a new presentation.

theme   A named collection of fonts, graphics, colors, and effects that can be applied to a presentation.

Thesaurus   A feature used to find a synonym, or a word with a similar meaning.

thumbnail   A small graphic image.

title bar   The area at the top of the each window that contains information about the window as well as window controls such as the Minimize, Maximize, and Close buttons.

transition   *See* slide transition.

V

Value axis   The identifying numbers listed on the vertical axis in a chart.

vector graphics   Graphics created in a file format that consist of lines, curves, and shapes.

W

WordArt   Feature that displays text as a graphic; includes options for formatting, text fills, shapes, and effects.

X

XML Paper Specification (XPS)   A format developed by Microsoft designed to preserve the visual appearance and layout of each page and enable fast viewing and printing.

Z

Zoom Slider   A feature on the status bar that can be dragged to change the zoom percentage of the Slide pane in the PowerPoint window.

INDEX